YORK 1831-1981

The picture on the front cover is from 'Panoramic View of the Gardens of the Yorkshire
Philosophical Society, York', a coloured lithograph by J. Storey, c. 1860

YORK
1831 - 1981

150 Years of Scientific Endeavour

and Social Change

Editor

Charles Feinstein

William Sessions Limited
The Ebor Press, York, England
in association with The British Association for the
Advancement of Science (York Committee)

First published in 1981

Hard Cover ISBN 0 900657 55 3
Card Cover ISBN 0 900657 56 1

© C. H. Feinstein and British Association (York Committee)
1981

Printed by William Sessions Limited
The Ebor Press, York, England

Contents

v

Illustrations

Illustrations—*cont.*

Maps

Contributors

P. V. Addyman	Director, York Archaeological Trust
A. Digby	Research Fellow in Social History, Institute of Social and Economic Research, University of York
D. J. Dowrick	Brickell, Moss and Partners, Consulting Engineers, New Zealand; formerly of Ove Arup and Partners, London
C. H. Feinstein	Professor of Economic and Social History, University of York
R. I. Hills	Lecturer in Economic and Social History, University of York
S. P. Jenkins	Research Fellow, Institute of Social and Economic Research, University of York
J. A. D. Matthew	Reader in Physics, University of York
A. K. Maynard	Senior Lecturer in Economics, University of York
A. D. Orange	Senior Lecturer in History and Philosophy of Science, Department of Humanities, Newcastle upon Tyne Polytechnic
A. J. Peacock	Warden, York Educational Settlement
E. Royle	Lecturer in History, University of York
C. C. Storm-Clark	Lecturer in Economic and Social History, University of York
J. S. S. Whiting	Lecturer in Physics, University of York

Acknowledgements

Editing a volume such as this is only possible with the willing help of friends and colleagues and I have incurred many debts. I wish, in particular, to express my gratitude to Helen Humphries for the exemplary skill and care with which she drew our five maps; to Tessa Sidey and the Curator of York City Art Gallery for their help in finding pictures and portraits; to the staff of the City Reference Library and of the York Archives for preserving much of the material on which these studies are based, and for the readiness with which they made it available; to Jessica and Naomi Feinstein for compiling the index; and to Anne Digby for unflagging and invaluable help at every stage from first planning to final proof reading. I am also indebted to William Sessions Ltd. for a greater degree of indulgence and co-operation than any editor is entitled to expect from his publisher.

Thanks are due to the following for permission to use photographs taken by them, or pictures and diagrams in their care: National Portrait Gallery (for Plate I); York City Art Gallery (for the front cover and Plates 2, 5, 10b and 16); Anglia Television (Plate 4); M. S. Duffy (Plate 6); Shepherd Construction Ltd. (Plate 7); Royal Commission on Historical Monuments (Plate 8); P. Gibson, and Dean and Chapter of York Minster (Plate 9); D. A. Wilde (Plate 11); York Archives (Plates 13 and 15); Jane Bown (Plate 14); Yorkshire Evening Press (Plate 17); Institution of Civil Engineers (Diagrams 2, 4 and 6 in Chapter IV); and York City Library (1881 poster on the back cover). Also to Professor M. D. Stephens for permission to quote from the article by Lord Annan 'The University in Britain' in M. D. Stephens and G. W. Roderick (eds.), *Universities for a Changing World* (1975).

C. H. F.

Preface

The return of the British Association to its birthplace on its 150th Anniversary is a cause for celebration. A warm welcome awaits those who come to the York meeting in the first week of September 1981.

In March 1831, the representatives of the City, approached by the Yorkshire Philosophical Society, confirmed that 'they would have great pleasure in doing everything that lies in their power to promote the objects of the Society . . . and they rejoice that York is fixed upon as the place for holding its meeting'. That meeting was, indeed, the foundation meeting of the British Association.

The purpose of the traditional volume to mark each annual stopping place of the British Association is to set the meeting in an environmental context. In earlier times, the natural phenomena of the area had pride of place, but latterly wide ranging surveys of both the physical and the social background have become more common. The 1981 volume continues this trend but, as befits a birthday volume, there is an added element of history and retrospect.

The York Committee were also glad to find support for the plan of the book in the words of one of the founding fathers, William Vernon Harcourt, who in proposing the foundation of the Association on 27th September 1831 said 'The chief interpreters of nature have always been those who grasped the widest field of enquiry, who have listened with the most universal curiosity to all information and felt an interest in every question which the one great system of nature presents. Nothing could be a more disastrous event for the sciences than that one of them should be dissociated from another.'

We hope that the members of the Association, whatever their special scientific interest may be, will thus find in this volume many points of contact and familiar landmarks in their own field of knowledge, so that they come to York, as it were, to visit an old friend whose life and character – 'warts and all' – they view with understanding and hopefully, like us, with affection.

The Committee is most grateful to Professor Charles Feinstein, the editor, and the team of authors who have placed their knowledge and time at the Association's service. They have interpreted with skill, against the backcloth of a small City, the theme of science and the community which has been at the very heart of the Association's work during the last 150 years.

Surely at no time has that theme been more relevant and important. There is too another theme which runs strongly through the Association's history and, as this book demonstrates, no less through York's – the ability of dedicated and informed men and women to shape events for the common good.

With full confidence therefore – and a warm welcome – the York Committee dedicates this book to the 150th birthday meeting of the British Association.

DONALD BARRON
Chairman
York Committee of the British
Association for the Advancement
of Science 1981

CHAPTER I

Science in early nineteenth-century York: the Yorkshire Philosophical Society and the British Association

by

· Derek Orange

IT IS PLEASANT TO CELEBRATE the 150th anniversary of the British Association for the Advancement of Science and to find the child of 1831 still in possession of its faculties, though clearly less vigorous than in its youth. The British Association was the very epitome of science in Victorian Britain.[1] Fashioned at the same time (and perhaps by the same social forces) as the great Reform Bill, it was from its early years earnest and evangelising, rhetorical and rumbustious. It belonged to the age of Lyell and Darwin and Huxley and their painfully acquired new perspectives on man's place in nature; to the age of Joule and Kelvin and the physics of the steam-engine and the telegraph; to the age of which the engineer and the industrial chemist and the school-inspector and the medical officer of health, even the 'scientist' himself were the new men. Both the matters and the men claimed their places on its programmes and its platforms.[2]

That Manchester or Birmingham or Leeds or Sheffield or Newcastle, or any of the other towns formed or transformed by the Industrial Revolution, should have cradled the British Association would, then, have been unsurprising. That York, an apparent anachronism in that new world, should have done so is, on the face of it, very surprising indeed. But

1

if it is the historian who first points to the incongruity of such juxtaposi-
tions it is also the historian who must accept the task of diminishing their
incongruity, of demonstrating that if they are not inevitable they are at
least intelligible.

Nevertheless, in order to uncover authentic connections he must look
in the right places. If the present essay throws any light on the beginnings
of the British Association, it is a diffused light, for it is the parent
institution, the Yorkshire Philosophical Society, and the culture which
nurtured it, that occupies the focus of attention. That a society established
by three men whose roots were in the eighteenth century rather than the
nineteenth, in a provincial and pre-industrial city with a population
hardly in excess of 20,000, should within a score of years command a
museum and gardens of breath-taking elegance, that some of its collections should be counted the best outside London, that it should inspire
half a dozen scholarly books of enduring interest and should send men to
profess the sciences in new universities and old, that its chronicles should
embrace William Smith the father of English geology and Sydney Smith
the prince of English wits, Sir George Cayley the inventor of the aeroplane (see Plates 3 and 4) and George Hudson the propagandist of the
railway,[3] these are matters sufficiently remarkable in themselves to merit
consideration. Only then does it become possible to understand how the
Society came to stage-manage the foundation of the British Association,
to exert a profound effect on the subsequent course of that body, and to
furnish it with three presidents in no more than a generation.

York: Problems and Possibilities

In January, 1813, York was the scene of a special assize to bring to
trial 64 prisoners implicated in the 'Luddite' machine-wrecking in the
West Riding; 19 of the men were subsequently hanged outside the Castle.
In 1826 the Castle Yard was crowded for the declaration of the results of
the county election. The scale and excitement of a parliamentary election
half a century before the secret ballot is difficult now to conceive: Lord
Milton had spent £120,000 in his first campaign in 1807, when Yorkshire
returned only two candidates. Now the number had been increased to
four and along with Milton, the Hon. William Duncombe and Richard
Fountayne Wilson, all members of the county aristocracy, John Marshall,
a Leeds manufacturer of textile machinery, was elected. For those who
could read the signs of the times there was a deep symbolism in these two
episodes. York remained geographically and administratively at the
centre of a vast and prosperous region, but its contact with the realities of
the new industrial age was indirect, second-hand. The charge that the city

had lost its trade to Hull and its 'manufactures' to Leeds was so familiar and so obviously true that it merited no discussion.

The historical sense and the historical imagination are arbitrary and selective faculties. Every good Yorkist knew that he lived in the city of Constantine and Alcuin, the city of the Council of the North, the city which for a thousand years had been the seat of an archbishop. York was traditionally the second city of the kingdom: no one made *that* claim for Leeds, nor even, yet, for Glasgow or Manchester or Birmingham. There was a solidity about the Minster, the Castle, the Walls, that was reassuring. In 1844 Hugh Miller found 'York essentially an ancient city still'.[4] But antiquity was not without its embarrassments. 'Blades of grass appear in the middle of the space just surrounding the hotel in which I am lodged', Dibdin complained in 1838 in the course of his northern tour, 'and more provoking still, narrow streets, and mean overhanging houses, frequently intercept the view of the noblest Gothic Cathedral in the World.'[5] While the self-appointed guardians of the past – local men like Charles Wellbeloved or national figures like Sir Walter Scott – might complain of the destruction wrought by 'the unsparing hand of improvement', no one could deny the inconvenience of the bars or gateways through which traffic in and out of the city had to pass.[6]

If there was a degree of ambiguity about attitudes to the monuments of antiquity, the more recent past was lovingly enshrined in the memory of the older citizens. Georgian afternoons were as golden to the nineteenth century as Edwardian ones have become to the twentieth. The Theatre Royal and the Assembly Rooms, to say nothing of the elegant houses of Bootham and Lendal and Micklegate, were constant reminders of past glories. The admired institutions, indeed, clung precariously to life. In the 1820s the Assembly Rooms boasted a new façade and were connected with the concert rooms which the music festival of 1823 had inspired; the Theatre Royal was lighted by gas. But the cynical could argue that these were no more than cosmetic operations concealing an underlying malaise. The York newspapers and the several writers of 'histories' of the city found it notably difficult to record any contemporary function without suggesting that it was a poor affair compared with the glitter, the sophistication of those of a previous generation.[7] Francis Drake, surgeon and antiquarian, whose *History* of the city had been published in 1736, although he had entertained misgivings of his own, was now remembered as the chronicler and herald of an unparalleled age of elegance.

The modish diversions provided by the theatre, the concerts, the assemblies, the races followed hard on the establishment of the great country estates in the seventeenth century. 'What has been, and is, the chief support of the city . . .', Drake had written, 'is the resort and residence of several county gentlemen with their families in it.'[8] The truth of the matter was beyond dispute. Robert Davies, Town Clerk and magistrate in the 1830s, recalled one of the assemblies of 1754 which had numbered among the visitors

> the Duke and Duchess of Ancaster, the Duke and Duchess of Hamilton, the Marquis and Marchioness of Rockingham, the Earl and Countess of Carlisle, the Earl and Countess of Coventry, the Earl of Dundonald, the Earl of March, the Earl and Countess of Northumberland, the Earl and Countess of Scarborough, the Earl of Thanet and the Ladies Tufton, Viscount Downe, Viscount Fairfax, Viscount and Lady Irwin, Viscount Stormont, Lord Barnard, besides two or three dozens of Honourables, Baronets, and Knights.[9]

History is shaped to a considerable degree by geology and geography. York owed its pre-eminence as the greatest eighteenth-century centre of fashionable life and entertainment in the north of England in part to the fertility of the Yorkshire plain and its attractiveness to the aristocracy, in part to the difficulties of extended travel. Progressive opinion in the place might now regret the comparative remoteness of the coalfields so crucial to the growth of Leeds and Sheffield; improved roads and the beginnings of a railway system might take the noble families of the county to London where previously they had spent the season in York; but in 1831 there were at least 50 seats of superior families within 10 miles of the City, and many of its plebeians – the jewellers, tanners, chemists, linen manufacturers, comb-makers, builders, and domestic servants represented in the census of that year – continued to derive a comfortable livelihood from their proximity. George Hudson, York's best-known son of early Victorian times, may now be remembered as a railway king and a self-made (and self-destroyed) millionaire, but in his early manhood he had an annual turnover of £30,000 in his drapery business.[10]

It was Hudson who led the resurgence of the local Tories at the expense of the long-dominant Whigs in the last years in which those denominations retained their currency. Hudson, of course, subsequently sat as MP for Sunderland, but it was domestic rather than national politics which more habitually exercised the inhabitants of York. While recent historians have argued that the inward-looking, restrictive policies of the unreformed city council relegated York to a subordinate position in the new economic hierarchy,[11] it was the damaging nature of political division itself which most engaged contemporary commentators. 'In this great city,' complained one of them in *The Yorkshire Observer* in 1823, 'nothing is thought of but Whigism and Toryism'.[12]

The Yorkshire Observer had no doubt as to the role to which the city might aspire. York had been the Athens of the Middle Ages; even in the seventeenth century its citizens had petitioned the Crown for the establishment of a northern university within its walls:

> To make the city commercial, is impracticable; to make it manufacturing is not desirable; to make it considerably more extensive, is not necessary. What then remains to be done to restore it to a large portion of its ancient character and magnificence? There remains to confer upon it the distinguished rank of a literary City, and as the centre of scientific attraction between London and Edinburgh.[13]

The appeal to the saving virtues of science and literature was taken up by newspapers representing quite different shades of opinion. The materials were already at hand, it was urged, from which to reconstruct the past greatness. All that was necessary was to bring them together in a situation in which class and party did not interfere. A society was needed, suggested *The York Courant* early in 1821, 'for *free* and *friendly* discussion upon the varied subjects that science and literature present, and . . . guided in its choice of Members by no other considerations than those of individual respectability'.[14] A couple of years later the same publication again challenged its readers:

> York can boast her *Musical Societies,* and her Associations for Fashionable Amusements . . . [but] when will the literary and philosophical talent which *we know* are confined within the walls of *Old Ebor* be concentrated into one focus and shine forth in its innate brilliancy?[15]

As far as the newspapers were concerned, opinion was unanimous: it was not music, not the theatre nor the assemblies nor the races which would redeem the time, it was science. The immediate basis of the judgment was obvious enough: the Leeds Philosophical and Literary Society had been established in 1819, the Sheffield Literary and Philosophical Society in 1822, and similar bodies in Hull and Whitby at about the same time. 'Do not these useful institutions which are daily forming round us, convey a severe reproof to the tardiness of our own city?' asked the *Courant,* rhetorically enough.[16]

Given the mood of the editors, the recriminations when a series of lectures on astronomy was sparsely attended were predictable:

> It does not argue well for the *scientific* character of the city, that scenes of frivolity and ludicrous representations, should attract their crowds, whilst subjects calculated to expand the mind, to inform the understanding, and to awaken the sublime emotions of piety and reverence for the God of Nature, should be neglected and unpatronized.[17]

While it was hardly surprising that the markedly Whig *Courant* should campaign for the wider spread of science and learning, the *Yorkshire Observer,* under the proprietorship of a sometime editor of the Tory *Gazette* argued similarly, and during its short life energetically canvassed support for a 'Museum and School of Arts'.[18]

The soil then was to some extent prepared, but what kind of plant might be hoped to take root? Many of the propagandists seemed to look for an institute, if not for mechanics who were hardly a numerous class in York, then for artisans: a further example of middle-class provision for the well-being of the labouring classes to rank with the Dispensary and the Savings Bank. Indeed the York Institute of Popular Science and Literature was established in this mould by Charles Wellbeloved in 1827, but as early as 1822 there was, briefly, a 'York Literary and Philosophical Society' which perhaps made provision for the ambitions, real or supposed, of the same section of the community. Eventually, more erudite classes and interests were also to be represented: the York Medical Society was founded in 1832, the Yorkshire Architectural Society 10 years later.

The Yorkshire Philosophical Society:
Foundation and Founders

The Yorkshire Philosophical Society owed its existence to four men who lived in or near York and who, although they did not admit as much, were clearly carried some way by the tide of progressive opinion: James Atkinson, Anthony Thorpe, William Salmond, and William Vernon. (Plate 1. Vernon added the name Harcourt in 1831 when his father, the Archbishop of York, inherited the Harcourt estates.) In another place or other circumstances they might have projected a scholarly library. But York had for a generation sustained a Subscription Library (Thorpe being one of its founders) which under the effective direction of Charles Wellbeloved was unlikely to be guilty of triviality in its policies. The issue on which the founding fathers of the Philosophical Society concurred with the York newspapers was the need for some central repository for objects of scientific interest. The need had long been felt. Many of the Roman remains collected by Martin Lister, who had practised medicine in the city in the 1670s and 1680s, had found their way to the Ashmolean Museum in Oxford; another York physician and antiquarian, John Burton, the friend of Francis Drake, had called for a local museum in the eighteenth century:[19] Thorpe himself, finding no more appropriate repository, had placed a small Roman altar in the Minster Library.[20] Although the Yorkshire Museum did not spring up overnight, the study and display of antiquarian remains was almost from the beginning an avowed part of the Philosophical Society's programme.

The event which most of all demonstrated the need for a museum, however, had to do with a remoter history than that of Rome. By the end of 1822 Salmond and Atkinson, along with several other individuals in the city and its neighbourhood, had amassed considerable collections of bones from the recently explored cave at Kirkdale.

Kirkdale Cave was discovered twice, perhaps three times. There are minor inconsistencies between the earliest accounts, but the main outlines of the story are clear enough.[21] The cave forms part of a limestone quarry near Kirkbymoorside in the Vale of Pickering, some 25 miles from York. The quarrymen first uncovered an entrance to the long, low cavern in the summer of 1821, and found the floor covered by an enormous and confused mass of bones which they vaguely supposed belonged to cattle who had somehow met their death there. When stones from the quarry were used in the resurfacing of the road through the village of Kirkdale, the bones went with them. There they came to the notice of a man of some scientific background, John Gibson, who was visiting friends in nearby Helmsley. Gibson immediately recognised that the bones derived from animals which no longer existed in Britain. This second discovery prompted many excursions to the cave by county gentlemen, including William Salmond. Gibson took a great many of the specimens to London with him, and presented them variously to the notoriously neglected British Museum, the College of Surgeons and the Geological Society. Some also came into the possession of the Bishop of Oxford, and it was in the university city that they first came to the notice of the Rev. William Buckland, the Professor of Geology. Buckland, a man of immense physical and intellectual energy, could hardly have ignored the problem of the cave, but according to his daughter it was William Vernon who actually engineered his visit in December 1821.[22] To Buckland, then, must be credited the third discovery: his thorough study of the cave (assisted by Salmond who mapped it for him) established its true character as a sometime den of prehistoric hyaenas who, during their long tenancy, had brought into it the carcases of many other animals, including elephants, rhinoceroses, hippopotamuses, no longer indigenous to such northerly latitudes.

All this would have been dramatic enough in itself. But Buckland, like many geologists of his day, saw his science as an adjunct to his religion. The Kirkdale bones were geologically recent, fragile, many of them, but unfossilised. They were contemporary not with the limestone, whose antiquity Buckland knew to be measured in millions of years, but with the superficial deposits of boulder clay. The last of the hyaenas had been overcome by an invading sea of mud. The clay, the compacted mud, the extinguished creatures, were pieces of natural evidence for Noah's flood as described in the book of Genesis; they were, in Buckland's picturesque phrase, *Reliquiae Diluvianae,* relics of the deluge.[23]

A generation earlier, many of the Kirkdale specimens might have rested in the cabinets of the *dilettanti*. But now, to the widespread feeling that such objects should be united in public collections were added the intellectual claims of the developing science of geology: the bones were the raw material of the history of the earth. *The Yorkshire Observer* might dwell in an abstract way on the practical advantages of a local museum, but it was probably Buckland who first proposed (in a remark which Vernon passed on to Thorpe) the combining of the Kirkdale specimens still in York. But where were they to be accommodated? By the time Buckland published *Reliquiae Diluvianae,* the account of his explorations, in 1823 he was able to answer the question. The newly formed Yorkshire Philosophical Society was their custodian.

Salmond was known as a 'gentleman of private means' who occasionally made use of his old army rank of Colonel, Thorpe was a partner in a highly respectable firm of solicitors and land agents, Atkinson an eccentric but popular surgeon. None of them was under 50.[24]

While Atkinson, a veteran who seemed to know and be known by everyone in the county, had inevitably acquired many choice specimens, it was Salmond who brought the largest collection to the new institution, indeed it was Salmond who, on his own reckoning, *founded* it: 'I proposed the plan to Mr. Atkinson and the late Mr. Thorpe,' Salmond claimed in 1831 when the matter briefly became contentious.[25] Atkinson did not disagree: 'Mr. Salmond and myself first formed a collection of Kirkdale bones at our houses, and invited Mr. Thorpe to join us'.[26] The three men, Atkinson, Salmond and Thorpe, held the first recorded meeting on 7 December 1822, at Atkinson's house in Lendal. The fourth and by far the youngest of the founders, the Rev. William Vernon, attended the second meeting a week later, when the new body was officially designated The Yorkshire Philosophical Society. At a distance of a century and a half, a petty squabble over priority is not worth pursuing; what is important is the progress from a casual agreement between two men to bring together their geological cabinets to the launching of what was soon to become a prominent scientific institution. The evidence provided by the earliest minutes and prospectuses lends support, albeit circumstantial, to Vernon's claim to have effected the transformation: 'I proposed to extend the plan, and instead of a public *Museum* only at York, to found a Yorkshire Scientific and Antiquarian *Society*'.[27] There can be no doubt that from the second meeting in December 1822 the clergyman was the chief architect and inspiration of the institution: 'to his fire and spirit it is owing that the Society has arrived at its present state,' Atkinson declared in 1830.[28]

In the winter of 1822-23 the prospects were not particularly encouraging. When the existence of the Society became known in the city, the individual initiative which had launched it was roundly condemned. A society, 'Epicurus' argued in *The Yorkshire Observer,* should have its origin in a public meeting of 'Nobility, Gentry and Men of Letters and Science'. The *Observer* at this time had not quite abandoned its campaign for a museum and school of arts hardly distinguishable, as already suggested, from the mechanics institutes beginning to appear in some parts of the country. The Yorkshire Philosophical Society, 'Epicurus' complained, was by contrast, 'under the government of a Committee, which is an Aristocracy . . . it excludes from all its advantages not only the entire bulk of the community, but the first order of Tradesmen, Men of Letters, and Artists'. Indeed, in a city 'divided by political parties, religious sects, and rival possessions', any man, however honourable, might find himself excluded in the ballot for new members.[29] The editor of the *Observer* joined in the condemnation of what 'Epicurus' had dismissively labelled the 'Triumvirate'. 'With them, no man can be a Philosopher who is not in the rigid cast of "Gentry" . . . We respect these men in their private capacity, but as public teachers of Philosophy, we hold them in utter scorn and contempt.'[30]

The Yorkshire Philosophical Society: Science and its support

If York lacked the powerful industrial interests which helped to determine the course of the literary and philosophical societies in towns like Manchester and Newcastle upon Tyne, who *were* the men who made the Yorkshire Philosophical Society? On any reckoning the institutions were products of the expanding and changing towns and cities of late-Georgian England. In those places it was the members of the traditional professions – medicine, the law, the church – who were continually, and often urgently, called upon for their services; and who therefore needed, in a world blissfully without telephone and motor-car, to reside conveniently and centrally.[31] These were the men, qualified practically by their availability, socially by their profession and intellectually by their education, who typically assumed responsibility for the ordinary functioning of an institution. The Yorkshire Philosophical Society relied most heavily of all on William Vernon, but also on other clergymen of the Established Church like the Rev. W. H. Dixon and the two Grahams. It called too on prominent Unitarians such as the Rev. Charles Wellbeloved, the principal, and John Kenrick and William Hincks, tutors, of the Manchester Academy which was situated in York from 1803 to 1840; on Friends such as the Backhouses and the Tukes, bankers, nurserymen and merchants, and on men like Thomas Allis and John Ford whom they brought to York in the 1820s to manage The Retreat and the embryonic Bootham School. The Society quickly won the support of the leading doctors of the city: after Atkinson himself, George Goldie, Baldwin Wake, Stephen Beckwith, Thomas Laycock, and younger men like Thomas Barker, attracted by the rise of the York Medical School in 1834; then there were solicitors, some of them, like Robert Davies, and Thorpe's partner Jonathan Gray, occupying important civic positions. So it was that the men who formed the effective leadership of the institution were already intimately engaged in the daily life of the city. The Yorkshire Philosophical Society was no bastard offspring of York custom and culture.[32]

Despite 'Epicurus', the real presumption of the institution was to be found not in the arbitrariness of its origins but in the ambitiousness of its objects. Its name, the Yorkshire Philosophical Society, was pregnant with implications. A society formed somewhat later than those in the other contemporary centres of influence in the county – Leeds, Sheffield, Hull – appropriated to itself the generic 'Yorkshire'; a society disdaining the attachment to 'literary' pursuits commonly claimed by its kind, was simply and comprehensively 'philosophical'. It may be that the absence of manufacturers left the philosophers free to neglect the utilitarian aspects of science, and to cultivate natural knowledge for its own sake. Anyway, the adjectives 'Yorkshire' and 'Philosophical' were interestingly complementary. The Society began by professing as its principal objects the study of the geology of the county and antiquities of the city, but by 1825 the programme was bolder than that:

> The materials will . . . it is hoped, be gradually collected for a complete philosophical history of Yorkshire; specimens of all the natural productions of the County, its native quadrupeds, birds, and reptiles, its fishes, insects, shells, plants and minerals, will be assembled into one view: and the questions respecting the district, which may suggest themselves to the scientific inquirer, will be answered by a glance of the eye.[33]

But for all this catholicity, the business of the Society was not simply to assemble, tabulate and exhibit the objects of natural knowledge. It was also to *promote* scientific interests, 'to give to studies too much neglected a more popular currency and a freer facility of access, to attract attention to philosophical objects, to awaken scientific curiosity, and afford more ready means of information'.[34] Support was therefore invited not only from the instructed but also the uninstructed,

> not only those who are themselves engaged in philosophical studies, but all by whom the value of such studies is duly appreciated; not

only those who hope to extend the boundaries of knowledge of their own researches, but all who are willing to encourage the prosecution of such researches by others.[35]

It was in the end its scientific comprehensiveness as much as its social exclusiveness which marked off the Society from a mechanics institute. So it was that the Society could add to the active participation of the professional classes the interest and goodwill of the aristocracy, at least the Whig aristocracy. In 1824 it could number among its official patrons not only Vernon's father the Archbishop of York, but also the Earls of Carlisle and Tyrconnel and the Lords Milton and Stourton.

An institution which pursues geological and antiquarian interests must necessarily have premises to house its collections. The first home of the Yorkshire Philosophical Society, obtained with some difficulty, was a rented suite of rooms in a house in Low Ousegate, adjoining the 'new' bridge over the river. The Society first met there in March 1823, and continued to do so for seven years. Members (there were by this time about 120) paid £5 on their election and an annual subscription of £1. Out of the limited resources thus available, the body had to pay its rent, augment and display its collections, and mount its other activities. The favour with which it was soon regarded was evidenced by abundant donations to its collections. Science is concerned with generalisation and unrelated natural objects may possess little more than curiosity-value, but as the Society became well established, important collections systematically formed by individual enthusiasts were added to the Kirkdale bones: two herbaria containing between them several thousand specimens in 1827, and two extensive collections of insects.

Throughout the century the Society appointed honorary curators to superintend its various collections, but early in its existence it took a step which as much as anything else laid the foundations of its scientific reputation: it engaged John Phillips (Plate 2) as its keeper. Phillips' connection with the institution began obliquely. In 1824 Vernon brought the great practical geologist William Smith to York to deliver a series of lectures. But although Smith's discourses were successful enough, it was Phillips, his young nephew and assistant, who impressed by his energy, his eloquence and his varied scientific talents. At the beginning of 1826 he was officially designated keeper of the Museum of the Yorkshire Philosophical Society, at a salary of £60 p.a.[36] In 1829 he was joined by a permanent sub-curator, Henry Baines.

Even before his appointment, Phillips had resolved to employ his creative talents in the fulfilling of the Society's earliest ambition, the elucidation of the geology of the county. The first part of his *Illustrations*

of the Geology of Yorkshire, published in the spring of 1829 and dedicated to his uncle, reflected the experience of several years of field-work
and the examination and classification of specimens in the service of the
Yorkshire Philosophical Society.[37]

The year 1829 also saw the archaeological and antiquarian commitment of the Society beginning to yield important, though unanticipated
benefits. The preparation of the Manor Shore for the building of a
permanent home for the Society uncovered unexpectedly rich and various remains of St. Mary's Abbey. The utilisation of the site to accommodate the King's Manor in the sixteenth century, and of the fabric for
building and restoration in both York and Beverley was, of course,
known. What was not clear was how much of the mediaeval abbey itself
still remained. The excavations begun in 1827 (Plate 5) yielded dramatic
discoveries[38] (see the description quoted in Chapter III, p. 54 below).
The promise of the early discoveries suggested further excavations, not
directly required by the preparations for the museum, and although such
an enterprise sorely tested already stretched resources, sufficient additional work was done to leave the Society in possession of a vast number
of relics: architectural fragments, sculptured ornaments, statues, utensils.
The identification, correlation and eventual description of the remains
was overwhelmingly the work of one man, Charles Wellbeloved; his
definitive *Account of . . . The Abbey of St. Mary, York,* was published by
the Society of Antiquaries of London in 1829.[39]

The difficulties, both of housing the collections and of mounting
lecture-courses in the wake of Smith's discourses of 1824, had demonstrated the inadequacy of the rooms in Low Ousegate; and the erection,
at a projected cost of £3,000, of a lecture-room and museum on the
Manor Shore had been proposed by Vernon early in 1825. With the
powerful support which the institution could now command in the
county, donations to the Building Fund quickly reached some £4,500, a
circumstance which persuaded the planners that they had been too modest in their proposals: 'if a great Northern Museum is to be formed,' read
the annual report, 'a building will be required of more dignified character,
and of larger dimensions.[40] At this stage, Vernon consulted William
Wilkins, architect of two recent learned institutions, Downing College,
Cambridge and University College, London. So the classical façade of the
Yorkshire Museum was first conceived: 'You have such Gothic at York,'
Wilkins wrote, 'that any design in the same style must appear trifling . . .
the style of Architecture to be adopted . . . must be Grecian. I cannot
reconcile the notion of any other style either to the locality or to the
purpose of the building'.[41]

Unfortunately the momentum which the original appeal had generated was soon lost, partly by the legal delays encountered in securing the lease from the Crown of the proposed three-acre site, partly in the shadow of the public subscription for the restoration of the Minster after the disastrous fire of 1829. When the Yorkshire Museum finally came into use at the beginning of 1830, the total expenditure of nearly £10,000 exceeded the total donations to the Building Fund by some £1,500.

The museum was widely acclaimed and much visited. Science, as Henry Brougham the Lord Chancellor commented in 1831, was 'magnificently lodged' there. William Vernon was thanked by the members, at the first annual meeting in the new edifice, for his 'indefatigable exertions in founding and completing the Museum'.[42] But Vernon, who had held the presidency since the office was created in 1823, saw the move to the new premises as marking the end of the immaturity of the Society, and intimated that soon a man of higher station in the county should be called to its leadership. As usual, he had his way. In Febrary 1831 he told the members that in order to complete the plan of the institution it was necessary that they choose a president who 'adding to ardour for the objects of the Society, the influence of rank and property, might be at once a zealous director of its course, and a powerful guardian of its interests'.[43] The Society numbered such an individual among its longest-serving members.

Lord Milton (Lord Fitzwilliam after his father's death in 1833), having represented the county in Parliament for 20 years, was well-known and popular in York and Yorkshire. He presided over the Society until his death in 1857, a powerful guardian of its interests if not quite a zealous director of its course.[44] Vernon himself (as John Kenrick recorded) 'continued to hold the guiding hand in the deliberations of the Council',[45] and although of the founders, Thorpe was already dead, and Atkinson and Salmond did not long survive, the Society remained effectively under the control of its early leaders, Vernon and Dixon and Goldie and Wellbeloved and the indispensable Phillips, until the middle of the century.

The opening of the Yorkshire Museum determined the Society's path in ways foreseen and unforeseen. The year 1831 found the institution with a high reputation and a large membership (about 400), but also with an adverse bank balance, 'not insolvent, but . . . deeply embarrassed', as its Council confessed in their report.[46] The new building was a statement of the philosophy of the Society, giving the greatest prominence not to the housing of its library nor even the comfort of its members, but to the display of its collections. But such was the curtailment of expenditure that it was several years before cabinets and cases could be purchased to make the display at all comprehensive. Nevertheless by 1836 Thomas Allis, one of the most vigorous but also one of the most critical promoters of the museum, could boast to the naturalist Charles Waterton that

> it is now decidedly one of the best out of the Metropolis, in some departments the very best; and I shall never feel contented or satisfied with it till I see it the very best in every department, and so excellent in each that it shall be impossible from its very excellence, for there to be a single Gentleman in the County of York, who shall not feel ashamed of himself if he does not belong to it and feel that it belongs to him.[47]

One of the most notable enterprises which followed the move to Manor Shore was the excavation of the adjacent Multangular Tower of the ancient Roman fortress. But as well as pursuing its original scientific interests the Society added new ones. There was a menagerie, brought to premature extinction when a bear escaped and took brief possession of the grounds. The Earl of Tyrconnel provided a comprehensive set of apparatus for the chemical laboratory. It had been a condition of the lease granted by the crown that a botanical garden should be established and the visit of the British Assocation in 1831 gave some impetus to the venture, although it remained only sketchily implemented for many years. The meeting of the Association gave validity and purpose to the previously desultory attention to meteorology in the Society, and also led to the erection of a small astronomical observatory. (Meteorology and astronomy, interestingly enough, were two fields of inquiry represented in the earlier history of science in York. Both Charles Wellbeloved and Jonathan Gray had kept systematic records of atmospheric conditions at the turn of the century, while a few years earlier the city had boasted three distinguished astronomers, John Goodricke and Nathaniel and Edward Pigott, father and son.)

But the serious scientific activities of the thirties and forties were the concern of a small inner group of the Society, who gave lecture-courses in the Museum and exchanged papers at the evening conversation meetings, which now showed more life than the one o'clock monthly meetings. They included the omniscient Phillips and his friend William Gray Junr., son of Jonathan Gray; Wellbeloved and his son-in-law John Kenrick, antiquarians, and their colleague at Manchester Academy, William Hincks a highly capable botanist who later held chairs of natural history in Cork and Toronto; Thomas Allis, self-taught anatomist and ornithologist, John Ford, primarily a meteorologist, W. L. Newman an astronomer, and Thomas Barker, a chemist.[48] Some of the labours of this loosely-knit group of enthusiasts are reflected in their publications: the two volumes of *Proceedings* which appeared in 1849 and 1855,[49] *Eburacum,* Well-beloved's great work on Roman York of 1842[50] and Robert Davies's *Extracts from the Municipal Records of the City of York* of the following year,[51] Kenrick's *Essay on Primeval History* (1846),[52] Phillips' later volumes on Yorkshire geology, *Illustrations of the Geology of Yorkshire, Part II* (1836) and *The Rivers, Mountains and Sea Coast of Yorkshire* (1853),[53] and various slighter works by Allis, Hincks and others.

While scholarly publications might add to the scientific reputation of the institution, the Yorkshire Philosophical Society imprinted itself upon the consciousness and the affections of the local population in quite different ways. Even while it remained in debt the Society took bold steps to secure the remaining six acres of the Manor Shore, and so to extend the Museum Gardens down to the river. Its Council discussed with the Treasury leases of 33 and 99 years, and finding neither acceptable determined to purchase the coveted land at a cost of £2,500; the transaction was completed in 1837. In 1845 the City Corporation transferred to the Society the adjoining remains of the medieval St. Leonard's Hospital.

The purchase of 1837 gave the Society possession of the former gatehouse and the hospitium of St. Mary's Abbey. The gatehouse was in due course rented and restored by John Phillips and became the permanent home of the bachelor geologist and his sister. The hospitium remained for some time an acute embarrassment, rejected as a venue for William Etty's projected school of art,[54] and in its damp and drafty condition fit only to relieve the basement of the Museum of some of its clutter of antiquarian objects. Among the several tenants on the Manor Shore at this period was a company which operated a public swimming baths at the bottom of Marygate; after 1845 the baths were under the direct control of the Society.

At a time when municipal parks hardly existed, the Museum Gardens were a recognised and envied amenity. The first, restricted, admission of the public, prompted by the visit of the young Princess Victoria, took place at the time of the musical festival of 1835. Dibdin found the place 'perfectly delightful' three years later; the gatekeeper told him that 'several scores' of visitors paid for admission every day.[55] The general public were admitted without charge at the Whitsun holiday each year. In 1842, for example, 'the Gardens and Museum were as usual crowded with visitors . . . the utmost order and regularity prevailed, and . . . the Collections were in no way injured . . .'.[56] The gardens also accommodated an annual horticultural meeting, while the museum provided a convenient conference-centre for outside institutions: the Provincial Medical Association, the Yorkshire Agricultural Association, the Yorkshire Architectural Society.

But the event which at a stroke relieved the Yorkshire Philosophical Society of most of its financial worries and opened the prospect of its rise to a 'rank seldom attained by any similar Provincial Institution' was the receipt in 1843 of the sum of £9,000 under the will of the late Dr. Stephen Beckwith, 'the Second Founder of the Society'.[57] The Council were not allowed by the terms of the legacy to pay off their outstanding debt, but they engaged the services of Sir John Nasmyth to landscape the gardens, they appointed a competent naturalist, Edward Charlesworth, to be keeper of the museum (a position which had lapsed since Phillips relinquished it in 1840)[58] and they built a house for the sub-curator, Henry Baines. It was of these years of the mid-century that John Kenrick, one of the most sagacious and durable of members, could write in his old age, 'the Society had passed safely through those crises of weakness and danger to which infancy and childhood are liable, and had attained the matured strength of a manly constitution . . .'.[59]

York and The British Association
for the Advancement of Science

The British Association for the Advancement of Science visited York twice during the second quarter of the nineteenth century, in 1831 and again in 1844. Since both events were widely reported and discussed, the historian is presented with two composite accounts of how science looked at York and York looked at science. To understand the circumstances of the two meetings, and particularly the foundation meeting of 1831, it is necessary to return to the question proposed at the beginning of this essay: how did ancient York come to be involved so crucially in the creation of an organisation which was emphatically a harbinger and symbol of a new age?

An outline answer can now be usefully enunciated: the British Association was brought to York in 1831 by the reputation of the Yorkshire Philosophical Society. The new Yorkshire Museum, rather hurriedly and imperfectly furnished for the occasion, provided a much-admired meeting place for the visitors (the more prestigious of whom were housed throughout the week of the event in the archiepiscopal palace at Bishopthorpe) and the officers of the institution provided the necessary local organisation. As protocol seemed to require, Lord Milton the President of the Yorkshire Philosophical Society, became the first President of the British Association; William Vernon (henceforth under his new name, William Vernon Harcourt, Plate 1), vice-president of the Society, became vice-president of the Association. York, then as now, proved an attractive place in which to stage a conference.

There can be no doubt that the dissatisfaction with existing traditions and practices which found expression in the Great Reform Bill of 1832 had its counterpart within the life of science. As Charles Lyell had argued in 1826, cultural change demanded institutional change, as much in science as in politics.[60] The vitality, the ambition, the considerable accomplishments of the Yorkshire Philosophical Society in the period no doubt reflect the more general rise of science as a cultural force. But the prominence attained by such embodiments of provincial enterprise serves also as a reminder that 1831 was very different from 1981. Science was still amateur, dilettante even, rather than professional: its senior institution, the Royal Society, had recently elected a royal president in preference to a natural philosopher of genius; there were no universities in England apart from Oxford, Cambridge, and the still suspect college in London, and they were (to put it no more strongly) not noted for their science; the Scottish universities taught the sciences, after a fashion, but no more than their English counterparts did they promote research. There was no mechanism for government initiative in science.

Edinburgh, as a great Georgian centre of sober scholarship and high culture which had stolen from York the rather tired epithet 'the Athens of the North', was a base from which the conservatism of the English universities had more than once been attacked. It was from the Scottish capital that the first proposal for a new association of scientific men had come in 1830, at the climax of a polemical essay on the 'decline of science' in the *Quarterly Review*. David Brewster, its author, although he was one of the half-dozen most capable physicists of his generation, earned his living (and that not without difficulty) by his writing and editing. His complaints were therefore made with some knowledge and some feeling:

> the sciences and the arts of England are in a wretched state of depression . . . their decline is mainly owing to the ignorance and supineness of the government; to the injudicious organization of our scientific boards and institutions; to the indirect persecution of scientific and literary men by their exclusion from all the honours of the state; and to the unjust and oppressive tribute which the patent-law exacts from inventors.[61]

Brewster's language belongs to the age of reform, the age of improvement: it looks prospectively to a number of developments which were to characterise Victorian and post-Victorian science – a closer relation with the (mechanical) arts, technology and invention, the rise of more powerful and more effective institutions, the securing of its prosperity by the action of government and legislature. But Brewster could only start from where he was: it was 'an association of . . . nobility, clergy, gentry, and philosophers' which he proposed to relieve the malaise by begging nourishment from King and nation.[62]

By February 1831 the scheme had acquired a little more definition. In that month Brewster wrote to John Phillips, who at this time was not only keeper of the Yorkshire Museum but also secretary of the Yorkshire Philosophical Society:

> I have taken the liberty of writing to you on a subject of consider-able importance. It is proposed to establish a British Association of Men of Science similar to that which has existed for eight years in Germany, and which is now patronized by the most powerful Sovereigns in that part of Europe. The arrangements for the first meeting are now in progress, and it is contemplated that it shall be held at York as the most central city in the three kingdoms.

> My object in writing to you at present is to beg you that you would ascertain if York will furnish the accommodations necessary for so large a meeting, which might perhaps consist of above 100 individuals – if the Philosophical Society would enter zealously into the plan, and if the Mayor and influential persons in the town and in the vicinity would be likely to promote its objects.[63]

The letter was not Brewster's first communication with the officers of the Society in York. He was for a period secretary of the Royal Society of Edinburgh, and as such had some years previously initiated a combined (although not very consequential) exercise in meteorological observation between the two cities. There had, indeed, been a strange dress-rehearsal for the opening of the British Association when the Yorkshire Philosophical Society held the first annual meeting in the new museum in February 1830. Brewster was elected an honorary member. William Vernon Harcourt read an address on the history and influence of literary and scientific institutions, in the course of which he explored some of the issues which the British Association was soon to make its own: it was, he argued, regrettable that the Royal Society had long ago relinquished one of the principles established in Francis Bacon's *New Atlantis,* that the man of science should be so provided for that he was able to devote his best energies to his work, that science should command the 'whole and entire man'.[64]

Brewster, it appears, was not present to accept the honour and to listen to the address. It is probable that the Society sent him a copy, probable that he recognised there doctrines complementary to his own, possible that their author suggested to him, during the winter of 1830-31, that York would be a better place than most from which to launch an association of nobility, clergy, gentry and philosophers.[65]

Vernon Harcourt's correspondence in 1831 pursued further the problem of the organisation of science. Brewster and his Edinburgh friends had by this time virtually committed the conduct of the projected meeting to the Council of the Yorkshire Philosophical Society,[66] and its past-president was not the man to embark upon such an enterprise without due thought and consultation. To Charles Babbage, Brewster's closest ally in the 'decline of science' campaign, and to John Herschel, the defeated candidate in the Royal Society presidential election, Vernon Harcourt urged an association which would assume roles the senior institution had long ago abandoned – the coordination of the nation's science and the promotion of its claims before the administration:

> There is no society in Great Britain which has ever attempted, or at least persevered in attempting to give a systematic direction to philosophical research. . . . Neither has there hitherto been any society sufficiently independent, deliberative and powerful to possess an influence with the Government of the country; to claim for Science what is due to it and to the interests of Society depending upon it; and through the medium of public opinion to lead to a more creditable dealing with men of Science and their objects.[67]

The idea of a society which would exercise a direct influence on scientific research, although it was at least as old as Bacon, had not formed any part of Brewster's proposal. The intention of influencing the government of the day certainly had, although whether Vernon Harcourt's society working through public opinion can be equated with Brewster's genteel association petitioning the King and his ministers is perhaps debatable.

Some acquaintance with the issues which exercised and occasionally divided the founders is necessary for a proper appreciation of Vernon Harcourt's proposal, to the company assembled in the Yorkshire Museum, on Tuesday 27th September, 1831:

> that we should found a BRITISH ASSOCIATION FOR THE ADVANCEMENT OF SCIENCE, having for its objects, to give a stronger impulse and more systematic direction to scientific inquiry, to obtain a greater degree of national attention to the objects of science, and a removal of those disadvantages which impede its progress, and to promote the intercourse of the cultivators of science with one another, and with foreign philosophers.[68]

This is not the place to follow the creation of the unusual constitution of the British Association or to trace the ways in which Vernon Harcourt, percipient and persuasive, upstaged the literate but inarticulate and curiously naïve Brewster. Sufficient to record that at York in 1831 and during the following six years as general secretary, the clergyman decisively shaped the character of the new organisation.[69]

An awareness of the preliminary debates also serves as a reminder that the first meeting of the British Association in York was exploratory, experimental. To many scientific men in 1831 Brewster was a trouble-maker: some of the charges he had made in the *Quarterly Review,* and some of the reforms he had proposed, could not but give offence to the upholders of the *status quo* in Oxford and Cambridge and London. That York was the most central city in Britain was an important consideration in an age when travel was slow and expensive; that it was equally removed from London and Edinburgh and the traditions and loyalties they repre-sented, was perhaps not less important in the delicate business of launch-ing the British Association.

The measure of scientific support which the meeting would attract was thus critical. In the event Professor Daubeny came from Oxford, and Buckland, although unexpectedly prevented from participating, was a declared sympathiser; the *cognoscenti* of Cambridge offered cautious encouragement but nothing more, London science was significantly represented only by Roderick Murchison the President of the Geological Society. On the other hand Edinburgh was strongly in evidence and Dublin modestly so. That the attendance topped 300 when Brewster had originally anticipated about a third of that number, was due to the announcement circulated from York that 'all persons interested in scien-tific pursuits are admissible to the Meeting', and to the consequent support from the provincial centres. At one of the two Association dinners, in the York Tavern, 'the Provincial Philosophical Societies' were toasted. The toast was acknowledged by the Rev. William Turner, foun-der and secretary of the Newcastle Literary and Philosophical Society, in the absence from the function (although not from the meeting) of John Dalton, President of the Manchester Literary and Philosophical Society. Representatives from the societies at Hull, Scarborough, Leeds, Birm-ingham and Bristol, as well as York, also responded.[70]

So, numerically, the attendance was all that was hoped for; scientifi-cally it was not more than adequate. The viability of the Association could not yet be regarded as demonstrated. The viability even of the York meeting remained in some doubt until the last moment:

> at Oxford, shortly before his death . . . Phillips described . . . his anxieties about the first meeting, saying how in the morning he walked in the York Museum Gardens in the hope of meeting illus-trious strangers and scientific visitors, but found none . . .'.[71]

That John Phillips, recently President of the Association, should end his days in a now scientifically committed Oxford in 1874 was not uncon-nected with the recognition of his professional and personal qualities at

York in 1831. In 1832 he added to his other responsibilities the position of assistant general secretary of the Association.[72] It was the young geologist who on the first evening at York before the formal business of the meeting was underway, set the mood for the week. As the *Yorkshire Gazette* reported, 'Mr. Phillips delivered an animated lecture on the Geology of Yorkshire – got up on the spur of the moment. . . . The Company was delighted with the lecture and separated about eleven o' clock'.[73]

The fact was that both York and its Philosophical Society had a deep affection for the big occasion, a predisposition which the visitors duly noted. Brewster recounted to his wife the splendours of 'the assemblage of beauty, fashion and philosophy';[74] his lieutenant, J. F. W. Johnston, placed on record the hospitality of the local inhabitants and the social highlights of the meeting, 'preparatory . . . but so showy and glittering that a stranger might have thought men had here met together to turn philosophizing into sport rather than to cultivate science in earnest'.[75] To the business meetings and the lectures and conversations were inevitably added concerts, parties, dinners. The sophistication of the scene, social if not scientific, was heightened by the enthusiastic support of the ladies of the city and county who, after the custom of the time, were admitted to the evening meetings as long as they could be accommodated. It all made for a splendid occasion; but it established precedents which the British Association was to find somewhat embarrassing and somewhat obstructive in its circuit of annual assemblies.

In September 1844, York entertained the British Association for the second time, 'the nursing mother . . . welcomed back her wandering children with hearty goodwill,' as the *Athenaeum* had it.[76] Roderick Murchison had spoken grandly at the foundation meeting of the delight with which 'in our periodical revolution we shall return to this point of our first attraction'.[77] Since that time the Association had been the recipient of urgent summonses from great towns and small: Liverpool had been visited in 1837, then Newcastle, Birmingham, Glasgow. At the meeting in Manchester in 1842 the General Committee had been somewhat confused by simultaneous invitations from York and Cork. In the event, Cork had been given precedence, a decision which the meagreness of the attendance there in 1843 had caused the leaders of the Association to regret. Murchison, now general secretary in succession to Vernon Harcourt, recorded in a fine mixture of metaphors that the occasion was 'desperately uphill work . . . we were never so near to shipwreck'.[78] For all its apparent vigour the British Association, the self-confessed exploiter of 'the medium of public opinion', was never stronger than the strength of its most recent meeting. At least one prominent *scientist* (the word, newly minted, owed something to the Association) concluded that it was the revival of fortunes at York which ensured their continuance.[79]

In an ideal world Murchison would no doubt have sought Vernon Harcourt for the presidency in 1844. But a previous crisis within the organisation had thrust the clergyman into that office in 1839; now he shared the vice-presidency with the other Yorkshire ex-president, Lord Fitzwilliam. The President, George Peacock, Professor of Astronomy at Cambridge and Dean of Ely, despite his northern connections, was virtually a stranger to York and its citizens. The retiring President, the Earl of Rosse had, as it happened, been born in the city but unaccountably chose to regard himself as Irish. The Yorkshire Philosophical Society supplied the two local secretaries, Thomas Meynell and William Hatfeild, although Hatfeild (who, as William Marshall had been one of the first curators of the Society, 20 years earlier) met his death on a field-trip just before the meeting. John Phillips was the perennial assistant general secretary of the Association, now joining with Meynell in superintending the dispensation from the Guildhall of information, advice, tickets of membership and daily bulletins of events.

Among the numerous strangers were several European scientists of distinction, most notably the German chemist Justus von Liebig, a close friend of the Vernon Harcourts. The foreigners were lodged and entertained at local expense, 'a degree of hospitality for which they were quite unprepared, and which certainly casts honour on the city of York,' said one of the journals.[80]

As John Phillips recalled, in 1831 all the members of the Association had been able to gather in the theatre of the Yorkshire Museum; now 20 rooms were necessary to accommodate them.[81] The contrast was not simply due to the difference in scale of the two meetings (there were about 1,000 members present in 1844) but also to the subdivision of the business among sections devoted to the several branches of science. The zoology and botany sections now met in the theatre of the museum, with the geology and physical geography section in the hospitium. But the other sections were scattered around the city, mathematics and physical science in St. Anthony's Hall, chemistry and mineralogy in the rooms of the Yorkshire Architectural Society in the Minster Yard, mechanical science in the Merchants' Hall in Fossgate, medical science in the County Hospital, statistics in the Savings Bank in Blake Street. There was also a model room in St. Peter's School.

There was a degree of variation in the support which the sections enjoyed. On the first day a reporter found 'the medical, statistical, and mechanical sections . . . thinly attended; the chemical, zoological and physical moderately; and the geological largely'.[82] But two episodes within the sections aroused such excitement that the work of the others was temporarily suspended, and the spectacle provided by the one was eclipsed only by the sensation generated by the other.

The first highlight of the week, then, was the account given by the Earl of Rosse of his new reflecting telescope. Peacock, during the course of his presidential address, had described the scene which awaited him on his visit to Birr Castle, Rosse's seat in Ireland:

> ... telescopic tubes, through which the tallest man could walk upright; telescopic mirrors, whose weights are estimated not by pounds but by tons, polished by steam power with almost inconceivable ease and rapidity, and with a certainty, accuracy and delicacy exceeding the most perfect production of the most perfect manipulation; structures of solid masonry for the support of the telescope and its machinery more lofty and massive than those of a Norman keep.[83]

The nobleman had brought to York not his telescope, but working models of the instrument, with supporting piers and gantries, and of the grinding and polishing machine. Everyone, it seemed, wanted to be present when the devices were explained and demonstrated: 'long before the hour of meeting, the room was crowded to suffocation, and many ladies, and even gentlemen, could not gain admittance'.[84]

One of the contrasts between the first and second visits of the British Assocation to York which forces itself upon the attention of the historian is in the size of the annual reports to which they gave rise: the 1831 volume has 112 pages, its 1844 companion nearly 600. But for all the expansiveness of the later report, it manages only a two-line reference to what was for most people *the* event of the week, namely the Dean of York's trial of strength with the geologists.

William Cockburn had been Dean of York since 1822. In a city so much of whose life revolved around its great cathedral he could not be other than well-known, but recently his name had come to be familiar to a larger public when Vernon Harcourt and Dixon carried before the Visitational Court of the Archbishop charges concerning his irregular administration of the Minster's finances.[85]

Intellectually Cockburn was no simpleton: 'a liberal-minded man', sometime Wrangler and Fellow of his Cambridge college, an early vice-president of the Yorkshire Philosophical Society and still listed amongst its members. But it is the common fate of liberals suddenly to discover themselves conservative as their once progressive opinions are overtaken by the tide of events. The Dean had declared war on the British Association and the geologists whose influence coloured its activities at the time of the Newcastle meeting in 1838.[86] Now he had an opportunity which could not be missed to launch a simultaneous assault upon his two principal targets. On the third day of the meeting he put before the geological section his 'Critical Remarks on certain passages in Dr. Buckland's Bridgewater Treatise', subsequently published under the combative title *The Bible defended against the British Association;*[87] the pamphlet generated great excitement in and beyond York, and went through five editions in a year.

The particular object of the Dean's attack, then, was the system of earth history assumed by Professor Buckland (who had presided over the British Association in 1832) in his recent Bridgewater Treatise.[88] If the already piquant situation required further local flavouring, it was provided by the fact that William Vernon Harcourt's brother, Leveson Vernon Harcourt, Chancellor of the York Diocese, had joined in the criticism of Buckland in a work entitled *The Doctrine of the Deluge: vindicating the Scriptural Account from the doubts which have recently been cast upon it by geological speculations.*[89] There were ecclesiastical undercurrents in York in 1844, and cross-currents too.

Cockburn's appearance took place before 'a vast multitude' in the renovated hospitium:

> On a platform at the upper end, with a green cloth bench in front, sat the officers of the section, having generally large charts and figures suspended upon the wall behind them. . . . In due time the dean, a tall and venerable figure with an air of imperturbable composure, walked through the crowd, and took his place by invitation beside the president on the platform.[90]

Cockburn attempted to meet the geologists on (so to speak) their own ground. *His* account of earth history, positing the adequacy of a unique violent catastrophe compounded of flood and submarine-volcanic action, to explain the character of the earth's crust, was, he insisted, better science than theirs, less speculative, more consistent with the facts of observation:

> You will of course perceive that my theory accords precisely with the account given by Moses. I do not however, press it upon you in consequence of that accordance, but because I contend that every modern discovery may be accounted for by this theory, and cannot be accounted for by the theory of Dr. Buckland.[91]

The Dean by himself would have been enough to send the reporters away satisfied, but in the absence of Buckland, Adam Sedgwick, whose intellectual and personal qualities had taken him from the fells of north Yorkshire to the geological chair in Cambridge, had been deputed to reply. The considerable eloquence with which Sedgwick had demolished many an opponent was perhaps deliberately muted, 'delicacy itself to what might have been expected to be called forth with reference to any man of inferior years, profession, or rank'.[92] Sedgwick began by contending, as Cockburn himself had contended six years earlier, that the British Association was no place for cosmogony and speculative discourse: once admit matters which went beyond science in their implications and its meetings were at the mercy of anyone who, 'without any personal knowledge of the subject, or a single new fact to offer', had a taste for controversy. That the Professor saw the Dean as belonging to this category became evident as he went on to expose Cockburn's inadequate understanding of Buckland's rendering of earth history, and his unfamiliarity with even the most elementary facts of geology. It did, indeed, seem scarcely worth arguing against such ignorance. Nevertheless, he *did* argue, engaging his audience to the visible satisfaction of most of them, for an hour and a half. Sedgwick, it is worth noting, was himself a canon of Norwich Cathedral; while Buckland, his Oxford counterpart, was appointed Dean of Westminster in 1845, ironically enough by Cockburn's brother-in-law, Sir Robert Peel. To set the Bible against the British Association was really to falsify and perhaps to trivialise the issues.

George Hudson cannot be excluded from any account of early-Victorian York. By 1844 he had already linked the city to London by rail; the connection with Edinburgh was in prospect. But it was as a representative of the Corporation of York and a former Lord Mayor that, after the exchanges between Cockburn and Sedgwick, Hudson withdrew an invitation to dine previously extended to some of the leaders of the British Association: 'we've decided for Moses and the Dean', he explained.[93] The absurdity of the remark should not obscure its deeper truth. If the historian of ideas is searching for the men and moods of the 1840s which most clearly anticipate the uncertainties and certainties of the Huxley-Wilberforce period, he will turn not to the expostulations of Cockburn and Leveson Vernon Harcourt but to Robert Chambers's anonymously published *Vestiges of the Natural History of Creation* and to Tennyson's *In Memoriam*. For a generation York had shown that science could be importantly and elegantly cultivated in a provincial, traditional setting. But the provincialism and the tradition remained, nonetheless. Hudson's railways already heralded the dissolution of a distinctively local culture, but the motor-car and the aeroplane, radio and television had still to accelerate, if not to complete, the process. So when the British Association left town, part of the quintessential nineteenth century went with it.

Notes and References
1   A view illustrated in G. Basalla, W. Coleman, R. H. Kargon (eds.), *Victorian Science,* 1970.
2   The point can be substantiated by the annual reports of the British Association, or more succinctly by Basalla et al., op. cit. (n. 1).
3   On William Smith and the Yorkshire Philosophical Society, see p. 11. The Rev. Sydney Smith, one of the moving-spirits of the *Edinburgh Review,* was Vicar of Foston-le-Clay, a few miles from York, from 1806 to 1829; he was elected into membership of the YPS in April 1823. Sir George Cayley, chairman of the York Whig Club in the 1820s, was an active member and an early vice-president of the Society; his life and work is discussed in more detail by Jim Matthew in Chapter II below. On Hudson's more marginal participation in science in York, see p. 25.
4   H. Miller, *First Impressions of England and its People,* 1846, p. 21.
5   T. F. Dibdin, *A. Bibliographical, Antiquarian and Picturesque Tour in the Northern Counties of England and in Scotland,* 2 vols., 1838.
6   The renovation of Micklegate Bar and the removal of the barbican in the late 1820s disappointed Sir Walter Scott: T. P. Cooper, *York, the Story of its Walls, Bars and Castles,* 1904, p. 243. Charles Wellbeloved was a constant critic of the demolition of parts of historic York in the first half of the century.
7   W. Hargrove, *History and Description of the City of York,* 2 vols., York, 1818. (Hargrove was proprietor of the *York Herald.*) Also T. Allen, *History of the County of York,* 3 vols., 1828-31; E. Baines, *History, Directory and Gazetteer of the County of York,* 2 vols., Leeds, 1823. (After the manner of the period, 'histories' were as much concerned with the present as with the past.)
8   F. Drake, *Eboracum, or the History and Antiquities of the City of York,* 1736, p. 240.
9   R. Davies, *Walks through the City of York,* 1880, pp. 20-21.
10 R. S. Lambert, *The Railway King 1800-1871,* 1934, p. 31.
11 E. M. Sigsworth in P. M. Tillott (ed.), *A History of Yorkshire The City of York* (Victoria County History), 1961, p. 262f.
12 *The Yorkshire Observer,* 1 March 1823.
13 Ibid, 22 February 1823.
14 *The York Courant,* 5 February 1821.
15 Ibid., 24 December 1822.
16 Ibid.
17 Ibid., 1 April 1823.
18 *The Yorkshire Observer* appeared weekly between November 1822 and March 1823, and then spasmodically until June 1823, when it was discontinued. Its editor claimed that the political divisions in York made it impossible for a literary and scientific newspaper to survive.
19 J. M. Biggins, *Historians of York,* York, 1956.
20 Hargrove, op. cit. (n. 7), vol. 1, p. 220.
21 The first published account was in G. Young and J. Bird, *A. Geological Survey of the Yorkshire Coast,* Whitby, 1822, p. 271; cf. *Proc. Geol. Soc. 3,* 1841, 525-6. The most recent review is by P. J. Boylan in *Proc. of the Yorkshire Geol. Soc.,* 43, part 3, 1981.

[22] A. B. Gordon, *The Life and Correspondence of William Buckland*, 1894, pp. 145-6. Vernon had made the acquaintance of Buckland at Oxford about 10 years previously.

[23] W. Buckland, *Reliquiae Diluvianae, Observations on the Organic Remains contained in Caves, Fissures, and Diluvial Gravel, and on other Geological Phenomena, attesting the Action of an Universal Deluge*, 1823.

[24] William Salmond, 1769-1838; Anthony Thorpe, 1759-1829; James Atkinson, 1759-1839. On Atkinson, see *D[ictionary of] N[ational] B[iography]* and Dibdin, op. cit. (n. 5), vol. 1, p. 213.

[25] In a pamphlet addressed to Lord Milton following the meeting of the British Association in York in 1831.

[26] *The Yorkshire Gazette*, 6 February 1830.

[27] Ibid., 12 November 1831. On William Vernon (Harcourt), 1789-1871, see *DNB*, and *Proc. R. S. 20* 1871-2, pp. xiii-xvii; also E. W. Harcourt (ed.), *The Harcourt Papers*, 14 vols., Oxford, private circulation, 1880-1905, vols. 13-14.

[28] *The Yorkshire Gazette*, 6 February 1830.

[29] *The Yorkshire Observer*, 18 January 1823.

[30] Ibid.

[31] Cf. E. C. Gaskell, *The Life of Charlotte Bronte*, 1857, ch. 1.

[32] A. D. Orange, *Philosophers and Provincials The Yorkshire Philosophical Society from 1822 to 1844*, York, 1973, pp. 23-6.

[33] *Objects and Laws of the Yorkshire Philosophical Society*, York, 1825, pp. 5-6.

[34] *YPS, Annual Report for 1830*, p. 16.

[35] *Objects and Laws* (n. 33), p. 5.

[36] On John Phillips, 1800-1874, see *DNB; The Athenaeum*, 1874, pp. 597-8; *Nature 9*, 1874, pp. 510-11; T. Sheppard, 'John Phillips', *Trans. Hull Geol. Soc. 7*, 1931-3, pp. 153-187.

[37] J. Phillips, *Illustrations of the Geology of Yorkshire Part 1, The Yorkshire Coast*, 1829.

[38] C. Wellbeloved, *A Descriptive Account of the Antiquities in the Grounds and in the Museum of the Yorkshire Philosophical Society*, York, 1852, p. vi.

[39] C. Wellbeloved, *Account of the Ancient and Present State of the Abbey of St. Mary, York*, 1829.

[40] *YPS Annual Report for 1825*, p. 9.

[41] Wilkins to Vernon, 29 June 1827: Harcourt, op. cit. (n. 27), vol. 13, p. 183.

[42] *The Yorkshire Gazette*, 10 February 1830.

[43] *YPS Annual Report for 1830*, pp. 16-18.

[44] On Charles William Fitzwilliam, Lord Milton, 1786-1857, see *DNB*.

[45] J. Kenrick, 'A Retrospect of the Early History of the Yorkshire Philosophical Society'. *YPS Annual Report for 1873*, pp. 34-44.

[46] *YPS Annual Report for 1829*, pp. 13-14.

[47] Allis to Waterton, 11 November 1836: 'Allis Letters', York City Library.

[48] The Evening Conversation Meetings seem to have begun in 1836 and continued at least until 1848.

[49] *Proceedings of the Yorkshire Philosophical Society, 1847-48*, London and York, 1849; *Proceedings of the Yorkshire Philosophical Society, 1847-54*, London and York, 1855.

[50] C. Wellbeloved, *Eburacum or York under the Romans,* York, 1842.
[51] R. Davies (ed.), *Extracts from the Municipal Records of the City of York,* London, 1843.
[52] J. Kenrick, *Essay on Primeval History,* London, 1846.
[53] J. Phillips, *Illustrations of the Geology of Yorkshire Part 2, The Mountain Limestone District,* London, 1836; *The Rivers, Mountains and Seacoast of Yorkshire,* London, 1853.
[54] Etty, the York artist, was instrumental in the opening in York in 1842 of a branch of the School of Design in London.
[55] Dibdin, op. cit. (n. 5), vol. 1, pp. 205-6n.
[56] *YPS Annual Report for 1842,* p. 8.
[57] Kenrick, op. cit. (n. 45), p. 43.
[58] Phillips divided his time between York and London from the early 1830s, being both assistant general secretary of the British Association and Professor of Geology at King's College, London; he did not, however, sever his connections with York or with the YPS.
[59] Kenrick, op. cit. (n. 45), p. 43.
[60] C. Lyell, 'Scientific Institutions', *Quarterly Review, 34,* 1826, pp. 153-79.
[61] D. Brewster, 'Charles Babbage, Reflections on the Decline of Science in England', *Quarterly Review, 43,* 1830, p. 341.
[62] Ibid., p. 342
[63] Brewster to Phillips, 23 February 1831: Phillips Papers, University of Oxford. The German association to which Brewster referred had been created in 1822; Vernon (Harcourt) always denied that it had provided the model for the British Association.
[64] *The Yorkshire Gazette,* 6 February 1830.
[65] A. Geikie, *Memoir of Sir Roderick Murchison,* 2 vols., 1875, vol. 1, p. 185.
[66] The Council of the YPS set up a steering committee which included Vernon Harcourt, Phillips, Atkinson, Davies, Goldie and Wellbeloved.
[67] Vernon Harcourt to Babbage, August 1831: Harcourt, op. cit. (n. 27), pp. 234-8.
[68] *British Association Report for 1831,* p. 10.
[69] A. D. Orange, 'The Origins of the British Association for the Advancement of Science', *British Journal for the History of Science 6,* 1972, pp. 152-76.
[70] *The York Courant,* 4 October 1831.
[71] W. H. Harrison, *The Founding of the British Association,* 1881, p. 6.
[72] Phillips retained his office as assistant general secretary of the British Association until 1862; he was President in 1865.
[73] *The Yorkshire Gazette,* 1 October 1831.
[74] Brewster to his wife, 30 September 1831: M. M. Gordon, *The Home Life of Sir David Brewster,* Edinburgh, 1869, p. 147.
[75] J. F. W. Johnston, 'First Meeting of the British Association for the Advancement of Science', *Edinburgh Journal of Science 6* n.s., 1831-2, p. 7.
[76] *The Athenaeum,* 1844, p. 897.
[77] *British Association Report for 1831,* p. 39.
[78] Geikie, op. cit. (n. 65), vol. 2, p. 18.

79 Richard Owen to his sister, 4 October 1844; R. Owen, *Life and Letters of Richard Owen*, 2 vols., 1894, vol. 1, p. 242.

80 *Chambers's Edinburgh Journal*, 2 n.s., 1844, p. 324. 'The principal gentlemen of the county' had subscribed over £1,000, the sum being in the stewardship of the YPS.

81 *York Herald Report of the British Association at York 1844*, York, 1844, p. 45.

82 *Chambers's Edinburgh Journal*, 2 n.s., 1844, p. 322.

83 *British Association Report for 1844*, p. xxxi.

84 *The Athenaeum*, 1844, p. 900.

85 The ecclesiastical court found the charges substantiated and ordered that the Dean be deprived of his office. Cockburn appealed against the verdict and a Court of The Queen's Bench, while not reversing the judgement, prohibited the loss of office.

86 W. Cockburn, *Letter to Professor Buckland concerning the Origin of the World*, 1838; *A Remonstrance, addressed to his grace the Duke of Northumberland, upon the dangers of Peripatetic Philosophy*, 1838.

87 W. Cockburn, *The Bible defended against the British Association*, 1844.

88 W. Buckland, *Geology and Mineralogy considered with reference to Natural Theology*, 2 vols., 1836.

89 L. V. Harcourt, *The Doctrine of the Deluge*, 2 vols., 1838.

90 *Chambers's Edinburgh Journal*, 2 n.s., 1844, p. 322.

91 Cockburn, op. cit. (n. 87), p. 16.

92 *Chambers's Edinburgh Journal*, 2 n.s., 1844, p. 323.

93 Lambert, op. cit. (n. 10), pp. 122-3.

CHAPTER II

Science and Technology in York
1831-1981

by

Jim Matthew

SINCE YORK FINALLY SUCCEEDED in getting a University only in 1963, one might think that the city and neighbouring region would have been far from the forefront of scientific and technological innovation in the last 150 years, but such an assumption implies a basic misunderstanding of how science and technology developed until well into this century. Ashby (1959) in particular has emphasised how the the universities (in England at any rate) played a very minor role in technological change in the nineteenth century. 'The industrial revolution was accomplished by hard heads and clever fingers', and the same is true for many breakthroughs in pure science. Landed gentlemen, leisured clergymen, visionary craftsmen and professional men obsessively interested in their hobbies were the innovators of that era, and it is on them that this chapter mainly concentrates.[1] Inevitably the material discussed is highly selective, and emphasises the physical sciences and engineering somewhat at the expense of natural history and medicine. The important scientific contributions of the Yorkshire Philosophical Society in the second quarter of the nineteenth century, and York's current scientific and technological expertise are dealt with elsewhere in the book (see Chapters I, III, and XII).

The Inventor of the Aeroplane:
Sir George Cayley (1773-1857)

It might be thought inappropriate to recount the exploits of Sir George Cayley within the brief 'Science and Technology in York 1831-1981' on two quite separate grounds. Firstly, the centre for his activities was Brompton near Scarborough, almost 40 miles from the city of York; secondly, he was a man of 58 years in 1831, an age at which he might have been expected to be well past his scientific prime. However, his connections with York were strong, for, as a vice-president of the Yorkshire Philosophical Society, he had been among those responsible for the creation of the British Association for the Advancement of Science (see Chapter I and Orange 1973), and for the organisation of its inaugural meeting in York. Furthermore, between 1843 and 1853 he was destined to make important fresh contributions to aeronautics, culminating in the successful flight of the first man-carrying (though non-piloted) glider; its design incorporated the basic features of the modern aeroplane. The role that he played in the development of aviation has been fully appreciated only in recent years thanks to the painstaking researches of John Edmund Hodgson, John Lawrence Pritchard and Charles Gibbs-Smith.

It was nearly 70 years after his death in 1857 that his private papers became available, and rediscovery of his full achievement and influence followed a letter to *The Times* 10 March 1927 from John Edmund Hodgson, Honorary Librarian to the Royal Aeronautical Society. 'By courtesy of Sir Kenelm Cayley I am now permitted to give, for the first time, some descriptions of them. As original documents they are of great interest and are probably the most important aeronautical papers of the last century extant.' Through the publication of Cayley's manuscript notebook under Hodgson's editorship, and critical scientific biographies by Pritchard (1961) and Gibbs-Smith (1962; 1968; 1974) Cayley's proper place in the history of aviation has been established. This account leans heavily on their painstaking researches.

As the son of a baronet, George Cayley had the advantage of an unusually thorough and stimulating education through the good offices of two highly talented tutors, George Walker FRS and George Cadogan Morgan. He was only 19 when he succeeded to the title as the sixth Baronet, and the management of his estate at Brompton was to occupy much of his time throughout the rest of his life. However, in the periods when family matters were not pressing, he was able to tackle an astonishing range of technological problems with vigour, independence of mind, and an originality that can properly be compared with that of Leonardo da Vinci, himself an early pioneer of flying machines.

Man's fascination with flight and yearning to fly like a bird have their
origins in legend, but few aerodynamic insights appear to have been
learned in those early years. In the Bible (Proverbs 30: 18, 19) Agur, son
of Jakeh, sums up the position well:

Three things are too wonderful for me;
Four I do not understand:
The way of an eagle in the sky
The way of a serpent on a rock
The way of a ship on the high seas
And the way of a man with a maiden.

The transition from legend to formal aviation history was marked by
unsuccessful attempts to design human imitations of bird flight involving
'wings', which were responsible both for propulsion and for supporting
the system in the air. Sir George Cayley's first fundamental contribution
to aeronautics was to separate clearly the problem of lift from that of the
mechanical propulsion needed to overcome the air resistance or drag that
hinders motion.

In this appreciation of Sir George's work we concentrate on his
post-1831 work, but to put this in context it is necessary to summarise his
earlier achievements (see Gibbs-Smith, 1968). Cayley was the first to use
model gliders in aerodynamic research (1804), and from these experiments he produced a model in the configuration of the modern aeroplane
with a main lifting surface, longitudinal stability and direction-controlling
tail surfaces (1808). He realised the importance of aerodynamic streamlining, and designed shapes of minimum air resistance (1809). He saw
clearly the difficulty of providing a means of propulsion with a sufficiently
large power to weight ratio, and was the first to suggest a form of internal
combustion engine to solve the problem (1809). By 1810 he had not only
formulated the basic aerodynamics of the fixed-wing aeroplane, but had
published his findings in great detail in reputable scientific journals,
notably *Nicholson's Journal.* Although the significance of this work was
not immediately appreciated, the articles were destined to have profound
influence on later pioneers of flight.

For some years, following this burst of aeronautical activity, Cayley
became preoccupied with other technological problems and with things
administrative rather than mechanical, as co-founder of the British
Association for the Advancement of Science, as Whig MP for Scarborough (1832), as co-founder of the Regent Street Polytechnic (1838),
and as a passionate advocate of relief from the widespread distress
accompanying the industrial development of West Yorkshire (*Yorkshireman,* 1842). Through lack of space it is not possible to discuss

Cayley's contribution to other branches of science and technology – railway engineering, ballistics, temperature scales and the optics of the eye (for these aspects see Pritchard, 1961), but one story blends rather nicely the picture of a humanitarian landlord and gentleman with that of the innovative technologist. In 1845 a workman on his estate lost a hand in an accident, and this prompted Cayley to present a series of designs for the 'Artificial Hand for Working Men' (1849).

It is remarkable that as a 70-year old man (Plate 3) he should get a prodigious creative 'second wind'. Two events prompted his intellectual resurgence. Firstly, on 25 July 1842, he received a letter from Robert Taylor, a young Englishman who had just returned from the United States, and who presented him with some ideas for flying machines that were derived indirectly from Cayley's earlier work. They involved

... a double contrary horizontal rotation of two series of inclined planes, or vanes, turned by a double or hollow perpendicular shaft – the inner shaft revolving in the opposite direction to the outer. The inclined planes or vanes to be brought to a general plane when sufficient altitude is attained for lateral progression.

Cayley replied politely to Taylor, but he was not optimistic about the possibility of developing a means of propulsion for a flying machine. 'Two horsepower is required to effect a flight of one man, and steam is too heavy within the weight required'. Yet his mind had been set working on the old problems.

The second source of stimulation came from W. S. Henson, who, under strong influence from Cayley's 1809-10 work, published designs for an Aerial Steam Carriage, which was to play an important role in popularising the concept of heavier than air flight. The design was of a fixed-wing monoplane propelled by airscrews, recognisably an 'aircraft' to modern eyes. Cayley's response was to criticise rather than to praise, but what was expressed was not just the conservatism of an old man. In 1843 two papers were published in the *Mechanics Magazine,* the one a 'Retrospect on the Principles of Aerial Navigation', the other addressed directly to the Henson design. Cayley questioned the structural stability of the large wings on the steam carriage (150 feet long and 4,500 square feet in area), and asked '. . . would it not be more likely to answer the purpose to compact it into the form of a three decker, each deck being 8 to 10 feet from each other to give free room for the passage of air between them?' This form of multi-plane was close in concept to the biplanes and triplanes of the first half of the twentieth century. Cayley also put forward another alternative, a 'convertiplane' incorporating four helicopter rotors that would provide vertical takeoff; the rotors were then rotated to play the role of circular wings, while pusher airscrews provided the forward propulsion. The design, shown in Diagram 1, essentially follows the ideas of Robert Taylor, albeit in more sophisticated and practical form, and it is surprising and totally uncharacteristic of Cayley that no acknowledgement of his correspondence with the young man is made.

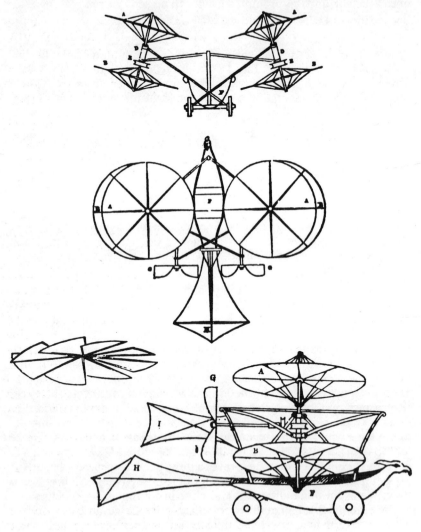

Diagram 1   The Cayley Convertiplane 1843.

Now Cayley had been totally revitalised: he proceeded to construct a full size triplane in 1849 in which '. . . a boy of about ten years was floated off the ground on descending a hill . . .', he conducted glider experiments with improved rudder control; and built an aerofoil testing machine to test experimentally the streamlining concepts he had put forward over 40 years before.

Our appreciation of the final stage of these developments came from the accidental discovery by Charles Gibbs-Smith of an article in the *Mechanics Magazine*. Its title 'Sir George Cayley's Governable Parachutes' is totally misleading, because the paper is much more about gliders than about parachutes. The advanced features of glider design contained therein are summarised by Gibbs-Smith (1968) as follows (see Diagram 2):

> . . . fixed wing, with dihedral setting for inherent lateral stability (purposely not shown in the crude illustration); nacelle for the pilot, attached rigidly to the wing, and fitted with a lightweight three-wheel undercarriage; fixed (but adjustable) tailplane-cum-fin to provide inherent longitudinal and directional stability; pilot-operated elevator and rudder (combined).

Gibbs-Smith further notes that the sophistication of control and stability inherent in the design was not incorporated into aeroplane design until 1908. Mysteriously, while on the one hand Cayley's 1809-10 researches directly influenced the flying pioneers at the turn of the century, his 1852 paper, although published in a reputable journal, remained totally unappreciated. As a result the successful gliders of Otto Lilienthal in the 1890s were in many ways much less sophisticated than Cayley's 'Governable Parachute'.

In 1853, four years before his death at the age of 87, Cayley built what he called his 'new flyer', of which no full design survives. It was in this machine that the world's first man-carrying (though not piloted) glider flight took place on his estate at Brompton. Sir John Hodgson was able to get both verbal and written accounts of the event from Cayley's grand-daughter, Mrs. Dora Thompson (1843-1933). Gibbs-Smith (1968) reports her description as follows:

> Of course, everyone was out on the high east side and saw the start from close to. The coachman went in the machine and landed on the west side at about the same level. I think it came down rather a shorter distance than expected. The coachman got himself clear, and when the watchers had got across, he shouted 'Please, Sir George, I wish to give notice. I was hired to drive, and not to fly'. . . .
> That's all I recollect. The machine was put high away in the barn and I used to sit and hide in it (from Governess) when so inspired.

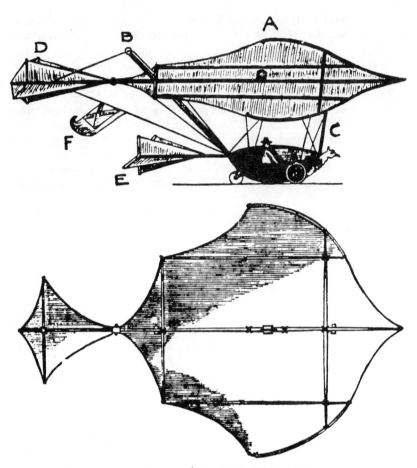

Diagram 2   The Cayley 1852 Glider Design.

The accuracy of this account by an elderly lady can never be determined, but it has been possible to test experimentally the authenticity of
Cayley's earlier gliding experiments and to evaluate just how effective his
1852 design was. Lt. Cmdr. J. Sproule (1974) took up the challenge:
'Quite early in my study of Sir George Cayley it occurred to me that it
would be an interesting project to make a replica of one of his machines to
see if it flew, and if it did, to fly it from the original place in Brompton
Dale'. From original sketches he first tackled the Riding Rudder glider,
one of Cayley's designs of the late 1840s, and on 18 August 1971 the 16 lb

glider was heaved off the eastern shore of the valley: 'It sailed away in a stable and graceful flight, exactly as its ancestor must have done 120 years before'.

Anglia Television then suggested that Sproule make a replica of a Cayley 'Governable Parachute' with a view to re-enacting the flight of the coachman as part of a television biography of Cayley. Working drawings were prepared from the *Mechanics Magazine* article of 1852, and the resulting machine was 40 feet long and 460 square feet in area, but weighed considerably more than Cayley's quoted weight of 160 lbs. This was mainly because a more robust product capable of many flights was required for filming. In successful tests the guidable 'parachute' was towed by a car, became airborne at 28 miles per hour, and reached an altitude of 50 feet; it proved manoeuvrable in flight (see Plate 4). Then it was tried going down 'the coachman's hill' in Brompton Dale. Sproule (1974) describes the event as follows:

> The car sped off down the hill with rope stretched to the limit, the Cayley was airborne immediately. At an altitude of 30 feet or so the machine sailed across the Dale to the western side, in Cayley's words like a 'noble white bird'. Across the valley towards the rising ground, the nose dropped, there was a loud bang as the front axle broke, and the tail fell off. All very dramatic, but our latter-day coachman was quite unhurt and was heard to observe on his recording transmitter the words 'oh dear'. So that was that.

> However, everyone was so pleased that the flying in the Dale was so successful, and that everything we had set out to do had been accomplished and filmed.

Of course, Sproule's experiments do not prove the story of the coachman's flight, and they do not confirm that Cayley put his 1852 design into practice in his 'new flyer', but these re-enactions show clearly that Sir George Cayley had, by the early 1850s, evolved highly successful and sophisticated glider designs. Because of the absence of any satisfactory means of propulsion in the 1850s there is no implication that an aeroplane in the Wright Brothers' sense could have emerged quickly, but more sophisticated stability and control would have been incorporated in early aircraft design if Cayley's 1852 work, rather than his ideas of 1809-10, had motivated later pioneers.

There is a risk that nationalistic fervour may induce historians to get the contribution of their own heroes a little out of perspective, and it is to authorities outside Britain that we should go to seek a final assessment (see Gibbs-Smith, 1968). Their verdict is unanimous, whether one goes to Wilbur Wright (1908): 'About 100 years ago an Englishman, Sir George Cayley, carried the science of flying to a point which it had never reached before and which it scarcely reached again during the last century'; to the celebrated German aerodynamics expert, Theodore von Karman (1854): 'The principle of the airplane as we know it now, that of the rigid airplane, was first announced by Cayley'; or to the new Air and Space Museum in Washington, opened in 1977: 'Sir George Cayley has earned the title "Father of Aerial Navigation" '. The message is clear and consistent, and we can justly salute the great achievements of this quiet humanitarian Yorkshire gentleman.

The Telescope Maker: Thomas Cooke (1807-1868)

As a young lad in Allerthorpe in the East Riding of Yorkshire, Thomas Cooke had no great liking for his father's shoemaking trade, and he began to study navigation, and hence astronomy, with the intention of going to sea. He was, however, persuaded by his mother to lead a less hazardous life. He moved to York in 1829 to work as a mathematics master (he, himself, had only two years at an elementary school and his skills were almost exclusively self-taught). He also studied optics, and made a small achromatic lens for a refracting telescope, that is one that corrects for the fact that different colours of light are focussed to different points as in a simple lens. Its performance was sufficiently impressive for his friends to encourage him to open a small optical business. He started in 1837 at 50 Stonegate, York and soon moved to Coney Street. His sons were to join him in the business, and Thomas Cooke and Sons described themselves as 'Opticians and Philosophical Instrument Makers' (E. Wilfred Taylor and J. Simms Wilson, 1954). This implied that spectacle lenses were a staple product, that the firm was willing to tackle any instrumental challenge, but that the making of refracting and reflecting telescopes was what they liked doing best.

York had continued to be active in astronomy following the important work of Nathaniel and Edward Pigott and of Thomas Goodricke in the eighteenth century. William Gray Jr., secretary of the Yorkshire Philosophical Society from 1827-1837 was one of Cooke's first customers, and his $4\frac{1}{2}$-inch aperture telescope was later to be used in total eclipse observations in Norway, while John Phillips (see Plate 2), himself an eminent geologist and Keeper of the museum of the Yorkshire Philosophical Society, purchased a $6\frac{1}{4}$-inch refractor. The Society had set up an observatory in the Museum Gardens (Taylor, 1970; Orange, 1977), but the original instruments were very primitive, and in 1843 the curator had to concede that the observatory was 'as yet unadapted to any but the simplest observations'. Thomas Cooke was assigned the task of building a new transit instrument, which was completed in 1844, the same year in which Cooke brought the new projection lantern to York.

From these parochial beginnings his reputation grew, and, as the years passed, larger, more ambitious, telescopes were produced: a 7-inch equatorial for Piazzi-Smith to be used at Teneriffe, and a $9\frac{1}{2}$-inch for J. T. Miller of Whitehaven, as well as a large number of smaller instruments (King, 1955; Hargrove, 1910). The quality of workmanship led to a build-up of orders that could not be handled in the Coney Street workshop, and in 1855 a move began to the Buckingham works, where factory methods were first applied in the optics industry. A very elaborate $5\frac{1}{4}$-inch equatorially mounted telescope was then built at Osborne for the Prince Consort. Meanwhile the 'Philosophical Instrument Makers' were also engaged in activities such as the manufacture of large turret clocks, including that for the Great Industrial Exhibition in London in 1862, and of an early form of steam car capable of travelling at 10 to 15 miles an hour and of carrying up to 10 passengers (Naylor).

Cooke's ability to match the quality of the finest European telescope makers followed the integration of two quite separate skills – one, an ability to make lenses of high quality from large discs of optical glass; the other, an ability to design and manufacture mountings, whose movements were free from backlash, and which worked on principles now known as 'kinematic design'. Technically, the summit of this achievement was the 25-inch Newall refractor with a 29.9 foot focal length, which took seven years to build and was, at that time, the largest refracting telescope in the World (Dimitroff and Baker, 1945). In his *The History of the Telescope* Henry King (1955) describes the building of the instrument.

> The project began when, at the Exhibition of 1862, R. S. Newall, a wealthy amateur astronomer, saw two large disks of optical glass on the stand of Messrs. Chance Bros. These Cooke offered to work into an objective and to mount them on a large equatorial stand of his own design. Together, the two lenses weighed 146 lbs and, to avoid their flexure during polishing, Cooke floated them on mercury. In the 32 foot tube they rested on three equidistant supports, while three counterpoised levers acted through the cell direct on the glass. The focal length of the lens was 29 feet and could be increased by a Barlow lens arranged to slide on a brass framework inside the tube. There were two finders of 4-inches aperture and a third of $6\frac{1}{2}$-inches. A comparatively small pendulum clock, housed in the upper part of the 19 foot high cast iron pillar, regulated the 7 foot driving sector of the polar axis. Right ascensions were indicated on a 26-inch hour circle, read from the floor by means of a small diagonal telescope attached to the pillar – an innovation due to Cooke and still used on large instruments.

Newall mounted the instrument on his estate at Gateshead, but blurring of the star images by the pollution-ridden atmosphere of Victorian north east England prevented the instrument from ever showing its full potential. In 1890 it was moved to the Solar Physics Observatory in Cambridge, where some good observational work on the measurement of stellar radial motions was carried out. Cooke himself died before the telescope was finally completed, but by then he had clearly established himself as one of the foremost telescope makers of the nineteenth century.

The Lens Designer: H. Dennis Taylor (1861-1943)

Too often innovative family ventures collapse following the death of the founder, but Thomas's sons Frederick and Thomas consolidated and diversified the business to produce clocks, machine tools, pneumatic pumps, pantographs (engraving machines) as well as a wide range of optical and astronomical instruments, which now included surveying and gun range-finding equipment. The firm's reputation in the field of telescopes and optical mountings remained high, and observatory domes proved a successful ancillary product, which was supplied to many famous observatories including Greenwich, the Cape of Good Hope, Brussels, Sofia, Odessa, Rio de Janeiro and Madras (Taylor and Wilson, 1954).

In this period Dennis Taylor took over as manager of the optical workshops. Whereas Thomas Cooke was responsible for adding good mechanical engineering practice to the art of the telescope maker, Taylor was to play a significant role in elevating optics into a precise quantitative science.

Harold Dennis Taylor attended St. Peter's School, York before starting training as an architect, but he had strong scientific interests, and he was quick to accept the offer of a job with Thomas Cooke and Sons, the only strongly scientifically-oriented local employer. He rapidly made his mark, filed numerous patents, and was soon in charge of the optical workshops. He had no formal scientific training at university level, and optics had, at that time, no text books which set out the theoretical background in detail. He evolved an individual philosophy of combining empirical methods with theoretical analysis, that culminated in his book *A System of Applied Optics* (1906), which Smith (1943) describes as '. . . the most important book that appeared on the subject in a hundred years'.

Making a good lens would seem to be a simple straightforward operation. The objective of the lens designer is to trap as many rays of light as possible emanating from a point in space (a point in the subject of the 'picture') and causing them to converge on a single point on the image by passing the rays through a series of curved transparent surfaces that constitute the lens system. Posed in this way, it would seem that there is a unique 'correct' solution to the scientific problem, but what the above description fails to convey is that the two goals of 'as many rays as possible' and 'converge on a single point on the image' are inherently incompatible. Furthermore, the 'best' compromise is in no sense unique, because the number of consequences following each decision taken in the design is very large, and as Price (1976) has emphasised, lens designing is in reality more akin to playing chess than to solving typical undergraduate physics problems that have a 'right' answer. If unique solutions do not exist, some important styles of compromise with wide applicability can be achieved. Dennis Taylor was responsible for one of the most important of these practical principles.

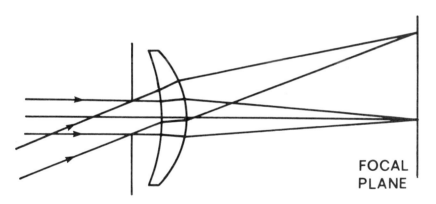

Diagram 3a   A simple meniscus lens.

The simplest meniscus lens consisting of two spherical surfaces, not necessarily of the same radii, is illustrated in Diagram 3a. Its performance deviates from the perfect behaviour required because of a series of so-called aberrations:

(1) Chromatic aberration— parallel light of different wavelengths (or colour) is focussed to different points. This can be corrected by combining simple lenses with different abilities to disperse light into its different colours. The simplest example is of a two-element lens (Diagram 3b), in which the lens compensates for the dispersion of the first, while maintaining focussing power.

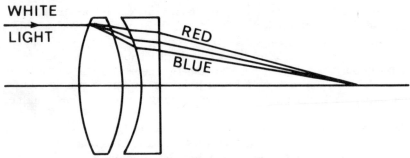

Diagram 3b   An achromatic lens doublet.

(2) Spherical aberration — if the lens surfaces are sections of spheres, light passing through the outer part of the lens comes to a focus at a different point from that near the centre of the lens (Diagram 4a). This will occur even for object and image points on the axis of the lens.

(3) Coma — images formed off the axis of the lens lead to a comet-shaped focus rather than a sharp point focus.

(4) Astigmatism — a further defect of off-axis images, which causes light to be spread along a line either in the plane of the image point and the lens axis or perpendicular to it.

(5) Curvature of field — the sharpest points of focus of different parts of the image do not all lie on a plane, leading to blurring at the edges of the pictures.

(6) Distortion — the magnification of the image varies with the angle between the point on the object and the centre of the lens. This tends to make straight lines appear curved in the image.

Let us examine one of these effects, spherical aberration, in a little more detail to get some insight into what the lens designer can achieve.

Closely following Price (1976), let us consider a lens system that intends to bring all rays from a point **O** on the axis to a unique focus at axis point **I** (Diagram 4a). The failure of various rays to strike **I** can be measured by setting up a 'shooting target' with **I** as the bullseye. The extent of the aberration may then be measured by the distance **h** of the intersection of a given ray crossing the 'target' from the point **I**; **h** depends directly on the distance **y** from the lens axis of the ray entering the lens system. A typical graph of **h** against **y** is shown; as long as **y** is very small a good focus is obtained, but eventually strong deviations occur. This is why better focussed photographs are obtained when the camera lens is 'stopped down', that is large values of **y** are eliminated; but then of course not

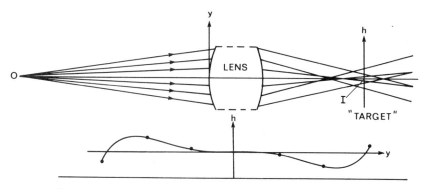

Diagram 4a Illustration of the effects of spherical aberration.
The distance **h** of a ray crossing the target plane from **I** varies
with the aperture distance **y**.

much light is trapped, and it is not possible to take pictures under poor
light conditions. The relation between **h** and **y** can be expressed as

$$\mathbf{h} = \mathbf{a}\mathbf{y}^3 + \mathbf{b}\mathbf{y}^5 + \mathbf{c}\mathbf{y}^7 + \ldots,$$

where **a**, **b** and **c** are constants characteristic of the lens system. Even
powers of **y** are absent due to the symmetry of the imaging process, and
the term linear in **y** is absent, because **I** is the correct focus for rays with
small **y**. It is possible to design the system to eliminate the lowest order of
aberration, that is to arrange that **a** $=0$. This is usually by far the most
important term in the series, and its absence will delay the onset of
appreciable spherical aberration until the lens size is much larger. It is
then said that third order spherical aberrations have been eliminated.

Moreover, similar equations govern all seven possible aberrations
(from the list given above the reader might think there were only six, but
two kinds of chromatic aberration occur with different distortions in the
longitudinal and transverse directions). Taylor (1893) tackled the problem by taking a three-element lens, and adjusting the design so that all
seven of the third order aberrations were removed. The lens system had
to have a required focal length (the distance in which parallel rays along
the axis are focussed) and so the problem is one of eight independent
variables. At least that number of variables must be available in the
system to achieve the desired goal. For a three-lens system there are
exactly that number of degrees of freedom: two radii of curvature for
each lens, the distance from the first lens to the second lens, and the
distance from the second to the third. The solution of the controlling
equations to achieve this condition was still very complicated, but Taylor
(1893) was able to carry out the tedious algebra to design the Cooke

Triplet Lens (Diagram 4b), named after the pioneer telescope maker. It has been the most studied of all lens combinations in the optics industry, and it remains one of the most used lens systems today. It does not, of course, eliminate aberrations altogether, but they are reduced greatly, and the way was opened for good quality lenses of high light-gathering power. It has been of great use in optical astronomy, and the relative simplicity of the design makes it ideal for use in mass-market cameras.

One of the first applications of the Cooke Triplet to a sophisticated astronomical system was in the Franklin-Adams telescope, an equatorial mounting containing two Cooke photographic lenses, one of 6-inch aperture and 27-inch focal length, the other of 10-inch aperture and 45-inch focal length. The instrument was used in making the comprehensive Franklin-Adams star charts of the northern and southern hemispheres (Franklin-Adams, 1902). The star images were of unsurpassed quality.

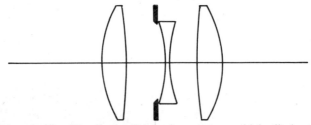

Diagram 4b   The Cooke Triplet lens system, which eliminates all seven aberations to lowest order.

With the invention of the digital computer, lens design has changed radically. Computers are ideal for juggling the many parameters necessary to specify a lens system, and lens design was one of the early applications of computers to science. By the early 1960s (Kingslake, 1962) it was possible to carry out an automatic predesign of a Cooke Triplet lens avoiding the painstaking manual iterations which Taylor had to go through, and now one can deal with much more complicated systems with many more variables. This is the approach used in specialist applications, where cost is not crucial, but if reasonable performance is required at reasonable cost, the Cooke Triplet remains an excellent compromise, and that is why many readers of this book, whose photographic tastes are not exotic, will have a Cooke Triplet in their possession.

In addition to Taylor's important book *A System of Applied Optics,* which develops in detail Taylor's approach to lens design, the firm also produced a handbook, which through its various editions was for many decades indispensible to good amateur and professional astronomers: *The Adjustment and Testing of Telescope Objectives* (1891; 1896; 1921).

Another important effect was first identified by Taylor when he noted that a lens which had weathered somewhat, thereby acquiring a surface tarnish or bloom, actually transmits more light than a pre-weathered lens. Good lenses therefore behave rather like good wines, maturing into a period of optimum optical quality before beginning to deteriorate in performance.[2] When light is incident at right angles to a glass surface about four per cent is reflected, the rest transmitted. By tarnishing crown glass lenses artificially in an aqueous solution of hydrogen sulphide Taylor was able to raise the transmission of a single surface to 97.5 per cent (Taylor, 1904). The reason for this blooming effect is now well understood; if the thickness and refractive index of the tarnished region are adjusted properly the wave reflected from the surface of the tarnished layer interferes destructively with that of the true glass surface, and so reflection is reduced or eliminated. It was not until 1936 (Strong) that more controlled techniques of blooming became available through evaporation of thin films of calcium fluoride (later the more durable magnesium fluoride). In 1981 it is routine to evaporate a complex series of multi-layers on lens surfaces to reduce radically reflection throughout the visible range, and this has made possible lens systems with 20 or more lens elements with good overall optical transmission; for example, television zoom lenses. The principles of these sophisticated activities were laid down in Taylor's 1904 patent.

For his contributions to optics Dennis Taylor was awarded the Trail Taylor Medal, the Duddell Medal of the Physical Society of London and the Progress Medal of the Royal Photographic Society. He retired to his family village, Coxwold, and died in 1943. A small display in tribute to his memory is to be found in the concourse of the Physics Department of the University of York.

Moving into the twentieth century, the products of T. Cooke and Sons Ltd. changed somewhat in emphasis and reflected the increasingly technological nature of military warfare. Improvements in internal base naval rangefinders were introduced incorporating 'built up' end reflectors, the swinging range prism and binocular vision. Another naval product was a cine camera capable of taking 5,000 photographs per second, which was used for following the bursting of shells, while Cooke theodolites were used in the Scott and Shackleton Antarctic expeditions and on attempts to climb Mount Everest in the 1920s and 1930s (Taylor and Wilson, 1954). In 1921 an equatorially mounted telescope of 18 inches was produced for the Brazilian National Observatory, and transit instruments were installed in Mauritius, Singapore and Colombia for relaying accurate time signals for ships to use in ascertaining their exact position.

The Second World War required great expansion in the optics field, and Edward Wilfred Taylor (1977) has recorded the output achieved by a workforce that rose to 3,300 during the 1939-45 period:

Clinometers 16,000	Tavistock theodolites 735
Flash spotters 1,150	Optical scale theodolites 860
Dialsights 5,600	Tank periscopes 147,260
Sighting telescopes 65,400	Spare tank prisms 228,900
Predictor telescopes 41,500	Tail drift sights 20,000
Identification telescopes 2,050	Telescope sights 10,000
Stereoscopic telescopes 2,010	Traverse indicators 1,600
	Long-base rangefinders 20

Just as Thomas Cooke's sons Thomas and Frederick continued their father's standards and traditions, so Edward Wilfred Taylor (1891-1980), Dennis Taylor's son, made further important contributions to optics, and to 'Cooke, Troughton and Simms Ltd.', as the firm became known after Vickers Ltd. had acquired both T. Cooke and Sons Ltd. and Troughton and Simms Ltd. of London in 1922. Following World War II the information-gathering power of the optical microscope was enhanced by the invention of the Phase Contrast Microscope by Zernike (Nobel Lectures, 1964), for which he was awarded the Nobel Prize in 1953.

Micro-organisms such as bacteria and cells are colourless and transparent, and are therefore difficult to distinguish from their surroundings in the optical microscope. Nevertheless, when a light wave passes through a transparent object there is a change of phase relative to a light beam going along an equivalent path *in vacuo,* and when two such waves recombine, destructive or constructive interference may result just as in the blooming of lenses. Zernike introduced the idea of splitting coherent microscope illumination into two beams, one of which passes through the specimens, while the other, called the direct ray, passes through a 'phase plate', which can be adjusted so that different parts of the sample go light and dark depending on whether there is constructive or destructive interference between the rays. In this way 'invisible' objects can be seen in the microscope.

It was imperative that the British optics industry should assimilate these techniques and become competitive in this area. E. W. Taylor's papers 'On the Control of Amplitude in the Phase Contrast Microscope' (Taylor, 1947) and 'Applications of Phase-Contrast to the Ultra-Violet Microscope' (Taylor, 1950) were vital developments in the field, and this work, allied with other contributions to optical science, was rewarded with a Fellowship of the Royal Society in 1952. E. W. Taylor is, to my knowledge, the only citizen of York so honoured in this century until after the University came to the city. Among the more novel projects of the postwar period was the design of special high-power microscopic objects for observing cosmic ray tracks in the film emulsions used by C. F. Powell (Nobel Lectures, 1964) in his discovery of the π-meson and other particles, work that was to be recognised with the award of a Nobel Prize in 1950.

It is too early to put into perspective the most recent contributions to optics of Vickers Instruments Ltd. (as the company is now called), but the firm remains active in the microscope field amid strong Japanese competition, and handles a wide range of military contracts in applied optics.

The Hunnings Micro-Telephone

Nineteenth-century clergymen were, at least in relative terms, quite prosperous men endowed with more than an average amount of leisure time. The range of their 'part-time' cultural pursuits was immense, and they were not immune from dabbling in technology. It is nevertheless surprising to find that one of the more important inventions in the development of telecommunications was made by the curate of a small village church near York (Matthew, 1981).

Henry Hunnings had undergone a typical clerical apprenticeship –'an MA at St. Edmund's College, Oxford followed by a series of short chaplaincy appointments – before becoming curate at the handsome parish church of Bolton Percy in 1874 (*Alumni Oxonienses,* 1891). The Parish Records (held at the Borthwick Institute, University of York) confirm his participation in weddings, funeral services and vestry meetings, where he was involved in such important decisions as 'Resolved that the Sexton be not allowed to send for oil for the bells except with the sanction of the Churchwarden'. One suspects that, amid the tedium of parish business, his mind would often wander to his intellectual passion – electrical science.

The transmission of speech along a wire by Alexander Graham Bell in Boston in 1875 was a widely publicised event, reported fully in both the popular and technical press in Britain. Based on detailed descriptions of the Bell device in journals, such as the *English Mechanic,* many amateurs set out to reproduce the early Bell experiments, and as early as September 1877 Henry Hunnings began work along these lines (Baldwin, 1925; 1938). He discussed his early attempts with another local enthusiast, Edward Cox-Walker, a manager with the expanding company of Thomas Cooke and Sons, whose achievements have already been discussed in this chapter. Whether the telephone was to remain an amusing middle class toy or whether it would revolutionise communications, depended on whether telephone messages could be transmitted over the large distances for which telegraph communication was possible. Hunnings correctly diagnosed the basic weakness of the original design. Bell used similar induction coil devices as both transmitter and receiver; in the case of the transmitter the pressure of sound waves sent a magnet into oscillation, which in turn induced oscillatory voltages in an electric circuit. Although this approach was adequate as a receiving device, it was not satisfactory as a transmitter if speech-transmission over many miles was contemplated. Thomas Alva Edison, probably the most prolific inventor of all time, was the first to make radical improvements in transmitter design. The variation of the electric resistance of carbon with pressure had already been established, and Edison exploited the effect in patenting a carbon transmitter in which pressure waves set up by speaking into the device changed the voltage across a piece of compressed lampblack. In Britain, David Hughes independently made a transmitter based on the same principle, and it was he who first called such a device a 'microphone' (Hope, 1978).

Meanwhile Henry Hunnings was working along the same lines, but found that much greater sensitivity could be achieved if discrete granules of carbon were placed between two metal diaphragms, the much augmented signal arising from the many independent points of microphonic contact. Patent number 3647 was filed at the Office of the Commissioners of Patents on 16 September 1878, and was sealed on 24 December 1878; the abridgment of the patent is reproduced in Diagram 5. US patents 246512 and 250250 followed.

Edward Cox-Walker believed the Hunnings design so promising that he decided to give up his secure position to launch a company along with a Mr. E. Harrison to manufacture the Hunnings transmitter. A public demonstration of the Hunnings Micro-Telephone (price 15 guineas) took place at a meeting of the Cleveland Institution of Engineers (1879) after the system had been tested between York and Darlington using the ordinary telegraph wires that stretched along the side of the railway. The members adjourned to the offices of Messrs. Stevenson, Jacques and Co., where Mr. Harrison communicated with Edward Cox-Walker at the Acklam works of the company. The instrument clearly worked well, for Cox-Walker was heard to reply 'Don't laugh so loud please'.

The high quality of the Hunnings micro-telephone soon attracted the attention of the United Telephone Company, which held both the Bell and Edison patents in Britain (Baldwin, 1934; 1938). In response to the commercial threat the United Telephone Company sued Harrison Cox-Walker Ltd. for infringement of their patents. The case, often known as 'The Telephone Case' because of its importance to the way the telephone industry developed in Britain, came before Mr. Justice Fry on 24 April 1882. The receiver of the Hunnings micro-telephone was indeed a close copy of the Bell design, and Cox-Walker lost the case with regard to

3647. Hunnings, H. Sept. 16.

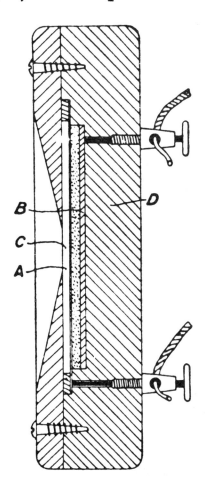

Telephones. — A telephone transmitter is constructed with a layer of finely-divided carbon C placed in a loose state between two thin metallic diaphragms, in a suitable box D with a mouthpiece. The front vibrating diaphragm A is preferably of platinum foil and the posterior diaphragm B is of brass. The layer of carbon is of oven-made engine coke crushed very fine, or metallized carbon powder may be used.

Diagram 5   Abridgment of Hunnings's patent for the carbon microphone.

it, but the action with regard to the transmitter was dismissed (Baldwin, 1934; 1938). Henry Hunnings, by now curate at Rothwell near Leeds, appeared before the court to defend the distinctive character of his transmitter, and the *Telegraphic Journal and Electrical Review* (1882) reports as follows on his cross-examination:

> Mr. Hunnings stated that he had not considered what was the reason why the instrument worked, and that the description given in his patent was entirely that suggested by the patent agent. The material he used in his transmitter, viz. powdered coke, he had never looked upon as being simply one form of carbon. He had tried lampblack after hearing of Edison's experiments, and had not found it to answer. All the experiments that had led up to the present form of transmitter had been made in total ignorance of any experiments having been made by other workers.

Complex legal wrangling followed, and the eventual compromise involved the sale of the Hunnings patents to the United Telephone Company (British rights) and to the American Bell Telephone Company (American patents) for £1,000.

At that stage it was by no means clear that the Hunnings form of microphone would triumph over other forms of transmitter. The Bell Company improved the packing characteristics of the carbon granules in 1885, and gold plated the electrodes to reduce contact contamination (Fagen, 1975). The use of granules of anthracite coal carbonised by roasting led to a form of the Hunnings transmitter suitable for large-scale production, and to the present day it is the dominant form of telephone transmitter.

Microphones are examples of what we now call transducers, devices which convert mechanical deformations into electric signals. It is astonishing that, amid the micro-electronic revolution, the Hunnings invention remains competitive in sensitivity against its rivals. Just over 100 years after Hunnings's work York is once again at the forefront of telecommunications following the completion of an optical fibre link between Haxby and York, which is capable of carrying simultaneously enormous numbers of telephone conversations – but each one of them is brought about by someone speaking into a carbon microphone that closely resembles the pioneering design of Henry Hunnings.

Epilogue

In concentrating mainly on the achievements of Sir George Cayley, Thomas Cooke, Dennis Taylor and Henry Hunnings in this chapter there has been a conscious attempt *not* to write a parochial history of science in

York, but to choose a small number of contributions that have had genuinely international impact. Others might conceivably have been included.

The work of Tempest Anderson (1846-1913) on vulcanology was of the first rank (Suthren, 1977). In spite of his 'amateur status' he was in the official British observing party to study the eruption of Soufrière and Montagne Pelée in 1902 (Anderson, 1908), and his photographs of volcanoes collected from travels all over the world are now being reanalysed. However, he was a distinguished collector and classifier rather than the instigator of some important new generalising principles or interpretations. Rowntree Mackintosh Ltd (as that company is now called) owe their tremendous success more to good product marketing and analysis, and sound assimilation of newly developed technology,than to fundamental scientific research, but some important steps in food and confectionery processing have been achieved, and recorded through patents. Other companies such as Armstrongs Ltd and Adams-Hydraulics Ltd have been responsible for engineering innovations of some importance, and in the 1930s there was a mild flirtation with the manufacture of aeroplanes in the city (Shute, 1954). However, four contributions to science in York since 1831 shine through: Cayley's amazingly sophisticated glider designs, Cooke's magnificently engineered telescopes, Taylor's superbly clever approach to the removal of aberrations from lenses, and Hunnings's opportunist invention of a very sensitive microphone. None of these four gentlemen was trained as a scientist or an engineer, but all four were highly innovative and very professional in converting their ideas into reality. They are among the most distinguished men associated with York in the last 150 years.

Notes

[1] The author has much pleasure in acknowledging assistance from and/or helpful discussions with Kenneth Hutton, Austin Chambers, K. Geddes of the Science Museum South Kensington, Alf Peacock, the late Edward Wilfred Taylor, Alan Gebbie, Christine Upton and members of the Yorkshire Philosophical Society.

[2] I am indebted to my colleague Dr. A. Chambers for this admirable analogy.

References

Alumni Oxonienses 1715-1891 (1891).

ASHBY, E. (1959), *Technology and the Academics.*

ANDERSON, T. (1908), *Phil. Trans. Roy. Soc.,* A208 275.

BALDWIN, F. G. C. (1925 and 1938), *The History of the Telephone in the United Kingdom.*

COOKE, T. AND SONS LTD. (1891), *The Adjustment and Testing of Telescopic Objectives,* 1st edition 1891, 2nd edition 1894, 3rd edition 1921.

DIMITROFF, G. Z. and J. G. BAKER (1945), *Telescopes and Accessories,* The Harvard Books on Astronomy (eds. Shapley and Bok).

FAGEN, M. D. (ed.) (1975), *A History of Engineering and Science in the Bell System. The Early Years 1875-1925,* Bell Telephones Incorporated.

FRANKLIN-ADAMS, J. (1902), *Monthly Notices of the Royal Astronomical Society,* vol. LXIV, 613.

GIBBS-SMITH, C. H. (1962), *Sir George Cayley's Aeronautics 1796-1855,* Science Museum Publications.

GIBBS-SMITH, C. H. (1974), *Sir George Cayley, Father of Aerial Navigation (1773-1857), Aeronautical Journal,* 4, 125.

GIBBS-SMITH, C. H. (1968), *Sir George Cayley 1773-1857,* Science Museum Booklet.

HARGROVE, W. H. (1910), *The History of York,* Supplement to *Yorkshire Herald,* 10 September 1910.

HOPE, A. (1978), *One Hundred Years of Microphones, New Scientist,* 78, 378.

Hunnings Microtelephone (1880), *Proc. Cleveland Inst. of Engineers,* 15 March 1880, 113.

KING, H. C. (1955), *The History of the Telescope.*

KINGSLAKE, R. (1962), *Proceedings of the Conference on Optical Instruments and Techniques* (ed. K. J. Habell).

MATTHEW, J. A. D. (1981), *York History,* no. 5.

NAYLOR, B. (no date), *The York Steam Cars, York History,* No. 1, 9.

NOBEL LECTURES (1964), *Physics 1942-1962.*
        C. F. POWELL, 1950, 137.
        F. ZERNIKE, 1953, 235.

ORANGE, A. D. (1977), *Philosophers and Provincials,* Yorkshire Philosophical Society.

PRICE, W. H. (1976), *Scientific American,* 8, 72.

PRITCHARD, J. L. (1961), *Sir George Cayley — the Inventor of the Aeroplane.*

SHUTE, N. (1954), *Slide Rule.*

SMITH, T. (1943), *Nature,* 151, 442 (Obituary notice for H. D. TAYLOR).

SPROULE, LT. CMDR. J. (1974), *Aeronautical Journal,* 7, 315.

STRONG, J. (1936), *J. Opt. Soc. Amer.,* 26, 73.

SUTHREN, R. (1977), *Annual Report,* Yorkshire Philosophical Society, 53.

TAYLOR, E. WILFRED (1947), *Proc. Roy. Soc. A,* 190, 442.

TAYLOR, E. WILFRED (1950), *Proc. Roy. Soc. B,* 137, 332.

TAYLOR, E. WILFRED (1970), *The Astronomical Observatory,* Annual Report of Yorkshire Philosophical Society.

TAYLOR, E. WILFRED and J. S. WILSON (1954), *At the Sign of the Orrery,* Cooke, Troughton and Simms.

TAYLOR, H. DENNIS (1893), *British Patent* 22607
        US Patent 568052
        German Patent 81825, 86757.

TAYLOR, H. DENNIS (1904), *British Patent* 29561.

TAYLOR, H. DENNIS (1906), *A System of Applied Optics.*

The Telephone Case (1882), Report in *The Telegraphic Journal and Electrical Review,* 13 May 1882, 332.

CHAPTER III

Archaeology in York
1831-1981

by

Peter Addyman

The Beginnings of York Archaeology

York, remote enough from the metropolis always to have had a distinct provincial character, has even so never been a cultural backwater. Although the city had no university until 1963, it nevertheless housed more educated and enquiring minds than were perhaps to be found in the average provincial city, particularly among a large ecclesiastical, medical and legal establishment, and the Quaker and Unitarian intelligentsia. It is hardly surprising, therefore, that in each generation for several centuries there have been at least a few York inhabitants, and the occasional outsider, who, stimulated by the uniquely well-preserved remains of York's periods of greatness as the northern Capital, have felt the urge and had the time and resources to study them as a means of extending knowledge of the city's history.

The tradition of archaeological writing about York and its region was already a century and a half old when the Inaugural Meeting of the British Association for the Advancement of Science took place in York in 1831. Francis Drake's *Eboracum* (1736), an exemplary history for its time which incorporated the results of earlier antiquarian enquiry (Lister, 1682), was still a standard work familiar to the several York scholars who were instrumental in starting the Association. Their awareness of the

53

potential and importance of the archaeological method had, moreover, recently been heightened by a series of linked events. These began with the discovery in June 1821 of the Kirkdale Cave; the cave's contents, and the controversies aroused by the find, are described by Derek Orange in Chapter I. The discoveries led to the establishment of the Yorkshire Philosophical Society in 1822, with one of its aims the formation of a geological and archaeological museum capable of accommodating such finds as had remained in local hands. The museum was in being in 1823, housed at first in Ousegate. Through the exertions of the Reverend William Vernon Harcourt (Plate 1), the Society obtained from George IV the grant of an area by the Manor Shore, part of what is now Museum Gardens, for a new museum. This area contained the ruins of St. Mary's Abbey and parts of the King's Manor, residence of the Lord President of the Council of the North. The Society, faced with the dilemma of building over the site of St. Mary's Abbey, took the advice of the Society of Antiquaries of London, on the strength of which it excavated not only the threatened portion of the Abbey but much else.

The excavations, as so often in York, were more successful even than their sponsors had hoped. They uncovered (Plate 5),

> not mere heaps of mutilated stones, but considerable portions of the walls of the Monastery, of spacious and elegant door-ways of columns of varied forms, rising to the height of five or six feet, standing as they had been before the dissolution of the Abbey, intersected by the massive foundations of the Palace; while, in the intervening spaces, were scattered numberless fragments of capitals, mouldings, and rich tracery-work. Of similar materials the foundation-walls of the Palace, upon being broken up, were found to consist. The curiosity of the public was most powerfully excited: not an hour passed without bringing to light some long-buried beautiful specimens of the art and fancy of the monastic sculptor – some memorial of departed splendour, to gratify the eye, to exercise the imagination, to send back the thoughts to times, and persons, and manners long past (Wellbeloved 1829, p. 9).

In 1829 with commendable promptness rarely seen today a report on the work was published by the Society's Curator of Antiquities, the Reverend Charles Wellbeloved (Wellbeloved, 1829). Meanwhile, funds having been quickly raised, the new museum was constructed over part of the excavated Abbey, opened in February 1830, and was already a year old when the British Association held its first meeting there. Within it, in addition to displays on geology and natural history, there were already very considerable archaeological collections. If archaeology was not at the start a main concern of the British Association for the Advancement of Science, it cannot but have been topical in the local circumstances.

Those who attended the first meeting of the Association must, moreover, have been conscious of another recent and significant anti-quarian achievement. Following a petition to Parliament in 1800 to remove the bars, walls and posterns of York, a preservation lobby was formed, with both local and national support including Sir Walter Scott's promise to walk to York, if necessary, to save the walls (Curr, 1980). This resulted in the saving of everything except three of the postern towers and the barbicans on three of the bars. In 1829 the York Footpath Association had drawn up a comprehensive plan to restore the walls, and by 1831 work was in progress on the whole length of walls south-west of the Ouse. The growing zeal for conservation of the city's historic buildings had received another challenge in 1829, with the fire in the choir of York Minster on 2 February. Not only was a restoration scheme quickly drawn up and quickly financed through a local and national committee, but the antiquarian lobby, led by Wellbeloved, ensured the preservation of the choir screen, which it was proposed to remove (Kerr, 1973).

In 1831, therefore, York was exceptional amongst provincial cities in having a scientific society with the study of archaeology as one of its declared aims; in having a tradition of excavation as a means of research; and in having experience of the problems of conservation of ancient sites and buildings. Within a year or two the city was also faced with another of the themes still familiar to York's archaeologists today, the opportunities and threats to the archaeological heritage presented by major develop-ment projects. Until that time the street pattern and tenement layout of medieval York had largely survived. Edward Baines's map of 1822, the first which accurately shows individual properties, recorded it just in time (see Map 1). A series of improvement schemes was undertaken in the 1830s and 1840s which fundamentally changed the street pattern (these and later changes are shown in black on Map 1). This gave rise to quite new property layouts in some areas, and caused a major breaching of the city walls. The arrival of the railway and the need for a station saw another breach in the ancient defences and the construction of a station, now itself demolished, within the walled area. In the 1830s also a new prison was constructed which caused great changes to the topography of the castle area. That decade, too, saw a start to the construction of sewer systems throughout the city. It was also a period when much private building was done in and, especially, immediately around the walled city.

All of these developments encountered archaeological remains and the archaeologically inclined members of the Yorkshire Philosophical Society were alert to the opportunities not only to record information

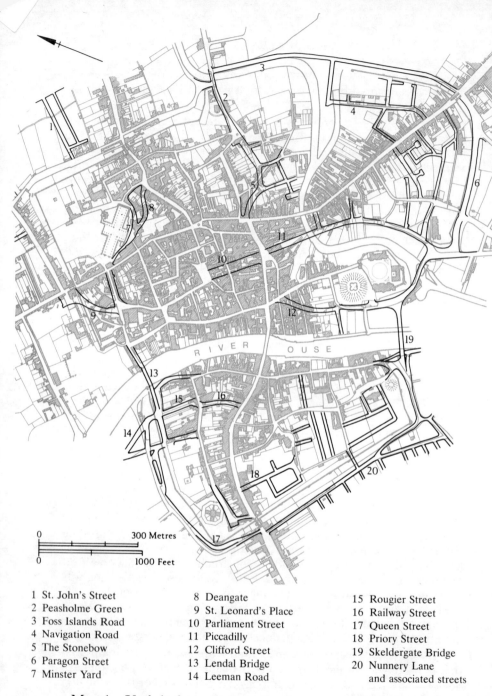

1 St. John's Street
2 Peasholme Green
3 Foss Islands Road
4 Navigation Road
5 The Stonebow
6 Paragon Street
7 Minster Yard

8 Deangate
9 St. Leonard's Place
10 Parliament Street
11 Piccadilly
12 Clifford Street
13 Lendal Bridge
14 Leeman Road

15 Rougier Street
16 Railway Street
17 Queen Street
18 Priory Street
19 Skeldergate Bridge
20 Nunnery Lane
  and associated streets

Map 1   York before modern development, based on the
plan of c. 1822 by E. Baines, with later streets shown in black.

about the topography of the Roman and medieval city, but also to recover the artefacts and even structural remains for preservation in the York-shire Museum. Their successes are recorded each year in the *Annual Report of the Yorkshire Philosophical Society*. Much of the work was evidently done by the museum's honorary Curator of Antiquities and Coins, the Reverend Charles Wellbeloved, with on-site recording and day to day watching carried out by the museum's sub-curator Henry Baines and by John Browne, whose experience here doubtless proved valuable when he came to record the remains of the Norman minster after the 1829 fire (Browne, 1847). The results of their watching brief, as it would now be termed, when the York and North Midlands Railway built its station in Toft Green, on the near vacant site of the Dominican Friary in 1839, are still the basis of our knowledge of what seems to have been one of the largest and most monumental Roman bath buildings in the Roman Empire north of the Alps. Their vigilance in 1832-34 when St. Leonard's Place was cut through the city walls to the south-west of Bootham Bar, and subsequently in 1842 when it was provided with sewers, gave us our first knowledge of the character and construction of the walls of the Roman legionary fortress; indicated for the first time the interval tower system of which many other parts are now known; and provided the basis of our present knowledge of the Roman topography of that area. The discovery of the fortress wall in Feasgate in sewer-laying in 1833, and later when Parliament Street was constructed in 1834-36, and when sewers were put into Patrick Pool and Aldwark, proved for the first time the extent of the fortress. The great Trajanic inscription from the *porta principalis sinistra* found at the corner of King's Square and Good-ramgate in 1854 (Wellbeloved, 1855b) provided the essential dating evidence for the rebuilding of at least the gateways in stone.

The Society promoted strongly the idea that the Yorkshire Museum was the appropriate resting place for all archaeological finds made in, or connected with, York. They collected from current excavations, bought the private collections of local antiquaries when they came on the market, and even sought out and recovered objects which had long since gone from York. The successive editions of the Yorkshire Museum Handbook, first prepared by Wellbeloved (Wellbeloved, 1852) chronicle the success of this policy.

The growing archaeological collection of the Yorkshire Museum stimulated scholarly interest in York's archaeological problems, and sev-eral members of the Yorkshire Philosophical Society produced papers on the subject in the Society's early years. Vernon Harcourt, a chemist by specialisation, turned his expertise to the examination of inclusions in a type of Roman pottery 'frequently found at York, but of a colour nearly black, and of a very loose texture' (Wellbeloved, 1842, p. 124). Well-beloved considered this the pottery 'full of mica or cat-silver' recognised as a York type by Dr. Martin Lister as early as the seventeenth century (Lister, 1682-3, pp. 70-4). Evidently it was in fact the now well-known calcite-gritted or *Huntcliff* ware, Lister's being perhaps the micaceous *Eboracum* ware (p. 66, below). Vernon Harcourt's examination showed the inclusions were calcareous spar, which he noted were unaltered, implying a relatively low firing temperature. These early observations, both Lister's and Vernon Harcourt's, are precocious forerunners of tech-niques of pottery fabric analysis now being developed by Dr. D. P. S. Peacock at the University of Southampton (Peacock, 1977).

The spate of Roman finds made in the 1830s and the accessions to the museum led to pressure on Wellbeloved first to provide lectures on their significance, then to publish an account of them. The resultant *Eburacum or York under the Romans* (1842) is a still valuable scholarly summary, epitomising the breadth of learning, systematic method and practical approach of Victorian antiquarianism at its best.

Wellbeloved's concern for the past also extended to later periods. The discovery of a series of Anglo-Saxon, Norman and later medieval coin-hoards in the 1830s to 1850s established the basis of York's excellent public coin cabinet, and stimulated Wellbeloved, and scholars with whom he was in correspondence, to the intense numismatic studies (Well-beloved, 1855a) which are still the basis of knowledge, particularly of the Anglo-Saxon series. The story has recently been reviewed (Pirie, 1975, pp. xv-xxii).

York Archaeology after the 1830s

The vitality of York's scientific community, and the excellent facilities provided by the Yorkshire Museum, led to the return of the British Association to York in 1844. Two years later the city was host to the Archaeological Institute of Great Britain and Ireland (Archaeological Institute, 1848). Local antiquaries were immediately conscious of the benefit to local workers of contact with distinguished archaeologists, of the value of the Institute's resultant report, and of the remarkable nature of the exhibition of antiquities the Institute brought to York on this occasion. Even without this stimulus, however, interest in archaeology was flourishing. Local antiquaries kept up a dialogue not only with the Institute, but its rival the British Archaeological Association, whose Gloucester meeting of 1847 heard of and inspected recent York finds (Roach Smith, 1846). By correspondence, members of the Yorkshire Philosophical Society helped Charles Newton of the British Museum with his map of British and Roman Yorkshire (Ramm, 1971, p. 68). In 1848 the Yorkshire Architectural Society had been formed, to study ecclesiastical architecture and to restore architectural remains in Yorkshire. By 1848 the Yorkshire Philosophical Society had elevated archaeology from one of its subordinate 'objects of scientific curiosity' to an equal place with natural history among its objectives (Ramm, 1971, p. 68).

In 1849 the Yorkshire Antiquarian Club was formed, to carry out research and excavation in the county, the products to come to the Yorkshire Museum. The club began energetically with numerous excavations of barrows in East Yorkshire (Proctor, 1855), part of the vogue which in the second half of the nineteenth century resulted in rudimentary excavation of a majority of Yorkshire barrows. The publication of the results by Bateman (1861), Greenwell (1877), Mortimer (1905) and others, and the accumulation of large series of prehistoric artefacts, some deposited in the Yorkshire Museum, some in the British Museum, and others first in Mortimer's Driffield Museum, and then in the Hull Museum, provided the basis for all future work on Yorkshire prehistory. The story of the late nineteenth-century scramble for Yorkshire antiquities has recently been well told (Manby, 1979, pp. 78-9).

One of the earliest of the barrow excavations, and technically one of the best, took place in York itself. John Thurnam, born at Lingcroft Farm near Fulford, was Superintendent at The Retreat, the well-known York mental hospital, until 1851. While there he excavated Lamel Hill, an enigmatic supposed barrow in its grounds. He reported his discoveries both nationally and locally, using, ahead of their time, a drawn section, drawings of the artefacts, and measured drawings of the skeletal material (Thurnam, 1849; 1855). His archaeological experience in York, and doubtless his contacts with like-minded members of the Yorkshire Philosophical Society (Ramm, 1971, p. 69-71), prepared him for a distinguished archaeological career when, while superintendent of the Wiltshire County Asylum at Devizes, he excavated and accurately reported on several Wiltshire barrows and began systematic physical anthropological studies on the skeletal remains discovered.

By 1911, according to Benson's estimation, some 1,272 burials had been excavated on the Wolds. The *Annual Reports* of the Yorkshire Philosophical Society in the late nineteenth century record the progressive acquisition by gift or purchase of the products for the Yorkshire Museum. The rare local finds – the 1868 hoard of neolithic tools found (Radley, 1968) during the construction of the York gas works is an example – also found a home with the Society. The successive editions of the Yorkshire Museum Handbook, culminating in the eighth in 1891, demonstrate progressive reorganisations of the display to accommodate not only new finds but also new ideas about the subdivision of prehistory.

Like most other museums of its time the Yorkshire Museum, under the joint honorary curatorship of the Reverend James Raine and Canon Greenwell (1873-96), chose to display its artefacts according to classification systems which owed much to the ones used for the adjacent geological and natural history collections. Nevertheless, by the time the British Association made its fourth visit to York, in 1906, the museum had a tolerably complete coverage of Yorkshire prehistory, including the finds from the Arras and Danes Graves Early Iron Age cemeteries; and the terms in which it was interpreted for Association members by the local secretary of Section H, Dr. George Auden, father of the poet (Auden, 1906, pp. 1-14), were recognisably our own.

Since then the Yorkshire Museum has continued to take in the products of prehistoric excavations in its gathering grounds, undertaken sometimes through its own initiative, as with the beaker barrow at Thornton Dale near Pickering (Kirk, 1911), excavated by the Keeper, Oxley Grabham, in 1911. In recent years the artefacts have increasingly come from rescue excavations, as barrows, settlement sites and other prehistoric monuments have been wiped from the face of the county by intensive agriculture, afforestation, mineral extraction and other destructive land-use changes. The collection has provided a quarry of evidence for generations of prehistorians, and in recent decades there have been a number of important studies of palaeolithic (Roe, 1968), mesolithic (Radley, 1969; Wymer, 1978), neolithic (Clough and Cummins, 1979), bronze age (Roe and Radley, 1969; Longworth, 1961) and local matters (Radley, 1974) which have drawn heavily on Yorkshire Museum material. The Museum's own Keeper, G. F. Willmot (1950-1971), understood its beaker and food vessel series as well as anyone, bringing to its study a pan-European knowledge of the early bronze age, and a perception which, despite his failure to publish, enabled him to anticipate many of the conclusions of Dr. David Clarke's magisterial doctoral study of British beaker cultures (Clarke, 1970, p. 2).

From an early period the Yorkshire Museum has contained some of the most important burial finds of the distinctive La Tène Arras culture of Eastern Yorkshire. The Yorkshire Philosophical Society has a long association with the study of this culture, most recently by its publication of Dr. I. M. Stead's successive surveys (Stead, 1965; 1979).

These twentieth-century studies show the wisdom of York's nineteenth-century antiquaries in gathering all local archaeological finds into the museum. Time and again they bemoaned the dispersal of local finds; time and again they persistently followed up private collections and acquired them either by purchase or gift from the owners or their dependants. For most of the twentieth century, local finds have tended to come more or less by tradition to the Yorkshire Museum. Once again, however, private collectors, equipped with metal detectors, are threatening the comprehensiveness of the museum's holdings and now pose for the Keeper of Archaeology much the same problems as faced her nineteenth-century predecessors.

The second half of the nineteenth century, the great gathering period for the prehistoric collectors, also saw major advances in knowledge of the topography and character of York in the Roman period, and in Anglian, Viking and medieval times. One stimulus to a new kind of thinking was evidently the Ordnance Survey's large scale (5 ft to 1 in) plan of York, published in 1852. This incorporated the results, findspot by findspot, of the previous two decades of rescue archaeology, and recorded in addition great amounts of historical information, the notes about which were unfortunately lost when the OS namebooks were destroyed in World War II. The new maps enabled antiquaries to see the topographical relationships of surviving ancient remains and to correlate with them the findspots of archaeological material. Twelve years later Robert H. Skaife produced a new map, based on the Ordnance Survey (Skaife, 1864) with much additional archaeological information, and various hypotheses about the sites of lost ancient structures, particularly documented medieval ones. They have often proved surprisingly accurate, and are evidently the result of a thorough knowledge of documentary, traditional and archaeological sources.

Rebuilding and development continued apace in later Victorian York. The Yorkshire Philosophical Society also continued, through its curators of antiquities, to monitor the archaeological discoveries and acquire whenever possible the archaeological finds. As new discoveries were made the Society always seemed to have a scholar ready among its members to report on them. As often as not between 1858 and 1877 it was the Reverend John Kenrick, son-in-law and archaeological heir of the Reverend Wellbeloved; while between 1870 and his death in 1898 the Reverend James Raine shared his time between his professional duties (latterly as Chancellor of York Minster), his assiduous work as Secretary of the Surtees Society and his Honorary Curatorship of Antiquities, producing a prodigious stream of archaeological and historical papers.

Roman York and Yorkshire

As far as Roman York is concerned the major event in this period was the construction of the North Eastern Railway Company's new Railway Station in Bishops Fields, south of the Ouse and west of the city walls. Excavations for the new lines and station began in 1871, and until 1877 there was a succession of finds in what was evidently an extensive and rich Roman cemetery. The Yorkshire Museum expended considerable sums on acquiring finds direct from the workmen, but as usual many private collections were made, and it was not until 1906, after a generation's assiduous collecting, that the Society was able to say, on purchasing the collection of Robert Smith of Scarborough, that 'practically all the products of the Railway Station excavations are now in the Yorkshire Museum' (YPS *Ann. Rep.* for 1906). The finds are still the definitive cemetery collection for Roman York; including sarcophagi, artefact groups and inscriptions. Still today, as then, they provide insights into 'Roman life and manners' and then, as perhaps still now, they enable the Yorkshire Museum to boast of a 'collection of objects illustrative of Roman life . . . much larger than that from any one place in the kingdom' (*Ann. Rep.* for 1874, p. 11). Many of the finds still have pride of place in the Yorkshire Museum, as for instance the discovery reported to the Yorkshire Philosophical Society by Raine on 7 December, 1875 of a sandstone coffin containing a gypsum-filled lead coffin with 'a long folded tress, the back hair, in fact, of a young Roman lady. It might almost have been combed when it was first discovered, it was so limp' (YPS *Ann. Rep.* for 1875, Communications, pp. 6-7).

Works connected with the Railway Station provided another fundamentally important contribution to York archaeology. When the city wall was breached in 1874 for the road to the new station it was possible to see that 'the mound on which the City wall is erected . . . had been raised at three or four different periods' (*Ann. Rep.* for 1874, p. 9), the first of a number of field observations and research excavations – the last as recent as 1973– which have progressively defined the complicated development of the city defences (p. 77, below).

New chance finds continued to come towards the end of the century. The Yorkshire Museum's well-known life-sized military statue was found in extensions to the Bar Convent in 1880 (*Ann. Rep.* for 1880, p. 13; King, 1882). A year later the Yorkshire Philosophical Society noted '. . . the figure will long remain, it is to be hoped, one of the chief ornaments of the Entrance Hall of the Museum' (*Ann. Rep.* for 1881, p. 10). It still does. Another important find, made in Sycamore Terrace in 1901 (*Ann. Rep.* for 1901, pp. 104-5), and acquired by the museum, was the burial of a young woman the contents of whose coffin included the openwork inscription SOROR AVE VIVAS IN DEO (Hail sister! May you live in God!), the first demonstrably Christian object from York.

Antiquaries were conscious, however, that the great days of hand excavation and deep foundation digging were nearly past. Thus in 1890 '. . . the number of antiquities obtained from York itself is, perhaps, below average, as the use of concrete has practically put an end to deep digging' (*Ann. Rep.* for 1890, p. 14). There were still a number of productive archaeological salvage operations to come, capable of producing useful information when close watching was possible. The drainage works of 1893 picked up the Roman road systems in the Bootham-Clifton area, while the stone bridgehead of the main Roman bridge across the Ouse turned up in North Street and Tanner's Moat (*Ann. Rep.* for 1893, p. 8). Not all recorders however were quite so perceptive. There are tantalisingly inadequate accounts of the discovery of a major columned building under the York Equitable Society's store in Railway Street (now the Co-op in George Hudson Street) and the scrappy descriptions of the huge excavations for the North Eastern Railway's offices in 1900-01 (*Ann. Rep.* for 1901, p. 104), made by the project architect, hint that much was lost there. Enough had been recorded by the turn of the century, even so, for George Benson, the most active York antiquary of his time, to draw together a coherent account (Benson, 1911, pp. 9-20) of Roman York as a preamble to his comprehensive study of York's development. The layout of the fortress and its alignment had at last been recognised. The road systems and main cemeteries were known; and the concentration of structures on the south-west bank of the Ouse, within the medieval walled area, was seen for what it was, the main late Roman civil settlement. The character of both military and civil life was becoming apparent from the unrivalled series of artefacts in the museum.

In the opening years of the century the potential of problem-orientated, investigative archaeology to redefine the history of Roman Britain became evident, and *Eburacum,* legionary base for the military north from AD 71 to 410, and civil capital for the divided province from the time of Severus at least, began to attract the especial attention of Romanists. The great Roman pottery collections of the Yorkshire Museum were systematically catalogued by Thomas May. He related them to the now fast-accumulating corpus of dated specimens elsewhere, and used them to define a ceramic history for Roman York (May, 1908-11). Excavations specifically designed to answer questions about the development of the legionary fortress took place under Stewart Napier Miller in 1925-27 (Miller, 1925; 1928). The results are still fundamental to the chronology of the fortress defences. Once again the Museum Gardens were the locale of important investigations, this time with Roman objectives and under the watchful eye of Canon James Raine's son, the Reverend Angelo Raine (Raine, 1926). When there were opportunities for watching briefs or rescue excavations there was a York Excavation Committee waiting to take them, as in the discovery, efficient excavation, and, happily, the preservation of the St. Sampson's

Square legionary bath building in 1930-31 (Corder, 1933). The city was fortunate in this period in the presence of a distinguished amateur archaeologist, Philip Corder, a master and housemaster at Bootham School from 1918-38, who subsequently became curator of the Verulamium Museum and Assistant Secretary of the Society of Antiquaries. Corder was one of a group who began systematic study of Roman Yorkshire under the aegis of the Yorkshire Archaeological Society's Yorkshire Roman Antiquities Committee. Mary Kitson Clark's Gazeteer (Kitson Clark, 1935) co-ordinated the scattered records and finds of the past, while a series of research excavations, at the Langton villa, and at Malton fort and town, and the resultant *Roman Malton and District* reports, began to show the rich agricultural basis for the prosperity of later Roman York. Corder's especial contribution, however, was his work on the Yorkshire pottery industries. His excavations at the kiln sites of Throlam and Crambeck defined the most common pottery types of late Roman Yorkshire (Corder, 1928; 1931; Corder and Birley, 1937) and as late as 1956 he proposed a new type 'Parisian ware' (Corder, 1956).

The Yorkshire Philosophical Society was conscious that 'our knowledge of Roman Britain has been revolutionised during the past 25 years, and the value of the museum collection for educational purposes would be largely increased if it could be better displayed' (*Ann. Rep.* for 1925, p. 21). The curators, moreover, adopted a new principle of display for the finds from the 1925 excavations which were shown 'grouped according to the trenches in which they were discovered, with plans and sections of the excavations' (*Ann. Rep.* for 1925, p. 26). The problems of displaying the Roman collections were solved in 1931 by repairing and extending the hospitium, a partly ruined outbuilding of St. Mary's Abbey. The new museum was opened in 1931; it 'gives to Yorkshire one of the finest museums of Roman Antiquities in the Country' (*Ann. Rep.* for 1931, p. 7) and is still used for this purpose. In the Second World War it was catalogued for safety, and after the war rearranged under Richmond's guidance. A new Roman gallery in the main museum was opened under Willmot in 1958, demonstrating at last what could be achieved with outside help and new displays.

Postwar years saw rapid redevelopment of many parts of the city centre of York, especially in or near the Legionary fortress. There were several local Roman specialists at the time with the skill and the motivation to take the archaeological opportunities. They increasingly received government support as the Ministry of Works (later the Ministry of Public Building and Works and latterly the Department of the Environment) began to assume a responsibility for recording and excavating ancient sites threatened with destruction. The Yorkshire Museum was under the curatorship of G. F. Willmot from 1950 to 1971 and he undertook some of the watching briefs. An important series of excavations was carried out in the 1950s and 1960s by L. P. Wenham, lecturer in history at St. John's College (now the College of Ripon and York St. John). In 1950 the York office of the Royal Commission on Historical Monuments was opened and its archaeological specialist, H. G. Ramm, also undertook several excavations and watching briefs. The city itself generated a perceptive excavator at this time in Dr. I. M. Stead who also directed several of the rescue excavations urgently needed in his home city. The *Yorkshire Archaeological Journal* increasingly during the 1950s became the means of publication of the results. Most of the work was done on an *ad hoc* basis. The efforts of Sir Ian Richmond and others to re-form a Roman York excavation committee to work out a co-ordinated research programme foundered on personal incompatibilities. Nevertheless there were considerable achievements which can be judged from Volume I of the Royal Commission on Historical Monuments' Inventory for the City of York, *Eburacum: Roman York* (RCHM, 1962). This compendium of all evidence about Roman York known in 1960 was largely Ramm's work, enriched and given perspective by the additions and comments of one of the commissioners, Sir Ian Richmond. Sir Ian's contribution to understanding of the significance of Roman York had already been considerable – his recognition of the identity of the Stonegate larger-than-life statue of Constantine the Great is but one example (Richmond, 1944). Here, backed by the detailed evidence of the inventory, he and Ramm drew out for the first time in proper balance and perspective the role of *Eburacum* as a fortress, and of *Colonia Eburacensis* as a town, provincial capital and sometime imperial seat.

In the 20 years since *Eburacum* there have been several substantial gains in knowledge. Wenham has continued his studies of the fortress defences and strengthened his case for the existence of a defence work of the date of Petilius Cerialis (AD 71) on the site of the later fortress rampart (Wenham, 1966). Four major excavations have taken place in the fortress. The underpinning and restoration of York Minster (described by David Dowrick in Chapter IV) gave opportunities for an herculean rescue excavation, carried out under the most adverse of circumstances. A York Minster Excavation Committee was set up, first under the chairmanship of Sir Mortimer Wheeler, then of A. R. Dufty and finally of Professor R. J. C. Atkinson. Investigations revealed the basilica of the fortress *principia* and parts of the adjacent barracks of the 1st Cohort. The work, begun under Ramm, was completed by A. D. Phillips (Phillips, 1975), whose report on the project is nearing completion. In the *praetentura* of the fortress in 1972 the York Archaeological

Trust uncovered more of the legionary bath building found in 1931-2, and a remarkable sewer which served it (Whitwell, 1976). Part of a tribune's house in Blake Street was investigated by the Trust in 1975. There have been two excavations on the fortress defences, one revealing more of an interval tower first excavated by Wenham in Lendal (Sumpter and Coll, 1977) and a series of others in Bedern and Aldwark which supplemented the information provided by Miller in the 1920s. The stratification in each case was linked with that of the fortress interior. Outside the fortress the Trust has investigated an industrial suburb in Aldwark, a grain warehouse and Ouse-side road in Coney Street, and Foss-side commercial structures in Coppergate. Evidence for a legionary pottery industry was discovered in 1971-72 by York Excavation Group in Peaseholme Green. Its product, *Eboracum* ware (Perrin, 1977, p. 105) includes that micaceous pottery defined as long ago as 1682 by Lister (pp. 57-8, above).

The *Colonia*, too, has been the subject of systematic excavation for the first time. Wenham revealed substantial buildings near St. Mary's, Bishophill Junior in 1961 and 1967, as did Ramm on the site of the demolished St. Mary's, Bishophill Senior. Ramm's excavations were extended onto adjacent sites by the York Archaeological Trust in 1974, revealing more of the buildings and a riverside street in Skeldergate (Carver et al., 1978). Part of another town house, evidently an extra-mural one, discovered as long ago as 1851 (*York Herald,* 20 September, 1851) was uncovered in 1976 in Clementhorpe. Outside the *Colonia* Wenham's publication (Wenham, 1968) of his Trentholme Drive excavations provide the first modern study of a large second to fourth century Romano-British cemetery.

These post-1960 excavations have been on a scale and to a standard to provide the strategraphic and chronological framework and cultural context into which the many previous finds can be set. They extend and extensively illuminate the history of Roman York – the fortress, colonia, extra-mural settlements, cemeteries, culture and chronology – they provide data on the physical characteristics and demography of the inhabitants, and give an indication of the contemporary environmental conditions. They do not, however, fundamentally alter the story built up painstakingly since the seventeenth century, and brilliantly summarised by Sir Ian Richmond at the 1958 meeting of the British Association at York in his Sheldon Memorial Lecture (Richmond, 1959).

Anglian York

Chance finds and museum acquisitions during the nineteenth century also stimulated local antiquaries to consider the archaeology of Anglian and Viking York. All the major early Anglian finds were made at this time. The Anglian cremation cemetery within the Roman burial ground at Dalton Terrace off The Mount, was found in 1859-60 (YPS *Ann. Rep.* for 1859, p. 72; Stead, 1958a) while railway construction in 1878 (YPS *Ann. Rep.* for 1878, pp. 8-9) located the Heworth Anglian urnfield. Other Anglian finds were made during construction of Clifford Street (1884; YMH 1891, pp. 216-18) and in 1829 during alterations to York Castle Mound. Few finds of substantive importance of the Anglian period have been added since, at least until very recently, though discussion of these nineteenth-century discoveries has continued unrelentingly.

Modern reconsiderations stemmed from Myres's work in the 1940s and 1950s on Romano-Saxon pottery and other evidence for early Germanic settlement near Roman towns. In York this stimulated Stead to undertake further examination of the Dalton Terrace site (Stead, 1958a). The York cemeteries were repeatedly adduced as evidence in discussion about the end of towns in Roman Britain. They contain some of the earliest Germanic pottery in the country and, it was claimed, indicate the garrisoning of the late- and sub-Roman city by Germanic mercenaries (Myres, 1969, *passim*). The earliest of the cremation urns, whose date is still under discussion, may well belong to the fourth century, before the end of Roman official rule. The cemeteries were probably still operative in the sixth century. The nature of these Germanic enclaves in an area not otherwise brought into Anglian occupation until the 570s awaits a satisfactory answer. Increasingly effective archaeological observation in recent years has failed to show where the Germanic occupants of the cremation urns may have lived. Though discussion of the finds continues (Faull, 1979; Eagles, 1979) and individual pots have variously been discussed in print (Myres, 1977; Eagles, 1979; Kennett, 1978), the finds of the Heworth cemetery, 103 years after its discovery, still await full publication.

Coins of the later Anglian period, before the Viking attack of 866, continued to be discovered in York throughout the nineteenth century and were then the main archaeological evidence for knowledge of Eoforwic. Other later Anglian finds also accumulated in the Yorkshire Museum, but few were at the time recognised as of that date. They were only belatedly brought together, and their significance revealed, by D. M. Waterman's *Archaeologia* paper of 1959, the basis of modern archaeological studies of Anglian, and Anglo-Scandinavian, York. The mid- and later-nineteenth century did see, however, the recovery of stone sculptures and inscriptions which contemporaries thought, sometimes rightly, sometimes wrongly, were of Anglian date. Many were found during the spate of restoration of city churches. One group with obvious Anglian associations came from St. Mary's, Bishophill Junior. They include the finest Anglian inscriptions yet found in York and a cross shaft preserving a charming and rare vignette of two figures in Anglian dress, one holding a horn. The most significant of the stones discovered at this period, however, was the dedication slab from St. Mary's, Castlegate (Haigh, 1870), found during Butterfield's restoration of 1868-71. This was first considered, probably correctly (Okasha, 1971, p. 131), to belong to the mid-eleventh century, but the Reverend John Kenrick, in his communication to the Yorkshire Philosophical Society of December 1870, revised his opinion to assign it a date of AD 756. On this basis he produced a stimulating if erroneous hypothesis about the topography of eighth-century York (Kenrick, 1870), an intractable subject which nevertheless still finds investigators willing to put forward hypotheses (Harrison, 1960).

The St. Mary's, Castlegate, stone emphasised the great age of some of the city churches. An early date had long been accepted for St. Mary's, Bishophill Junior, not only because of the pre-Viking sculptures but because the Anglo-Saxon character of its architecture was recognised as early as 1842 (Anon, 1842). There had been speculation about the Anglian date of structures discovered by John Browne under York Minster in the 1840s, first by Browne himself, later by Sir Charles Peers (Peers, 1931) and finally by Taylor and Taylor (1965). All were incorrect, as it turned out (p. 75, below; Taylor, 1978, p. 1086). When Taylor and Taylor came to review the Anglo-Saxon churches of York in 1965 they were able to point to Anglo-Saxon structural evidence in several others (Taylor and Taylor, 1965, pp. 697-700; St. Mary, Bishophill Senior; St. Cuthbert), but none of pre-Viking date. It was even then not realised, however, that possibly the oldest Anglo-Saxon stone building in York had been located as long ago as 1839. It was the so called 'Anglian tower', re-excavated by the late Jeffrey Radley in 1969. The structure was shown for what it was by Radley, and he established its relationship to a series of defensive works, themselves in part probably Anglian (Radley, 1972). Radley died in an accident during the work. The excavation was resumed by the Inspectorate of Ancient Monuments under B. K. Davison who demonstrated in detail the nature of the defences of post-Roman and pre-Viking York (Webster and Cherry, 1972, pp. 165-7).

To the several studies of the sceatta and styca coinage of pre-Viking Northumbria, and to the growing collection of Anglian sculpture, Raine added his edition of early historical sources relating to York *The Historians of the Church of York* (Raine, 1879-94), making readily available the historical evidence against which the archaeological finds had to be set. Finds since that time have been summarised several times in recent years (Cramp, 1967; Ramm, 1972; RCHM, 1975, pp. xxviii-xxx) and others continue to be made. Archaeologists have signally failed, however, to establish the role and character of York during Northumbria's Golden Age. Progress awaits the location of the contemporary royal palace, cathedral, churches and monastery, and occupation areas. The York Minster excavations of 1967-73 probably came near to achieving a part of this, producing sculpture of stupendous quality, and various evidence of occupation; but most of it remains a challenge for the future, made particularly difficult by the vestigial nature of the remains – pottery seems to have been used rarely if at all (Addyman, 1975, pp 219-21 and 24; 1976, p. 12) – and the occupation levels are therefore difficult to recognise. Most of the sites are probably inaccessible under historic buildings in the heart of the modern conservation area; and by mischance the recent excavations in areas where Anglian remains might have been expected all encountered, with a few precious exceptions (Addyman, 1976, pp. 12 and 28-9) later disturbances which would have removed all trace.

Anglo-Scandinavian York

Although the role of York as a capital for the Viking settlement in Yorkshire was well known to early antiquaries, and the coinage produced by Danish and Viking kings (between the capture of York in AD 866, and the final expulsion of Erik Bloodaxe in 954) has been recognised since the eighteenth century at least, little headway was made in the nineteenth century with the archaeology of Viking-age York. Objects and sculptures recognised as of Scandinavian affinity were discovered from time to time and added to the museum collections. It was realised that the plethora of Anglian coin hoards whose contents included coins no later than the 860s probably represented losses at the time of the attack. It was not until the cutting of Clifford Street in 1884, however, and the wholesale reconstruction of the Water Lanes and closely-knit properties nearby, that it became evident where the centre of Viking York might perhaps be found. Extensions of the Friends Meeting House to its new Clifford Street façade, for instance, produced many finds and a good part of the Yorkshire Museum's large Anglo-Scandinavian collection comes from this general area. The full significance of these finds became clear in 1902, when Benson was able to record timber structures and deeply stratified deposits of the period during building between High Ousegate and Coppergate. His excellent report (Benson, 1903) shows they were of a kind now familiar from the Coppergate excavations of the 1970s. The finds from these and adjacent building sites (Benson, 1907), with their clear Scandinavian associations, attracted considerable interest. Benson reported them to the Yorkshire Philosophical Society, while Auden provided reports for the *British Numismatic Journal,* the *Saga Book of the Viking Club,* and *The Reliquary* (Auden, 1907; 1908; 1910). Reginald Smith reported some of the finds to the Society of Antiquaries (Smith, 1907). Later Benson drew together the historical, archaeological, numismatic, placename and topographical evidence and correctly defined the location and character of the commercial centre of Viking Jorvik (Benson, 1911, p. 52). Here, as always, he brought to the problem, if not a breadth and precision of scholarship (see Dolley, 1971, p. 90) at least a profundity of local knowledge, a sound practical judgement and an innate geographical sense.

Despite the interest created by the 1902-06 finds, however, York archaeologists in the first half of the twentieth century, preoccupied often by Roman matters, paid scant attention to the problems of Viking York. Chance finds continued to be collected by the Yorkshire Museum. Existing finds were drawn upon by Viking scholars in their syntheses on Viking art and culture (Brøndsted, 1924, pp. 191, 196ff.; Kendrick, 1949, pp. 87-95) demonstrating York's place in the mainstream of Viking civilisation in the late ninth and early tenth century. The cultural achievements of the Viking Kingdom of York also began to be recognised, and the central role of York itself in bringing them about. W. G. Collingwood's series of papers on Anglian and Anglo-Danish sculpture culminated in a comprehensive study (Collingwood, 1927). Shetelig's scholarly corpus placed York's Viking finds in an international context (Shetelig, 1940, pp. 93-9). It was not, however, until a thorough watching brief was kept in one of the several huge postwar developments on the land between Foss and Ouse – in this case the Telephone Exchange site in Hungate in 1949 to 1951 – that York's potential to define the character of the English Viking period was realised. The observations, carried out by John Anstee and a trainee of the Wheeler School, Miss K. M. Richardson, and followed up by Robin Hill and G. M. Knocker (Richardson, 1959) provided, despite the miserable circumstances of the excavation, the first report to modern standards on Viking York. Its publication coincided with the Waterman corpus of earlier finds (Waterman, 1959), and attracted the 4th Viking Congress to York two years later (Small, 1965). With this example it is unfortunate that the York archaeologists of the 1950s and 1960s, still preoccupied with Roman archaeology, were to fail to grasp the opportunities for further work in the heart of the Viking area. The Marks and Spencer or Midland Bank developments in Parliament Street, various new buildings in Spurriergate and Coney Street, or even the telephone exchange extensions on the old Hungate site in 1971 (see Map 1), could all have provided valuable new evidence. In a number of rescue excavations designed to answer Roman problems, however, Anglo-Scandinavian deposits were encountered, recorded and published. The great depth of these deposits around the Roman corner tower in Feasegate (Stead, 1958b) and against and near the Roman defences in King's Square (Stead, 1968) and Low Petergate (Wenham, 1972) suggested that much of the land between the legionary fortress and the river Foss was intensively occupied in Viking times.

The full import of these and earlier discoveries was realised by Jeffrey Radley. His posthumous 1971 paper for *Medieval Archaeology* on the economy of Anglo-Danish York showed the importance of the Micklegate-Ouse Bridge-Ousegate-Pavement axis in Viking times and demonstrated the potential of the uniquely well-preserved organic deposits of this area. With the application of suitable scientific techniques they could provide a quite unusual range of information about the culture, economy and environment of the Viking capital. This led the York Archaeological Trust, set up in 1972, to take the first opportunity that came its way for rescue excavation in this area. A bizarre investigation deep under the standing eighteenth-century buildings which became Lloyds Bank, Pavement (Addyman, 1975, pp. 218-24), confirmed Radley's views. Not only were there deeply stratified deposits with a full range of well preserved timber structures and conventional finds, but the techniques of environmental archaeology vastly extended the data product (Buckland et al., 1974; Kenward, 1978, pp. 35-6).

The Lloyds Bank experience encouraged the Trust to undertake the very large project of excavating totally four properties in Coppergate shortly to be developed as a shopping centre. The Coppergate project of 1976-81 at last provided the detailed study of a part of the Viking City which has for long been an obvious lacuna in York – and British – archaeology. Evidently the Roman suburb in this area and any subsequent buildings were cleared away at the start of the Viking age to accommodate the new street, Coppergate. Properties were laid out in the long narrow strips typical even today of central York. Street front shops were built on the sites of their present day successors (Plate 6). Behind them were workshops, and behind again, yards, wells, latrines, even at one time perhaps, warehouses. A vast range of crafts and industries was carried on, and trade in both local and foreign commodities. The project has defined at last the international stature of Viking York – and has handsomely made amends for lost opportunities in this area in the past. In its wake has come a spate of research papers and publications presenting the results and drawing out the morals (Hall, 1976; 1978). The City of York, moreover, has accepted plans for the creation of a Jorvik Viking Centre, below the new shopping centre at Coppergate, to present to a wider public an account of this important but little known phase of York and English history.

The York Minster excavation project of 1967-73, though it failed to locate the Viking-age Minster, did encounter a cemetery of the period. From this, and from foundations of later Minster structures, were recorded many Anglo-Scandinavian sculptures which immediately made clear the importance of the York metropolitan school in the development of Viking art. Pattison's initial publication of these outstanding stones (Pattison, 1973) came at a time when the British Academy's corpus of Anglo-Saxon sculpture, shortly to be published, was being prepared. A lively debate has ensued on these and other recent sculpture finds from York and its region (Lang, 1978a; Lang, 1978b; Bailey, 1980). The British Academy has also served Viking – and indeed medieval – York well in numismatic matters by publishing recently its sylloge on coins in the Yorkshire Museum and Yorkshire collections prepared by Miss E. J. E. Pirie. Miss Pirie has documented the growth of the Yorkshire Museum's collection in the nineteenth century, the strengths and weaknesses of the various curators who cared for it, and the vast literature it has engendered (Pirie, 1975, pp. xv-xxiii). So far as the Viking series is concerned the most important papers emanate from the distinguished school of numismatists who in the 1950s and 1960s transformed understanding of Anglo-Saxon coinage. Professor R. H. M. Dolley in particular has given special attention to the Scandinavian series, to York finds, and to coins of the York mint. From this the British Academy sylloge benefitted greatly. Numismatics, however, does not stand still, and recent excavations, particularly those in Coppergate, have produced many coins and objects of the greatest numismatic rarity – including trial pieces, and a die for the minting of St. Peter's pence. Miss Pirie's accounts of these (Pirie, forthcoming) will provide an important new chapter in York's Anglo-Scandinavian numismatic history, to be followed, it is to be hoped, by a corpus of the complete known product of the York mint.

York and Medieval archaeology

Excavation on a medieval site, St. Mary's Abbey, was, we have seen, one of the first archaeological enterprises of the Yorkshire Philosophical Society. The Society continued to recover medieval finds from commercial excavations and observe the demolition or alteration of countless medieval buildings throughout the nineteenth century. Its museum became almost a mausoleum towards the end of the century for the discarded fittings of 'restored' city churches. Nevertheless, not for 80 years since its first excavation did the Society – or indeed, with the exception of John Browne in the Minster, any York archaeologist –

consciously undertake excavation of another medieval site. When it happened, once again it was St. Mary's Abbey. In 1900 the architect, Walter Brierley, began to clear the chancel of the abbey church, inspired by the research objectives spelled out well before his death by Chancellor Raine (YPS *Ann. Rep.* for 1880, pp. 45-7). Not only the thirteenth-century chancel but the whole east end of the preceding Norman church was found. The remains were not well preserved and Brierley consulted the best authorities as to how they should be displayed. Both William St. John Hope, Secretary of the Society of Antiquaries, with the experience of Fountains Abbey behind him, and C. J. T. Micklethwaite, restorer of Kirkstall Abbey, agreed with Brierley's scheme for laying the various periods out in different coloured bricks, flags and rock asphalt. To the protests that this brought from members of the Yorkshire Philosophical Society he answered 'we should break the spirit of our convention and ill deserve the title "philosophical" if we sacrificed antiquarian considera-tion to those of mere effect' (YPS *Ann. Rep.* for 1902, p. 9). In another defence of the restoration he claimed 'it is our duty to hand it on to future generations free from spurious imitations of old work, or from additions which would, when weathered with age, only deceive and puzzle the observer' (p. 77). Evidently he had the support of both the Society of Antiquaries and the Yorkshire Archaeological Society; and the Royal Archaeological Institute, on its return visit to York in 1903, approved what had been done. Brierley's restoration philosophy, to conserve but not to reconstruct, together with his use of distinctive materials, fore-shadows the principles still adopted by the Inspectorate of Ancient Monuments in its work on the ancient monuments in its guardianship.

The St. Mary's Abbey excavations continued in 1911, when construc-tion of a new lecture theatre for the museum, the Tempest Anderson Hall, revealed part of the cloister. It was effectively incorporated in the undercroft of the new building. Here W. Harvey Brook transferred, catalogued and redisplayed the museum's medieval sculpture collections. He and E. Ridsdale Tate, architect for the new extension, continued excavations in the abbey chancel in 1912 and 1913. They discarded the cautious conservation precepts of Brierley and rebuilt the south wall of the church 'in the best style of restoration, as it not only preserves the original work, but enables the student to form a true conception of a very important feature of the abbey, which had hitherto been largely left to the imagination'. Whatever the virtues of their restoration philosophy, the plan they produced remains the basis for modern work. The various evidence has recently been summarised by the Royal Commission on Historical Monuments (RCHM, 1975, pp. 3-24). In the intervening years aspects of it had been explored in a succession of specialist papers, particularly on the remarkable thirteenth-century abbey statues which remain the most spectacular expression of the brilliant York school of medieval sculpture (Sauerländer, 1959; RCHM, 1975, pp. xlii-xliv; Zarnecki, 1979, xvi, p. 3). Later excavations in the Abbey site, particularly those by Willmot in the 1950s, unhappily still unpublished, have mainly been concerned with the underlying Roman remains. However, the generosity of the Leverhulme Trust has enabled the Yorkshire Museum to commission a long-overdue architectural analysis of all the abbey remains and Dr. Christopher Wilson's definitive study – aided as recently as 1979 by supplementary excavations – is nearing completion. His work benefits from the various recent studies of the King's Manor nearby, which incorporates much of the fifteenth-century Abbots lodgings. So much of the abbey still lies below the museum gardens, however, that even this will be but a late twentieth-century situation report, with a fuller story awaiting the archaeologist of the future. The archaeological exploration of St. Mary's Abbey over the past 150 years, incomplete though it is, is something of a success story. The same can hardly be said for the other monastic houses of York. Though Skaife (1864) was able to define the approximate sites of all the other seven main houses, only for two, Holy Trinity Priory, Micklegate, from nineteenth-century work, and Clementhorpe Nunnery, from excavations in 1976 (YPS *Ann. Rep.* for 1976, p. 39), have we dependable archaeological information.

York Minster, the pre-eminent gothic building in the North, has been studied and well recorded from the earliest days of ecclesiological enquiry. The vast literature it has engendered has as much interest as an indicator of the changing antiquarian attitudes as for the subject itself. The latest contribution, the RCHM inventory, shortly to be published, will provide a thorough modern study as eloquent of the preoccupations of its age as any of its predecessors. Antiquaries have almost as long been conscious that the remains of earlier churches were likely to exist below the present structure. By the late nineteenth century it had become evident that the *principia* of the legionary fortress must also lie there. There has therefore also been a long tradition of archaeological observation whenever alterations or restoration had disturbed buried archaeological deposits. The restoration schemes in the wake of the 1829 fire provided the first opportunity for excavation, effectively taken and well recorded by John Browne (Browne, 1847, pp. 5-11). The structures then discovered provoked much speculation. Archaeologists expected to find below the Minster the first little wooden church dedicated to St. Peter, which Edwin of Northumbria put up on the occasion of his baptism by Paulinus in AD 626; followed by its stone successor, repaired and beautified by St. Wilfrid, reconstructed and elaborated in late Anglian and Anglo-Scandinavian times, and replaced by the great Norman cathedral of Archbishop Thomas. That in its turn should have been rebuilt by Archbishop Roger of Pont l'Evêque before being progressively replaced by the present structure. What had Browne found? He thought it included remains of Edwin's church, the main timber-laced foundations being those of Archbishop Albert's great church consecrated in AD 780. New investigations by Sir Charles Peers enabled him to reconstruct the east end of a remarkable stone church which he also identified as that of Albert. Subsequent commentators were less certain, principally because of the frequent herringbone masonry and timber lacing in the structure, considered normally to be early Norman in date. In the 1960s this and much more evidence was reviewed in detail by Taylor and Taylor (1965, pp. 700-09), just in time to be superseded by a new campaign of excavations (Taylor, 1978, p. 754). During the Minster restoration of 1967-73 A. D. Phillips was able to demonstrate that the Roman *principia* had stood in good repair until the ninth century. Wherever the pre-conquest minster might lie, it was not beneath the present one, though its cemetery evidently was there in the tenth and eleventh century. The structure Browne had located was the remarkable and innovative church built by Archbishop Thomas (1069-1100). Phillips was able to define the plan by a combination of excavation and deduction (Phillips, 1975) and its superstructure by relating structural considerations and architectural detail to elements preserved within the present structure. The culmination will be the report the York Minster Excavation Group is currently preparing, and some of the evidence is to be seen in an undercroft museum imaginatively formed by the Dean and Chapter within the engineering works which made the excavation possible. Almost as productive of academic dispute as Browne's structural discoveries has been one of the great sculptural finds probably associated with the church of Archbishop Thomas. The York virgin and child, found in the east wall of the Minster in 1829, has provoked a huge scholarly literature (Okasha, 1971, pp. 132-3) which itself epitomises the ebb and flow of art historical studies over the century and a half.

The Minster itself was the centre of a complex of buildings in the middle ages of which a few have survived; the chapel of the archiepiscopal palace is now the Minster library, restored under Dean Markham between 1803 and 1810; the Norman Treasurer's house exists in part encased in the later structures of Gray's Court; and St. William's College, college of chantry priests, was also restored in the flurry of conservation activity associated with Frank Green in the early years of this century. Many more of the Minster's medieval buildings have disappeared completely. One, the College of Vicars Choral, established in the Bedern by

Archbishop de Grey in 1252, survives in part. Its Common Hall, discovered encased in nineteenth-century industrial buildings, was elegantly
restored by the City of York in 1980; the rest of the College, including its
ruined Trinity Chapel, was excavated by York Archaeological Trust
between 1973 and 1980. The full story of the College's development,
from a quasimonastic layout in the thirteenth century, through an
arrangement of individual priest's residences into a post-medieval phase
of secular use, has been recorded. The archaeological and architectural
evidence has been correlated with the very detailed documentation in the
still-extant records of the Vicars Choral, to provide a classic exercise in
medieval urban archaeology (YPS *Ann. Rep.* for 1978, pp. 35-7; 1979,
pp. 48-9).

If both the structure and the archaeology of the medieval Minster
have survived well, and been adequately studied and recorded over the
years, the same can hardly be said for the complementary secular structures. The two York castles have suffered sadly from destruction without
record in the past century and a half. The rebuilding of the prison in
1828-35 entailed destruction of much of the then surviving remains of
York Castle, and the extensive levelling operations of the time will have
destroyed the archaeological stratification which could have elucidated
its history. At the time it was only the Roman finds which commanded
record (Wellbeloved, 1842, pp. 110-11). Similarly York's second castle,
The Old Baile, was progressively developed during the nineteenth century, with scarce an archaeological record of the medieval structures
which must have been encountered. Again Roman finds commanded
attention (YMH 1891, p. 68) though when the bailey of the castle was
completely filled with terraced housing in the 1880s the discovery of the
Bishophill conquest period coin-hoard (Dolley, 1971) and various
Anglo-Scandinavian artefacts hint that an important archaeological story
was largely lost. A far better service to archaeology was performed by
Platnauer and Benson in 1902 (Benson and Platnauer, 1902) at York
Castle, when Clifford's Tower was underpinned with concrete flying
buttresses concealed in the motte. The excellent schematic cross-section
drawings of the mound made at this time reveal a complex structure
evidently containing the well-preserved remains of several keeps pre-
dating the present mid-thirteenth-century structure. T. P. Cooper at
about this time provided a thorough and still useful study of both castles
(Cooper, 1911) based on the documentary sources. These good examples
were not followed in 1938, however, when the foundations for the new
city offices – in the event never built – were put in on what is now the
Castle Car Park. What, if anything, was encountered is not recorded. In
recent years the castles of York have come under scrutiny from both the

Royal Archaeological Institute, which conducted research excavations in the motte of The Old Baile in 1968-69 (Addyman, 1977) and from the Royal Commission on Historical Monuments, which has surveyed and brought together, through the perceptive work of Dr. R. M. Butler, all extant evidence about the two structures (RCHM, 1972a, pp. 59-89). Dr. Butler and his colleagues in the same volume have done the same for the rest of the city defences, presenting as well (pp. 1-5) a review of their conservation and study. Since the heady days of the first preservation movement in the 1820s the walls were breached on several occasions, allowing opportunity for archaeological observation: in 1832-34 (St. Leonard's Place); 1839 and 1845 (Old Railway Station); 1874 (New Railway Station access) and 1939 (air raid shelters near the station). Cooper's exhaustive history of the walls and bars (Cooper, 1904) provided an authoritative summary of development only recently superseded. Since then there have been various research excavations, by Miller (1925-26), Radley and Davison (1969-70) and Wenham (YPS. *Ann. Rep.* for 1971, 15). The walls and bars seem now sacrosanct, and further knowledge of York's defences – vitally needed in respect of the Walmgate section and the whole stretch south west of the Ouse – will have to await well considered and adequately financed research excavations.

To do them credit the nineteenth-century curators of archaeology in the Yorkshire Philosophical Society were as avid acquirers of medieval artefacts as of any others. They even managed belatedly to return to York Thomas Bateman's collection of York medieval pottery, by purchasing it in 1893 in the London sale (YPS *Ann. Rep.* for 1893). With further acquisitions in 1895 the Society boasted that its medieval pottery collection was 'far superior in extent and importance to that preserved in any museum in the country' (YPS *Ann. Rep.* for 1895, p. viii). It is still perhaps the country's best regional collection – albeit never catalogued for publication and only rarely and in part displayed. The curators had other successes. St. William's shrine and tomb, now perceptively reassessed (Wilson, 1977), were rescued when fragments surfaced at various times over the years from their Reformation place of dumping or concealment in Precentors Court. A similar astounding find, this time rescued by the museum's professional curator, G. F. Willmot, came with the discovery in 1957 of buried late fifteenth-century alabasters depicting the life of St. William – the reredos no doubt buried about the same time as St. William's shrine. The museum's medieval collections are eloquent of the success of its collecting policy over the 150 years of its existence in almost every field – numismatics, sculpture, small objects. They represent a huge resource from which the city's medieval archaeology will in future in part be written: and which, when the Yorkshire Museum obtains the necessary resources and space, could provide as effective a public exposition of the life of the medieval capital of the north as does the new Museum of London for the other city to the south.

So far as excavation and field work goes, however, with the exception of St. Mary's Abbey, medieval archaeology is a recent phenomenon in York. It began with the 1949-51 Hungate excavations (Richardson, 1959) and may well also have been stimulated by Raine's documentary survey of the city (1955). Wenham's Low Petergate project of 1957-58, partly published in 1964 but not fully available until 1972, showed what could come from a properly regulated examination of medieval deposits in the city centre. The Minster excavations (p. 75, above), however, were the first major medieval project – even then primarily thought of first as an exercise in Roman archaeology. From 1972 onwards a policy for medieval excavation has been followed by York Archaeological Trust which envisages: (1) the excavation of every unique building threatened by destruction – the Vicars Choral College (pp. 75-6, above) falls into this category; (2) the excavation of at least one example of each building or site type formerly common in the town – the recently excavated parish church, St. Helen-on-the-Walls, and its cemetery (Magilton, 1980; Dawes and Magilton, 1980) is an example; the Hospital of St. Mary in the Horsefair (Union Terrace) is another; and (3) the excavation of sample areas of various neighbourhoods of the medieval city – the Trust has completed samples off Goodramgate and Aldwark, in Coppergate, Skeldergate and Walmgate (YPS *Ann. Rep.* for 1972-79, *passim*). The Trust's policy is carried out entirely on sites threatened by destruction, in line with a demanding new national philosophy of preservation rather than excavation. Even so it should, with the associated artefact studies, physical anthropology and environmental archaeology, rapidly transform knowledge of the medieval city. To these results can be added the exemplary studies of the medieval standing buildings prepared by the Royal Commission on Historical Monuments. These are already available for the areas south west of the Ouse (RCHM, 1972b) and for extra-mural areas (RCHM, 1975).

For the core of the medieval city the inventory will be in our hands shortly. The Historic Towns Trust, moreover, is at an advanced stage of preparing the York maps for *The Atlas of Historic Towns*. With this in their hands, and with the results from the RCHM, the York Archaeological Trust, the York Minster Archaeology Group and the Leverhulme project on St. Mary's Abbey available to them, medieval archaeologists of the 1980s will be as well served in York, except possibly in terms of museum display, as anywhere in the world.

York Archaeology in the Later Twentieth Century

This seemingly complacent boast, reminiscent of those of the nineteenth-century curators of antiquities, is only possible because, first, changes during the twentieth century in the organisation of archaeology have created the means for effective archaeological work; and, secondly, because York has been recognised nationally, not only as of especial importance in the past, but as a place where the evidence is especially well preserved, and thus capable of providing the nation, as perhaps in no other city, with an intimate understanding of its urban past.

The Royal Commission on Historical Monuments was already 42 years old when, in a period of postwar expansion, and as a result of Sir Alfred Clapham's conversations at the 1948 York meeting of the Royal Archaeological Institute, it established its York office in 1950. Between then and 1977 a team has been engaged on an Inventory of all ancient monuments and historic buildings in the city. The Inventory is now complete, and its publication in six volumes nearly so. Inevitably the presence in York of so many able investigators has had its effect on the quality of archaeological thought, not only locally but throughout the region, and much of the achievement of the past 30 years has been the direct or indirect result of Commission initiative or influence. Government involvement in York archaeology also gradually extended from guardianship of Clifford's Tower (from 1915) and statutory responsibility for the small number of scheduled monuments (totalling 19 in the 1971 list), to a concern for the archaeological potential of every development in the historic core of the city. When such threats came to the attention of the Inspectorate of Ancient Monuments an *ad hoc* excavation was often arranged. There were a score or more between 1953 and 1970. This policy, applied not only in York but throughout the country, was shown to be increasingly inadequate as the urban property boom of the 1960s led to the archaeological annihilation of town centre after town centre throughout Britain.

In 1971, H. G. Ramm, the Commission's archaeological specialist in York, warned of the acute threat to the city's archaeology from ring roads and numerous proposed city centre developments. A joint committee of the Council for British Archaeology and the Yorkshire Philosophical Society was set up forthwith. It commissioned a survey *The Archaeological Implications of Proposed Development in York* (Addyman and Rumsby, 1971) and, with immediate grants from Rescue, The Trust for British Archaeology and the Department of the Environment, a York Archaeological Trust was set up in April 1972 by local and national archaeological societies, the northern Universities and the Royal

Commission on Historical Monuments. Professor Maurice Barley has been chairman of its executive committee since the Trust's inception.

The Trust has since then built up a team of professional archaeologists capable of undertaking major excavation projects where the opportunities justify it, and keeping constant watching briefs on lesser threats to York's archaeological heritage. It is backed by a number of specialist services. There is a Conservation Laboratory for finds, in Marygate; in 1980 this was greatly extended through a generous grant from the Danish Tjaereborg Foundation in recognition of the Trust's work on Viking York. It provides the York area for the first time with adequate facilities for all kinds of artefact conservation. It is making a modest contribution to the huge task of restoring and preserving the Yorkshire Museum collections, which have been the subject of a bewildering variety of treatments since the days of John Browne's 'persevering zeal' in treating corroded stycas (YPS Ann. Rep. for 1842, p. 12). The Trust also has photographic and drafting services, and an editorial team. The Department of the Environment has placed a contract with the University of York for its Environmental Archaeology Unit to provide reports on the environmental archaeology of the city. This laboratory, supported also by the Science Research Council, is now nationally pre-eminent for its co-ordinated work on a range of biological material. It deals with microfauna, including entomological and parasitic remains; fish and birds, larger game and domesticated fauna; pollens and seeds; soils; and a wide range of other remains. Its results provide a quite new kind of information about urban land use, economy and conditions in the past.

Interim reports on these and all the Trust's researches appear each year in the *Annual Report* of the Yorkshire Philosophical Society – as have the results of York archaeology for 150 years. The final accounts are given in a new series publication *The Archaeology of York* (Addyman, 1976 onwards). This provides reports rapidly on the completed research, but it will build up over the years into an integrated study of all aspects of the past of the city, period by period.

Working in parallel with the Trust is the York Minster Archaeology Group, a team of professional archaeologists set up to undertake and report on the archaeology of York Minster revealed in the restoration of 1967-73. Its report will also appear shortly, in a series of volumes devoted to the various periods encountered. Support for this work has come almost entirely from the Royal Commission on Historical Monuments and the Department of the Environment.

The twentieth century has also seen fundamental changes in the museum facilities. Because York already had an adequate museum, there was no need for the city to take advantage of the option provided by the 1845 Museums Act to provide a municipal museum (Willmot, 1953), and the Yorkshire Museum remained a private one, run by the Yorkshire Philosophical Society until 1961. With huge collections, a too-small staff and increasing maintenance costs it proved impossible for the quite small Society to sustain, and was transferred as an Educational Charity to the Lord Mayor and Corporation of the City of York in that year. With the devolution of functions following the reorganisation of local government in 1974 the museum, as an educational charity, became, with other educational matters, the responsibility of the County of North Yorkshire. In the 1980s the museum is embarking on the new and long overdue displays of local archaeological collections which are second to none in a provincial museum.

Local societies and amateur effort have always been a strength of British archaeology. In York both the Yorkshire Philosophical Society and the Yorkshire Architectural Society – since 1901 the YAYAS, having added 'York Archaeological' to its name – have been a source of archaeological strength in the intellectual life of the city. They were joined by the more practically minded York Excavation Group in 1970, the local expression of a burgeoning of interest nationwide in practical archaeology.

With the advent of the University of York in 1963 a number of scholars with an interest in archaeology or allied disciplines came to York helping to create the climate in which such great projects as the Minster excavations, or the York Archaeological Trust's work, could be undertaken. Archaeology was, however, specifically singled out by the first Vice-Chancellor as the kind of discipline the new University would *not* develop. Despite this, by 1978 the University had a Department of Archaeology. Professor P. A. Rahtz is the first professor. The first students will graduate in 1982. So many archaeologists, the present one included, have received their formative archaeological experience at York, even without the presence of a university, that this development cannot but augur well for the future. The new students have the opportunity of receiving their archaeological education in a city of now unparalleled archaeological resources. The six volume RCHM inventory of its ancient buildings and archaeological remains is finished. Definitive surveys are nearing completion on its main monastery and on the archaeology of its minster. An archaeological trust will be engaged for the foreseeable future on an active programme of excavation, research and publication. There is a first class conservation laboratory; an Environmental Archaeology Unit of international reputation; and a museum with local collections of first rank importance. There are active

local archaeological societies, and in the Yorkshire Philosophical Society
there is a venerable but still vigorous body whose activities have run like a
golden thread through the story of York's archaeology since it helped
form the British Association in 1831 – and before.

References

ADDYMAN, P. V. (1975), 'Excavations in York, 1972-1973. First Interim Report' *Antiq. J.* 54, 1975, pp. 200-31.

ADDYMAN, P. V. (1976), *Excavations in York, 1973-1974. Second Interim Report,* Counc. for Brit. Archaeol.

ADDYMAN, P. V. (1976 onwards), *The Archaeology of York,* Counc. for Brit. Archaeol. (continuing).

ADDYMAN, P. V. (1977), 'Baile Hill, York: A report on the Institute's Excavations', *Archaeol. J.* 134, pp. 115-56.

ADDYMAN, P. V. and J. H. RUMSBY (1971), *The Archaeological Implications of Proposed Development in York,* Report to Counc. for Brit. Archaeol. and YPS.

ANON (1842), 'Anglo-Saxon Church', *The Ecclesiologist,* 1, pp. 190-92 (re. St. Mary's, Bishophill Junior).

ARCHAEOLOGICAL INSTITUTE (1848), *Memorials illustrative of the History and Antiquities of the County and City of York.*

AUDEN, G. A. (1906), 'Pre-historic Archaeology' in G. A. Auden (ed.), *A Handbook to York and District,* pp. 1-14.

AUDEN, G. A. (1907), 'Recent finds in York', *Saga Book of the Viking Club,* V, pp. 53-5.

AUDEN, G. A. (1908), 'A leaden cross bearing a styca impression and other antiquities found in York', *Brit. Numis. J.* 4, pp. 235-37.

AUDEN, G. A. (1910), 'Abstract of a paper on antiquities dating from the Danish occupation of York', *Saga Book of the Viking Club,* 6, pp. 169-79.

BAILEY, R. N. (1980), *Viking Age Sculpture in Northern England.*

BAINES, F. (1822-3), *History, Directory and Gazeteer of the County of York:* vol. 1, West Riding, Leeds 1822; vol. 2, East and North Ridings, Leeds 1823.

BATEMAN, T. (1861), *Ten Years diggings in Celtic and Saxon Grave Hills,* Derby.

BENSON, G. (1903), 'Notes on excavations at 25, 26 and 27 High Ousegate, York', YPS *Ann. Rep.* for 1902, 1903, pp. 64-7.

BENSON, G. (1907), 'Notes on an excavation at the corner of Castlegate and Coppergate', and 'Further notes on the foregoing articles', YPS *Ann. Rep.* for 1906, 1907, pp. 72-6.

BENSON, G. (1911), *York from its origin to the end of the eleventh century,* York.

BENSON, G. (1914), 'Coins: especially those relating to York', YPS *Ann. Rep.* for 1913, pp. 1-104.

BENSON, G. and H. M. PLATNAUER (1902), 'Notes on Clifford's Tower', YPS *Ann. Rep.* for 1902, pp. 68-74.

BRØNDSTED, J. (1924), *Early English Ornament,* London and Copenhagen.

BROWNE, J. (1847), *History of the Metropolitan Cathedral of York,* 2 vols.

ARCHAEOLOGY IN YORK 83

BUCKLAND, P. C., J. R. A. GREIG, and H. K. KENWARD (1974), 'York: an Early Medieval site', *Antiquity*, 48, pp. 25-33.

BUTLER, R. M. (1971), *Soldier and Civilian in Roman Yorkshire.*

CARVER, M. O. H., S. DONAGHEY and A. B. SUMPTER (1978), 'Riverside structures and a Well in Skeldergate and Buildings in Bishophill' in P. V. Addyman (ed.), *The Archaeology of York*, vol. 4, fasc. 1, Counc. for Brit. Archaeol.

CLARKE, D. L. (1970), *Beaker Pottery of Great Britain and Ireland*, 2 vols.

CLOUGH, T. H. McK. and W. A. CUMMINS (1979), *Stone Axe Studies: archaeological, petrological, experimental, and ethnographic*, Counc. for Brit. Archaeol., Res. Rep. 33.

COLLINGWOOD, W. G. (1927), *Northumbrian crosses of the pre-Norman age.*

COOPER, T. P. (1904), *York: the story of its walls, bars and castles.*

COOPER, T. P. (1911), *The History of the Castle of York.*

CORDER, P. (1928), *The Roman Pottery at Crambeck*, Roman Malton and Dist., Rep. 1, York.

CORDER, P. (1931), 'The Roman pottery at Throlam, Holme-on-Spalding-Moor, East Yorkshire', *Trans. East Riding Antiq. Soc.* XXVII, p. 6.

CORDER, P. (1933), 'The Roman Bath discovered in 1930-31 during reconstruction of the Mail Coach Inn, St. Sampson's Square, York', *Proc. Yorks. Archit. and York Archaeol. Soc.* 1, pp. 1-21.

CORDER, P. (1956), 'Parisian Ware', *Yorks. Archaeol. J.,* vol. 39. 1, 153, pp. 48-52.

CORDER, P. and M. BIRLEY (1937), 'Fourth century Romano-British Kilns near Crambeck', *Antiq. J.* 17, pp. 392-413.

CRAMP, R. (1967), *Anglian and Viking York*, Borthwick Papers 33.

CURR, G. (1980), *Who Saved York Walls?* Sheldon Memorial Trust Prize Essay, York.

DAWES, J. D. and J. R. MAGILTON (1980), 'The cemetery of St. Helen-on-the-Walls, Aldwark', *The Archaeology of York*, vol. 12, fasc. 1, Counc. for Brit. Archaeol.

DOLLEY, M. (1971), 'The mythical Norman element in the 1882 Bishophill (York) find of Anglo-Saxon coins', YPS *Ann. Rep.* for 1971, pp. 88-101.

DRAKE, F. (1736), *Eboracum: or the History and Antiquities of the City of York.*

EAGLES, B. N. (1979), *The Anglo-Saxon Settlement of Humberside*, Brit. Archaeol. Rep., 68.

FAULL, M. L. (1979), *British Survival in Anglo-Saxon Yorkshire.* Doctoral Dissertation, University of Leeds.

GREENWELL, W. G. (1877), *British Barrows.*

HAIGH, D. H. (1870), 'The dedication stone of the Church of St. Mary in Castlegate', *Comm.* YPS, 27-32.

HALL, R. A. (1976), *The Viking Kingdom of York*, York.

HALL, R. A. (1978) (ed.), *Viking Age York and the North*, Counc. for Brit. Archaeol., Res. Rep. 27.

HARRISON, H. (1960), 'The Pre-Conquest Churches of York', *Yorks. Archaeol. J.* 40, pt. 150, pp. 232-49.

KENDRICK, T. D. (1949), *Late Saxon and Viking Art.*

KENNETT, D. H. (1978), *Anglo-Saxon Pottery,* Shire Publications, Princes Risborough.

KENRICK, J. (1870), 'On the Dedication Stone of the Church of St. Mary, Castlegate', YPS *Ann. Rep.* for 1870, 'Communications', pp. 50-6.

KENWARD, H. K. (1978), 'The Analysis of Archaeological Insect Assemblages: a new Approach' in P. V. Addyman (ed.) *The Archaeology of York,* vol. 19, fasc. 1, Counc. for Brit. Archaeol.

KERR, J. S. (1973), *Improvers and preservers: a dissertation on some aspects of cathedral restoration 1770-1830 and in particular the great screen squabble of York Minster from 1829 to 1831.* York, Inst. of Adv. Archit. Studies.

KING, C. W. (1882), 'The Roman statue found in York, in 1880' YPS *Communics* for 1882.

KIRK, J. L. (1911), 'The opening of a tumulus near Pickering', YPS *Ann. Rep.* for 1911, pp. 57-62.

KITSON CLARK, M. (1935), 'A gazeteer of Roman remains in East Yorkshire'. *Roman Malton and District, Report 5,* Leeds.

LANG, J. T. (ed.) (1978a), 'Anglo-Saxon and Viking Age Sculpture and its context', *Brit. Archaeol. Reps., Brit. Ser.* 49.

LANG, J. T. (ed.) (1978b), 'Anglo-Scandinavian Sculpture in Yorkshire', in R. A. Hall (ed.), *Viking Age York and the North,* Counc. for Brit. Archaeol. Res. Rep. 27, pp. 11-20.

LISTER, M. (1682-3), 'An Account of. . . some Roman antiquities at York' *Phil Trans.* 13, No 145, pp. 70-4.

LISTER, M. (1683), 'Some observations upon the ruins of a Roman wall and multangular tower at York', *Phil. Trans. Roy. Soc.* 13, 1683, pp. 238-42.

LONGWORTH, I. H. (1961), 'The Origins and Development of the Primary series in the Collared Urn Tradition in England and Wales', *Proc. Prehis. Soc.* 27, 1961, pp. 263-306.

MAGILTON, J. R. (1980), 'The Church of St. Helen-on-the-Walls, Aldwark', *The Archaeology of York,* vol. 10, fasc. 1, Counc. for Brit. Archaeol.

MANBY, T. G. (1979), 'Flint and stone axes in Yorkshire' in T. H. McK. Clough and W. A. Cummins (eds.) *Stone Axe Studies,* Counc. for Brit. Archaeol. *Res. Rep.* 23, pp. 65-81.

MAY, T. (1908-11), 'The Roman Pottery in York Museum', YPS *Ann. Rep.* for 1908, pp. 35-48; for 1909, pp. 34-40; for 1910, pp. 14-44; for 1911, pp. 1-48.

MILLER, S. N. (1925), 'Roman York; Excavations of 1925', *J. Roman Stud.* 15, pp. 176-94.

MILLER, S. N. (1928), 'Roman York; excavations of 1926-27', *J. Roman Stud.* 18, pp. 61-99.

MORTIMER, J. R. (1905), *Forty Years Researches in British and Saxon burial mounds in East Yorkshire.*

MYRES, J. N. L. (1969), *Anglo-Saxon Pottery and the Settlement of England.*

MYRES, J. N. L. (1977), *A Corpus of Anglo-Saxon Pottery of the Pagan period.*

OKASHA, E. (1971), *Hand-list of Anglo-Saxon non-runic inscriptions.*

O. S. (1852), Plans of York at the Scale of 5 ft. to 1 statute mile, Ordnance Survey.

PATTISON, I. R. (1973), 'The Nunburnholme Cross and Anglo-Danish Sculpture in York', *Archaeologia* 104, pp. 209-34.

PEACOCK, D. P. S. (1977), *Pottery and Early Commerce: Characterisation and Trade in Roman and Later Ceramics.*

PEERS, SIR R. C. (1931), 'Recent discoveries in the minsters of Ripon and York', *Antiq. J.* 11, pp. 113-22.

PERRIN, J. R. (1977), ' "Legionary" ware in York' in J. Dore and K. Greene (eds.) *Roman Pottery Studies in Britain and Beyond*, Brit. Archaeol. Reps., Suppl. Ser., 30, pp. 101-12.

PHILLIPS, A. D. (1975), 'Excavations at York Minster 1967-1973', The Friends of York Minster 46th *Ann. Rep.*, pp. 19-27.

PIRIE, E. J. E. (1975), *Sylloge of Coins of the British Isles, 21. Coins in Yorkshire Collections: the Yorkshire Museum, York, The City Museum, Leeds (and) the University of Leeds.*

PIRIE, E. J. E. (forthcoming) 'Post-Roman coins from York' *The Archaeology of York*, vol. 18, fasc. 1, Counc. for Brit. Archaeol.

PROCTOR, W. (1855), 'Report of the Proceedings of the Yorkshire Antiquarian Club in the Excavation of Barrows from the year 1849' YPS *Proc.*, 1, p. 176.

RADLEY, J. (1968), 'A York hoard of flint tools, 1886', *Yorks. Archaeol. J.* vol. 42, pt. 166, pp. 131-2.

RADLEY, J. (1969), 'The Mesolithic Period in North East Yorkshire', *Yorks. Archaeol. J.* 42, pp. 314-27.

RADLEY, J. (1971), 'Economic Aspects of Anglo-Danish York', *Mediev. Archaeol.* 15, pp. 39-45.

RADLEY, J., (1972), 'Excavations in the defences of the City of York: an early medieval stone tower and the successive earth ramparts', *Yorks. Archaeol. J.* 44, pp. 38-64.

RADLEY, J. (1974), 'The Prehistory of the Vale of York', *Yorks. Archaeol. J.* 46, pp. 10-22.

RAINE, J. (1879-94), *Historians of the Church of York and its Archbishops*, Rolls. Ser. 71, 3 volumes.

RAINE, A. (1926), 'The excavations near the Multangular Tower, 1926' YPS *Ann. Rep.* for 1926, Proceedings, pp. 14-16.

RAINE, A. (1955), *Medieval York: A Topographical survey based on original sources.*

RAMM, H. G. (1971), 'The Yorkshire Philosophical Society and archaeology 1822-55' YPS *Ann. Rep.* for 1971, pp. 66-73.

RAMM, H. G. (1972), 'The Growth and Development of the City to the Norman Conquest' in A. Stackpoole (ed.) *The Noble City of York*, York, pp. 225-54.

RCHM (1962), Royal Commission on Historical Monuments, *The City of York: volume I, Eburacum.*

RCHM (1972a), Royal Commission on Historical Monuments, *The City of York: volume II, The Defences.*

RCHM (1972b), Royal Commission on Historical Monuments, *The City of York:* volume III, *South-West of the Ouse.*

RCHM (1975), *City of York,* vol. IV, *Outside the City Walls, East of the Ouse.*

RICHARDSON, K. M. (1959), 'Excavations in Hungate, York', *Archaeol. J.* 116, pp. 51-114.

RICHMOND, I. M. (1944), 'Three fragments of Roman official statues, from York, Lincoln and Silchester', *Antiq. J.* 24, pp. 1-9.

RICHMOND, I. M. (1959), *York from its origins until the close of the eleventh century: a review,* Sheldon Memorial Trust (Sheldon Memorial Lecture for 1959).

ROACH SMITH, C. (1846), 'Roman inscriptions discovered at York', *Trans. British Archaeol. Assoc.* 3, Congress at Gloucester, pp. 149-51.

ROE, D. A. (1968), *Gazeteer of British Lower and Middle Palaeolithic Sites,* Counc. Brit. Archaeol. *Res. Rep.* 8.

ROE, F. and J. RADLEY (1969), 'Pebble mace-heads with hour glass perforations from Yorkshire, Nottinghamshire and Derbyshire, *Yorks. Archaeol. J.* 42, pp. 169-77.

SAUERLÄNDER, W. (1959), 'Sens and York. An enquiry into the Sculptures from St. Mary's Abbey in the Yorkshire Museum', *J. Brit. Archaeol. Assoc.* 22, pp. 53-69.

SHETELIG, H. (1940), *Viking antiquities in Great Britain and Ireland,* Oslo, A. Schehong, 1940.

SKAIFE, R. H. (1864), *Plan of Roman, Medieval and Modern York, drawn on the basis of the Ordnance Survey of 1851 & partly resurveyed,* York.

SMALL, A. (1965), *The Fourth Viking Congress.*

SMITH, R. A. (1907), 'Notes on some objects of the Viking period recently discovered at York', *Proc. Soc. Antiq.* 2nd Ser., 22, pp. 5-9.

STEAD, I. M. (1958a), 'An Anglian cemetery on The Mount, York', *Yorks. Archaeol. J.* 39, pp. 427-35.

STEAD, I. M. (1958b), 'Excavations at the south corner tower of the Roman fortress at York, 1956', *Yorks. Archaeol. J.* 39, pp. 515-38.

STEAD, I. M. (1965), *The La Tène Cultures of Eastern Yorkshire,* Yorks. Philos. Soc.

STEAD, I. M. (1968), 'An excavation at King's Square, York', *Yorks. Archaeol. J.* 42, pp. 151-64.

STEAD, I. M. (1979), *The Arras Culture,* Yorks. Philos. Soc., 1979.

SUMPTER, A. B. and S. COLL (1977), 'Interval Tower SW 5 and the South-west defences: Excavations 1972-75' in P. V. Addyman (ed.) *The Archaeology of York,* vol. 3, fasc. 2, Counc. for Brit. Archaeol.

TAYLOR, H. M. (1978), *Anglo-Saxon Architecture,* vol. 3.

TAYLOR, H. M. and J. (1965), *Anglo-Saxon Architecture,* vols. 1 and 2.

THURNAM, J. (1849), *Archaeol. J.* 6, 1849, pp. 27 and 123.

THURNAM, J. (1855), 'Description of an Ancient Tumular Cemetery, at Lamel Hill, near York', YPS, *Proc.* 1, p. 98.

WATERMAN, D. M. (1959), 'Late Saxon, Viking, and Early Medieval Finds from York', *Archaeologia,* 97, pp. 59-105.

Webster L. E. and J. Cherry (1972), 'Medieval Britain in 1971', *Mediev. Archaeol.* 16, pp. 147-212.

Wellbeloved, C. (1829), *Account of the Ancient and Present state of the Abbey of St. Mary, York, and of the discoveries made in the recent excavations,* Society of Antiquaries.

Wellbeloved, C. (1842), *Eburacum, or York under the Romans.*

Wellbeloved, C. (1852), *A Descriptive Account of Antiquities in the grounds and in the Museum of the Yorkshire Philosophical Society.*

Wellbeloved, C. (1855a), 'On the hoard of stycas discovered in the parish of Bolton Percy', YPS *Proc.* I, pp. 66-9.

Wellbeloved, C. (1855b), 'Observations on a Roman Inscription lately discovered in York', YPS *Proc.* I, pp. 282-6.

Wenham, L. P. (1964), 'Hornpot Lane and the Horners of York', YPS *Ann. Rep.* for 1964, pp. 25-36.

Wenham, L. P. (1966), 'The South-West Defences of the Fortress of Eboracum', in M. G. Jarrett and B. Dobson (eds.) *Britain and Rome,* pp. 1-26.

Wenham, L. P. (1968), *The Romano-British cemetery at Trentholme Drive, York,* MOPBW Report No. 5.

Wenham, L. P. (1972), 'Excavations in Low Petergate, York, 1957-58' *Yorks. Archaeol. J.* 44, pp. 65-113.

Whitwell, J. B. (1976), 'The Church Street Sewer and an Adjacent Building' in P. V. Addyman (ed.), *The Archaeology of York,* vol. 3, fasc. 1, Counc. for Brit. Archaeol.

Willmot, G. F. (1953), 'The Yorkshire Museum', *Museums Journal* 53, Sept. 1953, pp. 143-6.

Wilson, C. (1977), *The Shrines of St. William of York,* Yorkshire Museum.

Wymer, J. J. (1978), *Gazetteer of Mesolithic Sites in England and Wales,* Counc. for Brit. Archaeol. Res. Rep. 20.

YMH (1891), *Handbook to the Antiquities in the Grounds and Museum of the Yorkshire Philosophical Society,* 8th Edition, York.

Zarnecki, G. (1979), *Studies in Romanesque Sculpture.*

CHAPTER IV

Skills of All Ages
in the
Restoration of York Minster

by

David Dowrick

LIKE OTHER GREAT MEDIEVAL CHURCHES, York Minster was built to arouse awe and reverence of God for ever. Finished in the Perpendicular Gothic period, its youngest elements were thus determined five centuries ago. As the present generation view the Minster they might well believe that it would last for all time, given proper maintenance. However, ascertaining the true state of health of any building requires more than the superficial observation of the layman, and often needs the added perception of expert eyes. This was indeed the case at York, and was provided by the architect Bernard Feilden who, already greatly experienced in ancient buildings through caring for Norwich Cathedral, was appointed Surveyor of the Fabric of York Minster in 1965.

During a painstaking initial survey of his new charge, Dr. Feilden discovered much for concern in its fabric. Apart from the normal dilapidations of weathering external stonework, the deathwatch beetle was rife in many of the roof timbers and numerous cracks were evident in the masonry structure. Furthermore, parts of the structure were substantially out of plumb and out of level. With doubts about the structural safety of several parts of the building, Dr. Feilden called in Ove Arup and Partners as consulting engineers. The author of this chapter had the privilege of being appointed as Project Engineer for the investigations into the Minster's structural health and for the subsequent restoration, which together form the main subject matter of this chapter.[1]

The successful execution of an engineering project involves a blending of art and science, and explicitly or implicitly uses many specialist skills. At York Minster the range of skills used was exceptionally wide and involved several that are most unusual on engineering works.

The Investigatory Problem

The immediate question put to the engineer was, 'Is the existing structural safety of the Minster adequate?'. This raised the technical problem of how to determine the existing safety level, which in turn would raise the philosophical issue of what constituted an adequate safety level. For the present let us consider the problems involved in ascertaining the safety level of the structure as it stood at the time of the investigations.

The investigations comprised two main stages, namely (a) discovering symptoms of structural distress, followed by (b) the interpretation of any such symptoms. These processes were beset by three major sources of difficulty:

The sheer size of the building;

Some necessary methods of investigating the fabric would themselves decrease the safety level;

The general lack of modern engineering knowledge of massive masonry structures.

Regarding the size of the Minster (Diagram 1), it is notable for being one of the largest medieval buildings in northern Europe and is volumetrically the largest medieval cathedral in Britain. Obviously, a building nearly 160 metres long and over 60 metres high would take a long time to inspect all over, as was eventually deemed necessary. Also, it was time-consuming and expensive to erect the scaffolding required to inspect and measure the superstructure, most of which was physically out of reach of mere unwinged mortals.

Specially careful thought had to be given to any means of investigation that might endanger the Minster. Firstly, any inspections of the interior of the structure involved cutting or drilling holes into the masonry, thereby weakening it. This meant that the location, depth, extent and method of creation of any such inspection holes had to be carefully considered. Secondly, inspection of the foundations involved

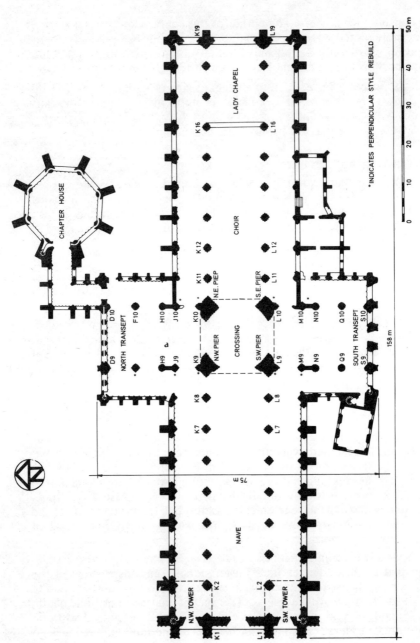

Diagram 1   Plan of the present Minster.

excavation of soil from around them, and such removal of soil is generally likely to induce subsidence and increase the risk of foundation failure. From the nature of the subsoil at York Minster, and from the evidence of the settlements which had already occurred, this problem was seen from the outset to be very important and special procedures were necessary during the excavation to ensure the well-being of the building.

The third major difficulty faced during the investigations was the shortage of modern engineering knowledge of massive masonry as used in medieval style cathedrals. This lack of knowledge arose simply because such structures have not been built in modern times, and no major structural restorations of ancient masonry had recently been undertaken. As a consequence little research had been carried out into either the strength of ancient masonry as a material, or the overall structural behaviour of such buildings. It therefore followed that many aspects of the investigations at York Minster blazed new engineering trails.

Because of the research nature of the project more skills than usual were directly employed, and because of the great age of the structure, very old as well as very new skills were needed, ranging from the mason's art to radio-carbon dating. This increased both the difficulty and the interest in the job. Perhaps the most notable novelty in the analysis of structural safety was the interplay between engineering and historical thought. As discussed later, in order to interpret the signs of structural distress it was necessary for the engineers to know the constructional history of the building, and in return, various engineering observations helped to unravel some historical and archaeological mysteries of the site.

A short list of some of the more important specialist skills used in the structural investigations is as follows: archaeology, architectural and social history, chemistry, computer technology, geometric surveying (including precise levelling), geology, metallurgy, photogrammetry, photography, radio-carbon dating, rock drilling and coring, soil mechanics, stone masonry, structural analysis.

Some Historical and Archaeological Aspects

Whenever an engineer investigates structural defects in a building, he needs to discover the history of the complaint. Indeed, he cannot interpret the symptoms fully without understanding the constructional history of the building. Like a doctor with a human patient, the engineer must find out the age of the structure, what it is founded upon, what it is made of and the nature and timing of any previous symptoms. With modern buildings the engineer does all of this research himself, as the sources of this data, if still in existence, are obvious to him.

However, in the case of ancient buildings the specialist knowledge and skills of the professional historian become a major advantage, and were harnessed throughout the work on the Minster. The research assistance into constructional history came from two main sources: firstly the archaeological team working on the excavations and secondly the architectural historians of the Royal Commission on Historical Monuments (RCHM). By great good fortune the latter had their northern office in York itself and were greatly interested in the project; their collaboration, notably that of John Harvey, was particularly helpful to the engineers.

As we were studying a famous building in a notable historic city, much valuable historical information relating to the building and its site was available in various publications, notably that of Willis (1848), and an enjoyable early task of the engineers was to assimilate this. As the behaviour of foundations can be influenced strongly by previous uses of a site, it was desirable to learn as much as possible of the usage of the site prior to the present building. The key information available at the beginning of the investigations was as follows:

c.AD70–c.400	Roman occupation of site, construction of major buildings within the fortress of Eburacum.
627–1075+?	Anglo-Saxon church, thought to have been built near the present Minster site.
c.1080–1100	Construction of Archbishop Thomas's Norman cathedral.
1137	Partial destruction by fire. New choir by Archbishop Roger, from c.1154.
1225–1250	Rebuilding of the transepts and central tower in Early English style.
1291–1338	Rebuilding of the nave in Decorated style.
1361–c.1420	Rebuilding of the choir, starting from the east end.
c.1400	Beginning of re-styling of Early English central tower main piers in Perpendicular style.
1470	Final completion of the present Perpendicular central tower.
1830–1850	Extensive restoration of the choir and nave after the fires of 1829 and 1840, removing much of the evidence of past deformations.
1930s	Ashlar repairs on the lantern. Recent movements of an old crack recorded by a crack in a new (30 year old) facing stone.

The above outline gave the essential historical framework on which to build the detailed explanation of the ailments of the Minster. But what crucial events in two millenia were missing from the historical record? What so-called facts of history would turn out to be misleading? In the attempt to answer the engineering questions, much new historical information came to light, some of it directly applicable to the engineering problem as well as having its uses in the general field of historical and archaeological thought (Aylmer and Cant, 1977, pp. 111-148).

The Tilting of the Transepts

As a first example of engineering historical analysis, let us examine the questions posed by tilting of the transepts (Dowrick, 1970). The basic question was: Was the observed outward tilt of the transepts (Diagram 2) part of a continuing present day process which would end in the eventual outwards collapse of the structure? Because the rate of tilting would be too slow to measure in an acceptably short period of time, this question

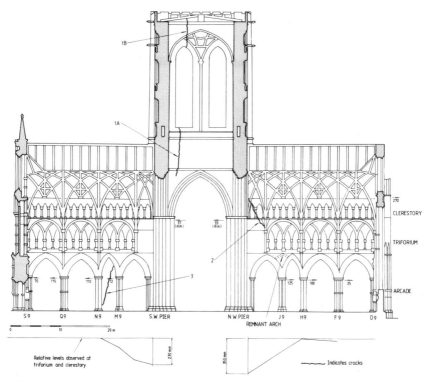

Diagram 2   Section through the transepts showing movements and cracks.

was answered by studying the overall pattern of cracking and tilting in relation to all available information on the dates of initiation and progression of these movements, and any past remedial works that may have been carried out.

In viewing the overall pattern of tilting and cracking, it was evident that the very discernible tilt measured on most piers in the transepts was not matched by a corresponding tilt of the main piers supporting the central tower (Diagram 2). Usually this type of behaviour in church transepts has been caused by a spreading of the arch of the central tower forcing out the transepts, sometimes sufficiently to bring about collapse. Further, there was no large crack-pattern suggesting a general tendency for both transepts to pull away from the central tower of their own accord. Unless any such cracking had been carefully concealed for the present by careful repairs (perhaps during Street's extensive restoration of the south transept in 1871), it seemed most likely that the tilt of the transepts had occurred prior to the completion of the present main piers and arches of the crossing early in the fifteenth century. Could this contention be supported by historical evidence, and if so, what was the nature and timing of the causative event or events?

The historical research undertaken by the RCHM at York to help answer these questions discovered two long forgotten events. Firstly, and most dramatically, it was found that the Early English central tower had suffered a collapse of its upper works during re-styling in 1407. Secondly, the master mason, William Colchester, was rushed to York after the collapse of the central tower, when he rebuilt pier M9 (which is still almost plumb, Diagram 2), and at the same time built the strengthening stone panel between piers M9 and N9.

In the light of these historical facts it was concluded that the tilt of the transepts had been associated with the Early English phase, and that little further tilt would have occurred since that time. This meant that the transepts must have been stable since the early fifteenth century and therefore their tilt need not be a matter for further concern.

The Settlement of the Central Tower

A second example of engineering historical analysis is provided by the interpretation of the cracks and presumed signs of differential settlement observed in and beneath the central tower (Diagram 2). At the beginning of the investigations the pattern of cracks in this vicinity had not yet been fully defined and gave no hints of its origin. Indeed, the cracks had no obvious overall relationship with the possible settlements, although a causal relationship was suspected.

The two main questions raised were as follows:
Would the cracks grow progressively worse?
Were the differences in level the results of settlement which would grow worse, leading to failure, or were they merely the product of the original workmanship?

In order to answer these safety questions, a prime issue to revolve was whether settlement had really occurred and, if so, was still occurring. The architectural historian, John Harvey, was able to assert that the differences in level along the triforia and clerestories would not have been due to slovenly building in such a prestigious building as the Minster. Certainly the conformity of levels along matching sides of the building was generally remarkably close (within 10 to 20 mm) except immediately adjacent to the central tower where the changes in level were worryingly large, ranging from about 100 to 300 mm.

If differential settlement therefore seemed certain to have occurred, the likelihood of its becoming worse or of associated incipient foundation failure needed to be ascertained. Crucial evidence for this would be provided by the nature and condition of foundation and subsoil, both of which therefore had to be investigated. From the broad history of the site noted above, it was possible that remnants of former major Roman, Anglo-Saxon and Norman buildings lay beneath the central tower piers, although nothing was then known of what actually existed below the floor, which had last been replaced by Lord Burlington in the eighteenth century.

The first small exploratory excavation was carried out adjacent to the north-east pier of the crossing (K10, Diagram 1), and the cracked and deformed masonry exposed immediately below the floor level was quite frightening (Plate 8). There was a difference in level of about 150 mm within a distance of two metres along the top of what was shown to be a strip foundation built c. 1080. The big diagonal crack through the masonry above the foundation ran down from a point near the base of the present north-east pier. Both the crack and the slope on the foundations were more or less certain to have been caused by a common action, notably by the NE pier pushing part of the foundations into the soil below. Was this damage caused by the present pier, or by the previous Early English pier of the tower that had collapsed?

Unfortunately there was no historical or archaeological evidence to associate this damage directly with either or both of these two building phases. However, a combination of historical and engineering information and arguments permitted the hypothetical reconstruction of the history of settlements that had occurred since the foundation had been built by Archbishop Thomas c. 1080.

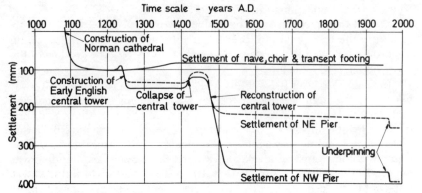

Diagram 3   Hypothetical reconstruction of settlements since 1080 AD.

This settlement history is illustrated for the NW Pier in Diagram 3 and was based on the effect of the weight of the building in its different Norman and Gothic phases, as it compressed the soil beneath the pier foundation. Although this calculation was to some extent conjectural, the probable forms and hence weights of the earlier buildings were known accurately enough for the purpose of establishing that the present central tower had caused most of the damage to the foundation.

Another outcome of this study, mainly inferred from the properties of the clay beneath the footings, was that little settlement was likely to have occurred since about 1550 (Diagram 3) and hence little further settlement would occur in the future. However, strength calculations showed that the margin of safety against sudden failure of the foundations (and hence collapse of the superstructure), was uncomfortably small. In view of the great value of the Minster to the community, it was therefore deemed fit to strengthen the foundations under the central tower to bring them up to modern safety levels.

Archaeological Reflections

It had proved necessary to discover the nature, condition, extent and construction history of the foundations under the central tower and vicinity, in order to find the cause of the structural defects and carry out an appropriate remedy. Excavations for similar reasons were also required at the east end and under the western towers.

Thus archaeology and engineering enterprises went hand in hand over a considerable area of ground and for a period of several years. Apart from the service supplied by the archaeologists in helping to piece together the constructional and damage-history of the substructure, this chapter would seem incomplete without discussing some aspects of the archaeology that are less directly related to the engineering analysis of the Minster. This was a major dig by any archaeological standards, in both area and depth, and much of it was carried out under the unfavourable conditions of a rescue operation. A vast amount of field data was nevertheless obtained over a six-year period from 1967 to 1973. In 1981 the story told by the dig is still unfolding, as the patient interpretation process continues under the direction of Derek Phillips who has been involved in the project almost continually since its inception (Phillips, 1975; 1976; and in preparation).

Most of the shaded part of the archaeological plan in Diagram 4 was not known to exist prior to this project. Indeed, the only part that was previously known, i.e. the foundations under the crypt to the east of the crossing, had hitherto been wrongly ascribed by some historians to the Anglo-Saxon Minster instead of to Archbishop Thomas's Norman cathedral. In fact, no trace of the Saxon church was found and it is virtually certain that it could not have been built immediately on the site of the present Minster (Phillips, in preparation).

The author was fascinated and delighted at the strength and extent of the remaining Norman and Roman substructures which were discovered. Because the ground level around the area where the Minster now stands had been built up by man during early medieval times to 3 m above the natural soil upon which the Romans built, the Norman footings were founded over 4 m below the present floor at about the level of the Roman ground surface.

This meant that previous structures were found intact to a surprising height. The Norman foundations were nearly 2 m deep and were made in two widths of about 3.5 m and 6.5 m, while the Roman footings had been dug over 1 m deep into the clay and were amply wide for the weight of the buildings that they would have supported. Walls still stood to a height of 1.5 m or more on some of these foundations.

The Understanding of Structural Behaviour

In reviewing the structural problems and remedies at York Minster, it is of value to compare the understanding of structural behaviour of the Norman builders with that of their successors and also to contrast their limited insight with that available today through the great advances in engineering science that have been made in the last century or so.

The Norman foundations were certainly adequate for the weight of either Thomas's or Roger's minster, as can be inferred by simple foundation strength calculations; and acceptable settlements would also have occurred without troublesome effects around the central crossing. It was only when the much greater loads of the Gothic central towers were rudely imposed on the Norman foundations that they were found wanting.

Having no engineering science, the great ancient builders had to rely on intuition and experience. The behaviour of soils is inherently more difficult to predict than that of structures, partly because we cannot examine as much of the soil as we can of the structure, and partly because of the mysterious effects of water on the behaviour of soil, which pose major conceptual difficulties additional to those encountered in thinking about building materials. The ancient builder was therefore more likely to be let down by his intuition for foundations than for structures, and the cause of damage to extant ancient buildings is most commonly found in the foundations. We need not be surprised therefore that the Gothic masons at York built superstructures which were beautifully proportioned and adequate in themselves, but lacked appropriate foundations.

The builders of the Gothic Minster were far more imaginative and knowledgeable about superstructures than their Norman counterparts, but oddly and ironically they had far less feel for the foundations upon which their buildings ultimately rested. This is exemplified at York by the way they, unlike the Normans, failed to make the footings significantly wider than the walls (Diagram 4). The present Gothic wall at the east end of the Minster would eventually have fallen outwards (Dowrick and Beckmann, 1971), because of its inadequate foundations. Our modern remedy was to underpin that wall with a wide foundation strip, and it is interesting to speculate whether it would have tilted outwards sufficiently to cause alarm if the men who built the Norman Minster had built its foundation. Probably not!

The essential skill that distinguishes the art of the modern engineer from his medieval counterparts is the ability to use numerical criteria derived from theories of the behaviour of structures (particularly where this is due to the loads acting upon them). Whereas the medieval builder no doubt understood that a big beam would support more sacks of grain than a small beam, he had no formalised system of knowledge which would permit him to calculate the *number* of sacks of grain which would cause any given beam to fail. Although the intelligent intuitive application of their building experience led to the construction of many successful medieval buildings, it should be noted that only the most successful ones survive today, and that many of these have deformed excessively by modern standards or have needed substantial repairs or reconstruction. We have already noted the collapse of York Minster's Early English central tower. To cite examples, Beauvais Cathedral in France suffered

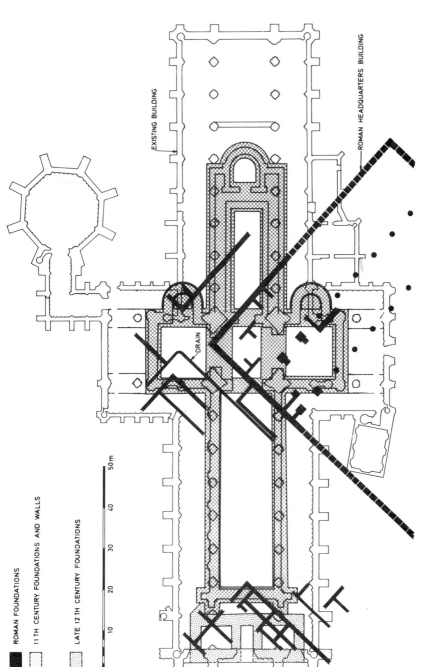

EXISTING BUILDING

DRAIN

ROMAN HEADQUARTERS BUILDING

0   10   20   30   40   50m

Diagram 4   Plan showing relationship of the present Minster to the main underlying Roman and Norman construction found during the works.

two major collapses, one in 1284 and one in 1573 (Heyman, 1967-68); and St. Paul's Cathedral and Winchester Cathedral both needed substantial structural repairs in the present century. (St. Paul's, while not medieval in age, is of that era in terms of engineering knowledge.)

Most commonly, the engineer uses theories of the behaviour of materials to help decide the quantity and quality of material to use in a structure so as to be reasonably certain that it will behave well. Less commonly, these theories may be used to help discover why a structure has behaved in a particular way. At York, it proved necessary to use engineering theory in both these ways.

Firstly let us see how the modern engineer tries to use numbers so as to have an advantage over his medieval colleagues. The chief criteria for successful behaviour of a structure are:

Strength – this should suffice to control excessive cracking and the risk of collapse.

Stiffness – this should suffice to control excessive deformation (sagging, tilting).

Aging qualities – the structure should not deteriorate too rapidly with time (e.g. erode, corrode, rot, wear, discolour).

For the present purpose it will be sufficient to discuss the first two of the above criteria, both of which are closely related aspects of the same phenomenon, namely the resistance of the structure to loads. Through these criteria the engineer attempts to ensure that the resistance of the structure, in terms of strength and stiffness, will exceed the loading demands that are likely to act upon it. In York Minster the principal loads acting on the central tower are those due to gravity and wind. Very simple calculations show that the total mass of the central tower complex is close to 16,000 tonnes, giving a load of about 4,000 tonnes at the base of each of the four main piers (Diagram 5). Similarly, simple estimates show that during a very violent gale the horizontal wind load acting on the lantern of the central tower would be equivalent to about 80 tonnes in weight. This means that 40 tonnes need to be resisted by one pair of the main piers. From these figures it is obvious how relatively small the wind loading is in comparison to the weight of this part of the structure – note that the walls of the lantern are nearly 2 m thick and the main piers are roughly 3.5 m square.

The medieval builders *could* have calculated the weight of the central tower, but did not know how to calculate wind forces. Nor would they have known how to use these loads in judging their influence on the behaviour of the structure. For this the engineer next needs to assess the

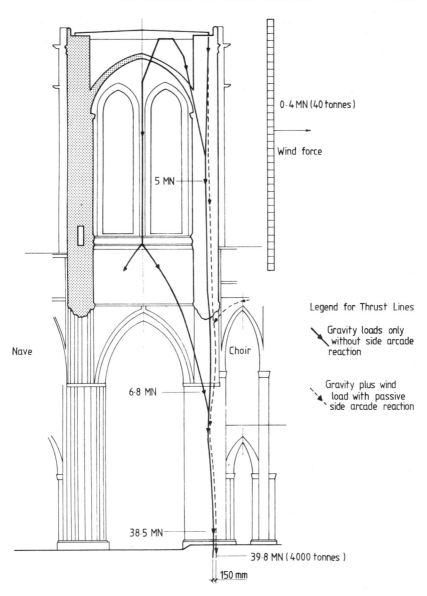

0·4 MN (40 tonnes)

Wind force

5 MN

Legend for Thrust Lines

Gravity loads only
without side arcade
reaction

Gravity plus wind
load with passive
side arcade reaction

Nave

Choir

6·8 MN

38·5 MN

39·8 MN (4000 tonnes)

150 mm

Diagram 5 Graphical thrust line analysis of the central
tower for gravity and wind loads.

way in which the loads are distributed throughout the structure. Diagram 5 shows the result of one such calculation, again a simple one carried out by a graphical method on a drawing board. Calculations of this type were first done in the mid-nineteenth century for the design of trusses; and the principles of their application to ancient masonry were beautifully crystallised in the light of modern knowledge by Jacques Heyman (1966), just in time for this project. The important features of Diagram 5, are the sizes and position of the forces as shown by the 'thrust lines'. If a set of thrust lines does not remain within the structure, then the structure would be unstable in that loading condition. As is indicated in Diagram 5 the superstructure of the Minster is stable in itself whether the wind blows or not (wind only slightly changes the position of the thrust lines).

Having ascertained that the superstructure of the central tower is satisfactory for gravity and wind loads, it remains to examine the adequacy of the foundations. From Diagram 5 the magnitude and position of the loads acting on the foundations were determined and then applied to the cruciform foundation arrangement shown in Diagram 4. As with the superstructure the position of the centre of loading is again important, for the closer the load is applied to the edge of any structural member, the greater the likelihood of failure. While this would seem to have been understood intuitively by the great medieval builders, they did not achieve the explicit mathematical formulation of this fact which is an essential part of the modern engineer's intellectual equipment. Rendering an intuitive idea into mathematical form enhances its power enormously. However, it is limited by human capacity to insert reliable values in any mathematical expression, for there are uncertainties in *all* the quantities that we evaluate, i.e. the loads, their positions and the resistance of the structure or soil to these loads.

We try to deal with these uncertainties by allowing a safety margin. In the case of the foundations of the central tower it was found that the calculated resistance was about 30 per cent greater than the calculated load, which is a far smaller safety margin than is deemed wise in the modern design of foundations. In the case of the Minster there was considerable uncertainty in assessing what area of the cracked and brittle ancient masonry footings was able to carry the load from each pier, as well as the usual uncertainties involved in ascertaining the strength of the soil supporting these footings.

This small safety margin against complete failure of course meant that the subsoil was so heavily loaded that the main piers settled into the ground between 150 and 300 mm more than the adjacent parts of the

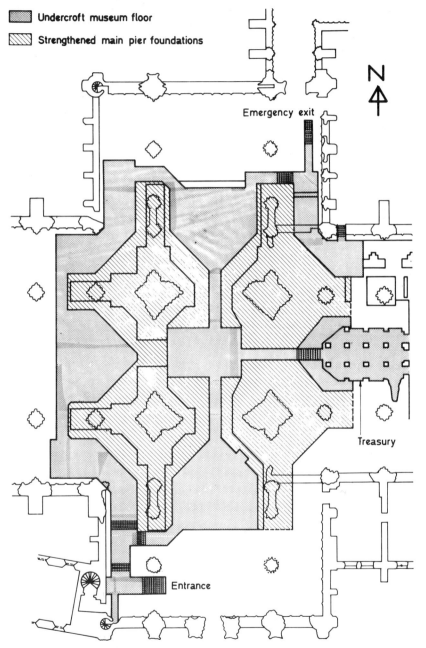

■ Undercroft museum floor

▨ Strengthened main pier foundations

N

Emergency exit

Treasury

Entrance

Diagram 6 Plan of the new Undercroft created around the remedial works.

structure (Diagram 2 and Plate 8). Although the foundations had survived so long, it was obvious in view of the Minster's great and unreplace-
able historical value, that the risk of leaving them unstrengthened should
not be taken, and the great strengthening works resulting in the new
Undercroft (Diagram 6) were devised.

Radio-Carbon Dating and other Skills

Although sophisticated modern dating techniques are sometimes
used in the analysis of soil or rock to determine when past earthquake
fault movement occurred, radio-carbon dating is *not* a skill that engineers
would normally expect to find useful on a building project.

However, because of the use of the constructional history in determining the causes of the damage to the structure, radio-carbon dating had an
important role to play. This arose in the analysis of the damage to the
central tower region of the building in general and its foundations in
particular. As noted earlier in discussing the settlement of the central
tower, at the outset of the investigations the nature of the foundation
under most of the building was not known. The wide strip footings that
were eventually cautiously exposed under the central tower piers (Diagram 4) were of great interest to all concerned. An accurate date for the
construction of these foundations was of considerable importance for
safety and historical purposes alike, but could not be determined conclu-
sively from the archaeological observations made during the excavations.
When during the long Saxon and Norman periods were these foundations
built?

Then the exciting discovery was made that these great wide footings
had been reinforced with large ancient oak baulks laid horizontally in
longitudinal and lateral rows, rather as steel bars are used today to
reinforce concrete construction (Dowrick and Beckmann, 1971). Apart
from the intrinsic and purely archaeological interest of this discovery, the
presence of these timbers was fortunate since they could be dated by
radio-carbon analysis. This in turn provided conclusive evidence, at least
for the engineering diagnosis, that the foundations were part of Archbishop Thomas's Norman church, built c. 1070-1080.

Photography

Various photographic skills have long been in use by engineers not
only for simple recording but also for analytical purposes. Two well-
known examples of the latter are the use of aerial photography for road
surveying and the mapping of water catchment areas. In studying the
faults of buildings, photography is invaluable. It can provide a visual

record of a convenient size which can be studied minutely in a more convenient and congenial place than is generally afforded by direct observation alone.

Photography was used very extensively for studying the structural form and defects of the Minster, and during this activity productive lines of investigation were frequently suggested for unravelling various analytical problems. As mentioned earlier the overall pattern of structural defects needed to be studied in relation to the constructional history in order to ascertain their cause. In this process the defects have to be related to the structural form of the building, i.e. to the arrangement of the load-bearing elements (roof beams, vaults, arches, walls, piers, foundations). Commonly these data are assembled on engineering drawings. In the case of York Minster the production of a comprehensive set of such drawings would be a mammoth task on account of the enormous size of the building and its complexity. The time and cost of this recording activity was considerably reduced by combining the use of photographs with less precise drawings than would be used for many other structures.

Photographs of course are not true-to-scale, and the distortions of photographic perspective make normal photography unsuitable for some engineering and architectural purposes. Photogrammetry, however, can be used for producing true-to-scale drawings and was used at York Minster, mainly for architectural recording purposes. In photogrammetry drawings are produced from stereoscopic photographs by a skilled operator using a very sophisticated viewing-cum-drawing machine. The production of such true-to-scale drawings is helpful to engineers, architects, archaeologists and architectural historians in perceiving patterns or features that may have escaped them in the field. While not required extensively by the engineers at the Minster, photogrammetric drawings did prove useful in analysing the state of stability of the transepts which was discussed above.

Craftsmen

As well as professional skills, the structural restoration of the Minster demanded much from the craftsmen, including those from Shepherd Construction Ltd., under the direction of Ken Stephens and George Preston, and the Minster masons, led by Bill Holland. Visitors to the Undercroft have ample opportunity to admire the high quality finish of the new concrete which has been added to the original foundations (Plate 7). Such a finish is the result of great care not only in the mixing, placing and curing of the concrete itself, but also in the workmanship of fabricating and setting out the formwork into which the wet concrete is cast.

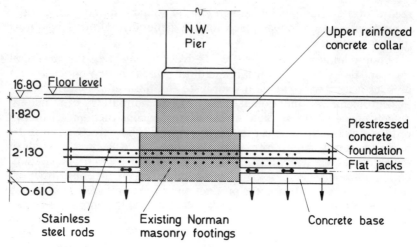

Diagram 7   Section through the north-west pier foundation.

This concrete was made to act integrally with the eleventh-century masonry by threading large diameter stainless steel rods through both components and stressing them together (Diagram 7). In order to place the rods in this way, holes had to be drilled through the ancient masonry. This drilling process proved to be exceptionally difficult and drew heavily on the hard-won expertise of the mining industry. These difficulties arose because it was necessary to drill many long holes, with great accuracy in position throughout their length, through extremely variable material. Ancient masonry is composed of stone rubble of variable size and shape, set in a matrix of very much softer mortar, and drill bits tend to change direction at each change in hardness encountered during drilling. This variability in the masonry was made worse by the presence of the oak reinforcement mentioned earlier, which not only itself caused the bit to deviate in line, but also necessitated the use of a wood bit rather than a masonry bit.

Much experimentation was necessary before a drilling method of satisfactory accuracy, speed and cost was found. Many combinations of types of bit and drilling action were tried. The favoured drilling action was a method known as the 'down-the-hole vole hammer' technique which combines a turning and a hammering action, the source of the latter being literally 'down the hole' within the cutting head.

This chapter would not be complete without paying tribute to the time-honoured skill of the mason. Such craftsmen are rare today as the modern world finds little need for massive stone masonry construction.

However, the maintenance of great ancient masonry buildings like York Minster requires the continuous employment of constructional and sculptural stone masons, and it is fortunate that the necessary old skills are still being perpetuated through the traditional system of masters training apprentices.

The most important principle in the conservation of old buildings is to disturb them as little as possible. This advice is part of the fund of wisdom found in the writings of William Harvey, particularly in his book on the restoration of St. Paul's Cathedral (Harvey, 1925). Harvey must be regarded as the first great masonry conservator of the modern era, and his advised objective was to achieve a sound conservation which did not in itself lead to further damage of the building fabric. While such consequential damage is generally slow to occur and undramatic in nature, it can of course be sudden, dramatic and dangerous. Both these types of secondary damage were borne in mind at York Minster. For these reasons alone, the availability of the Minster masons was of great benefit. The training and vocation of the masons ensured that they had a natural sympathy with their material, so that when the difficult task of cutting into existing masonry was necessary for the remedial works, nobody could surpass the masons at carrying it out with the minimum of disturbance to the surrounding stonework.

Knowledge, Wisdom and the Future

In the foregoing sections of this chapter the author has described the influence of a few of the specialist skills on the structural restoration of York Minster. While no attempt has been made to give a complete account of the skills used, those discussed should be sufficiently disparate and unusual in combination to convey something of the special flavour that this project had for those who were engaged upon it. Two other aspects which deserve at least a mention are the contribution of soil mechanics (discussed in more detail in Dowrick and Beckmann, 1971); and the vital role of surveying in measuring past movements and in monitoring the effects of the remedial works. Without the sensitive control of the excavation works, made possible by precise levelling instruments, the safe completion of the foundation works might not have been possible.

In discussing a few of the ancient and modern skills employed at various times on York Minster, some of the benefits acquired through advancements in scientific knowledge have been illustrated. However, despite our growing knowledge we need the humility to acknowledge that the store of potential knowledge in the universe is infinite, and great wisdom is required if we are to achieve a socially acceptable balance between caution and boldness in the exploitation of scientific knowledge.

We have had the privilege and responsibility of using our increased knowledge and corporate wisdom to extend the potential life of York Minster as far as seems feasible today. Apart from human failure to continue to maintain the building, the only *known* threats against which it now has no specific protection are those for which it is impossible for us to make provision, for example, a bomb or an earthquake. There is always, however, the possibility, of unforeseen dangers. We discover the short-comings in both our knowledge and our wisdom only through experience, but it is to be hoped that fate will smile kindly for centuries to come on our modern efforts to conserve the Minster.

Footnote

[1] The restoration of York Minster involved many people whose assistance is hereby gratefully acknowledged, not least those who contributed so generously to the Appeal Fund without which the work could not have been carried out. The principal professional parties involved in the structural work have been named in appropriate parts of the text, except for the author's colleagues, Paul Beckmann, Andrew Lord and the Resident Engineer, Norman Ross.

References

AYLMER G. E. and R. CANT (eds.) (1977), *A History of York Minster.*

DOWRICK D. J. (1970), *York Minster — The Structural History and Present Stability of the Transepts,* Ove Arup and Partners, London, April 1970. Additions, December 1971.

DOWRICK D. J. and P. BECKMANN (1971), 'York Minster structural restoration', *Proc. Institution of Civil Engineers,* Supplement (vi), Paper 7415 S, 1971, and Discussion, Supplement (xi), 1972.

HARVEY W. (1925), *The Preservation of St. Paul's Cathedral and other famous buildings.*

HEYMAN J. (1966), 'The Stone Skeleton', *Int. J. Solids Structures,* vol. 2, pp. 249-279.

HEYMAN J. (1967-68), 'Beauvais Cathedral', *Trans. Newcomen Society,* vol. XL, pp. 15-35.

PHILLIPS A. D. (1975), 'Excavations at York Minster, 1967-1973', Friends of York Minster *Annual Report,* pp. 19-27.

PHILLIPS A. D. (1976), 'Excavation techniques in church archaeology', in P. Addyman and R. Morris (eds.) *The Archaeological Study of Churches,* Council for British Archaeology, *Research Report* 13, pp. 54-59.

PHILLIPS A. D. (in preparation), *The Cathedral of Archbishop Thomas of Bayeux at York,* vol. 1 of the *Excavations at York Minster, 1967-1973,* Royal Commission on Historical Monuments.

WILLIS R. (1848), *Architectural History of York Cathedral.*

CHAPTER V

Population, Occupations and Economic Development, 1831-1981

by

Charles Feinstein

The Preceding Era, c. 1300-1830

Throughout its long and absorbing history the economic fortunes of York have depended partly on its position as a regional capital: a secular, ecclesiastical, military, judicial, social and commercial centre; and partly on the enterprise and activity of its manufacturers and merchants trading at home and abroad. The former has provided a stable basis for a buoyant local economy; the latter has been relatively volatile, bringing great prosperity in some periods and deep depression in others.

The high point in the city's position as a manufacturing centre of national significance was undoubtedly in the middle and late decades of the fourteenth century. It has been aptly described as being at that time 'the foremost industrial town in the North of England'.[1] The expansion of output rested predominantly on the progress of the clothmaking trades, but their success, and that of York's merchant adventurers, in turn stimulated local demand for many other products. The prosperity of the cloth trades was maintained into the first half of the fifteenth century, but thereafter its position deteriorated. By the end of the century a sense of decline, and of crisis, prevailed.

The opportunities open to the city's merchants followed a similar pattern and had parallel effects on the wealth and population of York. In the fourteenth century trade with the North, with London, and with Western Europe flourished. Wool was the main commodity, but cloth and lead were also sold widely. Early in the fifteenth century, however, York's standing in international commerce started to fade. By the seventeenth century a visitor, Thomas Fuller, could say of York that: 'the foreign trade is like their river ... low and little.'[2]

A modest measure of prosperity had been regained by the late sixteenth century, and the population had recovered to about 12,000 from a low point of some 8,000 in the preceding century. But in that revival it was only York's fortunate position as a regional centre which kept it in the first rank of English towns. The presence of the King's Council in the North was an especially valuable stimulus to the recovery of trade during the reign of Elizabeth I; and in the following centuries York sparkled as a social capital, providing shops, services and entertainment for the affluent citizens living in and beyond the city. The commerce of York with the surrounding farmers was also at all times a vital element in her prosperity, and there was a vigorous trade in butter, corn, fish and meat at the York markets. When the great wave of demographic and industrial progress surged across the country in the late eighteenth century, York shared in the growth of population but not in the development of industry.[3] Starting at about 12,000 in 1760, the population swelled to around 17,000 in 1801 and 26,000 in 1831. However, neighbouring towns had made much more impressive advances in size and income, and by the 1830s York was commonly regarded as a city in a state of decline.[4]

Modern York's inheritance from these preceding centuries has been both psychological and structural. First, the city was endowed with a belief in its importance, a confidence and a vitality which helped to make possible many achievements, including those discussed later in this chapter. The second legacy was the townscape which was created during (or, in a few notable instances, before) the medieval period, and which survived to the nineteenth century precisely because it was not destroyed to make way for the mills and the mean houses which came where industry thrived. This unique heritage has been a dominant influence on the development of modern York, especially in recent decades.

The Growth of Population
1831-1911

Between 1831 and 1911 the number of people living in York increased about threefold; in the process the economic and social character of the old city was completely transformed. This measure of the

Table 1   1831-1911
The Population of York, Census Years

	Municipal Borough (1)	Parliamentary Borough (2)	County Borough (3)	Registration District	
				Total (4)	Urban sub-districts (5)
1831	26,260	—	—	43,095	34,500
1841	28,842	30,152	—	47,778	38,406
1851	36,303	40,359	—	57,116	47,648
1861	40,433	45,385	—	59,909	50,847
1871	43,796	50,765	—	64,908	55,933
1881	49,530	60,343	—	76,695	67,963
1891	(51,105)	67,004	67,004	81,515	72,905
1901		75,521	77,914	92,012	83,526
1911		78,089	82,282	98,714	82,282

———— = boundary change

Source: *Census of Population* and Registrar-General *Annual Reports*.

Col. (1) The municipal borough was co-extensive with the ancient liberty, and essentially defined 'the city' until the formation of the County Borough (CB) – see col. (3). No return was made after 1891.

Col. (2) The parliamentary borough was created in 1832 and from 1885 was made co-extensive with the CB as extended in the previous year. It was not affected by the extension of 1893 until 1918.

Col. (3) The CB was created in 1888 and consisted of the municipal borough of 1881 plus the extensions of 1884. A further extension was made in 1893. See Map 2.

Cols. (4), (5) The Registration District was used by the Registrar-General for the returns of births, deaths and marriages, and was co-extensive with the Poor Law Union created in 1837. Until 1901 it contained seven sub-districts, three of which were predominantly urban and four predominantly rural (for details see Map 3). The District was reorganised in 1904, and two new urban sub-districts created (York East and York West) with a combined population equal to that of the enlarged CB.

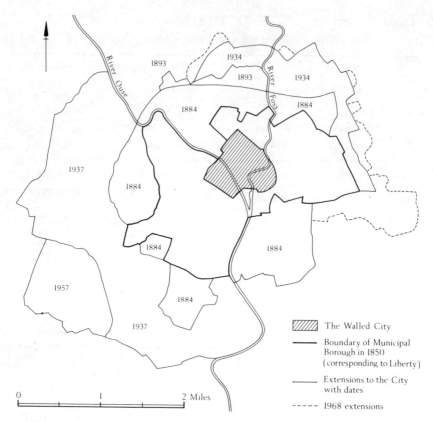

The Walled City

⎯⎯ Boundary of Municipal
Borough in 1850
(corresponding to Liberty)

⎯⎯ Extensions to the City
with dates

----- 1968 extensions

0   1   2 Miles

Map 2   York City boundary changes.

growth of population is broadly true however we define 'the city', but for closer investigation we need to take account of a dual complication: there were different definitions of 'York' for which the population was counted; and over time there were changes in the boundaries adopted for any particular definition.

Table 1 sets out the series for five of the differently constituted definitions of York, in each case showing the population within boundaries as they were drawn at each of the dates given. Map 2 shows the areas to which columns (1) and (3) refer, and also shows successive boundary changes; Map 3 shows the areas covered in columns (4) and (5) at the end of the nineteenth century. The main boundary alterations in 1884 and 1893 (Map 2) were not artificial administrative changes, but natural

Table 2
1831-1911
Population Growth in the County Borough

	Population within the 1893 boundaries (1)	Inter-censal increase	
		Persons (2)	Per cent (3)
1831	29,020	—	—
1841	32,130	3,110	10.7
1851	40,980	8,850	27.5
1861	46,225	5,245	12.8
1871	51,480	5,255	11.4
1881	62,598	11,118	21.6
1891	67,841	5,243	8.4
1901	77,914	10,073	14.8
1911	82,282	4,368	5.6

Source: *Census of Population*; Board of Trade (1908, p. 499); Rowntree (1941, p. 7); and author's estimates (for 1831 and 1841).

extensions, incorporating the inhabitants of areas with close economic and social ties with the city. For our purpose it is more appropriate to consider the growth of the city within a constant boundary. This enables us to capture the growth of population when it actually occurred and to avoid a break in continuity at the time of the extension. This is done in Table 2.

The 1840s and the 1870s immediately stand out as periods when rates of growth were exceptionally rapid: in the former a rise of almost 9,000 increased the city's population by more than a quarter; in the latter the increase was over 11,000, more than a fifth. By comparison, the rate of increase was very slow in the 1880s and 1900s. In order to obtain a better understanding of the reasons for these periods of faster and slower growth it is necessary to distinguish between two possible components of population change. The first is natural increase, i.e. the excess of births over deaths; and the second is net gain or loss through migration.

A reasonable approximation to the required estimates of natural increase can be obtained from the Registrar-General's *Annual Returns* of births and deaths within the York Registration District. The data for the

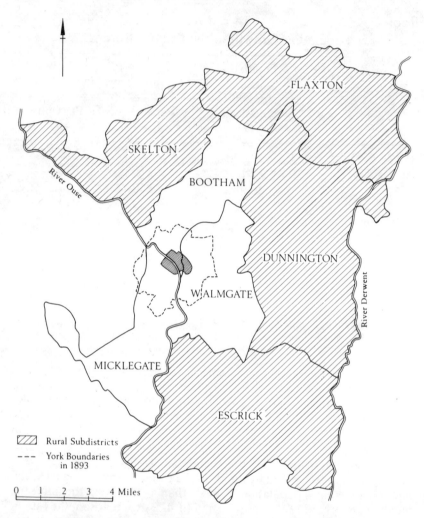

Map 3   York City and York Registration District
(Poor Law Union), 1893.

three urban sub-districts (see Map 3) were used to estimate the natural
increase within the 1893 boundaries of the county borough.[5] This is
shown in column (1) of Table 3 as the 'urban' area. The remaining natural
increase in the Registration District was taken as applying to the 'rural'

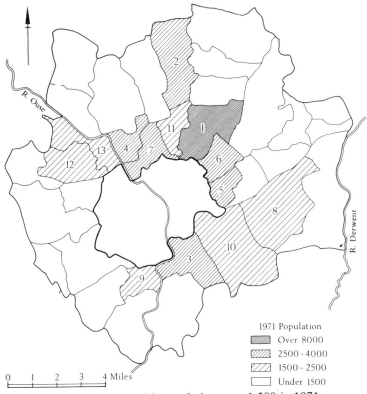

1971 Population
- Over 8000
- 2500 - 4000
- 1500 - 2500
- Under 1500

0   1   2   3   4 Miles

Parishes with population over 1,500 in 1971.

1. Huntington
2. Haxby
3. Fulford
4. Rawcliffe
5. Osbaldwick

6. Heworth (without)
7. Clifton (without)
8. Dunnington
9. Bishopthorpe
10. Heslington

11. New Earswick
12. Upper Poppleton
13. Nether Poppleton

Map 4   York City and 'York Study Area', 1971.

area and is shown in column (2) of Table 3. In each case the difference between this natural increase and the actual increase then represents the net gain or loss due to migration (columns (3) and (4) of Table 3).[6] Deriving both the urban and the rural estimates together in this way has an advantage in that it reveals the relationship between population growth in the city of York and that in the surrounding villages which were the nearest source from which immigrants would be drawn.[7]

Table 3   1831-1911
Natural Increase and Net Migration
within York Registration District

	Natural increase		Net gain (+) or loss (–) by migration		Actual increase	
	Urban (1)	Rural (2)	Urban (3)	Rural (4)	Urban (5)	Rural (6)
1831-40	(3,070)	(1,460)	(+ 40)	(+ 110)	3,110	1,570
1841-50	1,960	1,250	+6,890	– 760	8,850	490
1851-60	4,110	1,130	+1,130	– 720	5,240	410
1861-70	3,860	1,590	+1,390	–1,360	5,250	230
1871-80	5,850	1,770	+5,270	–1,100	11,120	670
1881-90	6,750	1,810	–1,510	–2,230	5,240	–420
1891-00	7,990	550	+2,080	– 10	10,070	540
1901-11	10,390	330	–6,020	+2,000	4,370	2,330

Source: Registrar-General, *Annual Reports* and *Census of Population*. See also
footnote 5, p. 153.

Cols. (1), (3) and (5) relate to the population within constant boundaries as
given in Table 2. (3) is obtained as the difference between
(1) and (5).

Cols. (2), (4) and (6) relate to the remaining population of York Registration
District. In calculating (6) adjustments were made for the
boundary changes in 1854, 1861, 1869, 1895, 1901 and
1904. (4) is obtained as the difference between (2) and (6).

A number of interesting conclusions can be drawn from Table 3.
First, the fluctuations in the growth of the urban population were principally the result of net migration (see column 3). There were large inflows
in the 1840s and 1870s – the decades when the rate of population increase
was especially rapid; and there were net outflows in the 1880s and 1900s
– the decades when the rate of growth was slowest. The net loss in the
1900s was particularly large. Secondly, the balance of migration out of
the immediately surrounding rural area usually accounted for only a small
part of the movement into, or out of, the city. The estimates in Table 3
show only the *net* flows, and it is likely that the total outflow from the
designated rural area was larger, but was partly offset by movement into

these villages from areas further from York.[8] Subject to this qualification, it is striking that in the 1840s, for example, when the city gained almost 7,000 through migration, the net loss to the surrounding rural area was less than 800. There was a similar picture in the 1870s and 1890s, even though the movement from Ireland to York was then a good deal smaller.

The large swings in migration to and from York – and thus the varying pace at which the city expanded during the nineteenth century – can be explained partly by the general trends in internal migration and emigration for the country as a whole and partly by factors specific to York. The very large influx of Irish in the 1840s, and the persistent drift from the countryside throughout the century, affected York in common with many other towns in England. The railways were a crucial element in this process, increasing mobility, providing jobs and strengthening the economy of urban areas. The net loss shown by York in the 1880s and – on a much larger scale – in the 1900s, similarly reflected York's participation in a nationwide pattern in decades in which there was a massive outflow to the USA and the Dominions. Equally, the marked recovery of the rural areas at the beginning of the twentieth century, after decades of steadily falling population, was a feature of many parts of England.

The two phases in which York's experience appears to have been most distinctive were the 1870s and the 1890s. The gains in these decades, especially the former, were proportionately larger than those in many other towns. The influx in the 1890s shows the impact of the expansion of employment in the railway workshops and the confectionery industry, both of which 'took off' in the mid-1880s (see pp. 124-5 and 129, below). For the 1870s the explanation for the drawing-power of the city is less apparent,[9] but must be associated with the increased numbers required for railway operation; the general growth of manufacturing; the high level of house-building and construction (including the new station, the infantry barracks in Fulford and eight church schools prompted by the 1870 Elementary Education Act); the recruitment of soldiers to occupy the new barracks; and an increase in the number of domestic servants.

1911-1981

York's demographic history since 1911 stands in sharp contrast to the quite rapid expansion experienced during the nineteenth century. If the effect of boundary changes is again eliminated, as in columns (2) and (3) of Table 4, the picture is one of very limited growth until 1951, and thereafter of gentle but steady decline. The most rapid growth rate achieved in the twentieth century (1939-51) was below even the slowest rate in the nineteenth century. In the most recent decade the population has continued to drift downward, perhaps by as much as 5,000.[10]

Table 4   1911-71
                              Population Growth

| | City of York | | | York Study Area (5) |
	Current boundaries (1)	1937 boundaries (2)	1971 boundaries (3)	Per cent change (4)	
1911	82,282	86,850	—	5.6	—
1921	84,039	89,012	—	2.5	—
1931	84,813	94,066	—	5.7	—
1939	97,673	97,673	—	3.8[1]	—
1951	105,371	105,371	109,015	7.9[2]	134,921
1961	104,392	104,348	108,133	−0.8	143,792
1971	104,782	—	104,782	−3.1	154,822

———— = boundary change.

Source: *Census of Population* and NYCC (1977, p. 4).

Col. (4): Based on col. (2) for 1911-51 and col. (3) for 1951-71. The rate for 1901-11 is taken from Table 2.

[1] = 8 years,   [2] = 12 years.

The very modest increase of the interwar years can be largely explained by two factors, both applicable not only to York but to most other urban areas in the country. First, the York birth rate continued to decline steeply and by the end of the 1930s had dropped to half its level at the end of the nineteenth century. The death rate was also falling, but much less sharply, and the natural rate of increase was accordingly reduced to a very low level.[11] Secondly, outflow from the rural areas had been broadly completed by 1914, so that there was subsequently much less scope to supplement the city's own expansion by drawing in population from the countryside. In fact, York was on balance losing population to the surrounding villages in each of the decades from 1911 to 1931, and made only small net gains during the 1930s and World War II. The downward trend in the population since 1951 again reflected very low rates of natural increase,[12] combined with net outward migration.

Although York has declined in size since 1951 as a consequence of net outward migration, it would be misleading to suggest that the city has lost its magnetic quality. It continues to attract population, but much of it is now drawn to villages which lie outside the formal, and in this respect unrealistic, boundaries. This process is recognised in the concept of the 'York Study Area' employed in the County Structure Plan (NYCC, 1979). This area consists of the City of York 'and those surrounding parishes with particularly close social and economic links with the City', notably Huntington, Haxby, Fulford and Rawcliffe (see Map 4). These and other villages are all de facto part of York even if de jure they lie outside the boundary. The number of people living in this wider area increased by some 20,000 (about seven per cent per decade) between 1951 and 1971 (see column (5) of Table 4); and growth continued through the 1970s though at a slightly slower pace.

The Occupied Population, 1851 to 1971

How were the people of York employed? What were the industries and occupations which provided work for a growing population, and – as we have seen – contributed to that growth by attracting new residents from outside the city boundaries? To answer these questions we look first at the level of employment relative to total population at four dates: 1851, 1911, 1951 and 1971. We then look in more detail at the industrial structure of employment in York at these dates, at the way in which it changed over time, and at some of the main factors responsible for those changes.

The basic information on employment was assembled from the *Census of Population*. 1851 is taken as the starting point, rather than 1831, as it is the first year for which a comprehensive classification is available. 1911 is a convenient midpoint and also marks the end of the period of rapid growth of population and industry. 1951 shows the position at the beginning of the post-war period, after the impact of interwar depression and two world wars; and 1971 is the latest year for which a census enumeration is available. The figures for each date relate to the population within York's boundaries at that date, and thus reflect boundary extensions (see Map 2) as well as changes in population.

As a first step the relationship between the total population and those who were 'economically active' (i.e. either at work or available for work even though unemployed or sick), is set out in Table 5. The overall ratio (the 'average participation rate' in row 3 of the table) shows a very slight upward trend between 1851 and 1971. The rates for each year are very close to those for Great Britain, which helps to increase confidence in the reliability of the estimates of the occupied population for York.[13]

The near stability in the average rate is the outcome of a number of divergent and more striking trends in the underlying specific participation

Table 5   1851-1971
          Average and Specific Participation Rates, York

	1851	1911	1951	1971
I *Average participation rate*				
1 Total population	36,300	82,280	105,370	104,780
2 Economically active[1]	16,140	36,990	49,320	49,470
3 Participation rate				
(2 as % of 1)	44.5	45.0	46.8	47.2
II *Sex- and age-specific participation rates*[2] (percentage)				
4 Males				
a 10-19	59.5	49.0	38.6	28.4
b 20-64	} 95.1	97.1	(95.5)	95.1
c 65 and over		51.2	(29.7)	15.7
d Total aged 10 and over	85.7	82.9	79.7	71.9
5 Females				
a 10-19	34.2	41.9	40.3	29.3
b 20-64	} 33.3	30.9	(37.8)	54.8
c 65 and over		11.9	(6.0)	6.9
d Total aged 10 and over	32.8	32.1	33.8	41.0

Source: *Census of Population.*   Figures in ( ) are partly estimated by the author.

[1] The unemployed are included in all years. For 1851 the census figures were reduced by 2% to exclude the estimated number of retired workers listed under their former occupations – this is the proportion suggested for the country as a whole, see Census of Population for England and Wales, 1881, *General Report,* pp. 28-9. For 1851 the figures cover all children at work; for 1911 those aged 10 and over; for 1951 and 1971 those aged 15 and over. The figures for 1951 and 1971 are for persons usually resident in York irrespective of where they worked.

[2] Economically active males and females (as defined in note [1]) in the specified age groups as a percentage of the corresponding figures for the male and female population of York.

rates for males and females in particular age groups. These are shown in the lower part of Table 5. Among males there have been two persistent forces tending to reduce overall participation. First, the general increase in the extent and duration of schooling and of further education has halved the rate for the 10-19 age group (row 4a). Secondly, the improvement of pension-schemes has encouraged earlier retirement and cut the proportion of men at work aged 65 and over from 51 per cent in 1911 to only 16 per cent in 1971 (row 4c). Since there has been very little change in the proportion of men at work in the main age-group (20-64), the net outcome has been to reduce participation rates for men aged 10 and over from about 86 per cent in 1851 to 72 per cent in 1971, the greater part of the decline occuring in the last two decades (row 4d).

For females the same two forces (education and pensions) have operated to reduce participation rates among the young (row 5a) and the old (row 5c), though the effect has been less marked than it was for men. However, these trends have been more than offset by a powerful movement towards increased employment among women aged 20-64. This has lifted their rate from 31 per cent in 1911 to 55 per cent in 1971 (row 5b); and has been sufficient to raise the overall participation rate for women and girls by about a quarter (row 5d). The rise has occurred almost entirely in the period since 1951. In York, as in the country at large, the reasons for this dramatic increase include the fall in family size; the increased levels of income to which they aspire; the changes in the attitudes of society, and of women themselves, to being 'working wives'; and the changes in the occupational structure which have increased the clerical and other service jobs in which large numbers of women are employed. We return to this last aspect at a later point (p. 138).

These divergent trends in participation rates for males and females since 1951 have increased the proportion of women in York's labour force from 32 per cent in 1951 to 39 per cent in 1971. The significance of this trend is, however, moderated by the fact that many of the women who have entered employment in recent decades have taken only part-time jobs.

We now go behind these figures for total employment to analyse the structure of economic activity in York. We look first at the data for 1851 and 1911 and at the changes between these years.

Occupations and Economic Development, 1851 to 1911

The broad picture for these two dates is shown in Table 6.[14] In 1851 the structure of occupations was still very much that of a pre-industrial town, with an exceptionally large proportion of domestic servants (row 9); of tailors, milliners, dressmakers and shoemakers (row 3) and of other shopkeepers.[15] A high proportion of the shopkeepers was engaged in the provision of food and other locally-produced necessities. The number occupied in farming (and market gardens) in 1851 had recently been increased by the prosperity of the chicory farmers who, at that time, provided employment for some 400, including many Irish labourers who had poured into York in the 1840s.

Table 6   1851 and 1911
                    Employment in York

		1851[1]		1911	
		Persons	Per cent	Persons	Per cent
1 Farming		1,080	6.5	520	1.4
2 Manufacturing		3,170	19.3	10,270	27.8
3 Making and dealing in clothing and shoes		2,440	14.8	1,690	4.6
4 Construction		1,220	7.4	2,610	7.1
5 Transport and communication[2]		1,130	6.9	4,790	12.9
Railways	*420*			*3,170*	
6 Distribution[3]		1,570	9.5	3,830	10.3
Food and drink	*800*			*1,800*	
7 Professional services[4]		900	5.5	1,860	5.0
Education	*290*			*680*	
Medical	*150*			*330*	
8 Government and defence		230	1.4	2,370	6.4
Government	*110*			*750*	
9 Domestic service		2,800	17.0	3,810	10.3
10 Other services		910	5.5	2,430	6.6
Hotels, inns, etc.	*560*			*1,240*	
11 Other and unclassified[5]		1,020	6.2	2,810	7.6
General labourers	*770*			*1,040*	
Clerks	*100*			*1,150*	
		16,470	100.0	36,990	100.0

Source: *Census of Population.*

[1] The figure for the total in 1851 differs from that in Table 5 because no adjustment has been made to exclude the retired. See also footnote 14 (p. 154).
[2] Including general messengers (490 in 1911) and all carriers, carters, etc. (480).
[3] Including merchants, agents and accountants (36).
[4] Including finance (350).
[5] Including gas and water (230).

Railway service, notwithstanding all the activity inspired by George Hudson, James Meek, Samuel Tuke and others,[16] still provided only a small number of jobs by the middle of the nineteenth century. Most of what has been classified in Table 6 as manufacturing consisted of handicrafts and small-scale workshops; like the dealers, they found much of their custom among affluent families of York and nearby estates and farms.

There were a few manufacturing concerns of modest size. One of the most notable was York Flint Glass Company, formed in 1835 by a chemist, Joseph Spence, in association with Joseph Meek and others. Another was the confectionery firm of Joseph Terry and Company which was rapidly expanding in the 1840s, producing sweets, jams and marmalade. The iron foundry of John Walker was also a significant enterprise, making gates and railings which had already won him a national reputation by mid-century; many of them still ornament the city. There were also two expanding firms of manufacturing chemists. The oldest was Butterfield and Clarke (established in 1780) in which William Bleasdale purchased an interest in 1856; and the other was Raimes and Company, which started in 1818.[17] For the most part, however, neither the coming of the railway, nor the development of textile and other factory-based industries, had yet made much impact on the economy of York.

By 1911 the position was completely transformed. The total occupied population had more than doubled and there were radical shifts in the composition of employment. Agriculture declined absolutely, with chicory farming contracting after the imposition of a stiff excise duty in the 1860s; so too did the clothing trades, as York's tailors and shoemakers, working largely by hand, were driven out by the progressive mechanisation of the factory industry in Leeds and other towns. There was also a sharp fall in the proportion dependent for work on domestic service. The first sign of what was later to be a significant trend is evident in the rise in the number employed in national and local government; and a big increase in the number in the army reflects the capacity of new barracks constructed in the 1870s. The changing nature of employment is also seen in the presence of over 1,000 clerical workers, where there were only 100 in 1851.

All these trends are dwarfed in significance by comparison with the expansion of manufacturing and transport. It was here that York experienced a change in both scale and character of economic activity. Small-scale handicrafts gave way to establishments with a labour force counted not in tens, or even hundreds, but in thousands. In the rise of the factory system in York two industries tower over all others and the economic history of the city in the second half of the nineteenth century is the history of their rise to great prominence. The first is the manufacture of confectionery; the second is the railway, with its ancillary building and repair of rolling stock. We look at each in turn.

In 1869, at the age of 33, Joseph Rowntree left the grocery shop in Pavement which his father had bought almost 50 years earlier when he moved to York from Scarborough.[18] From then onwards Joseph's capital and his talents were employed in the cocoa and chocolate manufacturing firm which his younger brother, Henry Isaac Rowntree, had purchased in 1862 from the Tukes. The firm employed only a dozen men at its premises at Tanner's Moat; the business was initially not very successful and in several years was working at a loss. The main product, *Prize Medal Rock Cocoa,* was a very rich and fatty blend of cocoa and sugar.

The firm's position was transformed by two innovations. The first came in 1879, when the Rowntrees were approached by a Frenchman, Claude Gaget and with his assistance started to make crystallised gums and pastilles. Manufacture of the gums had previously been a French speciality, and when the Rowntree products came on the market in 1881 they were an instant success. Two years later Henry Isaac died, leaving Joseph in sole charge of the business. With increased sales of the gums to support him he made the second, and most crucial, innovation.

Once again he turned abroad, this time to Holland, and with the help of Cornelius Hollander he installed equipment which had first been developed by the Dutch firm of Van Houten in 1828, and introduced into England by George Cadbury in 1866, followed two years later by Francis Fry at Bristol. Joseph Rowntree had visited the Cadburys in Birmingham in 1875, two years before he travelled to Holland. He had presumably been aware of the advantages of the Dutch machine at least since then, but had lacked either the resources or the confidence to make the investment. The new process used hydraulic pressure to squeeze the cocoa butter from the cleaned and roasted beans. This had two effects, both highly significant for the burgeoning cocoa and chocolate industry: by reducing the fat content of the pure cocoa it produced a much more appealing beverage, and it provided the supplies of cocoa butter used for making popular eating chocolate. From 1887 Rowntree's was selling *Elect* cocoa, a pure powder with no sugar or other additive. Once again their new product was quickly accepted, and sales shot upwards.

With these two innovations the foundations had been laid: subsequent expansion was sustained and substantial. In 1880 the firm employed about 100 workers; by 1894 the number had risen to 864; ten years later the firm was over three times that size, with 2,945 employees in York; and in the next ten years, to 1914, it almost doubled to 5,640. Of these, 3,144 were engaged in the production of chocolate assortments and confectionery, 828 were making cake chocolate and cocoa, and the rest were involved in associated activities such as boxmaking and packing, clerical work and maintenance of equipment.[19] In the early twentieth century the firm had over 300 'lines' of confectionery and sweets on sale. Its initial site had soon become quite inadequate, even with some additional purchases. In 1890 a large area of land was acquired in Haxby Road, about 1½ miles from the city centre; with later purchases it extended to some 222 acres. Starting in the following year production was gradually transferred to the new site, and in 1908 all activity ceased at Tanner's Moat.

A limited liability company, Rowntree and Co. Ltd. was formed in 1897; and with turnover leaping ahead, raw material prices falling or stable (see below, p. 127), and the increasing mechanisation of various stages of production, the business became extremely profitable. In the Prospectus issued on 3 May 1919 the average annual profit for the five years 1909-13 was given as £136,080 'after providing for adequate depreciation of buildings and machinery, interest on loans, pensions to employees and other ameliorative purposes, income tax and all other charges'.

Rowntree's was in general a good employer, and the provision of 'pensions and other ameliorative purposes' was one of many benefits the cocoa works brought to the City. It was not only the most important source of employment in York, it was also a very stable industry. Cyclical fluctuations in demand for labour were never the serious problem for York that they were for many other towns. There is, however, almost no precise information on the wages paid by the company. When the Board of Trade investigated working conditions in York in 1908 it observed that:

> In the largest of the cocoa works, rates of wages are fixed without regard to the general rates for labour prevailing in the city. The expressed aim of the directors is to pay a standard minimum 'living' wage throughout their factories. The bulk of the labour employed is of an unskilled order, but, while the remuneration is on an appreciably higher scale than that obtained by such labour elsewhere in the district, it is also claimed that very great care is exercised in the direction of procuring a class of labour more efficient than the average. (Board of Trade, 1908, p. 501.)

At about the same time an enquiry in York from the Royal Commission on the Poor Laws reported:

> Beyond the fact that the minimum wage for men over 24 [sic] years

of age is 24s a week and the average wage of men over that age is 26s a week, we were unable to obtain information respecting the wages of those employed in the large cocoa and chocolate works. (Kay and Toynbee, 1908, p. 115.)

This average can be compared with the data assembled below (p. 132) for average wages in York and elsewhere. The comparison suggests that if Rowntree's did pay more than the usual rate the margin must have been very slender. In other respects, however, its record as an employer was thoughtful and imaginative. Welfare and recreational facilities were available; the working week was cut to 48 hours in 1896, an improvement made only much later by most other firms; free medical and dental services were provided from 1904 and a company pension-scheme was introduced in 1906.

If York thus owed much to Rowntree's for its well-being in the late Victorian and Edwardian period, it was not the case that the company was to any significant degree dependent on the locational or other advantages provided by the city. To a large extent the company's phenomenal growth must be attributed to the qualities of its principal founder, Joseph Rowntree. As we have seen, it was not great inventiveness or boldness which characterised his management of the firm. When he made his decisive move to produce cocoa powder in the 1880s he had before him the very successful, and widely publicised, example of Cadbury's, already employing about 1,000 workers. His initial opposition to advertising may indicate a similar lack of adventurous entrepreneurial spirit.[20] The qualities he did bring to the business included prudence and an insistence on quality and attention to detail; acute business skills in respect of both short-run costs and long-run strategies; a modest lifestyle and a readiness to plough profits back into the firm; and, perhaps above all, an exceptional degree of foresight and vision in planning for the future. He also succeeded admirably in gaining the loyalty of those who worked for him, and when expansion made it necessary, he had the ability to delegate to others, including his son Seebohm, who succeeded him as chairman and managing director in 1923.

These qualities enabled Rowntree and Co. to flourish and to take its place as one of the three dominant firms in the British cocoa and chocolate industry, but that record has also to be seen in the context of the remarkable pace at which the whole industry leapt ahead in the second half of the nineteenth century. At the beginning of the nineteenth century cocoa as a beverage was very much a minority taste and subject to high import duties; and chocolate confectionery was not made in England before the 1840s. The industry then shot forward, with output more than doubled between 1850 and 1870 (as measured by the total quantity of cocoa beans imported for consumption in Britain). It increased three-fold in the two following decades, to 1890, and it almost did so again in the next two decades. In 1900 the total retail value of cocoa and chocolate consumed in Britain is estimated at some £10m; by 1913 this had doubled to £20m.[21]

Four factors helped to revolutionise the scale and profitability of the industry: the introduction of new machinery for making chocolate and the vital Dutch discovery, mentioned earlier (p. 124), for making cocoa powder; Gladstone's reduction of the import duty on cocoa beans to a uniform rate of 1d a lb, held constant from 1853 until 1915; the steep fall in the price of the principal raw materials; and the improvement in the real incomes of British workers brought about by higher earnings and lower prices.

In the early 1880s the average import price of raw cocoa was a little over 8d per lb (including duty); when Joseph Rowntree started production of his *Elect* cocoa a few years later it had dropped slightly below 8d. By the late 1890s it had fallen to about 7d and remained at about that level until 1909-13, when there was a fall of a further 1d. Over the same period of some 30 years real wages went up by about a third. With workers enjoying these increased earnings, what had previously been luxury products for a minority could now be shared by millions. When cocoa prices drifted downwards after the turn of the century it was not necessary for the industry to make a corresponding reduction in its retail prices in order to increase its markets.[22] In this fortunate conjunction lay the conditions for the immensely profitable expansion of trade made alike by the Rowntrees and their main rivals.

One of these rivals was the nearby firm of Joseph Terry and Sons. As mentioned earlier it was already a concern of some note by 1851, and under the leadership of Joseph Terry junior (later Sir Joseph) it maintained a strong upward trend in the following decades when Terry's became famous for its candied peel, jujubes, medicated lozenges and other sweets. In 1864 the firm moved from St. Helen's Square, in the centre of York, to Clementhorpe on the bank of the Ouse, where a substantial factory, warehouse and offices were erected. In 1886 production of cocoa and chocolate was started, and a new factory was built for this purpose, although sugar confectionery remained the main business of the firm until the 1920s. In 1898 Sir Joseph Terry died; three years before that the firm had been incorporated as a limited liability company. The number of workers employed at that stage was about 300. In the years following Sir Joseph's death growth was much less vigorous, and rapid progress was not resumed until after the First World War, though the quality and reputation of the confectionery remained high.[23]

The third and smallest of York's well-known confectionery manufacturers is M. A. Craven and Sons. Mary Ann Craven was the daughter of
one confectioner, and in 1851 married another. The two firms merged,
and in 1862, when her husband died, Mary Ann took over the management of the business. It specialised in boiled sweets, sugared almonds and
other sugar confectionery of a high standard, and remained loyal to these
products while its local rivals turned increasingly to chocolate. By 1914, it
employed a staff of about 250.[24]

The growth of trade stimulated directly and indirectly by these three
confectionery manufacturers would have made only a minor contribution
to the spectacular increase in railway traffic through York. Far more
important was the city's focal position in the vast network of lines constructed from the 1830s to the 1860s. The main company operating from
York was the North Eastern, formed by the amalgamation of four companies in July 1854; but the city's importance as a railway centre was such
that six other mainline companies had trains running through York by the
end of the century.

As a rough measure of the growth of traffic – and so of the labour
required to operate the service – we have some figures showing for
selected years the number of trains using York station each day.[25] In 1854
the daily traffic was 76 trains, and in 1868 it was 94. By 1878, after the
great industrial boom of the early seventies, the number was over 60 per
cent higher at 154. It increased by 36 per cent to 210 trains in 1888, and
by a further leap of 40 per cent to 294 in 1898. By 1908 it had risen to 352
trains, an increase since 1854 of over 460 per cent. As traffic increased,
the first station (opened in 1841) was extended, but by 1866 it was
recognised that a much larger station was needed. This was built entirely
outside the city walls, and completed in June 1877; at that time it was the
largest in the country, with a grandeur befitting the importance of York as
a railway centre. The prospect from Platform 8, looking south into the
station, was recently praised as 'still the finest view in York'.[26] The
operation and administration of this great system – and its associated
locomotive, carriage and wagon works – made the railways York's first
really large-scale employer. The total number working for the North
Eastern climbed from a little over 500 in 1851 to almost 6,000 at the
pre-1914 peak around 1905. Those directly occupied in running the
railway as drivers, firemen, porters, clerks and administrators numbered
a little over 300 in 1851, over 1,200 in 1891, and about 2,900 in 1901.
There was then a slight increase to almost 3,200 in 1911 (see row 5 of
Table 6).

A further 2,600 were employed in the company's three workshops at
the turn of the century.[27] The number declined after 1905 to about 1,600

in 1911. The first phase in the history of these workshops began in 1839 with the opening of a small carriage-repair shop in Queen Street, and lasted until the end of the 1870s. Activity in this period was on a fairly modest scale. The first workshop for repair of locomotives was opened by the York and North Midland at Queen Street in 1842. Both the locomotive and carriage shops were given more to do following the 1854 amalgamation, and improvements were made to the carriage shop in 1855. At this time most of the company's engines were constructed by specialist firms, and only a few locomotives were built at York. Most of the work done was repair and re-fitting of old engines, typically adding new cylinders and boilers. In the mid-sixties the move away from Queen Street was initiated by the construction of a wagon shop on a large site at Holgate, a short distance to the north-west. The works was enlarged in 1875, bringing the site up to 16 acres, of which 4 were under cover. However, in spite of this, the three North Eastern workshops failed to keep pace with advances in engineering practice and equipment.[28]

A second, and more vigorous phase, opened in the early 1880s, making this decade a turning-point in the growth of the railway industry in York, as it was also in the production of confectionery. The occasion for the change was the appointment of Alexander McDonnell as Chief Locomotive Superintendent of the North Eastern in 1882. His predecessor had held office since 1854, and by the time of his eventual retirement had become excessively conservative in outlook. The workshops which McDonnell took over were 'outdated and inadequate', and he took brisk action to re-equip and modernise the company's engineering works at Darlington, Gateshead and York.

The improvement of the locomotive workshops at York was undertaken at a cost of some £12,000. The subsequent years were among the most active in the history of the works, and by 1902 the number employed on locomotives had reached 763. However, the company had by then taken the decision to concentrate locomotive work at Darlington, and in 1905 the York works was closed. In his *Report* for that year the Medical Officer of Health referred gloomily to 1,870 workers and their dependants leaving York as a result of the closure. In contrast, York's carriage works was larger and more successful under the new regime. The North Eastern had decided in 1880 to make York its main centre for carriage building, and a completely new works was started at Holgate to replace the out-moded Queen Street shops. Some £75,000 was spent on new plant and equipment in the 1880s but even this soon proved inadequate. The size and weight of the stock used on the East Coast was increasing rapidly, and the York works advanced from construction of four-wheel coaches to vehicles with six and subsequently eight or twelve wheels.

These developments made obsolete the recently installed equipment and, with economic conditions generally booming in the North East in the 1890s, there was pressure for further improvement in the quality and capacity of the York workshops. Expenditure of over £22,000 was approved in 1896, and of a further £65,000 two years later. By 1910 the works extended over 45 acres, 13 of them covered by sheds and buildings. The staff employed on building and repair of carriages and wagons numbered 1,838 in 1896 and rose to 1,970 in 1907, years spanning the period during which work on construction of carriages for the North Eastern was booming. After that employment declined slightly, as the boom ended, and in 1912 was down to 1,553.

This completes our brief survey of confectionery manufacturing and the railways. By 1911 they held a position of overwhelming dominance in the York labour market, accounting for over one quarter of all jobs in the city (almost 10,000 out of 37,000) and for roughly half of those in manufacturing proper (about 5,500 out of 11,000-12,000).[29] There are only a few other York firms which warrant individual mention.

One of the larger and technically more progressive manufacturers in York was T. Cooke & Sons, whose distinguished scientific achievements are discussed at some length in Chapter II above. After the death of Thomas Cooke in 1868 the business was run by his two sons, and from the 1890s Dennis Taylor played a leading role, particularly in the development of optical instruments. In the words of the authors of a brief history of the firm:

> At the turn of the century T. Cooke and Sons possessed one of the most complete factories in existence for the manufacture of surveying and astronomical instruments, with well equipped metal and glass-working shops, an up-to-date factory, wood and leather-working shops . . .[30]

Some 400-500 workers were employed at the firm's Buckingham Works on Bishophill inside the city walls, and the products they made sold in many parts of the world.

Another very enterprising and successful business was the flour mill, started by Henry Leetham in 1850 at Wormald's Cut, on the Foss. After a slow start, a decisive advance came (once again) in the 1880s when a new milling technique was introduced from Hungary, using steel rolling in place of millstones. Leetham was one of the first to see the opportunities opened by this technological innovation, and the scale of his activity expanded rapidly in the 1880s and 1890s, with corresponding enlargement of his premises. Following his death in 1896 the firm was incorporated in 1899 as Henry Leetham and Sons Ltd. The prospectus issued at that time showed that the firm was making clear profits of over £50,000 a year in the late nineties, and supplied almost 9,000 wholesale customers. It had built impressive mills, grain silos and warehouses in York; and also operated in Hull, Newcastle and Cardiff, so that it was no longer simply a local concern. Nevertheless, its mills held a commanding position on the city's southern skyline (as one does to this day); and Leetham's would have accounted for many of the estimated 600 jobs provided in York in 1911 by the flour milling industry.[31]

The firm made full use of its favourable site alongside the river, and grain and flour soon displaced coal as the main traffic carried on the Foss and Ouse. It helped to persuade the Ouse Navigation Trustees to build new locks at Naburn, just south of York. In 1888 it took advantage of its importance for the river traffic, and its ability to threaten that its further expansion might be located in Hull rather than York, to negotiate a valuable agreement with the City Corporation. From this it obtained both an enlargement of the lock on the Foss at Castle Mills, and also extremely favourable terms for transport of its goods. Its agreement was renewed in 1906, but in the 1920s was declared illegal as giving undue preference to one firm.[32]

Of the firms mentioned earlier (p. 123), the York Glass Works, on Foss Island, prospered for some time; but by the early twentieth century was badly afflicted by inadequate modernisation of buildings and equipment, foreign competition, and labour unrest. This culminated in a strike for higher wages and shorter hours by the unskilled labourers (the majority of the workforce of some 220) in the autumn of 1911.[33] Manufacturing and wholesale trade in chemicals and drugs continued at Bleasdale Ltd., with 'multifarious ramifications, including the grinding of medical herbs and roots, the preparation of all kinds of tinctures, the manufacture of standardized pharmaceutical preparations, emulsions, syrups, oils, extracts . . .';[34] and also at Raimes and Co. Nitrate and other fertilizers for the surrounding farming area were made by Henry Richardson and Co., founded in 1824. However, none of these can have provided a large number of jobs: the 1911 census shows a total of only 197 persons working in York as chemists and druggists, etc.

Printing was a more important source of industrial employment, and in 1911 provided over 500 jobs. There were two daily newspapers: the *York Daily Herald* which had changed from a weekly in 1874 under William Wallace Hargrove (and was retitled *Yorkshire Herald* in 1890); and the present *Yorkshire Evening Press*, which first appeared in 1882.[35] The York Herald Newspaper Co. was also active as general printers; and there were two other firms in York, among many engaged in printing, which deserve mention for their standing in the late nineteenth century and their later expansion. The York origins of Ben Johnson and Co. Ltd. date back to 1854, when John Lancaster arrived from Hull to take advantage of the growing work to be obtained in printing time-tables and other material for the railways. In 1858 he appointed Ben Johnson as manager, and between them a thriving business – primarily in lithographic printing – was built up. The ancestry of the second firm, William Sessions Ltd., can be traced back to a firm of booksellers, stationers and printers started by a Quaker, William Alexander, in 1811, though it was not until 1865 that the business was acquired by a member of the Sessions family. In 1894 the printing presses were moved to larger premises in Coney Street, and in 1907 William Sessions II decided to concentrate exclusively on the printing side and set up in factory premises in North Street. The transition to a major concern began with that move but the main phase of expansion occurred after 1911 and so belongs to a later stage in York's history.

Wages in York, 1899 and 1905

One further aspect which it is interesting to consider is the significance of the structure of employment for the level of wages and living conditions in York. A complete analysis of this topic is not possible here, but we can draw on two enquiries to give a broad outline of conditions in York, relative to those in the rest of the country, at the turn of the century.

First, we have the results of the survey made by Seebohm Rowntree in York in 1899 (and discussed more fully in Chapter VII below). In his book Rowntree (1901) gives only family incomes, but he communicated his findings on the weekly wages of adult males to the distinguished statistician A. L. Bowley, and these were published by Bowley (1902). They are summarised in Table 7. A rough comparison of the spread of these earnings with those for the whole United Kingdom is given in Table 8. It appears from this comparison that, on average, wages for adult men in York in 1899 were very close to those for the country as a whole (rows 3 and 6 of Table 8). There was also relatively little difference at the lower end of the range: one quarter of the adult men were reported by Rowntree to be earning less than 20s. a week, and the corresponding national figure was 20s. 9d. (row 2). The differences at the upper end were much more marked, however, (rows 4 and 5) indicating that there were appreciably fewer opportunities in York for men to earn high wages. This is consistent with the distribution of occupations shown in Table 7. Only 15 per cent of the men in York were in skilled occupations in which wages of 35s. and above could be earned by more than a handful of

Table 7   1899
Average Weekly Wages, Adult Males, York[1]

	Engine drivers, Engineers, Printing (1)	Clerks (2)	Porters, Guards, Other Railway (3)	Build- ing (4)	Other indus- tries (5)	Lab- ourers (6)	Total (7)
Total No.	773	706	1400	1611	2279	2775	9544[2]
% earning:							
Under 20s	0.3	2.7	1.3	0.2	3.5	31.2	10.4
20-24s	5.4	14.2	15.0	17.0	37.6	66.2	34.8
25-29s	23.4	16.4	18.4	16.8	22.4	2.5	14.7
30-34s	40.7	47.3	51.4	62.7	27.7	0.1	31.6
35-39s	10.9	7.1	7.3	2.0	4.3	—	3.8
40-60s	19.3	12.3	6.6	1.3	4.5	—	4.7
	100.0	100.0	100.0	100.0	100.0	100.0	100.0

Source: Bowley (1902, p. 361)

[1] In the original table separate figures (and narrower wage ranges) are given for 21 trades.

[2] Comparison with the 1901 Census indicates that this covers about two-thirds of all occupied adult male wage-earners in York.

workers (columns (1) and (2) of Table 7); and over half were concentrated in predominantly low wage, unskilled occupations (columns (5) and (6) of the table).

The impression of York's relative position gained from the Rowntree survey is confirmed by the second set of data. This comes from an elaborate enquiry into wages, prices and rents in 83 large towns in Britain (and 6 in Ireland) carried out by the Board of Trade in October 1905. All the information was expressed in the form of indices showing for each town the level of rents, retail prices for food and fuel, and wages for selected skilled and unskilled occupations, relative to the corresponding level in London. No attempt was made to weight the wages according to the numbers employed in the selected trades, so the results indicated only the relative levels of wages in these trades, not the relative overall levels in each town.

Table 8   1899
Distribution of Earnings of Adult Males,
York and United Kingdom

		York (1)		UK (2)	
		s.	d.	s.	d.
1	Lowest decile	18	0	17	6
2	Lower quartile	20	0	20	9
3	Median	25	9	26	0
4	Upper quartile	31	0	32	6
5	Highest decile	33	0	38	9
6	Average	26	6	26	6
7	Mode	30	0	—	

Source: Bowley (1902, pp. 359-61; 1937, p. 46).

Col. (1)   The estimates are for weekly wages after allowance for short-time, etc.

Col. (2)   Bowley (1937, p. 46) gives a distribution for adult men's wages for a full normal week in 1914 (based on the Wage Census of 1906). I have used his index of wages (1937, p. 30) to adjust this to the approximate 1899 level; and have made a further reduction of 7 per cent to allow for short-time working through unemployment, illness, etc. (see Bowley, 1937 p. 52).

     The wages paid to skilled workers in York in 1905 can be seen from column (1) of Table 9 to lie below those in other Northern and Midland towns; and there was not sufficient difference in the cost of living to compensate for this. 'Real wages' for skilled workers were thus several percentage points below those elsewhere in England and Wales, except for the depressed Eastern and Southern Counties (column (4) of Table 9). The position for unskilled work (taking building labourers as representative of this grade), was rather different. Only London and the Midlands paid better money wages and 'real wages' were relatively high (columns 2 and 5). It is possible that this contrast in the relative ranking of skilled and unskilled in York reflects the competition for unskilled workers created by the larger numbers in this category required for both the railways and the confectionery industry; and the absence of any comparable demand for skilled workers.

Table 9

1905

Urban Wages, Retail Prices and Real Wages, Great Britain

Geographical grouping of Towns	Weekly wages		Retail prices and rents	'Real wages'	
	Skilled	Unskilled		Skilled	Unskilled
	(1)	(2)	(3)	(4)	(5)
London	100	100	100	100	100
Lancashire and Cheshire (17 towns)	87	88	84	104	105
Midlands (15)	85	92	85˙	100	108
Yorkshire[1] (10)	84	89	87	97	102
Wales (4)	86	85	89	97	96
Northern Counties[1] (9)	86	88	90	96	98
York	82	89	87	94	102
Eastern Counties (7)	76	84	88	86	95
Southern Counties (10)	80	85	93	86	91
Scotland (10)	83	79	95	87	83

Source: Board of Trade (1908, pp. xxxix-xl)

Col. (1) An unweighted average of the standard weekly wage rates for skilled workers in October 1905 in the building, engineering and printing trades, expressed as a ratio of the corresponding rates for London.

Col. (2) A similar index for building labourers.

Col. (3) Retail prices paid by the working classes for food and fuel in October 1905 weighted according to the pattern of working class expenditure and expressed as a ratio of the corresponding prices for London, combined with an index for rents (also relative to London), in the proportion 4:1.

Col. (4) Col. (1) ÷ Col. (3)

Col. (5) Col. (2) ÷ Col. (3)

[1] Cleveland is included in Northern Counties, not in Yorkshire.

Changes in Employment Since 1911

We turn now to developments after 1911, and to our last two bench-mark years, 1951 and 1971. The structure of employment in York in these two years is shown in Table 10.[36] These figures are only loosely comparable with those in Table 6 for the two earlier years. In particular, the figures in Table 10 are based entirely on a classification by industry (cf. note 14); and all clerks, drivers, labourers, etc. are assigned to the specific industry or service in which they were employed. The main factors responsible for an increase in the overall *level* of employment in York (from 37,000 in 1911 as measured in Table 6, to over 54,000 in 1951 as in Table 10) were the boundary changes and growth of popula-tion discussed earlier. In the following paragraphs we focus mainly on the differences in the *composition* of employment and industrial activity; looking first at changes in the main sectors between 1911, 1951 and 1971, and then at corresponding changes within manufacturing.

The overall pattern

An historian who had studied the pattern of economic activity in York in the years immediately before the First World War, and then gone away from the city for an interval of 40 years, would not have been much surprised by what he found on his return. Certainly nothing had occurred to match the impact on York of the rise of Rowntree's and the railways in the preceding 60 years. With a single notable exception, both the broad structure of industries and services, and the detailed picture of individual firms, would have seemed very familiar. Confectionery and railway work of all types were still overwhelmingly the most important sources of employment, accounting in 1951 for one third of all jobs in York.

The one exception was the nearly complete disappearance of domes-tic service, for so long the main form of work available to women and girls. The process started during World War I, when women were able to find more attractive and better paid work in industry and commerce, and by 1921 the number of domestic servants had fallen by over 40 per cent, to just over 2,300. World War II and its consequent socio-economic changes completed the transformation, leaving only 700 in service in 1951.

Over the period 1911-51 this radical change represented a fall of nine percentage points in the contribution of domestic service to total em-ployment in York (see Table 6, row 9 and Table 10, row 9). The offset-ting rise occurred in other service sectors: education and medicine increased their share by three percentage points, mostly in medical ser-vice; national and local government each increased theirs by about two percentage points, as did garages and motor repair work; and there was a rise of one percentage point in the shares of both banking and insurance,

Table 10   1951 and 1971
                    Employment in York[1]

	1951		1971	
	Persons	Per-cent	Persons	Per-cent
1 Farming, forestry	330	0.6	270	0.5
2 Manufacturing	19,080	35.0	16,930	29.0
3 Construction	3,250	5.9	4,200	7.2
4 Gas, electricity, water	1,000	1.8	840	1.4
5 Transport and communication	8,200	15.0	8,400	14.4
Railways	*5,590*		*5,450*	
Road	*1,260*		*1,230*	
P.O.	*1,200*		*1,560*	
6 Distribution	6,820	12.5	8,080	13.9
7 Finance	970	1.8	1,720	3.0
8 Professional Services	4,110	7.5	8,070	13.9
Education	*1,320*		*3,340*	
Medical	*1,920*		*3,060*	
9 Domestic Service	690	1.3	510	0.9
10 Other services	5,190	9.5	5,680	9.7
Hotels, inns, etc.	*2,200*		*2,290*	
Motor repair, garages	*1,120*		*1,240*	
11 Public administration	3,200	5.9	2,890	5.0
Local government	*1,510*		*1,210*	
12 Defence	1,680	3.1	490	0.8
13 Other and unclassified	30	0.1	200	0.3
	54,550	100.0	58,280	100.0

Source: *Census of Population* (with adjustments to obtain approximate com-
     parability in classification).

[1] The figures cover only those in employment and provide a classification by
   industry of all those working within York City, irrespective of place of residence. See also note 36, p. 155.

and of hairdressing and miscellaneous services. Finally, if allowance is made for the change in classification of clerical and other general occupations, it seems likely that there was a small fall in the share of manufacturing and distribution, and a rise in that of transport and communication, largely in the form of increased employment by the Post Office. For the most part these are all trends which York experienced in common with the rest of the country.

Changes from 1951 to 1971 (see Table 10) were to a large extent a continuation of those observed between 1911 and 1951. There was a fall of over 2,000 in employment in manufacturing, cutting its share by six percentage points, and there was a further erosion of domestic service. These were balanced by increased employment in education, medicine, finance, distribution, business, government[37] and other services. The only service sector to show a marked fall over this period was defence. The number of soldiers quartered in York was reduced by some 1,200, following the amalgamation of two Yorkshire regiments and the closure of part of Fulford barracks in 1958.[38]

The enhanced role taken by professional, financial, business and other services in the broad pattern of activity in York was not, however, out of line with the national pattern. There was little difference in the 1971 figures for York and for Great Britain for the share in employment of distribution and other services (47.5 per cent in York and 46.3 per cent nationally), or of construction and the utilities (8.6 per cent and 8.5 per cent). The very striking and distinctive feature of York was the comparative scale of employment in transport and communications: 14.4 per cent in York against a national proportion of only 6.6 per cent. York's long-established position as a railway centre was still a dominant aspect of its employment structure. It had, indeed, been enhanced when York became the headquarters for the whole Eastern Region of British Rail; and an increase in administrative staff helped to compensate for sharply reduced numbers of porters, shunters, firemen and others actually working the railways. The over-representation of transport in York was offset by a below-average proportion employed in agriculture and mining (0.5 per cent and 4.3 per cent), and manufacturing, in which York has only 29 per cent of its labour force compared with the national proportion of 34 per cent.

Within the service sector, the city's continuing position – as in so many past centuries – as a regional capital helps to explain the specific character of employment in York. It is no longer quite as important as it once was as a social and shopping centre, though these still play some part. But for transport, education (including the university), the health service, the armed forces, the church, and a variety of business services, notably insurance, it remains a major centre and offers many attractions.

A second, and more crucial element is the highly significant role which tourism now plays in the provision of employment in the city. Tourism is not a new phenomenon for the city, and might even be traced back to Tudor times.[39] From their earliest days the railways encouraged visitors to come and see the magnificent townscape which the city had so miraculously preserved from its past glory. However, the real expansion in interest, and in the number of visitors, belongs to the period since 1950. Initially, it was stimulated by increased affluence and leisure, the greater mobility of motor travel, and wider appreciation of York's unique attractions. In the past decade growth has been even more extraordinary; the result, it is thought, of such factors as the triumphant restoration of the Minster (see Chapter IV, above), the opening of the National Railway Museum in 1975, and the fame of the York Festival and Mystery Plays.

In 1950 there was accommodation in York hotels and guest-houses for roughly 1,300 visitors and in 1970 the figure was about 1,900. Since then it has increased at a remarkable pace, to over 3,600 in 1980; and is due to rise still further as hotels now under construction are completed.[40] The number of visitors was estimated to be about 1,150,000 in 1970 and was over 3,000,000 a decade later, though only about 10 per cent of these stayed overnight. Their total expenditure in 1980 was of the order of £30m,[41] of which roughly 40 per cent was for accommodation, and the balance for food, shopping, etc.

The number of people directly engaged in providing accommodation, meals, drinks and recreation for tourists is estimated by the city's Department of Tourism to be about 4,000. Allowance must also be made for the additional numbers employed in shops, banks, garages, transport and other local services solely as a consequence of the demand generated by tourists. Consideration of these figures suggests that tourism has been the most dynamic element in the growth of economic activity in York over the past decade, and the contribution which it now makes to local employment comes close to matching that hitherto made by the city's larger employers. It can justly be noted that quite a high proportion of these jobs are part-time, unskilled and low paid; and there are other gains and losses, apart from employment, which would have to be brought into a full assessment of the impact of tourism. However, within the ambit of this chapter – employment and economic activity in York – there is little doubt that tourism has made a vital contribution to the recent prosperity of the city, and that one of the best prospects for the future must lie in its further growth.

Trends within manufacturing since 1911

The most notable aspect of change within manufacturing in the half-century after 1911 was the manner in which the clothing industry was finally swept away. Numbers had already declined by 1911 (see p. 123, above), but there were still some 1,700 tailors, dressmakers, shoemakers and milliners; by 1951 there were only 260. The victory of factory-made clothing had destroyed the basis of York's small-scale activity. Roughly half the decline had occurred during World War I and the process was largely completed by the end of the 1930s.[42] Much the same story can be told for a miscellany of small metalworking and woodworking firms.

These reductions, and those caused by the removal of some firms to new sites outside York's boundaries were offset by an increase in other manufacturing employment, which also provided for the growth of population. This increase came predominantly from only one industry – confectionery. Total employment in manufacturing (as measured in rows 2 and 3 of Table 6 and row 2 of Table 10) increased by some 7,300 between 1911 and 1971, while employment in confectionery rose by about 6,000. Increased activity at the railway carriage and wagon works accounted for a further 2,000 jobs. In 1951 these two industries together accounted for two thirds, and confectionery alone for one half, of all work in manufacturing in York. The details are shown in Table 11.

In the two decades after 1951 the share of confectionery increased still further, to 56 per cent, since although employment in the confectionery works was the same at both dates (after having been at a much higher level half-way through the twenty-year period, see p. 143, below), total employment in manufacturing was falling (Table 11). One reason for this decline was a reduction of over 1,000 in the numbers employed at the railway workshops, and there were also reductions in chemicals, clothing, and other smaller industries.

In order to bring these broad trends in manufacturing activity into closer focus we turn finally to some of the individual firms. For this we include not only those operating within the city boundaries (and so covered by Tables 10 and 11) but also some which moved, or set up, outside those boundaries, especially in the parishes of Huntington, Earswick and Rawcliffe (see Map 4).

Among those whose names were already familiar in York by 1911, the outstanding feature was obviously the continued growth of Rowntree and Co. The national demand for cocoa more than doubled between 1914 and 1918 (most of it going to keep the army warm), and output of chocolate confectionery was maintained at a high level for most of the war years.[43] In 1919 the company raised an additional £750,000 of capital,

Table 11   1951 and 1971
Employment in Manufacturing in York[1]

		1951		1971	
		Persons	Per cent	Persons	Per cent
1	Cocoa, confectionery	9,570	50.2	9,520	56.2
2	Other food and drink	1,560	8.2	880	5.2
3	Railway carriage and wagon	3,220	16.9	2,030	12.0
4	Other engineering, etc.	1,150	6.0	1,420	8.4
5	Printing, publishing	1,280	6.7	1,150	6.8
6	Glass, bricks, etc.	640	3.3	1,130	6.7
7	Timber, furniture, etc.	300	1.6	360	2.1
8	Chemicals	520	2.7	130	0.8
9	Clothing	260	1.4	20	0.1
10	Other	580	3.0	290	1.7
		19,080	100.0	16,930	100.0

Source: *Census of Population*
[1] See note [1], Table 10.

and a year later they went back to the market for a further £750,000. In the Prospectus of March 20, 1920 the directors stated that 'during 1919 there had been an unprecedented expansion in the Company's trade, following substantial increases shown annually for many years'. They reported aggregate profits, after meeting depreciation, taxes, interest, etc. (cf. p. 125) over an eight-year period, 1912-19, of more than £1,200,000. All the equity capital was held by the Rowntree family and the three Rowntree Trusts; and both these issues to the public (as well as the further issue in 1927) were of preference shares, entitled to priority in the payment of a fixed interest but not to a share in the profits, or the control, of the company.

In making their second issue in successive years the directors explained that it now appeared to them 'in the light of their post-war experience, that it is desirable to obtain further capital in order to enable the company to take advantage of the openings for the extension of its business'. This optimistic mood was soon shattered by the post-war slump. Like many other firms, Rowntree and Co. found that the grossly inflated sales and profits of 1919 could not be maintained. The average price of all chocolate sold in Britain was 45d (19p) per lb. in 1920; it plunged to 36.5d in 1922 and by a further 6d the following year. By 1922 Rowntree's had seen its turnover slashed by a third, and workers had to be laid off. The unemployment benefit scheme which the company had established in 1921 was immediately called on to pay out over £7,000 in benefits in that year.[44] By 1923 profits had collapsed to one-third of the 1919 level.

Trading conditions in the industry remained difficult, and although there was some recovery profits were low for most of the interwar period.[45] Prices drifted downwards almost without interruption and the value of the country's consumption of chocolate and cocoa never moved above the level of £35m. to which it had declined by 1923. At its worst, in 1932-5, it was some 10-15 per cent below that. For Rowntree's, the twenties were years of financial strain and consolidation after the excessive enthusiasm up to 1920. Total employment stabilised around 6,000 from 1923 to 1927, but was then cut back by some 1,500 over the next few years.[46] Payments from the firm's unemployment scheme doubled, to average about £11,000 p.a. during these four hard years. Output was virtually static throughout the twenties, but from the early 1930s conditions started to improve, and within a few years Rowntree was expanding very rapidly indeed. Output from the York factory doubled between 1934 and 1937, and shot further ahead until 1939.

This transformation was partly a reflection of the improvement in the general economic position in the country, but was mainly a result of two fundamental policy changes made within the company. Credit for the first belongs primarily to Seebohm Rowntree (Plate 14), managing director in York until 1936, and chairman of the whole company until 1941. He initiated the policy of recruiting able managers from outside the family to take charge of various fields of company activity. This was formalised with the establishment in 1931 of a York Board, organised on a functional basis and given sole responsibility for the management of the Haxby Road business.[47] This structure proved highly successful, and was a very important step in the conversion of an old family firm dominated by the personality of Joseph Rowntree, to a multinational corporation under professional management.

The second and most critical innovation was essentially the contribution of George Harris. He was one of the members of the York Board and became chairman in 1938, succeeding Seebohm Rowntree as chairman of the company itself three years later. From the 1930s his ideas about business strategy, and particularly about the then relatively new concept of marketing – as distinct from selling – had a profound effect on the company's future. Under his leadership branded products which have become household names around the world were introduced – *Black Magic* (1933), *Aero* and *Kit Kat* (1935), *Dairy Box* (1936) and *Smarties* (1937). By 1939, these five products contributed nearly a third of the total output of the York factory; employment picked up rapidly, reaching nearly 10,000 in 1939; profits improved, and capital expenditure was increased.[48] These two fundamental policy decisions, professional management and branded marketing, formed the basis of the postwar success of the company.

During and immediately after the 1939-45 war, conditions were markedly less favourable for the company than they had been during the First World War. Output was cut steeply in line with the twin constraints of a controlled supply of scarce raw materials, and tight rationing of consumption of confectionery (though not of cocoa). Employment dropped to less than half the prewar peak. However, once war and rationing were over the long-frustrated demand for confectionery surged ahead, and prewar levels of activity were quickly restored. By 1956 the quantity of confectionery and other goods made in York was 30 times what it had been when the company was formed in 1897. Sales rose continuously year by year, and employment bounced back to around 10,000 by the late 1950s; it would have been even higher if more workers could have been recruited in York.

However, this was to prove the highest point which employment at Rowntree's in York would reach. In the following decade the company allowed the size of its labour force at the 'cocoa works' to fall. This was done partly because it was considered that it was not in the best interests of either the company or the town for one employer to hold such a dominant position in the labour market; and partly because of the difficulty experienced in hiring labour in York. It was also a result of the continuing programme of automation (notably in packing) made necessary by the increasingly competitive market conditions. In the ten years after 1958 the factory workforce was reduced by over 2,000 (about 25 per cent); work previously done by women accounted for the greater part of the decline.

In 1968, the company entered into discreet discussions with John Mackintosh & Sons Ltd, another large confectionery company, family-controlled, about the possibility of a merger. This company (fourth in size in the UK market, Rowntree was second) had also followed a branded-line policy, notably with *Quality Street* and *Rolo*. Before discussions could be completed, however, General Foods Corporation, an extremely large

American company, announced an intention to bid for Rowntree at a price very substantially above any previous market price. The Rowntree Board, under the chairmanship of Donald Barron (now Sir Donald), decided not to recommend the bid, or a subsequent higher bid, and conducted a vigorous campaign to preserve the independence of the company. They were strongly supported by the workforce through their trade unions and by local opinion, and also by the three Rowntree Trusts. Despite some criticism in the national financial press the defence was successful, and the bid was withdrawn. The Board instead put forward a recommended merger with Mackintosh, arguing that this proposal was preferable in terms of both industrial logic and compatibility of management philosophy, and this was strongly supported by both companies and shareholders. The new merged company was created in May 1969. The price of Rowntree's shares, although immediately lower, subsequently rose very substantially above the General Foods' bid price. The merger also helped to make York more important as administrative headquarters of an even larger enterprise. It produced extra jobs outside the factory, but failed to offset a continued reduction on the production line, and employment in York dropped a further 500. This brought the total workforce at the end of the 1970s to about 7,500.[49] In 1968, the last year of Rowntree and Co, the world-wide sales of the entire group were almost £78m. and there was a pre-tax trading profit of £4.3m. Ten years later, after a decade of spectacular expansion, Rowntree Mackintosh Ltd achieved sales of £563m. and a profit of £43m.

After Rowntree, York's second largest industrial employer in the twentieth century was, until recently, the railway carriage and wagon works. In both World Wars the works were called on to adapt their skills and equipment to produce objects required by the armed forces. These included not only tank-carrying wagons and ambulance trains, but also stretchers, gliders, Bailey bridges, and many other items.[50] Between the wars, under the LNER, the number employed on the repair and construction of carriages and wagons was normally about 2,750, though as a result of the depression it fell to some 1,700 in 1931. The carriage works was considerably improved after the amalgamation, with the introduction of both new equipment and more efficient organisation of work. The greater part of the carriages required for the LNER was built in York, as well as special wagons and standardised underframes for the company's other carriage works.

In the postwar years, under British Rail, new machinery was installed and new skills were required as the works turned to production and maintenance of electric and diesel vehicles. 3,200 workers were employed in 1951, about 2,300 of these were in the carriage shops and the balance in the wagon shops. The former level has been broadly maintained since then; but activity at the wagon shops was reduced in the late fifties and they finally closed in 1965, exactly 100 years after work on wagons had started in Holgate. Closure of the wagon shops was accompanied by an expansion in the programme of carriage maintenance allocated to York. This created about 600 extra jobs by the mid-1960s, but subsequent reorganisation and retrenchment by British Rail has reduced the workforce below 2,000.

Thomas Cooke and Sons Ltd. was another long-established York firm which was called on to make an important contribution to wartime requirements. In 1915 the giant engineering and armaments firm, Vickers, acquired a 70 per cent holding in the company, having been a major buyer of its products for some years. Vickers was particularly interested in a system of fire control manufactured by Cooke's and in rangefinders, range and bearing clocks, anti-aircraft predictors and other instruments. Cooke's had been specialising in this field since 1910, in some cases working to Vickers's design. During 1915-18 Cooke's concentrated exclusively on military products, and a new factory was built opposite their old Buckingham Works. Then in 1922 they were authorised by Vickers to acquire the distinguished London firm of instrument makers, Troughton and Simms, and two years later the joint firm was reorganised as a wholly-owned subsidiary of Vickers.[51] This was an early example of a process, later to become common, in which control of York firms passed outside the city.

In the interwar years the firm employed some 400-500 workers, and in 1939 it moved to a new factory on Haxby Road. (This lies outside the city boundaries, and so employment there is not included in Tables 10 and 11.) There was an enormous demand for its telescopes, periscopes and other instruments during 1939-45. It expanded to become one of the leading manufacturers of optical instruments for the armed forces, and employment increased to some 3,300. (See the discussion by Jim Matthew in Chapter II, above.) This level of activity could not be maintained once the war ended and by 1948 the workforce was down to about 1,000. The firm enjoyed its most active peacetime years in the mid-sixties, but in recent years employment has dropped to about 600. The company has traded as Vickers Instruments Ltd. since 1963.

Several other York firms which started production in the nineteenth century have also expanded and prospered in the twentieth. Sir Joseph's son Frank (later Sir Francis) and his grandson Noel were joint managing directors of Joseph Terry and Sons Ltd from 1923, with Frank as chairman until 1958, followed by Noel. Together they led the company through a further period of highly successful development. Substantial new premises were built in Bishopthorpe Road, on the edge of the city, between 1924 and 1930, and production was also continued at Clementhorpe. A cocoa plantation was purchased in Venezuela, in order to ensure control of the particular type of cocoa bean required, and *All Gold*, *Spartan* and other assortments of chocolate gradually displaced the many varieties of sugar confectionery as the firm's main products. A history of almost two centuries as one of York's leading family enterprises ended in 1963 when Terry's was taken over by Forte's (Holdings) Ltd at a price of £4m. Further expansion followed and several hundred additional workers were taken on, bringing total employment to about 2,000. Then in 1977 the holding (now owned by Trust Houses Forte Ltd) was in turn sold to an American company, Colgate-Palmolive, for £17.5m.[52] York's third manufacturer of confectionery, M. A. Craven and Sons Ltd. experienced a fairly prolonged period of decline and stagnation following the death of the founder and her only son. By the late 1930s employment had fallen to about 70, less than a third of the pre-1914 level (cf. p. 128, above), and growth was not resumed until the 1950s. In 1955 Ernest Kramer was appointed managing director. He had joined the company after leaving his native Czechoslovakia in 1949. Under his leadership the business was rescued and revitalised, and a reputation for quality was again established at home and overseas. In 1966 the outmoded premises in Coppergate were abandoned for a new site in Poppleton. The workforce has grown to about 350, and is still making Craven's traditional sugar confectionery, though now using modern and automated equipment.[53]

One of York's few private engineering concerns of any size was formed by a merger of two firms, both founded in the 1880s. In 1887, Samuel Henry Adams, a sanitary engineer of 45 Danby Terrace, started a company on a nearby site in Peaseholme Green to manufacture his original designs for sewage plants. The business prospered, and operated as The Adams Patent Sewage Lift Co. Ltd. until 1903, when the present title of Adams-Hydraulics Ltd. was adopted. Most of the iron castings used by the firm were purchased from the neighbouring Kirk's Foundry, started by G. W. Kirk in 1885. In 1919 the two firms agreed to amalgamate. The Adams family ended their connection with the business in 1926/27 and management passed into the capable hands of J. Hopwood, a director since 1919, and chairman from 1940 until his death in 1971. Alone among the major concerns started in York in the nineteenth century the firm has been able to expand on its original site in the centre of the city, and is still making sewage lifting and other sanitary equipment at Peaseholme Green, with its own foundry to supply its workshops. The number employed in the 1970s was around 175.[54]

In 1955 a new office block was constructed for the company by a firm with an even longer history: William Birch and Sons Ltd. It was founded in 1874 by William Birch, son of a bricklayer with York Gas Co, and himself a bricklayer. The first premises were at the back of Barbican Road, and they moved shortly after that to their present site in Spen Lane, within the city walls. The founder died in 1913 and in that year the firm became a limited liability company, with William Henry Birch as managing director. In the 1920s the firm started to operate on a larger scale, and also undertook civil engineering projects, and by 1939 they were carrying out a wide range of building and civil engineering work in the North East. Further progress was made after World War II, with direction of the company still the responsibility of members of the Birch family; and the workforce is currently about 150.[55]

The three printing and publishing enterprises mentioned above (pp. 131-2) have all flourished, and account for most of the employment in this industry in the York area. This was fairly steady at around 1,500 until the mid-1960s but since then has dropped very slightly following the closure of several small firms. The largest of the three big concerns is Ben Johnson. The firm moved from Micklegate to Boroughbridge Road in 1932, after a fire, and steadily increased its output and reputation. In 1978 the company was taken over by R. R. Donnelley of Chicago, said to be the largest printing concern in the world. Employment at that time was about 500 and the new owners planned to expand the work done in York. The other family concern, William Sessions Ltd., has remained independent. They moved to new premises in Huntington, outside the city, in 1920. This followed expansion during the war as a result of specialising in label printing; in particular, a sugar-rationing instruction label issued nationally in 1916. There have been numerous extensions on the site since then, and in recent years book printing and publishing has been an increasing activity in addition to the firm's other work. York and County Press (a subsidiary of Westminster Press Ltd.) has published the *Yorkshire Evening Press* since taking it over in 1953. This and general printing is still undertaken on the same site in the centre of York where presses have been working since the middle of the eighteenth century.[56]

Not all York's long-established firms have fared as well. The Victoria Ironworks (p. 123, above) was managed by J. R. Walker after the death of his father (William Thomlinson-Walker) in 1911, but was damaged by a fire in 1916, and the firm ran into financial troubles in the post-war slump. After three generations there was no member of the family to continue the business (one son was killed during the war, another had emigrated); and after Walker's death the foundry closed in 1923.[57] York Glass Works was also in trouble after 1918, as it had been before the war (p. 131). C. J. Pratt, the sole owner and managing director, failed to persuade the skilled hand-blowers to accept the introduction of automatic bottle-making machinery in 1919; and the coal strikes of 1919-21 added to his difficulties. The business was running at a loss, and was unable to meet interest payments due to the holders of debentures, recently issued to cover loans for £45,000. A receiver was appointed in May 1922, and in September the plant closed. An abortive attempt was made to sell the entire works, but the buyer was found to be insane, and the company abandoned its attempt to enforce performance of the agreement to purchase. Glassmaking at Fishergate then ceased for the rest of the decade, though it was subsequently resumed under new management (see p. 149, below).[58]

In contrast, closures in the milling industry in the 1930s proved to be permanent and York's many centuries of local flour milling effectively ended by 1936. In September 1928 the York mills of Henry Leetham and Sons Ltd were acquired by Spillers; and in February 1930 the new owners announced that they found it 'impracticable economically to manufacture at York the quality of mill products required'. No doubt it was more profitable for them to concentrate their production for the North East elsewhere in the region, as Leetham's had earlier threatened to do. Another factor may have been the adverse judgement in the courts in 1924 depriving Leetham's of the extremely favourable terms on which its grain and flour had been shipped on the Foss and Ouse. The corporation had offered a new preferential scale, but this was perhaps not sufficient to offset the advantages of milling at a port like Hull.[59] The workforce at the time of the closure was about 1,000 and with unemployment in York already over 3,000 in 1931 the loss of jobs at the mills was a heavy blow; by 1932 the number out of work had reached almost 5,000, an unprecedented tragedy for York. The only other local milling concern of any size, C. D. Mills Ltd, had been making flour in Skeldergate since the 1860s, but was presumably unable to survive the increased competition in the 1930s from Spillers and other nationwide firms, and had closed by 1936.[60]

The decline of drug manufacturing in the city did not occur until after 1944. The formation of the National Health Service stimulated those firms capable of manufacturing pharmaceuticals on a large scale, but neither Bleasdales Ltd. nor Raimes and Co. was able to take advantage of this, and each reduced or abandoned the manufacturing side of its activity. They have, however, continued to operate on a modest scale as wholesale chemists. In another branch of the chemical industry, the manufacture of fertilizers, the old-established firm of Henry Richardson merged with Anderton's of Howden and ended its manufacturing operations in York. In 1967 Anderton-Richardson and two other concerns were taken over by Hargreaves Fertilizers Ltd, a company owned jointly by the Hargreaves Group and ICI. The headquarters are in York and the factory is at Elvington, on the eastern edge of the Study Area.[61]

Remarkably few new industrial firms have started in York since 1911. In 1927 the Yorkshire Sugar Co. (subsequently acquired by British Sugar Corporation), opened a factory to process sugar beet. It was an early response to the British Sugar (Subsidy) Act, 1925, which guaranteed for 10 years generous (though reducing) subsidies for sugar and molasses made from homegrown beet. It was also notable as one of the few industries to be located in York because of its proximity to a supply of raw materials: beet grown in Yorkshire. In recent years the plant has been substantially expanded and modernised. However, production is highly seasonal: the main 'campaign' to process the beet lasts only from September to January, and during this period some 400 workers are needed. In the rest of the year employment is reduced to about 280.[62]

A second new industry set up in the city was the moulding of plastic products. There was a number of small firms, of which the largest was Gansolite. This was started in 1931 when Mr. Gans was attracted from Holland under a scheme initiated by Rowntree's to help its discharged employees by providing alternative employment. Assisted also by the imposition of a tariff on imports of plastic articles, he started a small plant to make buttons and similar items.[63] York then had to wait until 1949 for its next new arrival: Armstrong Shock Absorbers Ltd (since 1961, Armstrong Patents Co Ltd). The parent concern had been founded in Beverley at the turn of the century by Gordon Armstrong, and since the 1920s had specialised in shock absorbers. The York factory was opened in wartime aircraft hangars at Rawcliffe, just north of the city boundaries, to manufacture a new type of suspension unit for Ford cars, and to establish the company's range of telescopic shock absorbers. Its workforce was about 350 at the end of the 1950s and then expanded rapidly to about 2,000 in the late sixties, including some 400 who were brought in daily from as far away as Doncaster and Barnsley to help overcome the shortage of suitable labour in York. In the 1970s the parent company built a new plant in Hull; employment in York was reduced to around 700 by the middle of the decade, and has since been further affected by the recession in the motor industry.[64]

This occasional infusion of new blood from outside York was supplemented by vigorous growth from within. In March 1930 National Glass Works (York) Ltd was formed to take over the premises in Fishergate at which glass had been manufactured in York since the end of the eighteenth century. Under William Leslie Pratt, son of the previous manager, the old works were extensively modernised to produce bottles, tumblers and other glassware. In 1931 there were about 200 workers occupied in the manufacture of glass in York, and this increased to about 300 in 1940 and to almost 600 in 1951. In 1967 the York company merged with Redfearn Brothers Ltd of Barnsley, and from the following year the two concerns operated as Redfearn National Glass Ltd, with Leslie Pratt as chairman. He retired in 1969, but the family link has been preserved and his son, J. L. C. Pratt, is the present chairman and managing director. The two furnaces at York are used primarily to produce high quality bottles and jars for the soft drink trade, and smaller containers in colourless (white flint) glass for food and pharmaceuticals.[65] Employment at the glassworks rose to almost 1,000 in the mid-1970s, though it has declined slightly since then.

A second notable example of internal growth is the development of Bootham Engineers Ltd. The firm was founded in 1931 by Arthur S. Rymer, a graduate in engineering from Leeds University, whose father and grandfather had each been Lord Mayor of York. Together with R. Yates, and with capital of some £500, the business was started with one man in an old warehouse and stables in Bootham Row. New and much larger buildings were erected on that site in 1938, and in the 1970s, when further expansion was necessary the firm moved to new premises in Hull Road, where work in York is now concentrated. The workforce there is about 100, and several hundred more are employed at factories in other parts of the country. The firm provides an exceptionally varied and enterprising service to industry, including general engineering and repair work, welding, reconditioning, and metal and ceramic spray coating.[66]

The outstanding story of successful expansion from within York in recent decades is to be found partly in manufacturing and partly in construction. The story begins in 1890 when Frederick Shepherd, aged about 35, started in business as a joiner and undertaker. In 1895 he was listed in White's *Directory of York* at 70 Skeldergate. Shortly afterwards he moved to Lead Mill Lane in the Walmgate area, and was assisted there first by his eldest son, William, and then, at the turn of the century, by a second son, Frederick Welton. By this time the business had grown to include brickwork and Frederick had trained as a bricklayer. Among the buildings on which he and the firm worked in this period were the vast flour mill built for Leetham's (mentioned on p. 131, above) and the Empire Theatre. By 1910 William had emigrated to North America, and thereafter the firm operated as F. Shepherd and Son. In 1924 it was incorporated as a private company.

During the 1920s F. W. Shepherd was increasingly the driving force behind the continued expansion of the company, and his father died in 1930. Following a fire at Lead Mill Lane in 1927 the firm's main premises were developed on a larger site in Blue Bridge Lane (off Fishergate),

York has moved progressively away from the city. This process accelerated after 1945 with the formation of the public corporations, and has continued in both the commercial and public service sectors. The city could not expect to escape a worldwide trend, and there are some significant exceptions, but it will increasingly find that critical decisions about what happens to employment in York will be determined from a national, not a York-centred, viewpoint.

Footnotes

[1] Bartlett (1959, p. 19).

[2] Thomas Fuller, *The Worthies of England* c. 1660, quoted in Palliser (1979a, p. 22).

[3] See E. M. Sigsworth in Tillott (1961, pp. 256-66) and Armstrong (1974, pp. 20-7) for an excellent discussion of the economic, political and geographical factors which may have inhibited the growth of industry.

[4] For further discussion of attitudes and conditions in York in the early nineteenth century see Chapter I, pp. 2-6, above.

[5] For 1841-90 the estimates rely on the assumption that the rate of births and deaths per 1,000 population was the same for the population within the 1893 county borough boundaries as for those of the three urban sub-districts for which returns were made in the Registrar-General's *Annual Reports*. For 1891-1910 figures are available for births and deaths in the urban sub-districts as they were defined from 1904 onwards, i.e. for the area corresponding exactly to the post-1893 county borough; see Medical Office of Health, *Annual Reports* (e.g. 1904, p. 7). For 1831-40 no official returns are available for York and the rate of natural increase estimated by Armstrong (1974, pp. 78-9) was assumed to apply to both the urban and rural areas.

[6] The present estimates for natural increase, and for migration to or from the urban area, differ from those made by Sigsworth (Tillott, 1961, p. 256) partly because they relate to a different area until 1881, and partly because his were estimated from birth and death rates for the whole Registration District and not, as seems more appropriate, from those for the urban sub-districts only.

[7] This is subject to the reservation that, as Map 3 shows, the York Registration District did not extend to the west of the City in the way that it did in the other directions.

[8] This would be consistent with the traditional view according to which internal migration occurs in a 'complex wavelike motion' with individual migrants typically moving short distances. It would be desirable to make a more thorough analysis on the basis of Census data on the birthplaces of the inhabitants of York.

[9] More precise analysis of the additional employment provided by York in the 1870s is difficult because the 1871 Census omitted all occupied persons aged less than 20 years; and no figures were published on occupations in York in 1881.

[10] Office of Population, Censuses and Surveys (1978, p. 8).

154   YORK 1831-1981

11 The figures per 1,000 population (as given in MOH *Annual Reports*) are:

	Birth Rate	Death Rate	Rate of Natural Increase
1891-1900	30.3	19.3	11.0
1936-38	15.2	11.6	3.6

12 The figures per 1,000 for York for 1970-72 were: birth rate 14.3, death rate 12.0, giving a natural increase of only 2.3.
13 See Matthews et al. (1981, Table 3.4) for average participation rates for Great Britain. The rate for 1851 was 43.9 (York: 44.5) and for 1911, 44.8 (York: 45.0). The following paragraphs draw on the discussion of the national trends in Matthews, et al. (1981, Chapter 3).
14 Two major problems regarding Table 6 must be noted. First, all censuses for 1841 to 1911 offer what is primarily an occupational, not an industrial, classification. This means that those occupied as clerks, carriers and carters, messengers, building workers, general labourers, etc. were classified as such; and were not assigned to the particular industry in which they were employed. The figures in Table 6 for manufacturing and distribution will thus be under-stated, and those for construction and for transport (which include all the carriers, messengers, etc.) will be overstated, by comparison with those in Table 10 for 1951 and 1971 which are properly classified by industry. The census takers were not entirely consistent, however, and clerks, porters, etc. in railway and government service were included in these sectors. The second problem relates to the distinction between manufacturing and distribution. In many occupations that distinction was not, or not always, made in the nineteenth century, and many workers were both makers and dealers. The difference is especially blurred for 1851, both in reality and in the census returns. The tailors, shoemakers and others in the clothing trades are the largest group in this category, and for this reason were shown separately in Table 6 (row 3). In other cases workers for whom no distinction could be made were generally assigned to manufacturing (row 2).
15 See Armstrong (1974, p. 30) for evidence that York had an abnormally high ratio of domestic servants to total population; and Alexander (1970, pp. 89-101) for similar evidence regarding the number of shops.
16 See Peacock and Joy (1971) for a reassessment of the controversial George Hudson's contribution to the development of railways through York.
17 See Angus-Butterworth (1954) for the glassworks, Knight (1944, p. 675) and Hargrove (1910) for Terry's; Tillott (1961, p. 273) and Malden (1976) for Walker; and Knight (1944, pp. 587, 623 and 676) for the chemists.
18 For this and much other information about the Rowntree family and business I am indebted to Vernon (1958). Other sources used include Hargrove (1906). Mennell (1922) and Duckham (1956) for the firm; and Knapp (1930), Williams (1931) and Wickizer (1951) for the industry.
19 The figures in the text for 1894-1914 are from Rowntree's *Cocoa Works' Magazine*, March 1914, p. 1645; they refer only to employment in York. The total for 1904 including employees elsewhere was 3,564; and for 1914 it was 6,345, including 381 growing cocoa in the West Indies. Figures given in Willmot et al. (1959), for 1894-1909 include the employees outside York.

[20] See Vernon (1958, pp. 80-1 and 121) for the evidence on this point.

[21] The actual figures for retained cocoa imports (in long tons) are: 1850, 1,375; 1870, 3,100; 1890, 9,030; and 1910, 24,600 (Knapp, 1930, p. 27). For the value of consumption 1900-19 see Prest (1954, p. 67).

[22] For raw material prices see Board of Trade (1912, p. 317); for retail prices, Prest (1954, p. 67); for real wages, Bowley (1937, p. 30).

[23] Knight (1944, pp. 675-6 and 716), Hargrove (1910) and Terry's (1967).

[24] See York Times, 1, Winter 1961, p. 27 and Willmot et al. (1959, p. 123).

[25] Davis (1909, p. 354).

[26] Nuttgens (1978, p. 67).

[27] Russell (1902, pp. 36-7) gives figures of 763 working on locomotives at York and 1879 on carriages and wagons. For the early history of the workshops I have relied mainly on Hargrove (1910), Duckham (1956, pp. 47-54), Tillott (1961, pp. 270 and 481) and Hoole (1976, pp. 40 and 49).

[28] The main source for this statement, and the following paragraphs, is Irving (1976, pp. 90-7 and 109-12), supplemented by Hargrove (1910) and Hoole (1976, pp. 49-50).

[29] The estimate for total employment in the two industries is made up as follows: 3,740 in manufacture of confectionery, 1,600 in the railway workshops, 3,200 in railway service and at least 1,200 in non-manufacturing work for the confectionery firms. For manufacturing the last two categories are excluded, and the total for York is put at 11,000-12,000 so as to allow for an uncertain proportion of workers in the clothing trades (cf. Table 6).

[30] Taylor and Wilson (1950, p. 51).

[31] See Hargrove (1910) and Duckham (1956, pp. 143-5).

[32] See Duckham (1967, pp. 128-35 and 181-2).

[33] Duckham (1956, p. 155), and Y[orkshire] G[azette], 2 September 1911.

[34] Knight (1944, p. 717).

[35] This paragraph is based on Sessions (1976, pp. 50-1 and 54-8).

[36] The estimates in Table 10 for 1951 and 1971 differ from those in Table 5, partly because they exclude unemployed workers; partly because they are based on a 10 per cent sample, not a complete enumeration; but mainly because they relate to the place of work, not of residence. All persons working in York are included, even if they lived outside the city boundaries; and any residents of York who worked elsewhere are excluded.

[37] There is an apparent decline in Table 10 of some 300 in local government employment but this is misleading: in 1964 the classification of some 800 workers operating the main York bus service was altered from Public Administration to Transport, although the York District Council continued to maintain an interest in the joint undertaking with the West Yorkshire Road Car Co.

[38] Tillott (1961, p. 542).

[39] Palliser (1979b, pp. 38-9).

[40] I am indebted to Jim Crichton of the York Department of Tourism for information on the number of visitors and the number of bedspaces. The latter cover only hotels and authorised guest-houses; other accommodation is available at the University (which provided rooms for 23,000 conference delegates during the vacations in 1979/80), at youth hostels, schools, caravan sites, etc.

⁴¹ A detailed survey of expenditure in 1971 was made by the English Tourist Board (1971). To estimate total expenditure in 1980 I used the official Retail Price Index to adjust the 1971 estimates of daily spending by different categories of visitor to 1980 prices, and these adjusted figures were then multiplied by the estimated number of overnight tourists and day visitors in 1980. See also the detailed discussion, and estimates for 1975, in NYCC (1976, Report 33, pp. 14-33 and 46-67).

⁴² These and other figures for employment are derived from the Censuses (including those for 1921 and 1931) supplemented by data based on estimates of the insured population for the York Employment Exchange Area (EEA). Until 1974 (when it was merged with Tadcaster) the York EEA was approximately the same as the York Study Area (see Map 4). Annual returns of the estimated number of employees in the York EEA for 1960-77 were kindly made available to me by the Statistics Division, Department of Employment, Watford. For insured employees in the City in 1931 and 1940 see City of York (1945, pp. 471-2); in York EEA in 1939 and 1948, City of York (1951, pp. 30-4); for selected years in the 1960s, York Junior Chamber (1972, p. 63); and for some later years, NYCC (1976, Report 17, p. 67).

⁴³ Prest (1954, p. 67).

⁴⁴ See Stone and Rowe (1951, pp. 143-4) for estimates of expenditure on confectionery and of prices and quantities sold in the U.K. during 1920-38; Briggs (1961, p. 224) for turnover in 1922; and Rowntree (1938, p. 67) for the benefits paid. I owe the last reference to Rodney Hills.

⁴⁵ The company introduced a profit-sharing scheme in 1923 but was unable to make a distribution to the workers until 1929, and there was then no further payment until 1936 (Rowntree, 1938, p. 60).

⁴⁶ Willmot et al. (1959, p. 122) has annual employment figures for 1923-58.

⁴⁷ See Briggs (1961, pp. 224-34).

⁴⁸ This and other information on activity, profits, etc. is based partly on data from company records (for which I am indebted to Sir Donald Barron), and partly on the Chairman's annual statement to the employees, published annually in the Summer issue of the Cocoa Works Magazine, Rowntree's house journal until 1971. See also The Times 1000 (1979).

⁴⁹ York Junior Chamber (1977, pp. 70-5) and Kompass (1980, pp. 1791-4) are the main sources for this and other figures quoted for employment at individual firms in the late 1970s. Other estimates are based on the sources referred to in n. 42 above.

⁵⁰ The information in this and the following paragraph is based largely on British Association (1932, p. 78), Hoole (1976, pp. 50-1) and Swann (1966, p. 12). For the decision to close the wagon shop see Y[orkshire] E[vening] P[ress], 19 September, 1962.

⁵¹ Scott (1962, pp. 132 and 139); Taylor and Wilson (1950, pp. 51 and 59).

⁵² Terry's (1967); YEP, 14 February, 1963; 16 January, 1965; 11 February and 7 April 1977.

⁵³ Willmot et al. (1959, p. 123), YEP 22 December, 1972 and The Chamber, No. 8 Autumn 1980.

[54] Benson (1925, p. 155) and information kindly provided by Adams-Hydraulics Ltd.
[55] Birch (1974).
[56] *YEP*, 5-6 January, 1978 and 14 July, 1978, and Sessions (1976, pp. 50, 56, 58-9 and 70).
[57] Malden (1976, p. 38).
[58] Angus-Butterworth (1954, p. 6); Benson (1925, p. 155); *YG*, 15 March, 1924 and *Yorkshire Herald*, 7 May, 1924.
[59] *YG*, 1 February, 1930 for the closure by Spillers, and Tillott (1961, p. 474) for the Ouse Navigation case and tolls.
[60] The company was established in 1904, taking over a number of older businesses, see Hargrove (1910); also Knight (1944, p. 677). 1935 was the last year in which it was listed at Skeldergate in the *York City Year Book and Business Directory*.
[61] Swann (1966, p. 13); *YEP*, 8 July, 1967.
[62] Charlesworth (1953); Plummer (1937, p. 274) for the 1925 (and later) subsidies; *YEP*, 25 November 1980.
[63] Charlesworth (1953); Rowntree (1938, pp. 70-1).
[64] *YEP*, 19 January, 1965, 2 December, 1966 and 31 July, 1968.
[65] Angus-Butterworth (1954, p. 6); *YEP*, 23 January, 1969, information provided by the company and *Stock Exchange Official Year-Book*.
[66] *YEP*, 19 October, 1938 and 19 August, 1954.
[67] The information about the Shepherd Group is based on trade directories, details kindly provided by the company, *YG*, 8 March, 1930, and *The Times 1000* (1979).

References

ALEXANDER, D. (1970), *Retailing in England during the Industrial Revolution*.
ANGUS-BUTTERWORTH, L. M. (1954), A Galaxy of Glass, Glassmaking at the Fishergate, York, *Pottery and Glass*, Jan. 1954.
ARMSTRONG, A. (1974), *Stability and Change in an English County Town. A Social Study of York, 1801-51*.
BARTLETT, J. N. (1959), The Expansion and Decline of York in the Later Middle Ages, *Econ. History Review*, XII, August 1959.
BENSON, G. (1925), *An Account of the City and County of York from the Reformation to the Year 1925*.
BIRCH (1974), *Birch Builds 1874-1974*, York.
BOARD OF TRADE (1908), *Report of an Enquiry by the Board of Trade into Working Class Rents, Housing and Retail Prices*, Cd. 3864, *Parl. Papers*, 1908, CVII.
BOARD OF TRADE (1912), *Report of an Enquiry by the Board of Trade into Working-class Rents and Retail Prices . . . in continuation of a similar enquiry in 1905*, Cd. 6955, *Parl. Papers*, 1913, LXVI.
BOWLEY, A. L. (1902), Wages in York in 1899. From Mr. B. S. Rowntree's Investigation, *Jnl. of the Royal Statistical Society*, LXV.

BRIGGS, A. (1961), *Social Thought and Social Action. A study of the Work of Seebohm Rowntree, 1871-1954*.

BRITISH ASSOCIATION FOR THE ADVANCEMENT OF SCIENCE (1932), *A Scientific Survey of York and District*.

CENSUS OF POPULATION, *Census of England and Wales*, decennial 1831-1971.

CHARLESWORTH, C. (1953), *York's Chief Industries and Trades*. Unpublished typescript of lecture, in York City Library.

CITY OF YORK (1945), *Civic Committee Report of Market, Trading and Industrial Facilities, Minutes*, 1944-45.

CITY OF YORK (1951), *Development Plan*.

DAVIS, E. L. (1909), The Evolution of the Railway Time Table, *The Railway Gazette*, 12 March, 1909.

DUCKHAM, B. F. (1956), *The Economic Development of York, 1830-1914*, unpublished M. A. Thesis, University of Manchester.

DUCKHAM, B. F. (1967), *The Yorkshire Ouse. The History of a River Navigation*.

ENGLISH TOURIST BOARD (1971), *The Future for Tourism in York: The City's Choice*.

HARGROVE, W. W. (1906), The History of York, *Yorkshire Herald*, 2 June and 16 June, 1906.

HARGROVE, W. W. (1910), The History of York, *Yorkshire Herald*, 19 March, 2 April, 23 April, 3 September, 10 September and 24 September, 1910.

HOOLE, K. (1976), *The Railways of York*.

IRVING, R. J. (1976), *The North Eastern Railway Company 1870-1914*.

KAY, A. C. and H. V. TOYNBEE (1909), *Report to the Royal Commission on the Poor Laws*, App. vol. XV, Cd. 4593, *Parl. Papers*, 1909, XLII.

KNAPP, A. W. (1930), *The Cocoa and Chocolate Industry*, 2nd ed.

KNIGHT, C. B. (1944), *A History of the City of York*.

KOMPASS (1980), 18th edition, vol. II, *Company Information*.

MALDEN, J. (1976), The Walker Ironfoundry, York, c. 1825-1923, *York Historian*, 1.

MATTHEWS, R. C. O., C. H. FEINSTEIN and J. ODLING-SMEE (1981), *British Economic Growth, 1856-1973*.

MENNELL, G. H. (1922), *Romance of a Great Industry*, Darlington (reprinted from Yorkshire Gazette, 1921).

MOH, Medical Officer of Health, City of York, *Annual Reports* from 1900.

NYCC (1976), North Yorkshire County Council, *Structure Plan*, Report 17, *Industry and Employment; Structure Plan*, Report 33, *Tourism*.

NYCC (1979), North Yorkshire County Council, *Structure Plan*.

NUTTGENS, P. (1978), *York, Buildings in the City*.

OFFICE OF POPULATION, CENSUSES AND SURVEYS (1978), *Local Authority Vital Statistics*, Series VS, No. 5.

PALLISER, D. and M. (1979a), *York as they saw it – from Alcuin to Lord Esher*.

PALLISER, D. (1979b), *Tudor York*.

PEACOCK, A. J. and D. JOY (1971), *George Hudson of York*.

PLUMMER, A. (1937), *New British Industries in the Twentieth Century*.

PREST, A. R. (1954), *Consumers' Expenditure in the United Kingdom, 1900-1919.*
REGISTRAR-GENERAL of Births, Deaths and Marriages in England and Wales, *Annual Reports* from 1838, *Parl. Papers.*
ROWNTREE, B. S. (1938), *The Human Factor in Business,* 3rd ed.
ROWNTREE, B. S. (1941), *Poverty and Progress.*
RUSSELL, J. (1902), The Gateshead Locomotive Works, *The Railway Magazine,* XI.
SCOTT, J. D. (1962), *Vickers. A History.*
SESSIONS, W. K. and E. M. (1976), *Printing in York from the 1490s to the Present Day.*
Stock Exchange Official Year Book, annual.
STONE, R. and D. A. ROWE (1953), *The Measurement of Consumers' Expenditure and Behaviour in the United Kingdom, 1920-1938,* vol. I.
SWANN, A. W. (1966), *The Growth of the Manufacturing Industries of York,* unpublished B. A. Hons. Thesis, University College of Swansea.
TAYLOR, E. W. and J. SIMMS WILSON (1950), *At the Sign of the Orrery.*
TERRY'S (1967), *Terry's of York, 1767-1967,* York.
TILLOTT, P. M. (ed.) (1961), *The Victorian County History, The City of York.*
THE TIMES (1979), *The Times 1000, 1979-80.*
VERNON, A. (1958), *A Quaker Business Man. The Life of Joseph Rowntree, 1836-1925.*
WICKIZER, V. D. (1951), *Coffee, Tea and Cocoa. An Economic and Political Analysis.*
WILLIAMS, I. A. (1931), *The Firm of Cadbury, 1831-1931.*
WILLMOT, G. F., J. M. BIGGINS and P. M. TILLOTT, (eds.) (1959), *York. A Survey, 1959.*
YORK JUNIOR CHAMBER (1972), *York. A Study of the Environment.*
YORK JUNIOR CHAMBER (1977), *Living in York.*

CHAPTER VI

The Relief of
Poverty in Victorian York:
Attitudes and Policies

by

Anne Digby

SEVERAL OF THE PUBLIC BUILDINGS in York are commodious and
elegant, particularly the Mansion-house, for the residence of the
lord mayor, and the Guildhall . . . here are also several excellent
charity-schools and hospitals. There are also a great number of
elegant private houses. The city, in general, is well built, although
some mean habitations may be seen towards the outskirts, especially in the south-eastern part, which lies between Foss bridge and
Laythorpe postern, contiguous to the Foss Island; as well as between the Foss Island and Fishergate postern. These parts of the city
are both disagreeably situated and thinly inhabited; and, from the
Foss bridge on both sides of Walmgate as far as the bar, scarcely any
thing is seen but ill-built houses and gardens.[1]

   This description of York in 1813 was unusual in focusing on well-
established disparities in wealth among its inhabitants rather than dwelling on the gothic magnificence of the Minster. Already, the areas of
Hungate and Walmgate, which were to become the two worst slum areas
of Victorian York, were conspicuous for their 'mean habitations'. But the
'thinly inhabited' character of York was transformed by a rapid population increase which between 1811 and 1851 almost doubled the number

of inhabitants.[2] By this time, the overcrowded, insanitary and unhealthy condition of parts of the city had attracted much anxious enquiry and earnest proposals for reform. In a congested town where most still lived in the confined area within its medieval walls, disease generated among the poor soon spread to the propertied inhabitants.

This chapter begins with a brief discussion of deficiencies in the physical environment of the poor and the extent to which it had been improved by public action during Victoria's reign (1837-1901). The increasing vigour of such collectivist action suggests an underlying change of values in favour of public intervention in the lives of individuals. However, more detailed examination of local ideas and assumptions about the role of publicly-financed poor relief, and privately-funded charitable and educational assistance to the poorest inhabitants of the city, indicates more complex attitudes towards poverty. These perpetuated individualistic policies in the relief of the poor during our period. At the beginning of the twentieth century social inquiries revealed hidden dimensions to the poverty problem, and by implication asked how adequate traditional policies of social welfare had been in relieving it.

The Environment of the Poor

The arrival of cholera in York in 1832 highlighted unhealthy living conditions in parts of York, where 'slaughter-houses, dung-heaps, pigsties, etc., which unfortunately subsist in the heart of the town ... generate contagion. The dampness of the dwellings ... is ... prejudicial to the health of the inhabitants'.[3] More detailed investigations followed during the 1840s as part of a national sanitary movement to improve urban health; like those in other large towns they revealed the deplorable living conditions of the poor. Local water supply was grossly deficient; the York Water Company drew its water unfiltered from the Ouse in a state 'so turbid and dirty as scarcely to be fit for washing, and still less for cooking or being drunk'. Its inadequate quality was matched by its quantity since only 3,000 of the 7,000 houses in the city were supplied. Water seldom ran from the common standpipes in the yards of the poorest quarters of the town. Those drawing water from wells could find their supplies polluted by neighbouring graveyards. Houses in low-lying areas, particularly those in Hungate, were periodically inundated by that 'great open cesspool,' the stagnant River Foss (see Map 5, p. 172, below). Except for the main streets of the town there was no attempt at street cleansing, and the accumulation of filth and water drained into those houses built at a lower level than the street. Underground sewers and drains were few, and water closets a luxury, so poorer inhabitants usually shared a midden privy. Its night soil accumulated until scavengers carted it off to a district dung-heap where its effluvia and stench added to local pollution.[4]

Sickness produced by an unhealthy environment led to increased expenditure by charities and the poor-law guardians. A substantial proportion of cases treated from 1839 to 1843 by the York Dispensary, were of people living in insanitary neighbourhoods.[5] Even larger sums than those financing this medical charity were paid by local ratepayers whose poor rates were increased because of pauperism caused by sickness. Mr. Alderson, the Poor Law Medical Officer for an area which included Hungate and Layerthorpe, testified in 1850 that,

> Families being in comfortable circumstances come on the parish in consequence of illness. The expenses to parishes, I should say, is considerable on account of sickness. . . . Very often in consequence of the death of the husband, families from having been previously supported by this labour, are thrown on the parish.[6]

In 1847 an outbreak of typhus forced the poor law guardians to open a temporary fever hospital and the surgeon there found that the insanitary parishes in Walmgate of St. George, St. Dennis and St. Margaret provided 45 per cent of the pauper fever cases although they included only 21 per cent of the town's inhabitants: a clear illustration of the intimate connection between environment, sickness and pauperism.[7]

By the end of the century this urban environment had changed for the better but much still remained to be done; conditions in the poorest areas, those of Walmgate and Hungate, were as bad as those in the slums of London.[8] Public improvements had included: the provision of purer water to three times as many houses between 1850 and 1900; the closure of church burial grounds in 1854 and their replacement by a cemetery outside the town walls; the establishment of a Fever Hospital in 1881; the construction of an extensive system of sewers in the 1890s; and the growth of an active public health department with a Medical Officer of Health and four sub-inspectors of sanitary nuisances. Housing provision for working-class inhabitants was now more satisfactory than in many other towns since three-quarters of them lived in houses with four or more rooms. The general death rate and infant mortality rate, which had been above average, were in 1901 slightly below the figures for England and Wales. A tentative start had been made on slum clearance: by 1901 88 houses in York had been declared unfit for habitation under powers given under the Housing of the Working Classes Act of 1890. In spite of the association of midden privies with typhoid (an endemic disease in the town), there were still 6,418 of them in 1900. At this time one-fifth of the city's houses shared a privy, in some cases with as many as 15 others. In

Hungate and Walmgate fewer than half the houses had a private water tap, and householders could share a tap with up to 25 houses. In Hungate nearly half the houses were back to back, whereas only one-tenth were of this character in the town as a whole. During the Victorian period the disparities between areas of the city had become more obvious and this increasingly differentiated environment was reflected in sickness and mortality statistics. For example, in Hungate the death rate in the period 1898 to 1907 was 28.9 per thousand inhabitants (or 35.1 in the poorest neighbourhoods), whereas for the city generally it was only 16.2.[9]

During the reign of Victoria the population of York almost trebled; in 1831 the number of inhabitants had been recorded as 26,260 and 70 years later the city, with an expanded geographical area, had 77,914 people.[10] This increase in numbers was accompanied by greater social segregation; whereas at the beginning of our period most parishes included both rich and poor inhabitants, during the nineteenth century these mixed neighbourhoods became less common. Substantial town houses in the neighbourhood were turned into tenements as their occupants moved to more salubrious areas further from the congested centre of the town. Some of the rapidly growing population was then housed in overcrowded courts and yards built in the gardens of these large houses. In certain areas of the old town this process of infilling produced overcrowded slums as in Skeldergate, parts of Walmgate or Hungate (see Plates 13 and 15). Alternatively, new working class suburbs grew up outside the town walls and these might also have undesirably high population densities, as in the Groves, or in the Leeman Road area.[11] As the propertied and the poor shared less in a common pattern of neighbourly living so social cohesion was weakened. This process was not unique to York and was strengthened by the introduction there of national measures such as the New Poor Law. A prominent citizen in the city described this measure as having 'a good deal of class legislation in it'.[12] During the Victorian period this weakened sense of community was revealed in changing local attitudes to the relief of poverty.

Attitudes to Poverty

The attitude of those who administered the poor law in the city, towards the poor whom it was their duty to relieve, was ambivalent. Their economical instincts as guardians of the ratepayers' purses were at odds with a genuine, if restricted, sense of paternalism towards less fortunate inhabitants. With such divided loyalties it is perhaps unremarkable that the local system of relief before 1834 was fragmented and based on the parish rather than the city. There was much conflict between the 32 parishes in the form of expensive legal disputes over the settlement, and hence the right to poor relief, of the several inhabitants in the city. Attempts at co-operation were few, although a fluctuating number of parishes had shared a workhouse in Marygate since 1768; and after 1821, a Vagrants Office to deal with the mobile poor was financed by all the parishes.[13] This minimal co-operation contrasted with more vigorous schemes in York during earlier periods of the Old Poor Law, most notably in the late sixteenth and early seventeenth centuries. It also differed from more efficient co-ordination of poor relief in comparable cities such as Norwich or Bristol which in 1696 and 1712 respectively, had obtained local legislation to incorporate all their parishes into one union which was served by a central workhouse. In York this integration occurred only with the imposition of national legislation, the Poor Law Amendment Act of 1834, which inaugurated the New Poor Law era.

This external threat to local autonomy revealed that the propertied took sufficient pride in their idiosyncratic relief arrangements to resent outside interference by the newly-appointed Poor Law Commission in London and their mobile inspectorate. A succession of inspectors noted the prickly independence of the York poor-law guardians. The first, John Revans, commented in 1840 that 'the York Union has given more resistance to the introduction of the amended system than the whole of the other unions in the South and North Ridings combined'.[14] Twelve years later the same attitude still prevailed and the inspector, H. W. T. Hawley, stated that York guardians were 'as a body extremely difficult to control – highly sensitive on points where the interference of the central board was necessary to restrain them'.[15] In part, this desire for self-determination on the part of the York guardians had been fostered unintentionally by Revans himself. This was because there had been an urgent need to form the York Poor Law Union in 1837 in order to implement the Registration Act through the Union Clerk's registration of births, marriages and deaths. So as to facilitate a rapid formation of the local union Revans gave an extremely conciliatory speech to local ratepayers in May 1837, in which he emphasised that discretionary powers over poor relief by local administrators would remain. He even misrepresented the provisions of the Poor Law Amendment Act to the extent of stating that deserving cases would continue to receive relief outside the workhouse, whereas the act was designed to prohibit such out-door relief to the able-bodied poor.[16]

In spite of this misleading propaganda, feeling in the city ran high against the impending imposition of the new relief system. Symptomatic of opponents' attitudes was the impassioned statement at Revan's meeting by a local tea-dealer, Mr. Jackson, 'I don't think it a crime to be poor, or that we have a right to grind them down'.[17] The local press was predominantly against the 1834 act and orchestrated public opinion to expect impending doom. For example, the *York Herald* referred to Revan's eagerness to erect 'a prison-workhouse',[18] and after only one week of the new system's operation in the city, it prematurely condemned 'its harsh and revolting features'.[19] But local action against the impending changes was too belated to be effectual. York ratepayers followed the example of large textile towns in Yorkshire and Lancashire in organising an anti-poor law meeting in May, and attempted a boycott of the guardians' elections in July 1837. The meeting produced a petition to the Poor Law Commissioners, signed by some 3,000 people, which protested against their unconstitutional powers and argued the case for the retention of local control of poor relief. Having weathered far worse opposition in the industrial towns of the north, the Poor Law Commission ignored the petition, and the York Union was declared in June 1837. In the following month the boycott of guardians' elections proved to be as ineffectual in York as it had earlier been in every other town except Oldham and Ashton. The election result showed that the inclusion of a substantial rural hinterland in the York Union (see Map 3, p. 114) had facilitated the return of a small Tory majority on the York Board of Guardians.[20]

Although the New Poor Law was a lively issue in the city's politics during 1837, there was not the simple party division that might have been expected along the lines of Liberal support for the 1834 act as a Whig measure and Tory opposition to 'Poor-Law Whigs'. Instead, George Hudson, the leading Tory of the day, expressed his approbation of the 1834 legislation, while his influential Liberal opponent, George Leeman, had some reservations about the York Union.[21] However, many Tories did oppose the New Poor Law and a Tory-inspired pamphlet circulated in York in June 1837 entitled 'A Dialogue between a Poor Law Commissioner and the Paupers'. A poor man asked for relief until he could get work and was told:

> You work, you lazy rascal. You never intend to work. I can read roguery in your face, as plain as though I looked into a looking glass, however bring in your baggage of a wife, and all her brats, and we'll put you in a dungeon where the light of day shall scarcely shine upon you, you in one cell, your wife in another, and all your brats in different places.[22]

While this had the hall-mark of similar Tory productions in other towns – as in Norwich[23] – it exposed a very real local concern for the fate of the 'deserving' poor, and a distaste for the allegedly prison-like arrangements in workhouses of the New Poor Law. This sympathetic attitude to the poor might well have resulted in the kind of Tory-Radical coalition which effectively impeded the implementation of new relief policies in some northern factory towns. But the large income inequalities and lack of social homogeneity in York effectively precluded this kind of solidarity.[24] Instead, a paternalistic and limited sympathy shaped the relief policies of the propertied inhabitants who were elected to the York Board of Guardians.

This traditional stance was to continue virtually unchanged throughout the Victorian period. It successfully fused the interests of the ratepayers in an economical administration with those of the poor in a humane system of relief and did this by relieving paupers cheaply in their own homes rather than expensively in the workhouse. The *York Herald's* admonition of 27 May 1837 was well-heeded, 'Let, then, the citizens be active, and watch well their own pecuniary interests, and guard also the sacred rights of the poor, in the spirit of that humanity which we know pervades their breasts'.

During the early Victorian period the York Union was notorious in the area for its niggardliness over relief.[25] Samuel Tuke, who was a poor-law guardian during the first dozen years of the York Union, commented that 'you cannot be frequently an attender at the Board without knowing that *lavish charity* is not the besetting sin of the guardians'. Although he was broadly in sympathy with the objectives of the New Poor Law he felt, nevertheless, that it had had the effect of focusing too much attention on money and as a result had cut off the kindness due from man to man.[26] Perhaps, because others agreed with Tuke that the bureaucratic routine of the new system was undesirable, the York guardians later reformed their relief machinery. In the eyes of the central poor-law board this revision erred too far in the opposite direction and emphasised personality rather than principle. The York Board of Guardians substituted for the impersonal investigations of a paid official, the relieving officer, a system by which each guardian effectively managed the relief given in his area.[27] Having received a printed application form from the relieving officer, the pauper in York took it to his local guardian who questioned him and then presented his case at the guardian's board. It was the considered, and probably accurate, verdict of the local poor-law inspector, Mr. Bagenal, that such a system led to a:

> personal view of each case, and thus to favouritism and petty jobbery. The attitude of the poor law administration differs mainly from voluntary charity in that it is impersonal in its action. The best guarantee for uniformity in treatment, impartiality, and justice to the poor, is an impersonal consideration of these relief cases.[28]

The personal contact of charitable donor and recipient, to which Mr. Bagenal referred, was valued by Victorians because it was supposed to make their benevolence discriminating. Ideally, charitable help was restricted to the deserving, respectable poor who had been reduced to extreme poverty through no fault of their own, as for example, through the sickness of the breadwinner or the failing strength of old age. Accepting charitable help was not held to demoralise or harm the self-respect of the recipient as did poor relief. In theory, the poor law was directed at the undeserving poor, whose destitution was thought to have been caused by moral failings. A clear example of this social philosophy persisting into the early years of the twentieth century was given in B. S. Rowntree's study of unemployment in York. A 'careful, economical' family through loss of work 'had been actually starving for days before they appealed to the Parish, and the Parish recommended them to the C.O.S. as superior, self-respecting folk'. This family, who had thought their respectability threatened by the acceptance of poor relief, felt that no such loss of self-respect was involved in receiving help from the Charity Organization Society. The breadwinner stated that 'to this society I shall always be greatly indebted for their kindness in coming to my rescue'.[29]

York, for many years the second city of the kingdom, had amassed over the centuries a vast quantity of charitable funds. While much of this went on the provision of almshouses and pensions for the aged, which was thought by all to be a worthy object, too much money was felt to be wasted in doles. One York vicar stated that 'every year we are manufacturing paupers in York by the rotten administration of the charities'.[30] Many city parishes had been endowed by the bequests of parishioners with small sums of money which had to be distributed periodically in the form of coals, bread or money. In the earlier part of our period the propertied considered that doles were a useful form of assistance to the poor, but by the end of the century, a minority of citizens showed concern lest monetary help was given to the undeserving, who might be sufficiently ungrateful to use it on drink. Steps were taken to prevent this, as in the parish of St. John, Micklegate where Duckworth's Charity was administered by means of tickets exchangeable only for food, clothing or coals at local shops.[31]

Much charitable help in our period was instrumental rather than benevolent. The hidden cost to the poor of receiving such assistance was acceptance of, or at least outward conformity to, the social values of benefactors. In the early Victorian period there was enough social deference to lubricate this system so that the coercive element did not obtrude. This was partly because the propertied members of York society assumed that the lower orders shared their values. They were particularly confident of this in relation to the very large numbers of female domestics.[32] In 1829 the Ninth Report of the Society for the Encouragement of Female Servants stated:

It appears to your committee that the society has been the means of encouraging many deserving servants; that it has distributed many copies of the Scriptures as premiums; that it has tended to check the inordinate love of dress, and the spirit of change.

However, the momentum of changed circumstances forced even this society out of existence; by 1871 no nominations were put forward of servants whose faithful service deserved the approbation of their betters.[33] The spirit of change was already gradually transforming the social stability of the city. Traditionally, York society had consisted of a hierarchy of ranks with vertical lines of duty and responsibility on the one hand and loyalty and deference on the other. The emerging class society eroded these attitudes.

The resultant insecurity among the better-off inhabitants of York resulted in active efforts to impose desirable virtues on the poor. An element of social control was particularly clear in very active attempts to educate the city's poor children. Although many charity schools, day schools and Sunday schools had been set up in the eighteenth and early nineteenth centuries, investigations in 1826 and 1836 revealed that nearly one in three children did not go to school.[34] So denominational bodies (especially the Anglicans), redoubled their efforts in the mid-nineteenth century. The educational needs of poor children continued to be met by these voluntary agencies until 1889 when a School Board was set up to provide additional, rate-aided schools.

The anxiety of the propertied about the threat which increasing numbers of poor inhabitants posed for their possessions provided a hidden dimension in the philanthropic creation of these voluntary schools. Here social discipline could be imposed on the rising generation, and 'civilised' values transmitted, which would preserve the *status quo* of Georgian and Victorian society. For example, the Bishophill British Girls' School established in 1813 aimed 'to improve the moral condition of many of the rising generation',[35] and to train them 'to habits of order and industry'.[36] Neither the religious denomination of the managers, nor the passage of years seems to have altered the social philosophy of this educational missionary work. These comments by the managers of a non-denominational or British School were echoed by those of an Anglican or National School in the 1840s. The Visitors' Book of the Walmgate Girls' School (which drew its pupils from one of the most impoverished neighbourhoods in York), recorded their approbation at improvements in the children's 'docility' and the way in which 'the children appear more orderly and obedient'.[37]

The desire to moralise the poor and convert the feckless and idle into industrious and upright individuals, who accepted their lowly position in the social hierarchy, and respected those in higher stations, was particularly evident in belated attempts to rescue the most deprived of all York's inhabitants – the ragged street-urchins. In 1848 the York Industrial Ragged School was instituted with pupils from the Wesleyan Ragged Sunday School set up in the Bedern the previous year. Its first report stated its aims which were:

> to reclaim the most neglected and degraded children resident in the city of York, by providing for them a sound Christian education, combined with training in such branches of industry and household employments as are suitable to their condition of life.

There was a pressing need for such a school; of 110 pupils in 1850, 89 were said to have been street beggars. The school combined its education with a strong measure of social discipline. It is revealing that one occupation of the younger boys was that of picking oakum; the classic employment of workhouse inmates.[38] The purchase of the old workhouse premises in Marygate for the school must also have underlined this unspoken message of social control. This became explicit when it became an Industrial School after legislation of 1857 had permitted magistrates or poor-law guardians to send vagrant children aged 7 to 14 for training there.

Managers and teachers of ordinary day schools had limited tolerance of those poor children whose parents did not aspire to respectability. For example, Mary Metcalfe was dismissed from school in 1852 for her 'very improper and profane language' and her 'injurious influence'[39] on fellow pupils. In this context it is interesting that (following legislation of 1876 which aimed to improve school attendance), the Town Clerk found it necessary to ask how far managers of York elementary schools would co-operate by 'receiving into their schools children of the poorest and waistrell [sic] classes'. The managers indicated that there would be great difficulty and generally were 'unfavourable to the indiscriminate admission of the wastrels into existing schools'. However, certain of them relented later to the extent of agreeing to accept them 'if they came in cleanliness and were obedient to the discipline of the schools'.[40] The terminology of this discussion exposed with stark clarity the dividing line between the respectable – whose own efforts of improvement might be reinforced by the support of their betters – and the great unwashed, whose needs would be met reluctantly and on a minimal scale. In this case, a Wastrel School in Aldwark was provided in 1877 for children who had been ordered to attend a school by magistrates and then refused entry by teachers. When lack of funds later forced its closure ordinary elementary schools had to take its pupils. Eventually the Attendance Committee reported with a sigh of relief that:

> the street arabs who have been driven into the schools [and] have been a source of annoyance to the masters and mistresses and also to your attendance officers, are now showing a marked improvement both in attendance and behaviour.[41]

But the very existence of such an unusual institution had strikingly illuminated the local categorisation of the poor into the worthy and the reprobate.

The Relief of Poverty

These complex ideas about the poor were resolved on the York Board of Guardians through a policy of relieving the majority of applicants for relief by the traditional means of outdoor allowances. Only an unregenerate minority was thought to be fit occupants of the workhouse and for this the old parochial workhouse in Marygate (with accommodation for 90 inmates), was thought adequate. Since the York Union had a population in 1841 of 28,842 in the city and 18,937 in the surrounding countryside, it was clear that the intended restriction of outdoor relief to the adult able-bodied poor under the New Poor Law could not be implemented.

In September 1837 the newly-elected Board of Guardians had found the Marygate workhouse to be 'extremely incommodious and very much out of repair'.[42] A board that was well-intentioned to the objectives of the New Poor law would undoubtedly have decided to erect a new, and much larger, union workhouse. But as even a moderate supporter of the 1834 act found during service as a poor-law guardian 'we do not, I think, go as far as we ought in carrying out the New Poor Law; in regard to the poor house system I mean especially'. So the guardians decided that 'the alterations required to obtain the necessary subdivision and classification are very slight and of no great expense'.[43] This classification was designed by the central poor-law authority to separate the members of families in the workhouse and hence by psychological deterrence to inhibit any but the utterly destitute among the able-bodied from seeking relief. In York, these building alterations did little to effect this separation so that the workhouse retained all the features of a general mixed workhouse. That these conditions, rather than workhouse classification, might be sufficient to deter all but the desperately poor is suggested by the guardians' own description of the workhouse in October 1841:

One very small yard is used by the boys, by aged men, by the sick, by paupers in the probationary ward often exceedingly filthy or labouring under infectious diseases, by the married couples, and it also gives access to the room used by profligate women in a state of disease. . . . For all these classes there is one common privy.[44]

In spite of this, and the existence of damp, overcrowded rooms and grossly defective sanitary arrangements, the guardians decided that they would continue to use it, and rent adjoining premises in order to increase marginally the available accommodation. In 1845, the poor-law inspector found that the workhouse children were suffering from the itch (scabies), from opthalmia, and also from venereal disease communicated from the common privy. The girls' yard was an open cess-pool and the boys' rooms were directly above the lying-in (or labour) ward. The Poor Law Commission had no powers to order the guardians to build a workhouse and therefore had to pressurise them. To this end they restricted the numbers whom the guardians could send to their expanded Marygate premises to 100 inmates. In spite of this, it was not until September 1847 that the York Board decided to erect a new workhouse for at least 300 paupers at a cost not exceeding £6,000.[45] This starkly functional building was opened early in 1849 on the Huntington Road (see Map 5). Extensions gradually increased its capacity to 600 paupers, of whom one-third were accommodated in an infirmary.

The York Union differed from most of the surrounding rural unions, where the 1834 act was implemented successfully.[46] Its policies were similar to those of urban unions in the West Riding where there was a subtle blend of political independence, financial stringency, and old-style paternalism which delayed the erection of union workhouses.[47] As in these West Riding towns, it was not until after the Irish Potato Famine of 1846 and the influx of destitute Irish (whose numbers exacerbated the increased vagrancy associated with industrial depression), that it was decided to build a new workhouse. Before this it was felt that the erection of a large workhouse would enable the central authority to issue a prohibitory order laying down indoor relief for most able-bodied applicants and that this would remove local guardians' discretionary power over poor relief. In the York Union this reluctance to build was also partly attributable to the economical instincts of the guardians representing the 48 country parishes of which 7 were in the West, 16 in the East, and 25 in the North, Ridings (see Map 3). Like the country guardians in many other such mixed unions they saw little point in adding to the rate burden of rural areas through the capital cost of a workhouse which, it may be assumed, they considered too distant to be of much use in the management of their own poor. This parsimonious attitude continued and tended

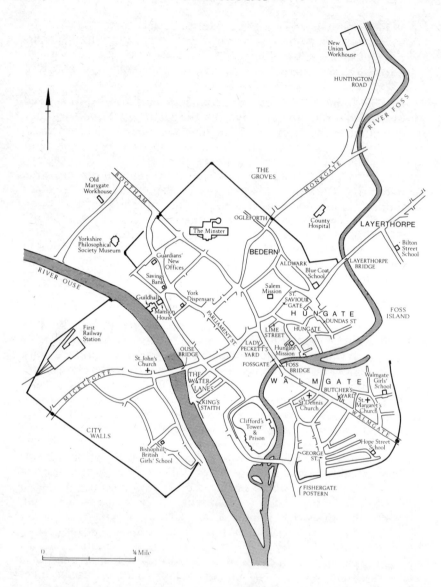

Map 5   York City in the mid-nineteenth century.

to restrict the provision of adequate facilities in the new workhouse. For example, the Gate Helmsley guardian who earlier had opposed the erection of the new workhouse, resisted in 1861 a proposal to provide baths there on the grounds that the inmates had need only of a good wash.[48] Nearly one half of the York guardians were farmers, and the remainder were divided between those in trade or manufacture, and those who were gentry, clergy or professional men. This admixture tended to inhibit policy initiatives and to result in a board which, while nominally a collective body, was effectively an assortment of individuals. But amongst them were humanitarians like Samuel Tuke with his unremitting and disinterested labour to alleviate the condition of the poor and sick of the city.

Tuke, who had visited Ireland in 1846, championed the cause of the destitute Irish who flooded into the north of England after the Potato Famine of 1846.[49] As a result of this influx a small Irish community in the city of 781 in 1841 had increased to 2,618 by 1851.[50] Many of them found accommodation in the slum areas of York:– the Bedern; St. Saviourgate in Hungate; the Water Lanes in St. Mary, Castlegate and St. Michael, Spurriergate; and particularly in the parishes of St. George, Dennis and Margaret in Walmgate (see Map 5). In St. George's the houses were said to be 'crowded by Irishmen, who are packed as close as herrings in a barrel'.[51] But it was in St. Margaret's that alarm was caused by the discovery of typhus among Irish immigrants in Butcher's Yard. A contemporary description referred to its being 'very filthy; two privies opposite the houses; no drain; five lodging houses'.[52] It was clear that the guardians needed to set up a temporary fever hospital to isolate the sufferers, but no-one wished to have such an institution near them so Samuel Tuke allowed them to use one of his fields next to Heslington Lane. Wooden buildings and tents were erected and used from May 1847 to December 1848. The Irish in York continued to pose problems for the York guardians; they made a disproportionately large number of relief applications in the ensuing period and constituted a heavy burden on the poor rates.[53]

The availability of a much bigger workhouse after 1849 did not at first alter the York Guardians' preference for outdoor relief; only 10 per cent of relief expenditure went on indoor relief compared to 6 to 8 per cent earlier. In 1852 the poor law inspector gloomily recorded the guardians' 'morbid views of humanity' which made them increase the burden on York ratepayers through their continued reliance on outdoor allowances.[54] But the proportion of indoor relief was increased gradually after the Poor Law Board issued a prohibitory order to York in 1852, which restricted outdoor relief to the able-bodied. By 1889 it constituted 38 per cent, and in 1901 48 per cent, of that administered in the York Union as a whole. By this time the amount of workhouse relief was higher than the average of 46 per cent in England and Wales.[55] But in the city district of the York Union there was some deviation from this trend since there had been a 43 per cent increase in the expenditure on outdoor relief between 1895 and 1901. This was a product of the recently established autonomy of the city's guardians over the relief administered in their own urban Out Relief Union.[56]

Those inside the York Union Workhouse came both from the city and from rural areas in the union. Of these a declining number were children; the proportion was only one-fifth at the end of the century compared to two-fifths some 40 years earlier.[57] To some extent this reflected contemporary concern about the undesirability of institutionalising the young. One apparent indication of this was the decision to send the workhouse children to an ordinary elementary school at Bilton Street instead of educating them in the workhouse. But economy as well as humanity was involved; the decision was made after legislation in 1891 had expanded the provision of free school places and hence made it cheaper to educate pauper children outside the workhouse.[58] In contrast, more benevolence was shown to the workhouse children by private citizens who lightened their dreary institutional existence. For example, during 1898 to 1899 there were invitations to a pantomime, a gala, an aquatic carnival, a chrysanthemum show, and a fat stock show and there was also a trip on the river, and a visit to Scarborough. At Christmas there were gifts of a Christmas tree, toys, sweets, oranges, and provision of an entertainment.[59] Essentially these were palliatives and a poor substitute for the failure of the York guardians to make constructive reforms such as had been pioneered by the Sheffield Guardians in 1893 with their Scattered Homes. There, small groups of pauper children lived in ordinary houses and were looked after by a foster mother.

Among the adult inmates in the workhouse there were fewer men than women. An increasing proportion of both sexes was either old or sick, frequently both. Even the minority who were classified as 'able-bodied' were usually either temporarily disabled through sickness or accident, or were socially inadequate because of feeble mindedness. Alternatively, some were sent to the workhouse because they were seen as undeserving cases such as unmarried mothers or the families of prisoners. The York guardians were reluctant to acknowledge that increasingly they were to all intents and purposes running a hospital and almshouse rather than a workhouse. The central poor law board pressurised them to expand the infirmary and to improve their nursing but encountered local lethargy. Eventually in the 1890s, the sanitary, washing, and laundry arrangements were improved,[60] and nursing staff increased.[61] Little was done for old inmates, and the Brabazon Scheme of occupational therapy which had penetrated even backward, rural workhouses had not been effectively implemented in York by the end of our period.[62] Costs were minimised by requiring relatives of workhouse inmates to contribute to their maintenance where possible. Correspondence with employers ascertained wages, and summonses might be taken out if a man neglected to contribute while being thought able to do so.[63] This necessarily brief review of indoor relief suggests that an economical defence of the ratepayer's interests took priority over the social welfare of the poor. And this impression is confirmed when it is seen that in 1901 the amount of 5s. 5½d. expended on each workhouse inmate in York was lower than in other large Yorkshire towns.[64]

Among the outdoor poor in the city about two in every five were children. A comparable number were adults who were defined as 'non-able-bodied' and were old, infirm or handicapped. This left only a small number of able-bodied adults receiving relief outside the workhouse. Of these, four out of five were widows. Indeed, it is noticeable that women vastly outnumbered men in the outdoor relief lists. This was mainly through greater longevity and consequent age, infirmity or widowhood and also because of confinements. Relief 'in kind' in the form of flour, tea and sugar, as well as money, was given in cases of confinement. Outdoor allowances were given to men when there was a funeral to be paid for, or when short-term sickness or accident prevented an 'upright' individual from working. At the end of the nineteenth century the usual weekly sums allowed in such cases were three shillings for a single individual, four shillings and sixpence for a married couple with two children, six shillings for three children and eight shillings for a family with four children. This showed little difference from the maximum rates paid 60 years earlier of three shillings for a single person, and five shillings for a married couple.

Outdoor allowances were not continued indefinitely, and if sickness or unemployment continued the family were offered 'the house'. The prospect of this eventuality deterred many from applying. For example, in 1910 the Lovell family, whose bread-winner was disabled from lead-poisoning contracted at work, and whose health prevented him from keeping steady work, were said to, 'dread applying to the Board, knowing that they would probably be told to "come inside". and while they can keep a roof over their head they are determined not to do this'.[65] Others would accept outdoor relief but endure semi-starvation rather than enter the workhouse. Such a family were the Archers where the man had had no regular work after being laid off four years previously; 'A month ago the Archers applied to the Parish for help, and they have had two grocery orders of four shillings. The Board refuses to help them further and offers them "the house".[66] In this kind of situation, rent payments were deferred as long as possible, credit extended at the corner shop, clothes or furniture pawned to get money for food, and assistance from better-off neighbours gratefully accepted. In families where this hand-to-mouth existence had become a way of life, it was unlikely that payments would have been initiated to friendly societies or trade unions. For the more highly paid, or regularly employed, worker such membership conferred benefits during sickness or unemployment. But trade union membership in York was rather lower than the national average with 3.3 per cent of the population who were members in 1899 compared to 4.4 per cent in England and Wales. (This low proportion was partly caused by the absence of unions in the important confectionery trade.) In contrast friendly societies were quite strong in the city and by 1905 they included 10.8 per cent of its inhabitants.[67] Among them was a remarkably vigorous Female Friendly Society which, having begun in 1788, was in the early twentieth century giving useful benefits to its 470 members of three to six shillings per week during sickness, and ten shillings during confinement.[68] Other contemporary indications of a spirit of self-help among the poorer inhabitants were the large numbers of small accounts at the York Savings Bank and at the Yorkshire Penny Bank, and the York Cooperative Society with 7,250 members in 1900.[69]

Assistance from charity was widely available to those for whom self-help was not attainable. For some it acted as an alternative to poor relief and for others as a supplement. In 1906 yearly income from York charities amounted to a colossal £21,714 or nearly three times the £7,525 distributed in outdoor relief by the poor-law guardians. Two-fifths of these charitable funds came from endowed charity and involved the bequests of earlier inhabitants of York, while the remainder was made up of current benevolence in the form of voluntary charity. Of these funds 72 per cent went on deserving categories of poor who included the aged, blind, orphaned and sick; another 11 per cent was of miscellaneous character and of general benefit to the poor; and the remaining 17 per cent was in the form of indiscriminate doles of money and goods.[70]

By the end of the century there was national concern lest an undiscriminating and over-generous distribution of charity should create more poverty than it relieved by way of sapping the independence and self-reliance of the poor. Influential in shaping this viewpoint were the national activities of the Charity Organization Society which had been founded in 1869. It believed that charity should be channelled to the deserving poor, whose poverty was attributable to unforeseen contingencies such as sickness or the death of a bread-winner, while the poor law should relieve the undeserving poor whose moral failures were thought to be responsible for their unfortunate state. This social philosophy had only a very limited impact on the relief of poverty in York. One example was the setting up of Hodgson's Charity. A tablet can still be seen in the former Board of Guardians' Offices on the corner of Museum and Blake Streets which commemorates this bequest of £5,000. It was for people on small incomes who fell sick, but were not on poor relief, and were 'without means to procure comforts and necessaries which they may require to help them in their distress'. The charity was administered by the York Board of Guardians; their account books show their careful stewardship, with amounts from £1 to £3 having been given to deserving individuals.[71]

Deserving cases were also the concern after 1879 of a York Branch of the Charity Organization Society, but it failed to realise its more important objective of trying to improve the administration of city charities and co-ordinate charitable assistance with that of the poor law. Until 1911 there was no complete register of York charities in existence and even after this date no purposeful use appears to have been made of it. Also, there was no formal co-operation between the poor law and endowed charities so that it was not uncommon for applicants for poor relief to have undisclosed income from local charities.[72] This economically inefficient allocation of public and private funds was tolerated because priority continued to be given to personal benevolence rather than bureaucratic procedures. When poverty wore a human face, rather than being a statistic in the case book of a paid official, it became more difficult to label it as 'deserving' or 'non-deserving'. This outlook must have sustained the York Benevolent Society founded in 1793 to distribute sixpenny tickets for bread and coal, and the Soup Kitchen started in 1846 to distribute quarts of soup to the abjectly poor. Neither organisation minded if those in receipt of poor relief received its charitable assistance.[73] But while extreme temporary deprivation attracted this kind of attention, the existence of crushing, everyday poverty went all but unnoticed.

It was first revealed by evangelicals who, in their attempts to redeem those most in need of religious and secular instruction, penetrated the worst slum areas. Both the timing and location of these Missions and Sunday Schools suggest that they were stimulated by the influx of destitute Irish into York after the Famine of 1846, since their efforts were concentrated on places with many Irish inhabitants. The Quakers were among the earliest missionaries in 1848, with their Friends' First Day School in one of the most deprived areas of the city. It was situated in Hope Street where the Friends already ran a day school; there the surrounding courts and yards were filthy from overflowing privies and

pig-sties and the houses were damp and unhealthy.[74] But the Friends
aimed to triumph over this unpropitious environment and to reach boys
and young men aged from 12 to 20 who had been neglected by other
Sunday Schools with a more respectable clientele. Through a house to
house canvas they managed to recruit a large, turbulent and 'motley
throng'.[75] Eight years later, an Adult School was formally started there
but soon moved to Lady Peckett's Yard, behind the Rowntree's premises.
This was convenient for the Rowntrees who helped in its teaching but of
greater importance was the fact that it could attract students not only
from Walmgate but also from the equally impoverished area of Hungate.
In 1856 a girls' school was begun, which moved to King's Staith in 1869
where it hoped to recruit from the notorious 'red light' and criminal
district of the Water Lanes adjacent to it. In this it was successful and its
first pupils there were described as being 'very ignorant, neglected,
ragged and dirty, and do not appear to have attended any day school'.[76] In
1880 a women's school was added to it. While the primary objective of
these schools remained religious and secular instruction, there was a
growing awareness that attendance at the schools needed to be encouraged by teachers' visits to the scholars' homes. With this visitation came
an appreciation of the problems arising from a hand-to-mouth existence
and the consequent creation of a savings fund, a sick club, a benevolent
box for the distressed, and a temperance society. Later, coffee carts were
organised which were sent into the slums 'to counteract the evil influence
of indulgence in strong drink'.[77]

Beginning with the York City Mission in 1848, many religious
denominations had made organised attempts to ameliorate religious and
material deprivation in the slums. Among them was the Hungate Mission
which had started in 1861 as the Salem Mission (see Map 5). This
unsectarian Sunday School was well-situated, first in St. Saviourgate and
then in Garden Place, to reach some of York's poorest homes in Hungate.
This area had become damp, insanitary and overcrowded; it was already
suffering from industrial pollution and was later to be over-shadowed by
Leetham's huge flour mills.[78] The evangelical promoters aimed to teach
local boys knowing full well that they had been too filthy and unkempt to
be acceptable to ordinary Sunday Schools. Their first pupils were 'all of
them ragged and dirty, and some of them revoltingly so'. From its inception visits were made to boys' homes, and discovery of the demon drink
there, rapidly led to the formation of a Band of Hope 'to lead the boys to
abstain from intoxicating liquor and tobacco'. A girls' mission school was
also begun in Ogleforth, north of the Bedern in 1862. Gradually,
activities for other members of the family were promoted: Parents'
Evenings with elevating talks on parental responsibilities; Teas for the

Aged; a Young Women's Sewing Class; a Women's Temperance Society; a Mothers' Meeting; and finally, Happy Evenings for Children.[79] During the 1880s and 1890s the indefatigable superintendent of the Hungate Mission, James Harrison, visited hundreds of homes in Hungate, and faced with such appalling poverty, soon appreciated that material needs were as great as spiritual ones. He relieved 'genuine cases of necessity by timely gifts of food, fuel, clothing, and dispensary and hospital notes'. So the distribution of tracts was accompanied in needy cases by bags of coal or coke, loaves of bread, and quantities of tea and sugar. Beginning tentatively in 1880 the mission began the occasional provision of free breakfasts for the poor children of the neighbourhood.[80] During January and February 1893, for example, 4,660 free breakfasts were given to hungry children on Sundays and on alternate weekday mornings. From its inception in 1861 the mission brightened the childrens' lives by organising an annual treat each July.

Plates 12, 13 and 15 show different aspects of the children's treat of 1904. The children were attired in their best clothes and carried paper roses as they paraded through streets bedecked with flags and greenery on their way to their annual assembly point on Peasholme Green. From there the younger children were transported to the country home of the Agars at Brockfield Hall near Stockton. Plate 12 shows them during their afternoon of carnival. Plates 13 and 15 reveal the adult inhabitants of Hungate as they came out of their homes to see the children's procession go by during the middle of the day. In Plate 13 the poorer inhabitants of Dundas Street can be seen wearing their everyday working clothes, while the greater substance of the residents in the principal street of the area, Hungate, is evident in Plate 15. So too is the centrality of Charles Dixon's corner shop which for over half a century met the needs of the neighbourhood for fruit and provisions. Plate 12 also suggests that the 1904 outing was a special occasion for Hungate people: a celebration of the foundation of a branch of the York Adult School Union in Hungate in June of that year. That adults should need an opportunity to acquire basic literacy indicated the difficulty which poorer people had experienced in acquiring elementary education during childhood.

Poverty militated against the attempt to educate children not only in Sunday Schools but also in ordinary elementary schools. A cryptic, but revealing, entry in the logbook of the Bilton Street School (which served the working-class community in Layerthorpe), stated 'attendance thin at commencement of school owing to numbers of children being at the soup kitchen'.[81] Undernourished children made poor scholars or no scholars at all. In some very poor families all the money went on food and there was none to spare for school pence so that children did not even attend school.

School logbooks indicated that a significant number of children were also kept from school because they had to contribute to the family budget: girls and boys helped their parents in casual work; girls might stay at home to mind younger children while their mothers worked; and even very young children might be taken away from school to help in the gleaning after harvest. Admittedly, the prevalence in York of handicrafts and retailing, rather than factory employment, meant that full time employment for children was much less of an impediment to schooling during the mid-nineteenth century than was the case in many other northern, or midlands, towns. But in spite of this a comprehensive survey of the city revealed an extensive shortfall in attendance.

Enquiries in March 1877 by the School Attendance Committee (appointed to implement Sandon's Act of 1876), found that on average only 73 per cent of the children who had been enrolled at school actually attended. 10 years later the activities of three attendance officers had raised this figure to 76 per cent. Getting children to attend school involved both sticks and carrots. Many parents of persistent non-attenders were summoned to appear before the committee, and, if recalcitrance continued, had to appear before a magistrate. Other families were found to be in such extreme poverty that they were nominated to the poor-law guardians who then paid the school fees. The expansion of free school places which followed national legislation in 1891 improved school attendance in York from an average of 83 per cent in that year, to 85 per cent in 1900, by which time nine-tenths of the school places in York were free ones.[82]

The Effectiveness of Relief

Brothers, let us lift our voices!
Lo! our benefactors come!
Let them know each heart rejoices,
That we here have found a home!
Lift your voices!
Houseless, hopeless, had we wandered,
But we here have found a home.[83]

So warbled the poor boys of the Blue Coat School in York during 1840; their dutiful gratitude for a free education expressed in the words of a song written for them by a York citizen. This gives us an interesting insight into the deferential and grateful response which the wealthier inhabitants expected from their poorer neighbours, and which, indeed, they usually seem to have received. During the Victorian period the intimate scale of the town, its largely pre-industrial character, and its independent political temper, perpetuated a tradition of social paternalism. But even with individualistic, rather than collective, responses to the changing dimensions of the poverty problem, levels of pauperism in the city remained at a moderate level. For example in 1901 only 2.1 per cent of the city's inhabitants were relieved by the poor-law guardians compared with an average of 2.5 per cent for England and Wales.[84] In these circumstances it is understandable that an influential York guardian, Alderman Wragge, should have felt complacent about the local record for the relief of destitution when he addressed a Poor Law Conference at the city's Mansion House in October 1901

> A few years ago the poor were very badly treated, but today circumstances were entirely different, and he, for one, was very glad that the improvement had taken place. The diminution of pauperism throughout the land showed that a more considerate treatment of the poor was not operating as an incentive to pauperism. He rejoiced especially to think that the children were looked after with a careful regard to their future. . . . In the treatment of the sick poor an immense improvement had been effected.[85]

Already the social work of evangelicals in the slums of York had revealed the hollowness of such self-congratulation. Many years before the Quaker industrialist, Joseph Rowntree, had concluded that much charitable effort to improve the lot of the poor was not only useless but positively harmful.[86] Increasingly he felt that charity was only a palliative, not a solution, and by 1904 he considered that:

> Much of our philanthropic effort is directed to remedying the more superficial manifestations of weakness or evil while little thought or effort is directed to search out their underlying causes. . . . The Soup Kitchen in York never has difficulty in obtaining adequate financial aid, but an enquiry into the extent and causes of poverty would enlist little support.[87]

By this time, however, his son Seebohm Rowntree had produced his first study of the extent and causes of York poverty (see Plate 14). He had told one of his adult classes in 1894 that 'you cannot live in a town like York, with its poverty, its intemperance, its vice, without a sense of responsibility being from time to time borne in upon you'.[88] Two years later he was stimulated by Charles Booth's study *The Life and Labour of the People of London,* to wonder whether there was equal deprivation in his own city.[89] The results of his investigation exposed a huge amount of poverty whose previously unsuspected existence suggested the inadequacy of existing Victorian agencies to relieve, or remove it.

In his *Poverty: A Study of Town Life,* B. S. Rowntree found that in 1899 27.8 per cent of the population of York was living in poverty; a figure very similar to Booth's 30.7 per cent in London. Most contemporaries found Rowntree's results in York a good deal more shocking than those of Booth, since the image of York as a typical provincial town would not have indicated the presence there of deprivation to equal that of the metropolis with its well-known slums. Yet Rowntree's painstaking survey of 11,560 working-class households, containing 46,754 individuals, or two-thirds of the city's population, indicated that 9.9 per cent of York's inhabitants were living in primary poverty and a further 17.9 per cent in secondary poverty. The former were defined as those 'families whose total earnings were insufficient to obtain the minimum necessaries for the maintenance of merely physical efficiency'. Those in secondary poverty had sufficient income 'for the maintenance of merely physical efficiency were it not that some portion of it was absorbed by other expenditure, either useful or wasteful'. Rowntree found that the labouring classes in the city were seriously underfed, and that the diet given to able-bodied paupers in York Workhouse was much superior. The diet which he assumed to be necessary to achieve physical efficiency was, in fact, less generous than that laid down in workhouse dietaries.[90]

The most common causes of primary poverty were low wages, a large family, and the death of the breadwinner; less common were the illness or old age of the breadwinner, irregular employment, and unemployment. Rowntree emphasised for the first time the dynamic nature of poverty in which 'the life of a labourer is marked by five alternating periods of want and comparative plenty'. At three points in his life the labourer was liable to be in poverty: during childhood; after marriage when children were too young to earn; and during old age.[91] Rowntree's analysis made clear that the moral character of the individual was irrelevant in causing primary poverty and by implication, that the division of the poor into deserving and non-deserving had little empirical foundation. Admittedly, some of the factors that he listed as contributants to secondary poverty were connected: notably drink, betting and gambling.

Rowntree's portrait of a working-class family on the poverty line indicated the superhuman discipline that was imposed on them:

> A family living upon the scale allowed for in this estimate must never spend a penny on railway fare or omnibus. They must never go into the country unless they walk. They must never purchase a halfpenny newspaper or spend a penny to buy a ticket for a popular concert. They must write no letters to absent children, for they cannot afford to pay the postage. They must never contribute anything to their church or chapel, or give any help to a neighbour which costs them money. They cannot save, nor can they join sick

club or Trade Union, because they cannot pay the necessary sub-
scriptions. The children must have no pocket money for dolls,
marbles or sweets. The father must smoke no tobacco, and must
drink no beer. The mother must never buy any pretty clothes for
herself or for her children. . . . Should a child fall ill, it must be
attended by the parish doctor; should it die, it must be buried by the
parish. Finally, the wage-earner must never be absent from his work
for a single day.[92]

In these circumstances it was hardly surprising that careless or improvi-
dent housekeeping – which was alleged to be a contributant of secondary
poverty – should occur. Indeed, the environment of the poorest inhabitants of York facilitated this descent into poverty (or worse), as the city's
Medical Officer of Health acknowledged in 1908 during an enquiry into
the slum conditions of Hungate: 'dark, dilapidated, and over-crowded
dwellings destroy "house pride," and engender the "slum habit of life,"
also alcoholism, indifference, indecency, immorality and crime'.[93]

By this time these slums existed in a city with a new-found prosperity
from the cocoa, confectionery, and flour-milling industries, and the rail
carriage works. But growth in the number of inhabitants during the
Victorian period had led to a wider geographical separation of the classes
and a weakened sense of local community. New-style evangelical missions and an expansion of schooling had been needed to combat faceless
slum-poverty. Nevertheless, the paternalistic tradition of an ancient
cathedral city had continued to inform the distribution of abundant
charity, while in the administration of poor relief the dominance of
personality over principle had blunted the local impact of a collectivist,
national poor law. Rowntree's findings exposed the typical inadequacy of
these individualistic policies of social welfare in failing to concern themselves with the fundamental causes of poverty. The Minority Report of
the Royal Commission on the Poor Laws of 1905-9 proposed that the role
of the poor law as a comprehensive agency for the relief of destitution
should be replaced by more efficient specialist agencies. The era of the
poor-law guardians had in fact ended in 1930 before Rowntree's second
survey of York poverty. In this investigation of 1936 only 3.6 per cent of
the population were in primary poverty compared to 9.9 per cent in 1899.
The major reasons for this reduction were improved wages and the
benefits available from expanded collectivist action in the form of unemployment benefit, health insurance, and pensions for widows and old
people. Although much had now been achieved by focusing on preven-
tive rather than palliative measures, much still remained to be done:
deprivation remained as a result of unemployment and an ageing population. But the slum environment which had blighted so many lives was

almost gone; whereas many of the slum areas described in 1899 still existed in 1930, a vigorous clearance programme had all but eliminated them by 1936-38.[94]

Footnotes

1. J. Bigland, *A Topographical and Historical Description of Yorkshire*, 1813, pp. 239-242.
2. P. M. Tillott (ed.), *The Victoria History of the Counties of England: A History of Yorkshire, the City of York*, Oxford, 1961, p. 254. (Subsequently referred to as *VCH.)*
3. Board of Health Report quoted by T. Laycock in *Report to Health of Towns Commission on the State of York*, 1844, p. 5.
4. Ibid., pp. 4, 8, 13; *VCH* pp. 281, 464; J. Smith, *Report to the General Board of Health on the City of York*, London, 1850, p. 37.
5. Laycock, *Report,* p. 21.
6. J. Smith, *Report,* p. 7.
7. Ibid, pp. 9-10.
8. B. S. Rowntree, *Poverty: A Study of Town Life,* third ed., London, 1908, pp. 216, 236. See Chapter VII.
9. *VCH,* pp. 461, 465, 466; *Reports of York Medical Officer of Health* (1900) and (1901); Rowntree, *Poverty,* pp. 196, 222, 225; E. M. Smith. *Report on the Sanitary Conditions of the Hungate District,* York, 1908, p. 5.
10. *VCH,* p. 254. For further discussion of population growth see Chapter V above.
11. Rowntree, *Poverty,* p. 204.
12. *Memoirs of S. Tuke* 2 vols., London, 1860, vol. 2, p. 241.
13. *VCH,* pp. 227, 257, 266.
14. R. G. Paveley, 'The Board of Guardians of the York Poor Law Union, 1837-1849' (Dissertation for the Certificate of Education, University of Leeds), p. 52.
15. Ibid.
16. *York Herald,* 20 May 1837.
17. Ibid.
18. *York Herald,* 27 May 1837.
19. *York Herald,* 7 October 1837.
20. *York Herald,* 27 May 1837; N. C. Edsall, *The Anti-Poor Law Movement, 1833-44*, Manchester, 1971, pp. 77-89.
21. *York Herald,* 20 May 1837.
22. Quoted in A. J. Peacock, 'York in the Age of Reform' (University of York D. Phil. thesis, 1973), p. 349.
23. A. Digby, *Pauper Palaces*, London, 1978, p. 127.
24. Edsall, *Anti-Poor Law,* pp. 77-8; A. Armstrong, *Stability and Change in an English County Town. A Social Study of York 1801-51*, Cambridge, 1974, p. 49.
25. R. P. Hastings 'Poverty and the Treatment of Poverty in the North Riding of Yorkshire c. 1780-1847' (University of York D. Phil. thesis, 1977), vol. 2, p. 216.

[26] *Memoirs*, vol. 2, p. 242.
[27] *Twenty-Seventh Report of Local Government Board 1897-8* (quarto edition), p. 129 (subsequently referred to as LGB).
[28] *Thirty-Second Report of LGB 1902-3*, p. 136.
[29] B. S. Rowntree and B. Lasker, *Unemployment. A Social Study*, London, 1911, pp. 238-9.
[30] A. C. Kay and H. V. Toynbee, *Report to the Royal Commission on the Poor Laws. Endowed and Voluntary Charities in certain Places and the Administrative Relations of Charity and the Poor Law*, Cd. 4593, London, 1909, p. 18.
[31] Ibid, p. 120.
[32] 72 per cent of female employment in York was in domestic service in 1841. (Armstrong, *Stability and Change*, p. 28.)
[33] *VCH*, p. 436.
[34] *Report of a Committee of the Manchester Statistical Society on the State of Education in the City of York in 1836-7*, London, 1837, pp. 5-6.
[35] Minutes of the British Girls' School Managers (1812-22), 27 April 1814, Accession 118/254, York Archives. (These archives are subsequently referred to as YA.)
[36] Ibid, 1 May 1820.
[37] Walmgate Girls' Visitors' Book (1843-50), 17 June 1844, 31 July 1844. Accession BG/YK, YA. This was later known as St. Margaret's School.
[38] E. Benson, 'A History of Education in York 1780-1902' (University of London Ph.D. thesis, 1932), pp. 200-203.
[39] Minutes of the British Girls' School Managers (1845-55), 30 November 1852; Accession 118/260, YA.
[40] York School Attendance Sub-Committee Minute Book (1876-87), 2 February 1877, 23 April 1877, 2 January 1879; Accession BG/YK, YA.
[41] Ibid., 9 November 1881.
[42] York Board of Guardians Minutes (1837-9), 7 September 1837; Accession 2/YL/PL/1, YA.
[43] *Memoirs of S. Tuke*, vol. 2, p. 242; York Board of Guardians Minutes, 2 November 1837, Accession 2/YL/PL/1, YA.
[44] Quoted in Pavely 'York Poor Law Union', p. 31.
[45] Ibid, pp. 38, 40, 51.
[46] R. P. Hastings, 'Treatment of Poverty', vol. 2, pp. 197-8; N. D. Hopkin, 'The Old and New Poor Law in East Yorkshire c. 1760-1850' (University of Leeds M.Phil. thesis, 1968), pp. 90-1, 100-102, 245.
[47] M. E. Rose 'Poor Law Administration in the W. Riding of Yorkshire 1820-1855' (University of Oxford D.Phil. thesis, 1965), pp. 320, 373.
[48] *VCH*, pp. 280-1.
[49] F. E. Beechey, 'The Irish in York 1840-1875' (University of York D.Phil. thesis, 1976), p. 107.
[50] Ibid, pp. 3, 26, 70.
[51] J. Smith, *Report*, p. 9.
[52] Laycock, *Report*, p. 44.
[53] Beechey, 'Irish in York', p. 282.
[54] *VCH*, p. 279.

[55] *Nineteenth Report of LGB 1889-90*, p. 139; Rowntree, *Poverty*, p. 435.

[56] *Thirty-second Report of LGB 1902-3*, pp. 134-5.

[57] The analysis of the social composition of pauperism within the city area of the York Union is based on a very limited analysis of the vast quantities of relief records in York Archives. This investigation was necessary because published figures on pauperism in the York Union had only a limited relevance to the town, as it was aggregated with that of the surrounding country area included in the union. Principal sources consulted on urban pauperism were the Application and Report Books of the Relieving Officers, Outdoor Relief Lists, Weekly Returns to the Poor Law Inspector, Relief Order Books, and Orders for Admission to the Workhouse. While it was possible to isolate figures for the city for outdoor pauperism and for applications to the workhouse, those for workhouse inmates refer to the entire union.

[58] *Twenty-first Report of LGB 1891-2*, p. 170.

[59] York Board of Guardians Minutes 1898-1900, Accession 2/YL/PL/30, YA.

[60] *Twenty Fourth Report LGB 1894-5* p. 57; *Twenty-Eighth Report LGB 1898-9*, p. 167.

[61] *Twenty Ninth Report LGB 1899-1900*, p. 137; Rowntree, *Poverty*, p. 427.

[62] Ibid, p. 428.

[63] For example, York Board of Guardians Minutes, 22 December 1898, 1 June 1899, 31 August 1899; Accession 2/YL/PL/30, YA.

[64] Rowntree, *Poverty*, p. 428.

[65] Rowntree and Lasker, *Unemployment*, p. 252.

[66] Ibid, p. 255.

[67] Rowntree, *Poverty*, p. 409; Kay and Toynbee, *Charities*, p. 134.

[68] Ibid, pp. 134-5; Female Friendly Society Sick Pay (1892-1925); Accession 50/40, YA.

[69] Rowntree, *Poverty*, p. 412; Kay and Toynbee, *Charities*, pp. 136-7.

[70] Ibid, pp. 15, 141.

[71] Hodgson's Charity, 2 vols. 1891-1919, Accession 2/YL/PL/87, YA.

[72] Kay and Toynbee, *Charities*, pp. 130-1, 138; York Charities Register Committee Book; Accession 2/YL/PL/88, YA.

[73] Kay and Toynbee, *Charities*, pp. 127-9.

[74] Laycock, *Report*, p. 44.

[75] J. S. Rowntree, 'History of York Friends' Sabbath School, 1856'; Accession 118/246, YA.

[76] Thirteenth Report of Girls' Sabbath School, Accession 118/10, YA.

[77] Annual Report of York Adult Schools, Accession 118/12, YA. See Chapter VIII.

[78] Laycock, *Report*, pp. 42-3. One of Leetham's mills was burned down in 1931.

[79] Hungate Mission Schools Minute Books, 5 vols., Accession Y268, YA.

[80] Thirty-Eighth Report of Hungate Mission, 1899, Y268.

[81] Bilton Street School Logbook (1863-1902), 5 January 1880, Accession 5/YK 2, YA.

[82] School Attendance Sub Committee Minute Books, 1876-87, BG/YK, YA; Benson, 'History of Education' p. 399.

[83] Quoted in Benson 'History of Education', p. 209.

[84] Rowntree, *Poverty*, p. 425.
[85] *Reports of the Poor Law District Conferences held during 1901-2*, London, 1902, p. 348.
[86] A. Vernon, *A Quaker Business Man. The Life of Joseph Rowntree*, London, 1958, p. 64.
[87] Ibid, p. 154.
[88] A. Briggs, *Social Thought and Social Action. A Study of the Work of Seebohm Rowntree, 1871-1954*, London, 1961, p. 13.
[89] Ibid, p. 17.
[90] Rowntree, *Poverty*, pp. 37, 131, 304-6, 351, 353, 355. See Chapter VII for further discussion of twentieth-century poverty in York.
[91] Rowntree, *Poverty*, pp. 131, 154, 169-71, 176.
[92] Ibid, pp. 167-8.
[93] E. M. Smith, *Report on Hungate*, p. 9.
[94] B. S. Rowntree, *Poverty and Progress, A Second Social Survey of York*, London, 1941, pp. 108, 110, 116-7, 252.

The Rowntree Surveys:
Poverty in York since 1899

by

Stephen Jenkins and Alan Maynard

FOUR DETAILED SURVEYS of the nature and extent of poverty in York have been undertaken since 1899. The first three surveys were carried out by Seebohm Rowntree (Plate 14) in 1899, 1936 and 1950 (Rowntree, 1901; Rowntree, 1941; Rowntree and Lavers, 1951). The fourth survey, which was concerned primarily with the way in which successive generations of York's low income families maintained or changed their economic status, was carried out in the period 1975-78 (Atkinson, Maynard and Trinder, 1980).

The purpose of this chapter is to survey and comment on the methods and results of these surveys. The first section is concerned with the aims, methods and findings of the three Rowntree surveys. The second presents a critique of these surveys: examining their organisation, the representativeness of York and the sensitivity of the results to the way in which poverty is defined. In the third section the aims, methods and some preliminary results of the most recent survey are set out.[1]

The Rowntree Surveys 1899, 1936 and 1950

The surveys which Rowntree organised were ambitious and path-breaking attempts to study the condition of the wage-earning classes in York. The first was undertaken at a time when methods of social investigation were in their infancy, and although his techniques might be faulted in some respects, if judged against the standards of modern survey procedures, the 1899 study was, for its time, a major advance. Both the first and second surveys contributed enormously to contemporary knowledge of the condition of the working class in Britain; and they had a significant effect on Lloyd George and Beveridge, and thus on social policy and the development of the welfare state.

The 1899 Survey

The object of Rowntree's first survey was to investigate in detail 'the conditions which govern the life of the working classes in provincial towns, and especially the problem of poverty' (Rowntree, 1901, p. vii). Inspired by the work of Charles Booth (1899) in London, and faced by the inadequacy of poor law and charitable data sources, both central and local, Rowntree decided to embark on an extensive survey of the working class population of York. By using this method of data collection he hoped to answer the following questions:

> What was the true measure of poverty in the city, both in extent and depth? How much of it was due to insufficiency of income and how much to improvidence? How many families were sunk in poverty so acute that their members suffered from a chronic insufficiency of food and clothing? If physical deterioration, combined with a high death rate, ensued, was it possible to estimate such results with appropriate accuracy? (Rowntree, 1901, p. xviii).

The extent of the survey which Rowntree undertook in order to answer these questions was impressively large. He sought to interview by house-to-house surveys the entire working-class population of York, identified as families with no domestic servants. This working-class sample was located by using local knowledge of the city, and consisted of 46,754 individuals in 11,560 families (Rowntree, 1901, p. 26), about 61 per cent of York's 1899 population of 75,182.

Some information was acquired from voluntary workers, clergymen, district visitors and others, but it seems that the bulk of the survey data was collected by one (un-named) investigator, largely in the period March to September 1899. No questionnaire returns from the 1899 survey appear to have survived, and thus it is impossible to comment on the quality of the data, which were collected in a very short period of time.

However, Rowntree claimed to have verified the results with his local experts who had advised on the location of the survey, and concluded that he was 'satisfied that the information obtained is substantially correct' (Rowntree, 1901, p. 15).

Where possible, Rowntree's investigator obtained details of the respondents' occupation and earnings. When earnings data were not acquired by interview, Rowntree estimated the earnings of skilled workers by assuming they were paid the local average for the particular trade. Earnings data for unskilled workers were obtained from employers, and Rowntree concluded that 'working on these lines, the earnings of every wage earner have either been attained or carefully estimated' (Rowntree, 1901, p. 27).

In determining the level of poverty, Rowntree wished to use a scientific measure of absolute poverty. Starting from nutritional science, he established a diet which would ensure physical efficiency, and then costed this diet in the local market place, assuming that the low-income people were efficient shoppers who were able to make their purchases at the average local cost (Rowntree, 1901, pp. 103-104). To these estimates of nutritional requirements, he added estimates of the necessary minimum expenditures on rent and household sundries such as clothing, light and fuel. These calculations gave absolute poverty line incomes for various family sizes (e.g. 21s 8d per week (£1.08) for a family of two adults and three children), and enabled Rowntree to determine the number of families with incomes below the relevant poverty line in York in 1899.

Rowntree also distinguished between primary and secondary poverty. The former was based simply on the poverty lines for different family sizes, and in 1899 9.9 per cent of the total population of the city (15.5 per cent of the working class) were shown to be in poverty. Furthermore, 21.5 per cent of the population of York were living on wages below, or not more than 6s (30p) above, the poverty line.

Rowntree's definition of secondary poverty was more subjective, but was perceptive. Some families had sufficient income to keep them above the poverty line and physically (nutritionally) efficient, but chose to spend it on 'drink, gambling and other wasteful expenditure' (Rowntree, 1901, p. 115). Such 'inefficient' behaviour could only be identified imprecisely; no detailed data on expenditure patterns were obtained by the investigator. However, Rowntree felt confident enough to conclude that 17.9 per cent of the population were living in secondary poverty, and thus that 27 per cent of the total population (43.4 per cent of the working class) were living in either primary or secondary poverty (Rowntree, 1901, p. 117).

From his survey data Rowntree identified six principal determinants of poverty. By far the most significant causes were low wages (52.0 per cent of those in primary poverty) and large family sizes, i.e. four or more children (22.2 per cent). Rowntree showed that the wages paid for unskilled labour in York were 'insufficient to provide food, shelter and clothing at an adequate level to maintain a family of moderate size in a state of bare physical efficiency' (Rowntree, 1901, p. 133). Another significant cause, accounting for 15.6 per cent of those in primary poverty, was the death of the chief wage earner. The remaining causes were illness or old age of the chief wage earner (5.1 per cent), the unemployment of the chief wage earner (2.3 per cent), and irregularity of work (2.8 per cent).

Whilst Rowntree did not elaborate this analysis and identify the industries in which these low-wage, unskilled, workers were employed, he did describe their life cycle in detail, noting that a labourer was in poverty (and therefore underfed) in childhood; in the early prime of life, when his income might be higher but his dependents numerous; and in old age, when his income would be low (Rowntree, 1901, pp. 136-7). Thus any cross-section survey of poverty would identify only those currently in poverty, and fail to detect those who were potentially poor, even if they were comparatively well-off at the time of the survey.

The care and detail of Rowntree's pioneering study, and the insights into the condition of the working class at the turn of the century derived from his meticulous analysis, make his 1899 survey a major landmark in the social history of Britain.

The 1936 Survey

The second survey was undertaken to identify the changes in the extent and causes of poverty in York since 1899. The sample was selected as all working-class families in the city whose chief wage-earner was receiving no more than £250 per year, and an attempt was made to interview all such families. They were located by sending investigators into 'all the streets where such people were likely to live' (Rowntree, 1941, p. 11), to interview all working-class families in those areas. This resulted in the acquisition of information for 16,362 families, living in 15,372 households, and consisting of 55,206 individuals. This was 61.5 per cent of York's 1936 population (Rowntree, 1941, pp. 11 and 13). It is remarkable that the sample sizes in 1899 and 1936, as a percentage of the city's population, were almost identical.

In this survey Rowntree used a team of investigators, the size of which is not clear from his book; and these assistants were instructed not to attempt to acquire income data. Most of the respondents were women, and Rowntree regarded them as unlikely to be accurate sources of income data:

> frequently the woman only knows what money her husband gives her, and not how much he actually receives. And even if those interviewed knew the wages the occupied person or persons were receiving, it is doubtful whether reliable information would have been given to the investigators (Rowntree, 1941, p. 25).

Because of these problems, Rowntree went directly to the employers for wages information. For 60 per cent of the sample, direct wage information was obtained in this way. For the remainder, estimates of wages were made on the basis of the normal earnings of the people in the relevant trades, with the required information being obtained from local experts and employers.

The poverty line was defined in a manner similar to that in the preceding study, but all discussion of secondary poverty was removed. Drawing on work in another of his books (Rowntree, 1937), and contemporary work on nutrition, Rowntree estimated the cost of the diet necessary to ensure physical efficiency, with added elements for housing, clothing, heating and lighting. As he emphasised, this poverty line, like that used in 1899, was not generous: 'the standards adopted throughout this book err on the side of stringency rather than extravagance' (Rowntree, 1941, p. 29). Poverty lines for various families were calculated using this method, e.g. for a family with two adults and three children it was 43s 6d per week (£2.18).

The results of the survey showed that 31.1 per cent of York's working-class, or 17.8 per cent of the total population, were living in poverty. The three main causes of poverty in 1936 were low wages (32.8 per cent), unemployment (28.6 per cent), and old age (14.7 per cent). Other causes – casual work (9.5 per cent), death of husband (7.8 per cent), illness (4.1 per cent) and miscellaneous (2.5 per cent) – were small in comparison to those three factors. As Rowntree noted, 1936 was a year of high unemployment compared with 1899, and this influenced the nature of the determinants of poverty.

Although the 1936 poverty standard was frugal, it was more generous than that used in 1899. Rowntree showed that if the stringent 1899 standard were expressed in 1936 prices, then the level of working class poverty had declined: from 15.46 per cent in 1899 to 6.8 per cent in 1936; 'the proportion of the working class population living in abject poverty had been reduced by more than one half' (Rowntree, 1941, p. 451).

The 1950 Survey

The aim of the third Rowntree survey (Rowntree and Lavers, 1951) was to examine the effects of the development of the welfare state on the character and extent of poverty in York. This was the least satisfactory of the three surveys, in terms of both the design and conduct of the data collection, and its analysis. Various aspects were questioned by a number of people, including the Cambridge economist, A. C. Pigou, and Douglas Jay. These criticisms led the authors to prepare a fourth social survey but this was never carried out, and Rowntree died in 1954.

In a supplementary chapter of his 1941 book Rowntree had examined 'the reliability of social statistics based on the sampling method' (Rowntree, 1941, pp. 478-492), and found that sampling gave accurate results. As a consequence, the 1950 survey was based on a one in nine sample of the working-class population of York, defined as those families whose chief wage-earner received less than £550 per year. As in the previous surveys local knowledge was used to select the areas in which low income families might reside. 'We took a list of all the streets in York, and a man who has lived in the city for more than half a century, who knows the city intimately, and has also a wide knowledge of, and sympathy with our work, marked on our list every street where working class families live' (Rowntree and Lavers, 1951, p. 2). The method of respondent location seems to have been to go to the ninth house in each street in a designated working-class area and, if the house yielded no return, to select a neighbouring dwelling as a substitute. The survey was carried out by a team of interviewers during July-September 1950.

A new poverty line was calculated, with the food cost element once again based on contemporary nutritional knowledge; with quite stringent allowances for housing, clothing, heating, lighting and personal sundries. The poverty line income for a family of two adults and three children was calculated to be £5 0s 2d, per week. The survey showed that the proportion below the poverty line in 1950 was much smaller than in 1936: 2.8 per cent of the working class, or 1.7 per cent of the total population of York. The main causes of poverty in 1950 were old age (68.1 per cent of the total), sickness (21.3 per cent), death of the chief wage-earner (6.3 per cent), a large number of children (3.2 per cent), and low wages (1.1 per cent). These calculations were based on a different poverty standard from that used in 1936, and so comparisons in levels and causes of poverty in each period are not unambiguous, though this did not prevent the 1951 authors from making them.

A Critique of the three Rowntree Surveys

There are many aspects of the work of Rowntree and his co-workers which deserve careful appraisal. However in this chapter we intend to deal with only three: the organisation of the surveys, the representativeness of York, and the sensitivity of the results to the chosen definition of poverty. Our discussion of Rowntree's work differs from that of other critics (e.g. Political and Economic Planning, 1952) in that we use previously unavailable data from the archives of the Joseph Rowntree Memorial Trust, and interviews with surviving assistants of Rowntree.

The Organisation of the Surveys

The selection of the sample and the administration of the surveys is a matter of some importance, to which relatively little attention is paid in the three books. The samples were selected in relation to the working class only, and no attempt was made to sample the whole population of York: in terms of the 1950 survey, covering households where the chief wage earner received less than £550 per annum, perhaps 10-15 per cent of the population were not sampled. Furthermore, the procedure for identifying the working class families of York relied heavily on local knowledge, and it is possible that some were omitted. To the extent that this occurred, the results derived from the surveys will be subject to an additional margin of error.

In 1899 and 1936 Rowntree sought to survey the working-class population in its entirety. According to Dennis Chapman, who was Rowntree's personal assistant in 1936, Rowntree was a very reluctant convert to sample survey techniques as used by Bowley. Chapman asserts that Rowntree's 1936 supplementary chapter was aimed at discrediting the sampling technique, and that Rowntree was surprised when the sample results coincided with those obtained for the whole (working-class) population. This, plus subsequent argument with Mark Abrams, appears to have led ultimately to Rowntree's conversion to sampling techniques.

According to Chapman's notes in the archives of the Joseph Rowntree Memorial Trust in York, Rowntree was not enthusiastic about carrying out the 1936 survey. Chapman also asserts that Rowntree was reluctant to use modern mechanical devices to carry out the numerical calculations. Despite this, the analysis of the survey data was completed promptly, but there was a delay of five years between the completion of the survey and publication of the results in 1941. The book on the 1936 survey is clearly written and shows considerable insight; Chapman claims that it may have been partly written by one of Rowntree's assistants, F. D. Stewart (Rowntree Trust archive material, 1955; correspondence, 1980).

By 1950, Rowntree was an old man (aged 80 years) and resident in Hertfordshire, 170 miles south of York. His role in the third survey was apparently limited; and his assistant, Lavers, an ex-naval officer with little experience in social survey work, was the prime force behind the initiation of this survey. His exact role in the work is, however, not clear. It appears that the principal local organiser was Tim Brooke, an undergraduate student of history at Oxford, with no experience of survey work. Brooke met Lavers when they were both politically active in Hertfordshire in early 1950, and he was hired after a briefing from Rowntree and Lavers. The latter, according to Brooke, had little knowledge of York.

The principal author of the report on the 1950 survey was probably Lavers, judging from handwriting similarities in the extant 1950 survey material. The book suggests that Lavers' role in the survey was substantial. Brooke, however, asserts that he was sent to York to organise and execute the survey. He hired a team of interviewers, largely his friends from schooldays at Nunthorpe Grammar School. The identification of working class areas was not easy, as the city had changed considerably since 1936, and despite the fact that Brooke was a native of York, he was relatively unfamiliar with these alterations. Brooke filtered the survey returns, discarding an ex-colonel and a magistrate who were inadvertently interviewed, before passing them on to Lavers. Brooke indicates that Lavers visited York infrequently (about 3 times) during the interview period; and that each time he stayed at the Royal Station Hotel, and did not get involved in the actual survey work (Interview with T. Brooke, 1980).

Lavers's checking of the data seems to have been limited, though he claimed to have revisited households to verify information, and found 'no cases in which they furnished inadequate or incorrect information' (Rowntree and Lavers, 1951, p. 2). The extant schedules, which we used in our fourth survey (1975-78), exhibit errors with regard to names, addresses and ages. There are also errors in the occupations, e.g. one Whitehall Department, when asked for earnings data on one respondent, supplied this information and informed Rowntree: 'I do not know how Mr. X's occupation came to be described as Secret Service Work. He has been identified as a packer in the Department's local store'.

In the book it is claimed that 95 per cent of the 1950 earnings data were collected directly from employers. Our analysis of extant records indicates that this was not so. From the surviving returns it is clear that estimation, employer refusals, and incorrect information about the place of work, resulted in about 14 per cent of chief earners having no wages data supplied by employers. These problems are analysed in greater detail elsewhere (Atkinson, Maynard, and Trinder, 1980), but it seems fair to conclude that the third study claimed more than it delivered.

The acquisition of wages data directly from employers alienated local trade unions and individual respondents, most of whom were not consulted about the release to Rowntree of information about their wages. This reaction was one of the the factors which made it impossible for Rowntree and Lavers to carry out a planned fourth survey (see p. 193, above) in 1953-54 (Rowntree archives, University of York).

Inevitably, the organisation of the surveys was not without defects. We know relatively little about the 1899 survey as, apart from the book, there are no surviving records of this study. The information in the extant records about the 1936 and 1950 surveys discloses attitudes and organisational problems which are not evident in the Rowntree books; and which are not examined elsewhere; for example, Briggs (1961) presents little analysis of the 1950 survey. The conflicting evidence about these surveys will be analysed at greater length in a subsequent paper by the present authors.

The Representativeness of York

In the introduction to his first survey, Rowntree (1901, p. viii) said that he had satisfied himself:

> that the conditions of life obtaining in my native city of York were not exceptional, and that they might be taken as fairly representative of the conditions existing in many, if not most, of our provincial towns . . .

For the second survey (1941, p. 10) he made a slightly more precise claim:

> On the whole, I think, we may safely assume that from the standpoint of the earnings of the workers, York holds a position not far from the median, among the towns of Great Britain. If, on the one hand, there is no important industry employing a large number of highly skilled and highly paid workers, on the other hand there are no large industries (though unfortunately there are isolated small businesses) where wages are exceptionally low.

This statement was quoted in 1950 with the claim that it 'still holds true' (1951, p. 6), but no evidence was offered to support this contention.

The estimates given by Charles Feinstein (see Tables 8 and 9, Chapter V, above) suggest that in 1899 average earnings of adult men in York were close to those in the country as a whole, and that the range of earnings below the average was also typical. Was York still a representative town in 1950? We have made a detailed analysis of this question, and find that in a number of ways York's socio-economic profile differed from that in the rest of the country. The first point to consider is the level and distribution of earnings. Although national earnings data for 1950 are poor, and comparisons are difficult, there are reasons to believe that the average level of earnings in York at that time was lower than that for the whole country; and that the distribution was more compressed. In other words, there was a higher proportion of workers in York with wages close to the average, and a lower proportion at either of the extremes. Secondly, the relative stability of employment in the two major industries (confectionery and the railways) has generally resulted in unemployment rates in York below those for England and Wales; and this was true in 1950, when the respective rates were 0.8 per cent and 1.5 per cent. Thirdly, York has fewer old people; in the census of 1951 the population aged 65 and over was 10.3 per cent in York compared with 11 per cent for England and Wales. Fourthly, there were some differences in the structure of employment. Agriculture, where average earnings are significantly below average, was under-represented in York, and so too was manufacturing; while transport and other services were over-represented (see also p. 138 in Chapter V, above). Finally, the populations of York and of England and Wales in 1951 can be analysed and compared in terms of the Registrar-General's classification of social class. It is evident from this comparison that there were proportionately many more workers in York in unskilled occupations, but also more skilled workers; and that intermediate occupations (e.g. teachers) and semi-skilled workers were under-represented.

Some of these five characteristics will tend to increase the relative extent of poverty in York; others (for example, lower unemployment, fewer old people and a smaller agricultural sector) will tend to reduce it. On balance, it seems clear, from the results of the comparison made below (p. 199), that the dominant factor was the first of those considered – the relatively low level of average earnings in York in the early 1950s – and that this may be responsible for a significantly higher degree of poverty than in the rest of England and Wales.

This conclusion might not apply in other periods; and it is, of course, improbable that any one town will provide an exact microcosm of the combined demographic, social and economic characteristics of the whole country. In very broad terms York may have been a representative town, but it is necessary to exercise considerable care before conclusions about the form and extent of poverty drawn from a study of York can safely be assumed to apply to the rest of the country.[2]

An Alternative Definition of Poverty

In his first survey Rowntree attempted to establish an objective measure of poverty; and this remained the basis for the two later studies, though with considerable refinement of the measure in 1936. As real incomes rise, however, the concept of *absolute* poverty (minimum requirements for food, fuel, clothing, etc.) becomes increasingly difficult to apply, and modern scholars have preferred to take some measure of *relative* poverty as the basis for their studies. One widely-used example of such a measure is the scale specified periodically by the government after 1948 for National Assistance (now called Supplementary Benefit). On the basis of this definition of poverty, families are considered to be living below the 'poverty line' if their incomes are less than those they would receive in National Assistance benefits. However, this represents a minimum standard, and there are circumstances in which discretionary payments in excess of the basic scale may be made to cover special expenditure (e.g. extra fuel or clothing). For this reason some authors have adopted as their poverty criterion the National Assistance scale plus (an arbitrary) 40 per cent, and we also use this criterion below.

In this section we examine the effect of reworking the results of Rowntree's third survey with a different definition of poverty: the 1950 National Assistance standard. This enables us to compare the York estimates with those made for England and Wales in 1953/54 using a similar definition.

The size of the 1950 survey was 2,011, but unfortunately only 1,363 of the interview schedules have survived. These surviving schedules seem to be reasonably representative of the survey characteristics described in Rowntree and Lavers (1950). We have taken the data on these schedules, and made an assessment of the net resources of the family (income minus housing costs), in relation to the relevant 1950 National Assistance scale. Whilst these calculations have followed National Assistance procedures as closely as possible, strict adherence to their methods has not been possible in all cases because of inadequate data.

The calculation of income is based on earnings (net of income tax and National Insurance contributions), plus State income benefits (including National Assistance), plus other income (e.g. occupational pensions), plus the contribution from lodgers. We use only personal tax allowances, and as a consequence net (post-tax) income may be understated, but low income families are unlikely to be affected, the tax threshold then being much higher than it is today. Inevitably the assessment is only approximate. No account is taken of capital. We have not allowed for provisions in the regulations disregarding certain types of income for assessment purposes. Also, no account has been taken of wage stop, under which National Assistance payments to the unemployed could not exceed previous employment income. On balance, we feel that our methods of assessment tend to under-state entitlement to National Assistance benefits.

On the basis of these assumptions we found 14.4 per cent of working class families, or 9.7 per cent of the working-class population, living below the National Assistance standard in 1950. According to Rowntree and Lavers the working-class population of York accounted for 60 per cent of the total population. If we multiply the preceding percentages by 0.6 (thus assuming that none of the middle and upper class families were below the poverty line), we find that 8.6 per cent of all families, and 5.8 per cent of all individuals, lived below the National Assistance standard in York in 1950.

Rowntree's own assessment of poverty in York (1.7 per cent of the population) was much lower. There are several reasons for this. Whilst the Rowntree poverty line was higher than the corresponding National Assistance scale by some 30 to 40 per cent, he tended to include some income in kind (e.g. home-grown vegetables and school meals and milk), and to treat non-dependent family members in a manner closer to a household means test than the National Assistance (family) treatment. These differences are discussed at length elsewhere (Atkinson, Corlyon et al., 1980), and result in an under-estimate (compared to the National Assistance method) of the level of poverty.

Consequently, it is not surprising that Abel-Smith and Townsend (1965) using 1953/54 data for the whole country found evidence of the existence of a substantial degree of poverty. Their results showed 2.1 per cent of the population of England and Wales below National Assistance scales (a standard lower than Rowntrees). It thus appears from this re-analysis of Rowntree's 1950 data that when comparable definitions are adopted, poverty in York in 1950 (5.8 per cent) was much higher than that nationally in 1953/54 (2.1 per cent).

We may also note that when the more generous standard of National Assistance scales plus 40 per cent (cf. p. 198, above) is used, our re-estimated figure for the proportion of York's population in poverty rises to 10.1 per cent.

This brief discussion of an alternative way in which the same set of data can be analysed indicates the degree to which the proportion of the population living in 'poverty' is sensitive to the definition of poverty used. The methods used by Rowntree and Lavers in 1950 relate closely to their earlier work, but the link with the analysis of poverty since 1965 (after Abel-Smith and Townsend) is not apparent without careful re-working of their data. When this is done it can be seen that the poverty 'discovered' in postwar British society by Abel-Smith and Townsend existed in York in 1950 to perhaps a greater degree.

The Fourth Social Survey, 1975-78

The aim of the fourth social survey was radically different from those of its predecessors; it was specially designed to ascertain the current economic position of the descendents of those who were surveyed by Rowntree in 1950. It will present an analysis of the way in which incomes and subjection to poverty change across generations, not of the degree of poverty at a single point in time. It might thus be seen as a natural development arising from the awareness of the life-cycle aspects of poverty demonstrated by Rowntree in 1899, although he did not analyse the inter-generational aspects of the problem.

The investigators found 1,363 schedules surviving (out of 2,011) from the 1950 interviews. After careful consideration they decided that although these data were imperfect, they would provide the best basis available to conduct an examination of income changes across generations. The study involved tracing and interviewing the sons and daughters of the 1950 respondents in order to provide data which could be compared with those obtained from the parents by Rowntree and Lavers in 1950. The 1975-78 survey was not carried out in York alone as the three Rowntree surveys had been because a significant proportion of the children of the 1950 families were by then living outside York.

The first problem to be faced was tracing the 1950 parents at the time of our new survey, and through them, their children. We used public sources, street directories and voting registers; and after two mailings we had acquired the addresses of children for 500 of the 1,363 original families. A further 111 parents had no children, and 37 refused to assist us. In the second stage of the tracing process we sampled (10 per cent) three groups: those who had not replied to the first mailing; those who gave an incomplete response to the first mailing; and those whose location was initially not known, for whom a special search was made (in case this 'missing' group had exceptional characteristics). In the end we obtained addresses for children of 826 of the 1950 parents (60.6 per cent). A further 16 per cent had no children, 4 per cent were unwilling to assist us and just under 20 per cent of the parents could not be traced. Of those children traced we interviewed 1,292, and for the remainder (because of resource constraints) we carried out a ten per cent sample. Thus the total number of interviews on sons and daughters was 1,360, or 2,242 when the sample is grossed up. For 920 (1,433 grossed up) of these we had complete income data.

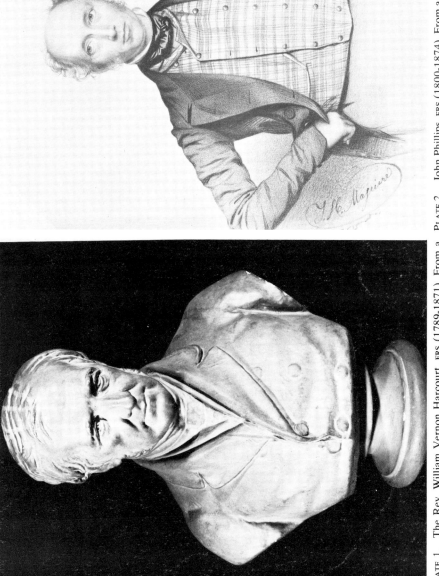

PLATE 1. The Rev. William Vernon Harcourt, FRS (1789-1871). From a bust by Matthew Noble c.1871. Harcourt was one of the principal founders of the Yorkshire Philosophical Society and of the British Association for the Advancement of Science.

PLATE 2. John Phillips, FRS (1800-1874). From a lithograph by T. H. Maguire, 1851. Phillips was for many years Keeper of the Yorkshire Museum, Secretary of the Yorkshire Philosophical Society and Assistant Secretary of the British Association.

PLATE 3. Sir George Cayley (1773-1857) at age 70.

PLATE 4. Reconstruction (by Anglia Television) of the Cayley 1852 glider in flight.

PLATE 5. Workmen on the Yorkshire Philosophical Society's excavations uncover St. Mary's Abbey, c.1827. From a lithograph by F. Nash.

PLATE 6. Trained excavators of the York Archaeological Trust uncover Viking-age shops in Coppergate, 1980.

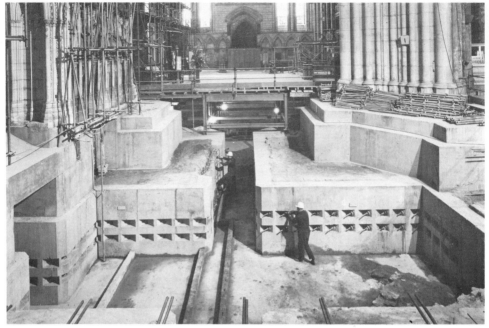

PLATE 7.   View from the Minster nave of the completed north-west and south pier foundations.

PLATE 8.   Shear crack in the Minster's Norman masonry immediately below the north-east pier of the central tower.

PLATE 9.   Late twelfth-century panel of stained glass from York Minster showing natural weathering (size of head: 0.14 m high × 0.10 m wide).

PLATE 10. Two views of George Leeman (1809-1882).
(a) As seen by *Vanity Fair.*   *(b)* Silhouette, artist unknown, c.1870.
Leeman was a leading member of the York Liberal Party. He was Lord Mayor on three occasions and MP for York in the 1860s and 1870s.

PLATE 11. Alderman Dobbie, York's first Labour Lord Mayor, receives the Prime Minister, Ramsay Macdonald, Mansion House steps, April 1924.

PLATE 12.   Hungate children's carnival at Brockfield Hall near Stockton on the Forest, 1904.

PLATE 13.   Inhabitants of Dundas Street, Hungate with their street decorated on the occasion of the children's carnival.

PLATE 14. B. Seebohm Rowntree (1871-1954). In addition to his work as Director and Chairman of Rowntree and Co. Ltd., Seebohm Rowntree was the author of a number of studies of poverty and social conditions in York.

For further comment on the children's carnival and the scenes in Plates 12, 13 and 15 see p. 179.

PLATE 15. Inhabitants of Hungate and Lime Street with their street decorated for the children's carnival.

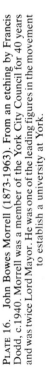

PLATE 16. John Bowes Morrell (1873-1963). From an etching by Francis Dodd, c.1940. Morrell was a member of the York City Council for 40 years and was twice Lord Mayor. He was one of the leading figures in the movement to establish a university at York.

PLATE 17. Lord James of Rusholme (b. 1909), the first Vice-Chancellor of the University of York.

The nature of the material obtained, and of mobility into and out of poverty, is illustrated in the three following case studies, the first covering three Rowntree generations (1936, 1950 and 1975-78) and the second and third covering two generations.

Family X. In 1936 the family consisted of a widow aged 61 years, her 19 year-old son and her 14 year-old daughter. The house was small (two-bedroomed) and rented for 7s 10d per week. Contributions from the children (employed as an assistant in a newspaper shop and a factory worker at Terry's), together with a widow's pension of 10s per week, led to them being adjudged 'not in poverty'. The results for 1936 have not been reworked on the basis of a more generous standard (equivalent to the criterion of 140 per cent of National Assistance scale rates applied in the postwar surveys), but if this were done it is likely that the family would be classified as 'in poverty' in 1936.

By 1950 the son lived in an adjacent street, in a comparatively large house which he was buying at a cost of £2 14s 0d per week. He continued to work at the same newsagent's shop, but his wage had risen from 15s 0d to £6 2s 6d. He was married with four daughters aged 4 months to 13 years.

In 1977 all four daughters were interviewed; three of them continued to reside in the same area as their parents and grandparents. The 1950 mother was alive but the husband was dead; he had been left a part-share in the shop when the proprietor died. The eldest daughter was married to a man working for a local glass company and earning £75 per week. The wife worked full-time as a clerk for a wage of £33.50. Of their two children, one was in work and one at school. The second daughter and her husband had bought her mother's 1950 house, and were paying a mortgage of £6.17 per week. There were two children, aged 11 and 14 years; and the father worked long hours for British Rail, earning £115 per week. The wife was in part-time employment. The third daughter lived in the same locality as her eldest sister, was married and had three children, aged 2, 6 and 8 years. The husband worked for British Rail and normally earned £88 for a week of around 60 hours; a recent period of sickness had reduced this income. Their mortgage cost £6.85. The eldest daughter lived within walking distance of her sisters, was separated from her husband, and had two children, aged 3 and 5. Because of the separation her economic circumstances were difficult, and she had also to meet mortgage payments of £7.88 per week.

Family Y. The respondent in 1950 was one of the highest earners in the survey – his wage as a works manager was £10-10s per week. He was 38 years old, his wife was 37 and there was a child of 7 years. They paid only £7 a year in rates on a small house which lacked a bathroom. The husband was reported to have taken 'special steps' to have his child educated at a school other than the local one which contained 'rough children'. The family lived on an income of 361% of the National Assistance scale.

When interviewed in the 1970's, the son was 34 years old and married, with one child aged eight months. He had been to grammar school and obtained five G.C.E 'O' level passes. Since leaving school he had worked as a wages clerk. He earned £67-30p per week from his job, and a further £3 from casual part-time employment. The couple were buying their house, at a cost of £16.54p per week, but with an income equivalent to only 126 per cent of the Supplementary Benefit scale, they had fallen below our specified poverty line, i.e. 140 per cent of the National Assistance scale rates.

Family Z. In 1950 the father was 43 and the mother 39; the former worked in the gum department at Rowntree's where he earned £5-19s-1d per week. There were seven children in the family, aged between 3 and 16 years and only the eldest child was working. Family allowances totalled £1-5s-0d and the rent was 17/10d for a six-roomed house with a bathroom. They lived at 113 per cent of the National Assistance scale and were thus below the specified poverty line for a family of that size.

The second child, a son, was interviewed in 1977. He was married and had two children, aged 12 and 14. The family lived, as their parents had done, in a council house, and paid a rent of £7.78p per week. They had lived in that house for only five years, having previously lived in a council 'prefab' for 16 years. The husband was employed by British Rail (Engineering) as a semi-skilled fitter. Although his basic wage was low (£38.08p for a 40 hour week), his average weekly earnings were £74.88p as a result of overtime, shift-work and bonus payments. The wife also worked full-time, as a cleaner with British Rail. Like her husband, her basic wage was low (£32.70 for 40 hours) but shift-work and overtime increased her average weekly earnings to £65. They believed that overtime work was essential, because of their low basic wage rates, and that the wife's employment was a crucial determinant of their standard of living. They admitted that they had 'become used to having money and could not now manage on less.' They had, however, had to make a decision as to whether to have 'more family life together and less money, or to have the money to buy luxuries.' Their decision gave them a standard of living at 253 per cent of the Supplementary Benefit scale and thus kept them well above the poverty level.

As an example of the way in which these case studies can be combined to provide information at a more aggregative level we shall look at the preliminary estimates obtained for movement into and out of the category 'living in poverty'. A crude indication of the extent of income mobility is given by the number of children who have moved from below to above the poverty line between 1950 and 1975-78 ('upward mobility') or from above to below the line ('downward mobility'). The 'immobile poor' are those who remain in poverty in both generations.

We adopted a poverty line in 1950 of 140 per cent of National Assistance scale rates, and in 1975-78 of 140 per cent of Long Term Supplementary Benefit rates (cf. p. 198, above). Using the grossed-up results of our sample, we found that 15.7 per cent were in the 'immobile poor' group, 17.7 per cent were 'downwardly mobile' and 16.8 per cent 'upwardly mobile'. (The remaining 49.8 per cent were not in poverty at either date.) One yardstick with which to compare these results is the proportion that would be in each group if there were no relation between parents' and childrens' incomes (i.e. if they were independent, in the statistical sense). Under these circumstances one would expect only 10.9 per cent of our sample in the 'immobile poor' group, with 22.6 per cent 'downwardly mobile' and 21.6 per cent 'upwardly mobile'.[3]

These are only preliminary results, and may be revised in the light of later work.[4] Nevertheless, they show very clearly the extent to which the status of one generation communicates itself to the next, increasing the prospect of remaining in poverty and reducing the chance of escape from it. The fourth survey thus illuminates an additional aspect of poverty in York, and so extends the information and understanding derived from the work of Seebohm Rowntree.

Notes

1 The authors would like to acknowledge a research grant from the Joseph Rowntree Memorial Trust to finance a re-analysis of the studies of poverty by Seebohm Rowntree.

2 The characteristics of York in relation to the country are discussed more fully in a report on the fourth survey (Atkinson, Maynard and Trinder, 1980, Chapter 3).

3 There were 466 children below and 967 above 140% of National Assistance standard in 1950. In 1975-78 there were 479 below and 954 above 140% of Long Term Supplementary Benefit scales. If income categories in each generation were independent, the proportion expected in the 'immobile poor' group would be $\frac{479}{1433}$ x 466 = 0.109 (10.9 per cent); for the 'upwardly mobile' group $\frac{954}{1433}$ x 466 = 0.216 (21.6 per cent); and for the 'downwardly mobile' group $\frac{479}{1433}$ x 967 = 0.226 (22.6 per cent).

4 They are discussed at greater length in Atkinson, Maynard and Trinder (1980).

References

ABEL-SMITH, B. and P. TOWNSEND (1965), *The Poor and the Poorest*.
ATKINSON, A. B., A. K. MAYNARD and C. G. TRINDER (1980), *The Rowntree Follow-up study; an analysis of inter-generational income continuities*, report to S.S.R.C.
ATKINSON, A. B., J. CORLYON, A. K. MAYNARD, H. SUTHERLAND, and C. G. TRINDER (1980), *Poverty in York: a re-analysis of Rowntree's 1950 Survey*, mimeograph.
ATKINSON, A. B., A. K. MAYNARD and C. G. TRINDER (1981), National Assistance and low incomes in 1950, *Social Policy and Administration*, volume 15, number 1.
BOOTH, C. (1899), *The Life and Labour of the People of London*.
BRIGGS, A. (1961), *A Study of the Work of Seebohm Rowntree*.
POLITICAL AND ECONOMIC PLANNING (1952), Poverty: Ten Years After Beveridge, *Planning*, XIX, 344.
ROWNTREE, B. S. (1901), *Poverty: a study of Town Life*.
ROWNTREE, B. S. (1937), *The Human Needs of Labour*.
ROWNTREE, B. S. (1941), *Poverty and Progress: a Second Social Survey of York*.
ROWNTREE, B. S. and G. R. LAVERS (1951), *Poverty and the Welfare State*.

CHAPTER VIII

Religion in York
1831-1981

by

Edward Royle

Patterns of Religion, 1831-1914

Victorian York was replete with outward manifestations of the Christian religion. Not only did the cathedral church of St. Peter (the Minster) dominate the skyline, but the 34 surviving civil parishes still contained 23 churches, 20 of which were within the walls and three of which (St. Olave, St. Maurice and St. Lawrence) lay only just beyond them. To these Anglican churches the various branches of Methodism had added five chapels by 1831, and the Unitarians, Society of Friends, Roman Catholics and Independents one each. More were to follow in the next 70 years, and by the end of the century there were to be 15 churches and chapels belonging to the principal non-Established denominations within the walls.

The purpose of this essay is to explore briefly the institutional history of the major Christian churches in York during the century and a half since 1831; to examine their attempts to attract the people of York to their life and worship; and to suggest the reactions of the churches to the changing social geography of the city – firstly as the population spilled beyond the old medieval confines into new suburbs such as Holgate, the Groves and Clementhorpe; and then as clearance programmes in the twentieth century moved inhabitants out of the slums of Bedern, Walmgate and Layerthorpe to new housing estates in the hitherto green fields of Tang Hall, Clifton and Acomb (see Maps 2 and 5).

The Church of England

The Church of England in 1831 was awakening from its slumbers. The safeguards which an Anglican state had appeared to offer to its Established Church were being weakened by the repeal of the Test and Corporation Acts (1828), the Emancipation of the Catholics (1829), and the reform of the electoral system (1832). The spiritual monopoly of the Church was also under attack as the evangelical revival stirred religious forces outside the Establishment among the various followers of John Wesley, while Evangelicals with scant regard for orthodox procedures were attempting to breathe new life into the old Church from within. For all these reasons what had been the unquestioned practices of the church during the preceding half century were never again to be thought good enough. Evangelicalism was to be an important strand within Victorian church life in York, encouraged particularly during the archiepiscopate of William Thomson (1863-90), who was an active Evangelical eager to make his mark on the church in the city through his use of patronage and by personal example. Though William Richardson, who had pioneered Evangelical opinion in the city, was dead by 1831, his mantle had been inherited by his brother James and his nephew Thomas. It was James, aided by Thomas, who conducted the first Anglican evening service in York in 1828.[1] The most eminent of William Richardson's successors, though, was John Graham, who as a preacher and organiser dominated Evangelical religion in York until his death in 1844. He too was aided by a son, John Baines Graham.

To write of 'abuses' in the Church of 1831 is to see matters in the wrong light; one should rather see them as problems to be faced by the Church in the context of a small cathedral city bearing the burden of a basically medieval ecclesiastical structure – problems which were not untypical of similar cities but which were not always the same as those of the nation at large.

Non-residence was technically widespread but was not really a problem. The ecclesiastical parishes were tiny: the largest of the 15 situated wholly within the walls was only 28 acres, the average being just over 11. Residence was sometimes physically impossible and incumbents seem to have counted themselves resident when licensed to live just down the street from their parish; most were certainly resident within the city. Only as expectations rose as to what a good parish priest should be does there seem to have been a determined effort to build residences within the actual boundaries of the parish so that the minister could live among his people.

The plural holding of livings, itself a cause of non-residence, was also prevalent but again not serious. Most of the small parishes were insufficiently endowed to provide a living on their own – the mean value of the twenty-two livings in York (the twenty-third, St. Maurice, was united with Holy Trinity, Goodramgate) was £122 and the median was £109; the mean had risen to only about £200 50 years later.[2] The average stipend expected by an Independent minister at this time was £150, and the best preachers were paid £400.[3] Nor was pluralism a sign of spiritual torpor. The great William Richardson had held both St. Sampson and St. Michael-le-Belfrey; while John Graham held two of the richest benefices, St. Mary, Bishophill Senior (£226) and St. Saviour (£173). Yet no-one could challenge the reforming zeal or industry of either man.

One of the most serious problems which faced the Church across the nation was that of over-large parishes. This was obviously not a problem for the majority of York incumbents, though it was to become one for those with parishes which stretched beyond the walls – St. Cuthbert, Holy Trinity, Goodramgate with St. Maurice, and St. Saviour to the east; St. Lawrence to the south; St. Mary, Bishophill Senior, St. Mary, Bishophill Junior, and Holy Trinity, Micklegate to the west; and St. Olave to the north. Of these eight parishes the first four were in the Walmgate registration sub-district, which contained the most depressed areas of the city with the worst housing and highest death rates (see Maps 3 and 5).

The problem of church accommodation was one which caused national concern in the mid-nineteenth century, and was one of the main reasons why a Census of Religious Worship was conducted at the same time as the population census in 1851. This unique document can be exploited to yield some sort of picture of the position of the Church in York in relation to the people and its denominational rivals in the mid-century.

As might be expected, the churches serving Walmgate were least well-placed as regards accommodation. Only St. Crux could offer accommodation to more than half its people (59.6 per cent). By contrast, of the 10 churches in the Bootham district, seven could provide for over half their people and only St. Olave's was really badly placed. Micklegate fell between the two extremes, but only St. Mary, Bishophill Junior, was in the same league as St. Maurice, St. Cuthbert, St. Dennis and St. Olave with a mere 13.2 per cent of its population offered accommodation. Horace Mann, who superintended the census, calculated that 58 per cent was the figure needed to meet the hoped-for demands of a parish.[4] Nevertheless the position within the walls compared very favourably with that in most cities. As the founding secretary of the York Auxiliary of the Church Pastoral Aid Association remarked in 1836, 'the inhabitants of York did not feel the wants of Church accommodation as was done in the manufacturing districts',[5] Though this problem was to occur in the suburbs with the growth of population following the coming of the railway and its associated workshops, the opposite difficulty was to be encountered within the walls, with depopulation destroying the parochial fabric.

The numbers of people attending worship in mid-century York can only with difficulty and much approximation be suggested from the census details, for it was concerned with the number of attendances made, and not with the number of attenders. Making due allowance for people who went to church two or three times on the same day, one can suggest that the number of adult attenders at Church of England services on an average Sunday in 1850-51 was about 10,000 – 37 per cent of the adult population of the parishes. However there were important local differences. If the parishes are grouped in their registration sub-districts the figure for Walmgate alone is 27 per cent, while for Bootham it is 44 per cent and for Micklegate 48 per cent – the reverse order to that in which the districts were placed for death-rate statistics. The conclusion from this might be that, although against the national picture the Church of England was successful in York, it enjoyed disproportionate success among the better-off classes. This should not be pressed too far, however, for at ten churches where evening services were held – and these were the unfashionable 'popular' services – attendances outnumbered those at the other major service in all but two cases. The Church clearly was reaching large numbers of working people, and the success of a church like St. Saviour's, with an average of 650 at the evening service, or St. Margaret's in the heart of Walmgate, crowded to capacity with 480, must not be overlooked in the statistics.[6]

Nevertheless the incumbents of these 23 churches were for the most part concerned not with the extent of their success but with the challenge presented to them by those who did not attend church. On the negative side they blamed drink and Dissent; on the positive side they sought to meet the challenge by reinvigorating the parish structure.

The Anglican ideal was the well-worked parish, and many Victorian clergy to some extent achieved this in the countryside. The effort to construct an urban equivalent was commendable, but difficult to achieve and often inappropriate to urban needs. High Church George Trevor of All Saints, Pavement, in 1865 asserted bluntly, 'I am convinced that nothing can raise the Church in York but the revival of the parochial system of fixed pastoral relations with the people' though to achieve this there would have to be a destruction of 'the excessive number of parishes which fritters away the parochial principle'.[7] However each incumbent jealously guarded his own parish from interference: rationalisation of church work without amalgamation of benefices was seen as anti-parochial, but rationalisation with amalgamation was to be a very slow process and largely the consequence of serious inner-city depopulation in the twentieth century. The instinct of the Victorians was to create new parishes in areas of growth without any concerted plan for the city as a whole. Thus as the Holgate area expanded with the arrival of railway employees a new parish was created in 1856 out of the parish of St. Mary, Bishophill Junior. Six years later the *Yorkshire Gazette* was reporting that 'This arrangement has unfortunately proved a great disadvantage to the mother church, and its resources have thereby been entirely cut off'.[8] The small inner-city parish was not, and could not be made, self-sufficient, and as the population grew and became geographically dispersed but socially concentrated the system broke down. The logical thing to do – and it was done in only one instance in the nineteenth century – was to abandon the mother church rather than divide the parish. This is what happened to St. Mary, Bishophill Senior, shortly after the opening of St. Clement's in 1874 to serve the new community of railway workers outside the city walls in Clementhorpe.

Though not a major industrial city, York experienced in the later nineteenth century all the disadvantages of settlement patterns based on social class. 'Some of the gentry will not come to the dirty locality where this church is', complained the energetic and diligent Andrew Robert Fausset of St. Cuthbert's in 1865. 'We have not any persons in the parish of any position, the principal class are railway labourers and small shop-keepers – consequently I have little help', lamented the clergyman at St. Mary, Bishophill Junior in 1894.[9] The loss of the upper classes to the suburbs and the middling classes to Dissent was widely lamented, and it left the parish priests in an isolated and difficult position. In a small parish they were certainly able to know all their people and their needs, but they lacked the support to provide an adequate ministry. Where they did succeed in establishing popular Sunday services for their people this too could prove anti-parochial, for they then destroyed their neighbours' congregations and swamped their own with outsiders. 'I think the great difficulty which I feel comes from the way in which people wish to go to those churches which are full,' W. F. Wilberforce at St. John's sadly recognised in 1877.[10]

Two factors within the life of the Established Church were also felt to militate against the satisfactory development of parochial work – the Minster, and the way in which the Church Day and Sunday Schools were organised in the city.

The trouble caused by the presence of the Minster became noticeable as the Dean and Chapter began to play a more active part in the life of the

city. Nave services for working men were started by Dean Duncombe in
1863: he described them to the Church Congress in 1866 as 'a most
important movement, a movement which I know to be popular with large
classes of working men and which has been the means in this ancient city
of bringing vast numbers of the labouring classes to church'. But most
York incumbents felt differently about what George Trevor in 1865
referred to as 'the influence of the Minster which overwhelms and suffo-
cates'. Echoes of this view are found in the Visitation Returns of the
clergy right through to 1915.[11]

Even more widely unpopular than the Minster, though, was the
arrangement of the Church Schools in York. The ideal parish had its
National and Sunday School, bringing the next generation up in whole-
some doctrine and attaching it to the church. But this was quite impracticable in many of the small parishes of York, and the Sunday Schools were
organised in districts by a Central Committee. Parishes containing a
district school were fortunate but neighbouring incumbents were not
happy as their children were shepherded into someone else's church.
Even where a district school lay within a parish all was not well for, as
H. W. Beckwith of St. Mary, Bishophill Senior, explained in 1865,
'These are not parochial schools, and the clergyman of the parish has *ex
officio* no voice in the management of any of them'. Three years later he
reported 'The Boys' school has of late been in a sad state, doing more
injury than good to the cause of religion – and to the efficiency of the
church – this is to be attributed to the defective constitution of the Sunday
School Society'. A similar complaint came from St. Lawrence's where the
clergyman decided to start his own parochial schools instead, but this was
not everywhere possible, for not all parishes had a room in which to hold a
Sunday School, the matter being made worse by the fact that the National
Schools in the city were also organised on a district basis and were open to
the same complaints.[12]

In these circumstances the parochial ideal was very hard to work –
impossible in the inner-city parishes – but this does not mean that the
Church in York was failing and in a sad state in the Victorian period, as
the results of the 1851 census showed, with Anglicans being about half of
the total number of adult church-goers. Within the limits of parochial
concepts the Church responded well to the challenges of the age.

The principal of these challenges came from the geographical expansion of the city and the increasing population under the impact of railway
employment. New suburbs grew up, still largely within the area covered
by the 23 churches, but with populations beyond what those churches
could cope with. A school-room in Holgate Lane, in the parish of St.
Mary, Bishophill Junior, was licensed for worship in September 1848 to

cope with the influx of railway employees; a new church, St. Paul's, soon followed with a new parish being created in 1856. On the opposite side of the city another new district, known as the Groves, was rapidly being built up at the same time, and the parish of St. Thomas was created in 1855 out of St. Olave's. St. Maurice, on the edge of the Groves, was rebuilt on a grander scale in 1878, as was St. Lawrence in 1883; while two villages which were rapidly becoming 'select' suburbs, Heworth and Clifton, were carved out of St. Saviour's and St. Olave's in 1870 and 1871 respectively. Lastly came St. Clement's, built as a daughter church to St. Mary, Bishophill Senior, in 1874 but becoming the principal church of the parish in 1876.[13]

These seven new churches provided accommodation for about 4,310 people, and their congregations in 1884 were estimated at 3,130. This expansion was, however, failing to keep pace with the rising population: though St. Thomas's was immediately full with 500 people in the pews in the 1860s, that represented only about 14 per cent of the population of the area. In the next half century the population increased three-fold, while the congregation was halved. Only St. Clement's, Clifton and Heworth were able to maintain absolute numbers up to the First World War and even they, relatively speaking, were falling behind.[14]

These outer, newer, parishes had problems of their own. Churches provided for working-class suburbs needed free seats, and yet such was their financial position that pew rents had to be imposed. Only a half of the seats in St. Thomas's were originally free, and only a third of those in St. Paul's.[15] The wealthier areas also had their problems. While the inner-city churches were complaining that they had lost their more substantial parishioners to the surburbs, the incumbent of Clifton was observing the opposite: 'The gentry attend the Minster, and professional and other well-to-do classes, are terribly split up among themselves, and many who have been born and bred in the city in other parishes, cling to their old churches'.[16] As the nineteenth century drew to a close the churches seemed to be competing amongst themselves for a maximum share of those prepared to attend worship regularly. 'The existence in York of several large churches with small populations', thought Canon Argles, meant that 'These in the struggle for existence find themselves compelled to prey upon their neighbours for money and congregation'; and the parochial principle was being undermined by what the Vicar of St. Thomas's lamented as 'The tendency to go off (on the part of the people) to special attractions got up in other places of worship.[17] He was referring not only to the Minster and rival Anglican establishments but – worse still – to the infamous wiles of Dissent.

Thinking differently from the national church (a church of England).

Dissent

Dissent from the Established Church had long been present in York, with the Presbyterian church in St. Saviourgate being built under the patronage of Lady Hewley in 1692. By the beginning of the nineteenth century it held a Unitarian congregation and had entered upon a golden period in its history during the Rev. Charles Wellbeloved's pastorate from 1792 to 1858. Wellbeloved personified the intellectual culture of late eighteenth-century Dissent, untroubled by evangelical fervour. He made York the seat of the last great Dissenting Academy, the Manchester College, between 1803 and 1840, and was also active in the affairs of the city (see Chapter I, pp. 9-15); but he was never able to make the part played by St. Saviourgate Chapel in the life of York of comparable importance to that played by Cross Street Chapel, Manchester, in the life of that city. The average congregation in 1850-51 was only about 120, 0.7 per cent of the adult church-going population, and there was no Sunday School. After Wellbeloved's death there was dissension and decline, and by the end of the century the congregations were no larger, while actual membership was only about 50.[18]

The Independents – or Congregationalists as they were becoming known – were comparatively late arrivals amongst Old Dissent, the embers of splinter groups from the Calvinistic Methodists being fanned into flame by the West Riding Itinerant Society in 1814. A new chapel, designed by one of the leading members of the congregation, J. P. Pritchett, was opened in Lendal (St. Martin's, Coney Street, parish) in 1816, and this experienced a period of prosperity under the ministry of James Parsons from 1822. An average of 30 members a year was added to the books between 1816 and 1838, by which time the total membership was 447. Adherents were as many again, and Pritchett designed a new, larger chapel which was built in St. Saviour's Place, looking down St. Saviourgate and opened in 1839 with the name of Salem Chapel (Map 5). Parsons removed to this new chapel, and predictably 80 per cent of the membership went with him, leaving only 79 at Lendal. The latter now began a long, lean period. There were quarrels in the congregation, in which Pritchett appears to have played a leading part, and ministers were slow to accept invitations and quick to depart, some in broken health. Congregations stagnated or declined, which meant only small stipends for the pastors and so even more problems in persuading them to come.[19]

Meanwhile at Salem the reverse was true, with about 60 members a year joining in the first decade, including a steady stream from Lendal. Indeed, at the Members' Meeting on 1 October 1846 'It was stated that the officers of the Church had thought it advisable not to present to the Church the dismission of members from the church meeting in Lendal

Chapel, *under present circumstances,* excepting after conversation which would satisfy them as to their motives for removing'.[20] At the 1851 census Lendal had a morning congregation of 220 and an evening one of 216, although admittedly the pastor had been ill since October 1850; the figures for Salem were 976 in the morning and 802 in the evening, the latter figure being about 100 below average due to the temporary illness of Parsons. The average number of attenders at Independent services in York in 1850-51 was probably a little under 9 per cent of the total adult church-going population.

In the tradition of Old Dissent, the Society of Friends in York was both old-established and influential – but small in numbers. There had been a Meeting in York since the mid-seventeenth century, and a new meeting house with seating for over a thousand was designed by Pritchett and opened in 1816, but on the morning of 30 March 1851 there were only 273 people present, and only 170 in the afternoon – making a congregation of around 2 per cent of the adult church-going population. Total membership of the Meeting in 1862 was 231 and did not rise above 300 until the 1870s; it was not to pass 400 until shortly before the First World War. Before the last decade of the nineteenth century the additional number of 'attenders' was only a third of that of the membership, but rose to a half in the Edwardian decade. This late growth in both membership and support clearly signifies the change in policy as Friends adopted a more open, evangelistic approach to mission work, especially through the Adult School Movement which made a major impact on York in the decade preceding the First World War.[21]

Representatives of the other two main groups of Old Dissent – the Baptists and the orthodox Presbyterians – were late-comers to Victorian York. The Baptist cause had died out in the early 1830s, believers dispersing to the St. Saviourgate or Lendal Chapels according to their theological predispositions, and the cause was not re-established until January 1862 when the Baptist Home Missionary Society rented the Victoria Hall in Goodramgate. A church of about 30 members was formed at the end of the year, and a chapel was opened in Priory Street, opposite the large new Wesleyan Chapel, in 1868. At first progress was brisk, especially during the Moody and Sankey revival of 1873; membership grew from 91 in 1870 to 199 in 1879. There was then a falling back to 137 in 1890, a brief recovery to 192 at the start of the new century, but then a further decline with a third of the members being lost in the next few years.[22]

The Presbyterian cause began in a similar way, with meetings in the Victoria Hall in 1873, leading to a chapel in Priory Street six years later. A congregation of about 80 had been assembled in Goodramgate, but the total at the new church did not pass 100 until the end of the century. Thereafter it grew rapidly, passing 300 by 1914. One source of strength was the presence of Scots regiments stationed in York, which used the Priory Street Chapel in preference to the Anglican chapel at the barracks.[23]

The most successful of all the old religious bodies outside the Establishment, though, was the Roman Catholic Church, As a county town and centre for the Catholic gentry of the area, York had long had a Catholic presence. At the Nunnery (or Bar Convent), outside Micklegate Bar, there had been a boarding school for young ladies since 1686, and the Mission of St. Wilfrid was founded in 1742 with a chapel being erected in Little Blake Street, close by the West Front of the Minster, in 1760; it was replaced in 1802 and again in the 1860s when Dean Duncombe had Little Blake Street widened to improve the view of the Minster. A new Church of St. Wilfrid was built on the opposite side of the road and was opened in June 1864 with Cardinal Wiseman preaching provocatively on the text 'Thou art Peter'. Both the text and the way in which the Church tower successfully intruded itself on Dean Duncombe's vista served as a reminder of all that the Tory Anglican *Yorkshire Gazette* had feared since Emancipation in 1829.[24]

In fact the old Catholic community in York had been highly respected and produced a Lord Mayor as early as 1830, but with the arrival of poor Irish, especially in the Walmgate area in the 1840s, things began to change. When a new church, St. George's, was opened in Walmgate on 4 September 1850, the *Yorkshire Gazette* devoted two and a quarter columns to the infamous affair as well as an editorial on 'The Progress of Romanism'. 17 days later the Papal Bull restoring the Catholic hierarchy was promulgated and York, like the rest of the country, fell in a frenzy.[25]

In 1851 the Catholic share of the adult church-going population was about 9 per cent – slightly larger than the share held by the Independents. Using Horace Mann's own calculations York emerges as the only major English town outside Lancashire with both an attendance figure in excess of 50 per cent and a Catholic share of those attendances of more than 10 per cent.[26]

The City of York was placed in the diocese of Beverley, but when in 1878 the diocese of Leeds was created for the West Riding and that of Middlesbrough for the East and North Ridings, York was divided at the river, leaving the Micklegate portion in the Leeds diocese without a church other than the school chapel at the Nunnery. The parish of the English Martyrs was formed in 1882 but a separate church was not built for a further 50 years.[27]

Despite the alarm which the Catholic presence caused, and despite the prestige enjoyed by Old Dissent, thanks to pastors like Wellbeloved and Parsons, and Quaker philanthropists like the Tukes and the Rowntrees, Dissent in York really meant the New Dissent associated with the followers of John Wesley, and especially the original Connexion. In 1851 around 14 per cent of the adult church-going population was Wesleyan, with a further 9 per cent belonging to the Wesleyan Reformers and still regarding themselves as part of the Wesleyan Connexion; the Primitive Methodists made up a little under 4 per cent, and the Wesleyan Methodist Association had a little over 1 per cent; there was no New Connexion in York at this time.

The Wesleyans had become firmly entrenched in York in the second half of the eighteenth century, and in 1805 had opened a major new chapel in the centre of the city in New Street. In 1816 a second chapel had been built across the river in Skeldergate, the Albion Street Chapel; and in 1825 had followed a mission school-chapel, St. George's, in the heart of Walmgate with 400 free sittings. This was replaced as a chapel (though kept on as a school) in 1840 by Centenary Chapel in St. Saviourgate, a colossal structure with accommodation for nearly 1,500 people.[28] The evening congregation at Centenary on 30 March 1851 was by far the largest assembled in any church in York on that day; even the largest service at the Minster, the afternoon service, usually averaged only a thousand.[29]

The total membership of the Wesleyan Circuit in 1831 was 1,800, 1,130 of whom belonged to the three central churches. This latter figure rose by unsteady steps until the opening of Centenary when it suddenly increased from 1,457 in 1840 to 1,734 in 1841. In 1849 the figure for the city was 1,976; a year later it had fallen to 1,408, a consequence of the great Wesleyan disruption which followed the expulsion in 1849 of three ministers for alleged libels upon the Wesleyan leadership. The Wesleyan Reform movement gained great sympathy in York where James Everett, one of the expelled preachers, had once been stationed, and by March 1851 – the month of the religious census – the gains of 20 years had been swept away as membership sank to under 1,200.[30]

The Reformers called an unauthorised conference in London early in 1850, to which three eminent York Wesleyan laymen were sent by over half the membership; and for this offence the three delegates were stripped of their circuit and society offices in April 1850 after a 'trial' at New Street by the superintendent minister. Immediately they formed a Wesleyan Branch Society, holding Sunday services in the Festival Concert Room.[31] At this stage they still considered themselves to be Wesleyan Methodists 'only separated as a branch for a time, in order to bring about a change in matters of discipline in the Wesleyan body'.[32] Gradually, though, they separated and in 1852 had constituted a circuit with 718 members and meeting rooms in Walmgate and St. Saviourgate as well as the use of the Festival Concert Room on Sundays. During the next few years the split became institutionalised with the majority of the leaders forming a society in the New Connexion in 1855. They opened a chapel in Peckitt Street, near the Castle, the following year and on the same day laid the foundation stone of a school-chapel to the south of the city beyond the walls near the cemetery. Other Reformers joined the Wesleyan Methodist Association, which had had a chapel in Lady Peckett's Yard in the centre of York since 1830; and when the two groups were united nationally to constitute the United Methodist Free Churches in 1857, the old chapel was sold for a warehouse and a new one built just inside Monk Bar in 1859. A third group joined the Primitive Methodists, among them James Meek junior, son of a former Lord Mayor, who had voted against his father at the trial of the three delegates, and who had been so impressed by the hospitality offered to the excluded by the Primitives that he and his whole Wesleyan class joined them in 1853.[33]

Primitive Methodism in York really began to expand only after the Wesleyan Reform disruption. The city had been missioned by William Clowes, one of the founders of the Connexion, in 1818 and it became the head of a separate circuit in 1822, but at this stage what strength they had lay in the countryside. Of 225 members in June 1832, only 100 belonged to the city society which since 1820 had been meeting in a damp, ill-lit and ill-ventilated chapel in Grape Lane, off Petergate in the centre of the city. This chapel had previously been used by Independents, Calvinistic Methodists, the New Connexion, the Wesleyans, the Particular Baptists and the Unitarian Baptists. All but the Wesleyans had failed to strike roots, and the Primitives remained in a precarious position for many years, with their membership falling below a hundred in 1837 and not rising above that figure again until June 1849, just after the beginning of the Wesleyan troubles. A year later the membership had risen to nearly 150, and at the end of 1851 when a new chapel, designed by Pritchett and called Ebenezer, was opened in Little Stonegate around the corner from Grape Lane, they were over 170 in number. The 200-mark had been passed by mid-1853, the membership now having doubled in only four years. By the 1860s the Primitives were ready to begin founding chapels elsewhere in the city.[34]

Meanwhile the Wesleyan cause was deep in trouble. Plans to build a new chapel in Micklegate to replace Albion Street were delayed. Even when the new building, called Wesley Chapel, was opened in Priory Street in 1856, causing the membership west of the river to rise from 266 to 354 and producing the first signs of recovery, the total city membership was still only 1,384. The number of Wesleyan members attached to chapels within the walls was never again to reach the level it had been immediately before the disruption. When York was divided at the river into two circuits in 1867 the combined total was still only just over 1,900, and thereafter the expansion of the city and the opening of chapels beyond the walls began to transfer the balance of membership away from the old city centre chapel in New Street.[35]

Like the Anglicans, both Wesleyans and Primitives were alive to the need to expand into the new suburbs, and they did so usually by gradual progression from outdoor and cottage meetings, to renting a room, then building a school-chapel, and finally, in the most successful cases, building a large chapel with accommodation for several hundreds.

One of the most promising areas was to the south of the city and east of the river. The Anglicans began to work the area in the 1870s, with the transfer of the area from Fulford parish to St. Lawrence in 1871. A year later the Wesleyans took over the New Connexion school-chapel near the cemetery, which was failing for lack of local preachers and Sunday-school staff. The Wesleyans with greater resources witnessed dramatic success, the premises proved too small, and in 1877 a large new chapel and schools were opened in Melbourne Terrace, built at a cost of £8,000 and with a membership of 80. By the end of the decade this had reached 300 and by 1884 had passed 400. It remained around this level until the end of the century, but had fallen back to under 250 by the First World War.[36]

At the opposite side of the city the Wesleyans were also active in the Groves, the district of over 5,000 people which St. Thomas's had been built to serve in 1853. They began with a room over a stable in 1860, erected a school-chapel in 1868, and opened a new chapel, costing nearly £6,000, in 1884. The growth of the new society here was not as spectacular as at Melbourne Terrace, but it proved more enduring. In 1869 there were 63 members; by the time the new chapel opened in 1884 there were 298; a peak of 349 was reached in 1905, but this had fallen back to 270 by 1914. A similarly large chapel was opened by the Wesley Circuit in 1887 to serve the south of the city west of the river at Southlands, Clementhorpe, and in the west near the railway works in Holgate, a mission room was opened in Wilton Street which, significantly for a lower-working-class area, was not replaced by a chapel until 1910.[37]

The Primitive Methodists were also active, particularly amongst the railway workers: they had mission rooms in the Leeman Road area, across the railway lines from Holgate; in the Groves; in Heslington Road near the cemetery; and in Clementhorpe. The last venture was the most successful, beginning with a mission in a rented wash-house. In 1865 a school-chapel was opened in Nunnery Lane with 42 members. As numbers rose above the 100 mark at the end of 1870 the mission grew more ambitious, acquiring land just inside Victoria Bar where in 1880 they opened a chapel to seat 900. Membership passed 150 but never reached 200. In 1883 the Primitives decided to divide their York Circuit, with Victoria Bar at the head of the Second Circuit, but with only 238 city members in total (and only just over 300 in the First Circuit) the cause was hardly viable. A loss of members was sustained with the transfer of some railway workers to Darlington in 1885, and in December 1889 the Victoria Bar Quarterly Meeting applied to rejoin the Ebenezer First Circuit. The application was refused, and by 1894 the number of city members had fallen below 200, despite the opening of a mission room in Leeman Road. The downwards trend continued until the First World War.[38]

The Wesleyans had also divided their New Street Circuit again, in 1888, with two large chapels in each part (Centenary – Melbourne Terrace with a combined membership of 1,092; and New Street – The Groves with a combined membership of 578). Each was therefore able to support itself, its share of inner-city missionary work, and church extension into the ever-increasing suburbs: Clifton falling to New Street, and Heworth and Fulford to Centenary. It is significant, though, that Wesleyan success in the nineteenth century was greatest in the better sort of working-class suburb. Clifton and Heworth especially were still small and select, and the Wesleyan cause grew there only slowly. Both Heworth and Fulford gradually edged upwards from 30 to 40 members in the 1880s, but had reached only 50 each by 1914, while the two working-class churches of St. George's (re-opened as a church on a new site outside Walmgate Bar in 1901) and Layerthorpe had 82 and 73 respectively. Clifton began even more slowly. Despite a school-chapel being opened in 1884 the society did not gain more than 40 members until 1902. It was an act of faith which led the Wesleyans to build a new chapel at Clifton and to close New Street in 1908, for New Street in 1907 still had 144 members against the 43 at Clifton. Under the new arrangement the membership at Clifton immediately rose to 158 and remained at not much below that level until the First World War. To close down what had been for over a century the historic centre of Wesleyanism in York and to transfer its work to an outer suburb was an act of imagination pointing to trends which were to become accentuated as the twentieth century progressed.[39]

Missions

Broadly speaking there were three classes of mission: the occasional special effort; the permanently but separately organised Mission, often with buildings and a paid missionary; and the continuing outreach of the ordinary church.

Special missions, often associated with revivalism, were held on many different occasions by various denominations and interests, including the American evangelists James Caughey in 1845 and Moody and Sankey 30 years later. Archbishop Thomson was especially keen, and arranged eight-day missions in York in November 1871, 1878 and 1888. That held on the last occasion is of special interest as the 1894 Visitation Returns to his successor give the incumbents' mature reflections on its impact.

The mission was led personally by the Archbishop. Services were held daily in every parish with special missioners brought in from other towns, and the Dean and Archbishop also played a full part. The latter addressed a meeting of business men in St. Martin's, Coney Street at which he reminded them of 'the bounden duty of employers to exercise the influence they possess over their assistants for their good'. He also addressed five meetings of working men at their places of work – two in the railway workshops during the dinner hour. Here he denounced drinking and gambling: his message was that 'The best workmen are those who deny themselves and start their week's labours with clear heads and steady nerves, the result of temperance and sobriety. A righteous life is the best and conducive to true happiness'. The Archbishop's view of the working man, his problems and his customs, was not untypical of that held by the majority of Churchmen in York.[40]

When asked about recent missions in their parishes five years later, 10 out of 23 incumbents did not see fit to mention it, though the rector of All Saints, North Street, thought he recalled one in 1877 [sic] with 'no apparent results'. Of the rest, two offered no comments or did not know; two simply reported 'very fair results'; two had positive views of a favourable kind; and six were more or less critical. The feeling of a number was summed up by the incumbent of St. Sampson's: 'I think the spiritual life of our communicants deepened but I did not observe any startling results. I have more confidence in quiet parochial work for bringing in outsiders'. There was, in fact, a danger of too many special missions: as J. E. M. Young of St. Saviour's remarked, 'very little results – they are so *often* held by dissenters'. The Dissenters may also have been better at them. Revival services in the Wesley Circuit in March 1878 resulted in 280 names being taken, and a net gain of 83 members to the circuit by June.[41]

The most constant missionary endeavour of all the churches, though, lay with the Sunday Schools. These were not, in modern parlance, 'junior churches' but a means of laying hold on the children of the poor, non-church-going classes, through a mixture of philanthropy and evangelism. A speaker at the New Street Chapel Mutual Improvement Society in 1846 was unusual in arguing that 'Sunday schools should be for the rich as well as the poor and ministers ought to impress that upon their congregations and recommend them to send their children'. The orthodox view was still that set out by the Church of England Sunday School Committee, founded in 1786 for 'rescuing the children of poor parents from the low habits of vice and idleness, and initiating them in the principles of the Christian religion from which we may reasonably hope the rising generation will be made useful members of society'.[42]

Critics of the Sunday school movement argued that it had failed in its task of making church members, but the ideal remained that 'every church should have its Sunday School'.[43] As has already been noted, York incumbents felt they had a special grievance in that the Sunday School Committee was inhibiting the realisation of this ideal. By 1841 the Church of England Committee had five schools with 436 boys and five with 564 girls, serving every part of the city. In three schools belonging to the Wesleyan Sunday School Committee (founded 1813) there were 459 boys and 530 girls. The total number of children on the books of Protestant Sunday Schools in York was 2,880, just over 50 per cent of the population between the ages of five and fifteen. Attendance was normally about two-thirds the nominal figure.[44] By the time of the Sunday Schools' centenary in 1880, the figures were as shown in Table 1 for the various participating Protestant denominations.[45]

Although the Church of England Committee was now at its peak, more and more parochial schools were being opened, and by 1900 there were only 544 children in the district schools. Meanwhile the Wesleyans were advancing rapidly, with 6,153 children in 35 schools by 1900.[46]

The most remarkable development was the work of the Friends in their Adult Schools. These had grown out of an adult class taught by John Stephenson Rowntree in connection with the Hope Street Boys' School in Walmgate, opened by the Friends in 1828. Rowntree moved the class to a room in Lady Peckett's Yard behind his father's Pavement shop in 1857, and by the early 1870s the Adult School had a membership of nearly 300. One of the main problems of society at this time was widely believed to be intemperance, and in 1872 the school began holding Sunday evening meetings to ensure healthy and sober leisure. This proved very popular, and the old chapel which the Wesleyan Methodist Association had vacated in 1858 was demolished and replaced with a new school building in 1876. The next decade saw the school reach its peak with an average attendance of 263 in 1887, but when this declined rapidly

– falling to 150 in 1900 – the reaction of the leaders was to extend the schools into the suburbs. In 1902 there were four schools with 729 members; a York and District Adult School Union was started under the presidency of Arnold Rowntree in 1903; and by 1906 there were 13 schools with 2,373 members, mostly in working-class areas. In reality they were both elementary schools and temperance working-men's clubs, combining religion with leisure and social work. In 1907 Joseph Rowntree wrote that their aim was 'to bring Christianity as an active, practical force, into daily life in the home, the workshop, and in the area of citizenship'.[47] The Adult Schools were the means by which the Friends broke into positive evangelism, and the effects are clearly reflected in the number of adherents and the size of the York Meeting in these years, while individual testimonies as to what the schools had meant for ignorant drunkards were worthy of any revivalist sect.[48]

Table 1   1880
                        Attendance at Protestant
                        Sunday Schools in York

Denomination	First School	No. of Pupils
Church of England	1786	3,850*
Wesleyan	1791	2,850
Primitive Methodist	1831	930
Society of Friends	1848	550
Congregationalists	1817	420
Methodist Free Church	1830	370
Hungate Mission (non-denom.)	1861	350
New Connexion	1850	250
Baptist	1862	200
Navigation Road Mission (non-denom.)	1869	150
Unitarian	1791	80
Presbyterian	1873	80
Total		10,080

* 1,974 of these pupils were at parochial schools not under the Central Committee

222

The more orthodox Sunday Schools for poor children were the spear-head of the churches' mission into new areas. For instance, the Church of England Committee opened a school in the Groves as early as 1832, 23 years before the new parish of St. Thomas was created. The usual pattern in Methodist expansion was for a school-chapel to precede the building of a chapel proper. When the Wesley Circuit Extension Committee built the Wilton Street Mission Hall in 1872 they immediately started a Sunday School which, within a year, had 135 children on the books. They next moved into the Foundries district on Leeman Road, starting a school with 54 scholars in 1876. But running a Sunday School in a rough working-class area was not easy: the Visitor reported in 1881 'attendance small – scholars very small, some unruly boys, one impersonating Daniel under the Table'. The venture was persisted with, despite misgivings, until 1887 by which time the Primitives had moved into the area. Even in 1928 when the Congregationalists were considering taking a room in the new council-housing area of Tang Hall, the Church Meeting at Salem deputed the matter to representatives of the Sunday Schools.[49]

Involvement in Sunday School work was never an end in itself, but inevitably led the churches on to other things. In its 1845 Annual Report the Wesleyan Sunday School Committee stated 'They cannot but regret that one class of its [York's] poor are suffered to grow up in ignorance and impiety, neither fearing God nor regarding man, whose tattered garments and depraved habits forbid them entering the Sabbath School'. As a result a committee was set up to start a Ragged School, and two rooms were taken in Bedern, the heart of the ragged area. The school opened in 1847, but attendances were irregular, especially in the mornings. The committee therefore started giving the children breakfast, the bill partly being met by George Hudson. Once established, the school passed out of Wesleyan hands, and was gradually transformed into an Industrial School, housed in the old workhouse in Marygate.[50]

One task which befell the Ragged School teachers, as all Sunday School teachers, was to visit the homes of the scholars. Out of this practice in 1848 arose the York City Mission, one of the most important of several permanent Missions established to act as a kind of bridge between the institutional churches and the people who never came near them. The nature of the Mission's work is illustrated by the fact that aid was received from both the York Auxiliary Bible Society and the Health of Towns Association. One missioner was appointed at £30 p.a., and during the first year he paid 2,046 visits; attended 100 cases of sickness, 94 cottage meetings, and 16 open-air meetings; and distributed 5,000 tracts and 1,800 handbills. The work was concentrated on 'Bedern, the Water

Lanes, and the vilest description of lodging houses in Walmgate, and other parts of the City'. The missioner, apparently, spoke some Irish.[51]

A second missioner was appointed in 1852 and a third in 1853. Between them they divided up the worst areas of the city, and by 1855 were making over 14,000 visits a year and distributing nearly 16,000 tracts. They also began work among cabmen, railway porters and policemen, whose jobs required them to work on Sundays. The missioners appear to have been particularly concerned with the evils of prostitution, drink and gambling, the York Races presenting a special problem and opportunity.[52]

The City Mission was primarily but not wholly an evangelistic agency, for the material necessities of the poor could not be neglected. In the Edwardian years the missioner was distributing old clothes, dispensary, hospital and invalid kitchen tickets, and bread and coal tickets. There continued to be a need for this sort of work during the inter-war depression, and not until after the Second World War did the Mission's aim become solely evangelistic. Crippled by lack of finance, it was forced to close in 1975.[53]

Alongside, and sometimes in rivalry with, the City Mission were a host of similar institutions. Some of these were denominational, like the Anglican Scripture Readers' Society (6,000 visits paid in 1849), or the York Wesleyan Visiting Agency (9,767 visits and calls in 1862).[54] Others were non-denominational (i.e. Protestant), like the York Religious Tract Society which in 1842 had the Revd. John Graham as president, J. P. Pritchett as secretary, and James Parsons and Joseph Rowntree on the committee; or the York Central Mission, a non-denominational but primarily Wesleyan organisation started in the 1880s.[55] There was also the Wesley Mission in North Street and later in Skeldergate; the Layerthorpe Mission run by the Wesleyans of Centenary Circuit; and the non-denominational Hungate Mission, founded under the presidency of James Parsons in 1861. Such Missions often grew to offer a variety of activities from Sunday Schools and Bible Classes to sewing classes, mothers' meetings, clothing clubs and goose clubs for Christmas. At Skeldergate in the winter of 1907-8 the Mission pioneered free dinners for poor children, supplying 10,000 meals at a cost of 1½d each.[56]

Such work was also undertaken by other more overtly materialistic agencies, like the York Charitable Society, linked to the Sunday School Committee between 1798 and 1841;[57] but a great deal of this latter kind of benevolence was the quiet duty of individual parish priests.[58]

The Salvation Army also made an important contribution to missionary work, following its 'opening fire' in York in July 1881. Tenancy of an old skating rink in Gillygate was taken, and the following year the foundation stone of a new Citadel was laid close by. The opening ceremony was performed by General Booth himself on 26 March 1883, and in 1981 the building remains the Army's headquarters in the city. In January 1883 a second corps was formed in Fishergate, at the southern end of the city, and this moved to the premises vacated by the Wesleyan North Street Mission in 1905. The corps moved again in 1936 to the former Wesleyan and then Railwaymen's Mission in Wilton Street, but this closed in the 1960s. For a time other meetings were held in mission rooms in Nunnery Lane and Skeldergate, and the equivalent of a Sunday School was run in Haver Lane, Hungate. A third corps, opened in Hamper's Yard, Walmgate, in May 1908, lasted until the 1930s. Outdoor meetings with band music were always an attractive feature of the Army's work, drawing both spectators and worshippers. Though some hostility (attributed to publicans) was experienced in the 1880s, the Army then became a settled feature of York religious life, with its characteristic blend of religious mission and social work.[59]

Outreach through mission, however, was only a part of the work of the churches, though one is given the impression that for many active Christians there cannot have been much leisure time left for anything else. Nevertheless pastors also felt it necessary to bind together their flocks with a host of other ancillary activities which were to attach converts and maintain the loyalties of the faithful. Central to this, of course, were the Sunday services and Bible study. Two important developments in this area in the nineteenth century were the growing importance of the Holy Communion, and the introduction of the evening preaching service. Whereas in 1849 none of the 23 churches in York administered the Holy Communion weekly, and only nine of them as frequently as monthly, weekly celebrations had become the norm – at least for Anglicans – a century later.[60]

Evening services were really an evangelical innovation, particularly on the part of Wesleyans who wished to hold their services at other than the hours of the Established Church. Morning or afternoon services were usual for the Church of England in 1831. As the *Yorkshire Gazette* explained, 'reading the Bible and religious books in the family circle ought to be the Sabbath evening occupation of every God-fearing household'.[61] But with the introduction of gas lighting (Lendal Chapel was the first to be lit with gas in 1816) it was easier to offer evening services, and these rapidly became popular with those classes who worked hard until late on Saturday nights in shops or on the market where the poor bought their provisions at the end of their week's labour. The Sunday evening lecture service rapidly became a normal feature of any church which wished to reach the lower classes.

In addition to Sunday worship, every responsible parish priest came to feel his church ought also to provide a whole range of other activities. The old puritan style had been quite against these: Dean Close in 1866 had eulogised the gentleman scholar-priest who stooped to grasp the horny hand of the labourer, but he thought 'it cannot promote their respect or reverence for his office or his work, to remember that he was bowled out at cricket by the Parish Clerk, or suffered at football from the hob-nailed shoes of one of his humbler parishioners'. But in July 1927 it was quite acceptable for the Rector's team to play the Wardens' team of St. Clement's at cricket on the Knavesmire.[62]

St. Clement's might indeed stand as example of what most churches and chapels of any size were attempting to offer to consolidate the work of attracting people to the churches. St. Clement's was consecrated in 1874 and became the parish church in 1876; G. M. Argles was priest there from 1871 until 1919, and his work was one of the successes of the late Victorian Church. Already in 1873 he had a parish magazine, Men's and Women's Guilds, and a Parish Temperance society. The first parish Flower Show was held in 1875 and became an annual event; a Penny Bank and Parish Library were in existence by 1877; and the first Mothers' Meeting was held in 1882. A Girls' Friendly Society came in 1894; a unit of the Church Lads' Brigade in 1900; a Choral Society in 1906; and a company of Girl Guides in 1920. By 1924 there was a Tennis Club and a Hockey Club, and by 1927 an Amateur Dramatic Society. The Church had to compete with new forms of leisure to survive.[63]

Changing Patterns in the Twentieth Century

The 1851 census remains the one fixed point for an analysis of the churches in the Victorian period, since the York papers regrettably did not join the fashion for reporting attendances at the various churches in their area in the autumn of 1881. But for the twentieth century there are the results of three such censuses conducted by B. S. Rowntree in 1901, 1935 and 1948 as part of his great surveys of York.[64] In Table 2 the total number of adult attendances in York in 1851 is added to Rowntree's results.

Allowing for the probability that fewer people were attending church twice or three times on a Sunday in 1901 than in 1851, it is possible that the churches had more or less maintained their numbers of attenders, but over a period in which the population had nearly doubled. The 1884 Visitation Returns suggest that the estimated number in Anglican churches in 1884 was not much different from that found by Rowntree in 1901. All but the Roman Catholic Church, though, suffered a setback which was both absolute and relative to population in the first half of the

Table 2   1851-1948
Church Attendances in York

	Church of England	Noncon-formist	Roman Catholic	Total
1851				
Adult attendances: Number	10,842	9,536	2,070	22,448
%	48.3	42.5	9.2	100.0
As % of adult population[1]	40.3	35.4	7.7	83.4
1901				
Adult attendances: Number	7,453	7,247	2,360	17,060
%	43.7	42.5	13.8	100.0
As % of adult population	15.5	15.1	4.9	35.5
1935				
Adult attendances: Number	5,395	4,386	2,989	12,770
%	42.2	34.4	23.4	100.0
As % of adult population	7.5	6.1	4.1	17.7
1948				
Adult attendances: Number	3,384	3,763	3,073	10,220
%	33.1	36.8	30.1	100.0
As % of adult population	4.3	4.8	3.9	13.0

[1] The population in 1851 is taken as that which lived approximately within the municipal boundaries of York in 1901. The smaller York of 1851 was served by the same churches, and if attendances are calculated as a proportion of this population the figure is 90.9%. Rowntree took the churches and municipal population of the day, including Acomb in his 1935 survey for the first time.

twentieth century, with the Nonconformists suffering more heavily than the Anglicans in the interwar years.

    Some sense of what broad trends might lie behind these figures can be gained from individual and congregational records, though membership figures in a period of declining commitment might give an unduly favourable picture. The plateau which most churches seemed to have reached around the beginning of the new century gave way for most to a period of decline from about 1905. Anglican, Methodist and Baptist figures all suggest that decline had begun before the outbreak of the First World War, though the war seems to have accentuated the trend which with some exceptions continued right up until the early 1950s. There was then a period of revival which gave way to renewed decline in the 1960s; a sharp downturn in the late 1960s was continued throughout the 1970s.

The fall in numbers was most pronounced within the city walls, the only exception being St. Cuthbert's, which was filled to overflowing with people from all over the city and beyond at the time of the 1969 Visitation. This was due to the efforts of the Revd. David Watson, a powerful Evangelical preacher who, in the 1970s, was allowed to take over and fill the large and almost redundant church of St. Michael-le-Belfrey at the side of the Minster.[65] In the suburbs two new churches were planted in the parish of Holy Trinity, Heworth, to the east; two in the parish of St. Stephen, Acomb, to the west; one in St. Clement's to the south west; and one in St. Olave's to the north west; while there was also some growth in the northern commuter villages of Huntington and Haxby. Even in areas of population growth, however, the churches had to fight hard to maintain absolute numbers and what growth there was did not cancel out the losses within the old city.[66]

The history of the Methodist Church shows a similar pattern, though it is somewhat complicated by the amalgamations which produced the United Methodist Church in 1907 and the Methodist Church in 1932, creating the need for rationalisation and the closure of chapels. Membership figures show clear evidence of decline. When the Primitive Methodists closed their Ebenezer Chapel in Little Stonegate in 1900 and moved to a new site in Monkgate outside Monk Bar they took with them 192 members; by 1934 they had only 166.[67] Even the great Wesleyan Chapels were not exempt from decline. The Groves Chapel, down to 270 members at the start of the First World War, had lost another 100 by the start of the Second; and Melbourne Terrace fell from 235 to 149. What had once been growth points in late Victorian York had now themselves become ageing parts of the city, though Fulford (54 to 49) and Clifton (149 to 135) scarcely offered much hope of new growth points further out.[68]

The same general picture of falling numbers is presented by the Baptist Church in Priory Street, which fell back from an already low 128 in 1914 to 101 in 1940; by 1950 they were down to 87 before the revival brought them up to 191, their highest since the start of the century. A second church was begun in Acomb in 1963 which by 1980 had 111 members, but by this time the central church had declined to 134.[69]

The greatest fall of all was that experienced by the Congregationalists, who collapsed between the wars. In 1914 Lendal had a membership of 120 and Salem one of 236; both had enjoyed better days but at neither church was there a hint of the calamity which followed the war. In 1920 Salem's membership had also fallen to 120, and financial problems were apparent.[70] Lendal was the first to go. Prompted by a letter from their bank, the members voted to sell the premises and begin again in the suburbs. Burton Stone Lane, Clifton, was chosen and New Lendal chapel was opened there in 1934 with a membership of 16.[71] Attempts to unite the two city centre causes had failed, but Salem also had grown too weak to continue on its own. By 1936 the members realised that 'apart from finances there is not enough young life to carry on'. The communion roll, which had risen from 103 in 1922 to 161 in 1927 had fallen to 120 in 1936; of these, only 53 actually received a monthly communion during the year. A remnant of the congregation continued to meet in the Guild Room, but of 83 nominal members in 1938, only 13 lived centrally. There was no reason to continue in what had long ceased to be a fashionable part of the city, except that 'to move to the suburbs would have definite disadvantages in that whatever location might be selected the majority of our present members would have larger distances to travel'. Numbers continued to dwindle, and the church petered out in June 1953.[72] Not until the formation of the United Reformed Church in 1972 was a city centre cause re-established, with the Priory Street former Presbyterian Church becoming by 1980 the church with the largest single Nonconformist membership in central York.[73]

The history of the churches in York in the twentieth century was closely related to York's slum clearance and housing schemes. Weakening churches and chapels found the areas in which they stood depopulated as the slums of such places as Bedern, Walmgate and Layerthorpe were cleared.[74] Rehousing was started on the Tang Hall estate, a mile to the east of Walmgate Bar, in 1919. St. Hilda's parish was carved out of St. Thomas, Osbaldwick, in 1936, by which time the population was already over 7,000, mainly unskilled labourers. The Methodists moved St. George's to its third site to serve the new community in 1937. But in 1969 the regular congregation at St. Hilda's was only 150 and the new church was still unfinished in 1980; while at St. George's the membership was only 80 and evening services had been virtually abandoned.[75] Other large housing schemes transformed Burton Stone Lane and Clifton, but it was Acomb which grew most rapidly, especially after the Second World War, and presented the greatest challenge to the churches. The vast area of new housing from the river south-westwards through Acomb to the Tadcaster Road at Dringhouses was served in 1981 by four Anglican

churches, three Methodist chapels, a Baptist chapel, a Roman Catholic
church, a Quaker Meeting and a Mormon tabernacle.[76]

The Catholic Church was the only one which could feel happy with
Rowntree's figures, and indications were that the trend he perceived
continued in the second half of the twentieth century. From having only
two churches – St. Wilfrid's and St. George's – in 1914, York had seven in
1981. The parish of the English Martyrs at last received a church in 1932,
and in 1954 a separate parish was created in Acomb, dedicated to Our
Lady. In the Middlesbrough diocese, St. Aelred's parish was created in
Tang Hall in 1932 (before the Anglican parish of St. Hilda), though a
permanent church was not opened until 1956; the Burton Stone Lane
estate was supplied with St. Joseph's in 1941; and the area between the
two parishes in the north-eastern suburbs was assigned to St. Paulinus in
1968.[77]

The success of the Roman Catholic Church, taken together with the
revival led by David Watson at St. Cuthbert's and St. Michael-le-Belfrey
at the other end of the theological spectrum, were a salutary reminder in
the later twentieth century that the history of religion in York between
1831 and 1981 was one of changing patterns as well as of decline. In 1915
the rector of St. Cuthbert's had written of a 'strong religious feeling
beneath the surface – which shows itself in time of trouble and on special
occasions such as memorial services, baptisms, weddings and funerals.
There is constant evidence of steadfast faith, bright hope, and true-
hearted lovingkindness'.[78] This level of religion cannot be measured or
lightly dismissed, but the Victorian pattern had certainly been broken and
many explanations can be suggested: the disruption to church activities
during two world wars when church and school premises were
requisitioned by the military; the rise of alternative leisure facilities which
undermined the virtual monopoly which religion had once enjoyed; the
disruption of settled communities, habits, expectations and disciplines;
changes in social fashion. The incumbent of Dringhouses noted in 1900,
'Very much attendance at Church is, I fear, due to custom only, it seems
"the right thing to do" '.[79] Within a few years that age had passed. Only
11 of the 23 churches in York in 1831 were still open for public worship in
1981; only two Methodist chapels remained within the walls, and both
were under sentence of closure.[80] Yet in a city which also included
congregations of Christian Scientists, Christadelphians, Open and Exclu-
sive Brethren, Spiritualists, Seventh Day Adventists, Pentecostalists,
Mormons and Jehovah's Witnesses, religion could hardly be said to be
dead. The Minster too continued to meet the spiritual needs of the city in
a way which transcended the institutional problems of the mainstream
denominations.

Sources

The locations of the principal sources are as follows: York Diocesan Records – Borthwick Institute of Historical Research; York Minster Records – York Minster Archives; Unitarian Chapel, St. Saviourgate – Borthwick Institute; Lendal and Salem Independent Chapel records – York City Archives; Wesleyan Methodist Records (William Camidge Collection) – York Minster Library; Methodist Records, New Street and Centenary Wesleyan Circuits, and Primitive Methodist First Circuit – North Yorkshire County Record Office, and Circuit Safes at Centenary and Trinity (Monkgate) Chapels; Wesley Circuit Records – Circuit Safe at Wesley Chapel; Quaker records – Friends' Meeting House; most printed sources and local newspapers – York City Reference Library; Census of Religious Worship, 1851, Returns (H.O. 129/515) – Public Record Office, Kew. I should like to thank the archivists, librarians and custodians of these records for their generous help.

Notes

1. *Y[orkshire] G[azette]* 12 January 1828.
2. White's *Directory of the East and North Ridings,* 1840, p. 94; *V[ictoria] C[ounty] H[istory, City of York]*, p. 304.
3. *Y[orkshire] E[vening] P[ress]* 23 November 1959; Salem Chapel Minute Book, 2 July 1882.
4. *Census 1851: Religious Worship,* Accounts & Papers, lxxxix, 1852-3; the original returns for York are in HO 129/515. W. A. Armstrong, *Stability and Change in an English County Town,* 1974, pp. 72-4 discusses points arising from these returns, but he unfortunately did not have access to the complete set.
5. *YG* 27 August 1836.
6. All calculations are based on the original returns and are not directly comparable with those published by Mann: Sunday scholars have been omitted and the adult population in 1851 has been taken as 68% of the total (Armstrong, op. cit. (n. 4) p. 48). I have tried to turn attendances into attenders by taking the sum of the best attended service + ½ the second-best + ⅓ the third-best, i.e. Mann's formula but without the bias towards attendance at morning service. For this and for the use of average rather than precise attendances, see D. M. Thompson, 'The Religious Census of 1851' in R. Lawton (ed.), *The Census and Social Structure,* 1978, pp. 250-2. Missing data has been estimated from diocesan records.
7. *V[isitation] R[eturns of the Clergy],* 1865; he said similar things in 1868.
8. *YG* 1 November 1862.
9. VR 1865, 1894.
10. VR 1877.
11. *Report of the Proceedings of the Church Congress held at York, 1866,* 1867, p. 196; VR 1865.
12. VR 1865, 1868. J. Howard, *Historical Sketch of the Origin and Work of the York Incorporated (Church of England) Sunday School Committee,* York 1887, second ed. 1896.

13 HO 129/515 (St. Mary, Bishophill Junior); Diocese of York, Orders in Council, passim; Cathedral and Church Returns, 1875; Clifton was partly formed out of St. Michael-le-Belfrey but mainly out of St. Olave. In 1853 a new parish was also assigned to St. Edward the Confessor, Dringhouses, out of Holy Trinity, Micklegate, St. Mary, Bishophill Senior and Acomb. A further church, Holy Trinity, King's Court, was rebuilt in 1861, but not to meet the needs of a new or enlarged parish.

14 VR 1865, 1884, 1915.

15 Cathedral and Church Returns, 1875; see also VR (St. Thomas) 1865, 1884.

16 VR 1900.

17 VR 1894, 1884.

18 *YG* 4 September 1858, 28 April 1906; Unitarian Chapel Committee Minutes, 3 December 1900.

19 Lendal Chapel Minute Book, 15 July 1839 and passim.

20 Salem Chapel Minute Book, 1 October 1846 and passim.

21 *A List of the Members and Attenders of the York Monthly Meeting* (1862 ff.) passim; F. J. Gillman, *The Story of the York Adult Schools,* 1907; S. Allott, *Friends in York,* York, 1978.

22 *Baptists of Yorkshire,* Bradford & York, 1912; *Baptist Handbook* (1869 ff.); [H. A. Jones], *History of Priory Street Baptist Church,* Centenary Brochure, 1962.

23 *YEP* 12 October 1962; *Presbyterian Church of England Official Handbook* (1893 ff.); F. H. Legge, *The Story of St. Columba's Church, York, 1873-1973,* Centenary Brochure, 1973.

24 Baines's *Directory of the County of York,* 1822, vol. 2, p. 48; *YG* 4 June 1864.

25 G. F. Willmot, J. M. Biggins and P. M. Tillott (eds.), *York, A Survey,* 1959, p. 145; *YG* 7 September, 16 November 1850.

26 See the table in B. I. Coleman, *The Church of England in the Mid-Nineteenth Century,* Historical Association G.98, 1980, p. 41.

27 *Middlesbrough D[iocesan] Y[ear] B[ook],* 1979; *Leeds DYB,* 1979.

28 J. Lyth, *Glimpses of Early Methodism in York,* York 1885; W. Camidge, *Methodism in York,* York 1908.

29 The attendance at Centenary (1037) was surpassed by the Wesleyan Reformers meeting in the Festival Concert Room (1317); the average claimed at Centenary was 1400, and by the Reformers, 1450.

30 Quarterly Schedules, Centenary Circuit, passim; *YG* 29 March 1851.

31 *YG* 13 April 1850.

32 This explanation occurs in the Religious Census returns from the Festival Concert Room and elsewhere.

33 Circuit Plan, 1852, and memorandum of agreement, 5 November 1851 (Wesleyan Methodist Records); W. Camidge, *A History of the Methodist New Connexion in York* (n.d.); J. Lyth, op. cit. (n. 28), p. 266; W. Camidge, *Primitive Methodism in York,* 1901.

34 Idem; and Local Preachers' Meeting Minute Book, and Quarterly Schedules, Trinity Circuit, passim.

35 Wesley Chapel Trust, York, Minute Book 1848-71 (Wesley Circuit Safe);
    Quarterly Schedules, Centenary Circuit; Quarterly Meeting Minute Books,
    Wesley Circuit.
36 W. Camidge, *Methodism in York;* Quarterly Schedules, Centenary Circuit.
37 W. Camidge, op. cit. (n. 28); W. B. Gardner, *Unfinished Story: the birth and
    growth of the Groves Methodist Church in the City of York,* 1949; Quarterly
    Schedules, Centenary Circuit; Wesley Circuit Extension Committee Minute
    Book, 9 November 1871; *Y.G.* 17 September 1910.
38 W. Camidge, *Primitive Methodism; YG* 12 April 1913; Quarterly Schedules,
    Trinity Circuit; Quarterly Meeting Minute Books, Trinity Circuit, 3 Sep-
    tember 1883, 15 December 1889; York Second Circuit Plan, April – June
    1894 (Wesleyan Methodist Records).
39 Quarterly Schedules, New Street and Centenary Circuits (NYCRO and Trinity
    Circuit Safe); W. Camidge, *Methodism in York.*
40 *YG* 17 November 1888.
41 VR 1894; Quarterly Meeting Minute Book, Wesley Circuit, March and June
    1878.
42 Transactions of the Select Society for Mutual Improvement, York Centenary
    Circuit, 13 February 1846; J. Howard, op. cit. (n. 12), p. 7.
43 Select Society for Mutual Improvement, loc. cit.
44 J. Howard, op. cit. (n. 12), pp. 59-60; *York Wesleyan Methodist Sunday
    Schools, Annual Report,* 1841, 1848 (Wesleyan Methodist Records).
45 W. Sessions, *York and its Associations with the Early History of the Sunday
    School Movement,* York, 1882; J. Howard, op. cit. (n. 12), p. 84.
46 *York Incorporated . . . Sunday School Committee, Annual Report,* 1900; Local
    Preachers' Meeting Minute Book, Centenary Circuit, 1900 (Wesleyan
    Methodist Records).
47 F. J. Gillman, op. cit (n. 21).
48 For examples, see ibid., pp. 47, 49.
49 J. Howard, op. cit (n. 12), p. 50; Wesley Circuit Extension Committee Minute
    Book, 3 January 1873; Wesleyan Sunday School Committee Minute Books,
    Wesley Circuit, December 1881; Salem Chapel Minute Book, 29 March 1928.
50 W. Camidge, *York's Ragged School. Its Inception and Development* (n.d.).
51 *YG* 10, 24 November 1849.
52 *YG* 1 December 1852, 1 October 1853, 4 November 1854, 17 November
    1855, 28 October 1865, 22 October 1870. A special Race Course Mission was
    started in 1904 – *YG* 25 September 1936, and *Annual Reports* in York
    Reference Library.
53 *City of York Mission,* Annual Report, 1902: *YEP* 4 July 1970, 13 September
    1975.
54 *YG* 17 November 1849, 20 December 1862.
55 *YG* 26 November 1842; *Yorkshire Herald* 8 October 1910.
56 *Yorkshire Herald* 8 October 1910.
57 *YG* 12, 25 January 1834; J. Howard, op. cit (n. 12), p. 34.
58 e.g. VR (St. Saviour) 1934.

[59] *VCH* p. 447; *YG* 15 July 1882, 31 March 1883; *Yorkshire Herald*, 11, 12 July 1882, 26, 27 March 1883, Other information from Mr. R. Hawkshaw, who is preparing a *Souvenir History* (1981).

[60] Visitation Returns of the Churchwardens, 1849.

[61] *YG* 29 September 1838.

[62] *Report of Church Congress, 1866*, p. 245; *St. Clement's Parish Magazine*, June 1927.

[63] idem; and *St. Mary, Bishophill the Elder, Ancient and Modern. The Jubilee Record* (1924). For a fuller discussion of such matters, see B. S. Rowntree, *Poverty and Progress*, 1941, pp. 424-8.

[64] B. S. Rowntree, *Poverty, A study of town life*, 1901; fourth ed., 1902, pp. 344-8; *Poverty and Progress*, pp. 417-424; and with G. R. Lavers, *English Life and Leisure*, 1951, pp. 339-74. Space does not permit me to repeat and expand upon Rowntree's own full discussion of the trends between 1901 and 1948.

[65] VR 1969; *YEP* 5 November 1969, 6 April 1971, 29 September 1978.

[66] VR 1946, 1952, 1969.

[67] Quarterly Schedules, Trinity Circuit (NYCRO and Trinity Circuit Safe).

[68] Quarterly Schedules, Centenary Circuit (NYCRO) and New Street Circuit (Trinity Circuit Safe).

[69] *Baptist Handbook* (1914-1980), passim: [H. A. Jones], *Priory Street Baptist Church;* Acomb Baptist Church records.

[70] *Congregational Year Book*, 1914, 1920; Lendal and Salem Chapel Minute Books, passim.

[71] Lendal Chapel Minute Book, 18 October 1928, 31 January, 4 July, 22 August, 26 September 1929, 12 November 1931, 5, 15 July 1934.

[72] Salem Deacons' Minute Book, 18 February 1936 et seq.; Communion Attendance Registers, passim; Deacons' Minute Book, 4 November 1935. A small group of former Salem members began meeting in about 1953 in the Friends' Meeting House on Sunday afternoons; in 1962 they joined New Lendal – information from Mrs. M. F. Baker.

[73] *United Reformed Church Year Book*, 1980. This congregation, though, drew on the settled Scottish population from the whole York area.

[74] See, for example, VR (St. Margaret) 1946; (St. Cuthbert) 1952.

[75] *YG* 2 August 1919; VR (St. Hilda) 1936, 1969; *YG* 22 January 1937; Centenary Circuit Plan, 1980. St. Hilda's parish also included parts of St. Lawrence and Holy Trinity, Heworth.

[76] The Mormon Tabernacle was opened in 1962; by 1968 there were 460 registered members – *YEP* 12 October 1962, 6 May 1968.

[77] *Middlesbrough DYB*, 1979. *Leeds DYB*, 1979. A further parish was created for the village of Haxby in 1979.

[78] VR 1915.

[79] VR 1900.

[80] *YEP* 4 January 1975, 26 January 1980. There was remarkably little non-Christian worship in York, even in 1981: the small Jewish congregation closed in 1975, and there was little settlement of Asian immigrants with other religious traditions.

CHAPTER IX

George Leeman and York Politics 1833-1880

by

Alf Peacock

ONE OF THE MOST IMPORTANT DATES in York history is 1835. In that year an Act was passed which opened up local government, and in York gave men of a certain political persuasion the opportunity, at last, to achieve political power. The Act was the Municipal Corporations Act, and in York the people it opened the door to were the Tories. The opponents of reform there benefited almost immediately from the fact of reform.

For years before 1835 York had been a Whig city, controlled by a self-perpetuating closed corporation, to which very very few of its opponents were admitted,[1] no worse, but certainly no better than similar bodies elsewhere in the country. The Act of 1835 brought all this to an end and the Tories, shut out of power for so long, took to electioneering with alacrity. They used all the usual techniques for influencing voters and were presided over by a man with a long purse who was destined to become a major force in British politics. Within two years he had destroyed the Liberal majority which had been returned at the first reformed elections, and was installed as the city's first Tory Lord Mayor. He was George Hudson, the famous 'Railway King', and he and his Party were to rule York for a decade or more. In those years the Liberals practically disappeared from the council, thrown out by a grovelling, grasping, scared electorate; or if they stayed they remained there as Liberals in name only, sycophantic followers of the great man, wearing his livery and boasting of the fact.[2] When Hudson began to make the moves that finally laid him low, the opposition in the council consisted of no more than four people,[3] but it was an opposition that seized its chances with great skill. One member of that little group was James Meek, the proprietor of the local glassworks; another was George Leeman (Plate 10).[4]

Leeman and Liberalism

Leeman was an attorney and a member of the Rev. James Parsons's Independent congregation, which met at Salem chapel in Lendal.[5] He was born on 22 August 1809 and joined the Independents in 1833. Leeman had been articled to Robert Henry Anderson, one of the most extraordinary characters in York's modern history. Anderson was a Catholic who was prominent in reform movements until he finally went over to Hudson in the late 1840s.[6] In 1820 he was in trouble with the Yorkshire Law Society which passed a vote of censure on him for 'advertising for, or soliciting business, by a printed circular',[7] and eventually he fell out with Leeman, as he fell out with everybody. The details of the dispute, such as they are, emerge from the reports of *Martin* v. *Barber,* a case heard in the Sheriff's Court at York in 1834, in which Anderson appeared for the defendant and R. H. A. Smith represented the plaintiff.[8] Leeman appeared in the case as a witness called by Smith (who had also once been Anderson's clerk).

Leeman revealed that in 1834, when *Martin* v. *Barber* was being heard, he was a clerk to Smith. In court Anderson questioned him and elicited the fact that Leeman had been articled to him and now entertained 'a degree of hostility against me, for what reason I cannot conceive'. He said he made Leeman a present of £100 when the latter's articles were signed, to which Leeman replied, 'It is false, Sir; you gained nearly £200 by me'.

Leeman gave his version of his relationships with Anderson in a letter to the *York Courant.*[9] In it he revealed that he had worked for Anderson for eight years, then produced £120 and asked to be articled. Anderson proposed that Leeman should work for two years without salary, then enter into a bond saying that he would not practise within York, or within five miles of York, for five years after qualifying. Leeman rejected the demand and a compromise was agreed to, whereby he paid the £120 and worked for a salary lower, he said, than he could have got anywhere else. He worked for Anderson until the summer of 1833, having been with him for a total of 11 years.

In 1833 a serious difference of opinion occurred between Leeman and Anderson, and Leeman applied to Mr. Justice Littledale, who made an order by which his articles were assigned to R. H. A. Smith. It was with Smith that Leeman eventually qualified. The dispute between Leeman and Anderson is an important fact in York politics, adding, as it did, to the troubles that faced the Liberal Party in the middle decades of the nineteenth century. Leeman became closely identified with the *Yorkshireman,* the city's radical paper, and its columns were closed to Anderson. This prompted him to start journals of his own, one of them designed specifically to puff himself and denigrate his erstwhile clerk.[10]

Leeman, who was admitted to the roll of attorneys and solicitors in 1835, was only one person who suffered from the activities of Anderson, the stormy petrel of York politics, but he seems to have benefited to some extent from his 11 years with that volatile figure.[11] Anderson was closely involved with politics; he nailed his colours to the Whig mast and spent much time in the fight for Catholic Emancipation. Leeman's liberalism was of the same kind as that of his master – he was a nonconformist himself and never deviated from allegiance to the party which he thought would end dissenters' grievances. One of his first appearances in court was in a case involving church rate protesters,[12] and thereafter he was always present at meetings and rallies called to discuss such issues. In 1837, for example, he tried to persuade the corporation to give its support to a petition on the question of church rates.[13]

On broader political issues Leeman was middle-of-the-road, a cautious reformer never willing to go so far as to endanger his own prospects. He shied away from supporting candidates like Henry Vincent, who were tainted with Chartism, and he never committed himself wholeheartedly to a cause while it was unpopular. He was for free trade, and spoke out for it at least from 1841,[14] but he never totally identified himself with the Anti-Corn Law League. He was for the secret ballot at least from 1835,[15] and was always for some extension of the franchise, adopting his own version of some kind of psychology of entitlement that varied as the years went by. During the Chartist years Leeman was embarrassed, as most Liberals were, by the logic of the case put forward by the followers of Feargus O'Connor when it was contrasted with his own; but when the threat of Chartism was removed he did not take part in the movement for Joseph Hume's 'Little Charter', as so many others did.[16] When a York branch of Joshua Walmsley's National Parliamentary and Financial Reform Association was first suggested Leeman stayed aloof from it;[17] a year and a half later, however, a branch was created,[18] to which he did give his support.[19] By this time he was strongly entrenched in power in the city.

When the creation of a reform organisation was mooted in York in 1848 the city was in the throes of an election in which Leeman, for a time, was a possible candidate.[20] Henry Redhead Yorke, the Liberal member, had committed suicide. The ensuing contest illustrated the dilemma in which Liberals of Leeman's type (who refused to accept the comprehensive Chartist platform) or Walmsley's (who was for triennial parliaments, electoral districts, the ballot and household suffrage) found themselves, arguing about just *where* the franchise should start and engaging in a dutch auction to get support. The contest ended with two declared Liberals fighting each other (William Mordaunt Edward Milner and Henry Vincent), with a sham radical who was introduced by Robert Henry Anderson confusing the issue.[21] Leeman ended up by supporting Milner on the hustings in a half-hearted address in which he publicly regretted the fact that the candidate was only lukewarm on reform. The 1848 election in York was an extraordinary affair, with Leeman speaking (almost) for Vincent, and supporting Milner!

Councillor, Alderman, Lord Mayor

That Leeman genuinely believed in some kind of reform cannot be doubted, and his belief in the need to redress dissenting grievances made any other refuge than the Liberal Party impossible for him. However, the sceptical could point to the fact that Liberal politics also produced (presumably) an income for him. After reform people like Leeman were regularly employed at the annual voters' registrations, challenging the known supporters of the opposing party and, in his case, earning the hatred of George Hudson and the *Gazette*. Leeman came to be known as a Liberal lawyer and lost work and got work as a result of it. Lord Wenlock made him Clerk of the Peace for the East Riding; he represented the interests of Samuel Holberry, the Chartist, who died in York Castle and became Chartism's greatest martyr;[22] he was always in demand in church rate cases; and he became solicitor to and investor in many anti-Hudson railway companies.[23] By the time Hudson fell, the firm of Leeman and Clark (William Fox Clark) was very, very prosperous.

Leeman had joined the York Corporation as a councillor soon after reform, but during the Hudson years little was heard of him. He never spoke out against the excesses of the Railway King, and neither for that matter did people like James Meek and the elder Joseph Rowntree. Perhaps they reasoned that people would not have listened to them – in which case they were almost certainly correct. Perhaps they waited patiently until Hudson became vulnerable and made a mistake, or until the consequences of his rule worked themselves out, as every intelligent observer *must* have realised they would. If that is the case they were good strategists, but the uncommitted reader of York history is forced to wonder why these men of principle did not feel compelled to keep up a

running criticism of a man whose major tactic was to personalise every
issue. Only one brave soul ever stood up to Hudson. He was Frederick
Hopwood (and he turned out to have feet of clay). Leeman kept out of his
campaign until the very last moment, when he could do little else.[24]

Hudson gave Leeman and Meek their opportunity to attack him in
1846, when he tried to foist on the council a pet scheme for bridging the
Ouse; which most people thought was for the benefit of his railway
companies. Following this he made a terrible mistake handling a York
election (as Lord Mayor for the third time he presided over it), and then
the revelations of his railway frauds began to appear. The *Herald* had for
years been a Whig paper, then switched its allegiances to Hudson, singing
his praises with all the regularity and monotony of a Robert Henry
Anderson. In 1846 it had attacked Leeman and the *Yorkshireman* for
daring to question Hudson, and the York and North Midland Railway
company for their 'kind, liberal, and disinterested manner towards the
city at large';[25] not long afterwards it was having to report not only the
findings of the railway committees set up to investigate the activities of its
hero, but also some of the scandals of the Railway King's system in York –
which it must have known about earlier, but had never mentioned. There
was the affair of John Pulleyn, for example, the city surveyor, who was
caught perpetrating 'a job'.[26] Pulleyn had been a complete Hudson man.
There was also the affair of B. T. Wilkinson.[27] From the time of the
Railway King's downfall the *Herald* never deviated from its support for
the Liberal Party, but its role in the 1840s is not one to be proud of.
Leeman, in its view, was now the man to be followed. He must frequently
have thought of how the Hargroves[28] had pilloried him earlier. His own
paper, the *Yorkshireman*,[29] continued in existence alongside the *Herald*.

As the revelations about Hudson came out he resigned from his
railway companies, and his erstwhile colleagues on the York council
turned on him, like the *Herald,* in a disgusting episode. He was expelled
from the corporate body, demands were made that his position as a
Justice of the Peace be declared vacant, and Alderman Matterson
demanded that his portrait be removed from the Mansion House. Never
was 'A more scorching humiliation . . . inflicted upon man', wrote the
Yorkshireman.[30] People like Matterson hoped that, by denouncing their
old leader, they could retrieve something from the wreckage and survive
as municipal legislators. They chose a Liberal as Lord Mayor, and James
Chadwick, a Hudsonian to the core, postured as a person who had always
disapproved of his leader's excesses. It was strange, E. R. Anderson said,
to hear Chadwick present himself as 'one of the very best reformers in the
council'.[31] Chadwick, chairman of the local gas company, became leader
of the Tories in the wake of Hudson's downfall; he was eventually

replaced by William Dallah Husband, another survivor from the era of the Railway King.

A swing away from the Tories began in York. Elections to the council were then held annually in November and from 1848 the Liberals made gains. In that year Guildhall, 'the pet ward of Mr. Hudson', went Liberal when Leeman's legal partner defeated Husband, and two gains were made.[32] At that stage the Tories had a majority of 19.[33] A year later Leeman organised the contests which were, the *Gazette* said, 'on the whole adverse to the Conservative party' and more gains were made (Leeman himself being re-elected unopposed in Guildhall).[34] Even before the election of that year the *Gazette* had seen the way things were going when it said that 'the Deacon of Salem' was determined to get a completely Liberal council – all we want, it whined, is 'a fair share of influence in the management of the city's affairs', apparently unaware that that was exactly what it had denied their opponents for a decade or more.[35] The Tory majority was further lowered when a Liberal replaced a Tory alderman;[36] then in 1850 the great breakthrough came. In that year ten Tory seats and two Liberal seats were up for election. Six out of the ten retiring Tories declined to stand and the Liberals swept the board, making seven gains. This gave them a small majority at last, and one of the successful candidates that year was none other than Robert Henry Anderson. He had managed to get himself elected in Castlegate by paying five shillings a head for a vote, and in doing so defeated Joseph Rowntree.[37] Anderson, the *Yorkshireman* said, represented 'not the respectability of the Ward but the beer-barrels of Mr. Edward Calvert, and the "five-shilling headmen of the Ward" '.

In 1850 six aldermen retired, and the Liberals did what Hudson used to do in those circumstances. They grabbed five of the seats for themselves, and Leeman was one of those chosen to go to what, not long before, he had called 'the ceremonial' part of the council. (Oddly enough R. H. Anderson was also created an alderman).[38] As if to underline their success the Liberals chose James Meek as Lord Mayor.

From 1850 onwards the Liberals were in a majority in York, and they added to their numbers, not always by using the 'purity of election' methods which they gave lip service to – that is if the *Gazette* is to be believed. In Walmgate in 1851 (where you *had* to use such methods to stand a chance) the Tories were defeated, it said,

> by recourse on the part of the Whig-Radicals – the professed purity party – to the most utter violation of all those principles of morality and decorum in praise of which they are wont to be so lavish when it suits their purpose.

Votes were bought for between five and ten shillings and 'men were led to the poll rather like beasts than human beings . . . the scene of drunkenness, debauchery, and immorality . . . baffles all description, and exceeded anything of the kind which . . . had ever before experienced. It was perfectly shocking.'[39]

Thereafter the Tories lost heart. In 1852 there were no contests anywhere, and by then the Liberals were in a majority of three to one, the *Gazette* saying they had 26 out of the 36 councillors, and eight of the twelve aldermanic seats.[40] In 1854 there were no contests,[41] and by 1856 there was established what the *Gazette* called 'an over-bearing tyranny', with three-quarters of the councillors followers of Leeman and Meek.[42] By the following year the same journal was complaining (again forgetting that Hudson had done exactly the same) that all council committees where 'patronage or influence are supposed to exist were closely barred against the intrusion of any Conservative councillor'.[43] In 1860 the Tories made some minor gains,[44] but that was a flash in the pan. They continued to make some inroads, but in 1861 the situation was that they had only 18 councillors to the Liberals' 30.[45]

From 1860 a change came over York municipal elections which might be worth noting. In that year a new system was introduced whereby nominations had to be in two days prior to the election. The result of this was a plethora of candidates – some nominated without their permission, some nominated simply to cause trouble, some nominated in two or three wards. In 1861, for example, 52 nominations were made, including eight for Micklegate, 26 for Walmgate and eight for Monk. Few of these actually went to the poll, but considerable confusion was caused.[46]

Leeman became an alderman in 1850 and three years later was chosen as Lord Mayor. In 1860 it was said that the Liberals had difficulty in finding a candidate to fill the office of first citizen, and Leeman agreed to stand again.[47] During this term of office he acted as anything but the unbiased person Lord Mayors were supposed to be; and half-way through his tenure of office he became ill, had to convalesce at St. Leonard's, and was absent from the city for long periods. Just after he left office his first wife died. Leeman, who married again, served a third term as Lord Mayor in 1870-71.

Just before the Liberals gained control of the corporation Leeman had entered into a controversy which regularly agitated the citizens of York. Throughout the whole of the period of Leeman's life there was controversy over the York strays, and, more often than not, Robert Henry Anderson was at the centre of it. In 1849 Leeman produced a Bill which was highly commended in the *Justice of the Peace*. It was introduced at a public meeting in the city,[48] and was intended to produce a more equitable system of management of the common lands.[49] It failed to pass through Parliament, however.

The controversy over the strays was a constant accompaniment to the mainstream of local politics, and it was often fought on party lines, reflecting what went on at a higher level.[50] When the Tories fell from power at that higher level a great change came over local government. Corporations at last gained real power from the Public Health Act of 1848. Until that Act was adopted in York the powers of local government, important though they were, had been very limited. From the time of its adoption the corporation had a modern look about it.

Public Health and Improvement of the City

The Public Health Act was introduced by Lord Morpeth, the nobleman who had applauded Leeman's bill for the management of common lands. It was intended to improve 'the sanitary condition of towns and populous places in England and Wales'. It created a central board of health which had powers to create local boards on the petition of ten per cent of the inhabitants of a district, and to enforce boards on places where the death rate was above 23 per 1,000. The local boards were empowered, and in some cases compelled, to carry out a wide range of duties, including[51]

> not only sanitation in the strict sense, – sewerage, drainage, and the like – but also much wider functions as the supply of water, the management of the streets, the making and maintaining of burial-grounds, and the regulation of offensive trades.

The 1848 Act gave local politicians great powers to modernise their cities, and of course the modernising would be expensive and bring inevitable reactions. The Tories of York realised this. In municipal boroughs the town council became the local sanitary authority, and the board a committee of it. Looking for an excuse to explain why so many of the Hudson rump would not be standing for election in 1850, the *Gazette* said that 'An opinion appears to be on the increase that the onerous duties which must devolve on the council, under the Health of Town's Act, will exceed the honour which municipal authority confers. . . .'[52] After the election, on 2 November, it said it wished the now victorious Liberals 'a happy deliverance from the odium which the costly working' of the Public Health Act 'will bring'.

The Public Health Act was introduced in the wake of a cholera epidemic, the effects of which were felt in York. The city had been hit by the first of the outbreaks of the disease in the nineteenth century, and by the time the second visitation occurred very little, in truth, had been done to improve the place. There had been a number of surveys of the state of the city, notably one by Thomas Laycock, who felt the lash of Hudson's tongue for daring to write it,[53] and a local Health of Towns organisation, mainly working-class, it seems, had been set up to advocate the need for reform.[54] Its activities, and the cholera, prepared York for the need for drastic measures, and the Public Health Act was adopted in March 1850, while the Tories were still nominally in control, but when in reality they had abdicated authority, knowing that their days were numbered.[55]

The population of York had been growing continuously throughout the nineteenth century and this contributed to, and underlined the urgency of the need for, adequate reform measures in the field of sanitation. The influx of Irish had done the same, those immigrants turning whole areas of the inner city (Map 5) into slums as bad as could be found anywhere.[56] Some indication of the huge task facing York's municipal legislators in the mid-nineteenth century is given in the opening sections of the chapter by Anne Digby, pp. 161-3, above.

Meek, Leeman and their colleagues set about tackling the problems of draining and improving the city, able to push through whatever measures they wanted without real opposition. (On the Board of Health in 1852 they had a majority of ten to three; on the finance committee one of nine to two; the watch committee consisted of eight Liberals and three Tories; while the Ouse Navigation committee had a majority of ten to one in favour of the ruling party.)[57] Straight away they were involved in increased expenditure. There was a debt taken over from the Commissioners of £2,000 on the general rate and £5,600 on the improvement rate, and another inherited by the Commissioners from the Market Trustees.[58] There was also the need to appoint a surveyor and many other servants – and all this before any work was done. In 1850 a rate of 1s. 2d. was levied.

It would be tedious to detail all the improvements that were made to the city between 1850 and 1870; suffice it to say that great improvements *were* made, and that for a considerable period the populace seemed to accept their need, *and* the increased expenditure involved. The extent of that expenditure can be discovered from perusing the columns of the opposition *Gazette,* and it did eventually bring the odium which the paper had forecast would come the way of Leeman and his colleagues. As early as February 1851 city funds were at a low ebb – partly because of the Jubbergate improvement. '. . . yet what do . . . our city Solons propose?' asked the *Gazette?* Why to provide accommodation for washerwomen, and books for mechanics and labourers. 'Baths and Washhouses and Public Libraries . . . forsooth!', while other more urgent reforms were needed.[59] Leeman proposed to meet some of the city's debts by selling corporate property, but expenditure continued to outrun income (income for the quarter following November 1851 was reckoned to be £1,547, while expenditure would be £2,305).[60] The Bedern needed improving; the Foss was a terrible hazard; everywhere work needed to be done to purify the city. In 1860 the total debt amounted to between £37,000 and £38,000 and, speaking on the council, in the debate at which those figures were presented, Leeman said that his party's policy was to throw the payment of money expended on improvements over 20 to 30 years. '. . . the present generation', he said, 'should not be called upon to pay for that which would be for the benefit of future generations'.[61] In 1868 it was reported that expenditure on lighting, scavenging, street improvements, salaries, interest, sundries and public sewerage works amounted to £10,529, while income was £8,234. In that year the *Gazette* reported that the Board of Health had borrowed £3,000 more than it should have – at five percent. Had they handled the matter more sensibly, it said, their own debt would have been £6,000 instead of £12,000.[62] In February 1870 a Mr. Edward Thomas Snowden wrote to the press about the taxes collected in the parish of St. Crux, showing how they had increased in the years of Liberal rule from £267 in 1851 to £402 ten years later.[63]

As had been said, the problems confronting York were so obvious and so overwhelming that there could be little argument about the necessity of reform, so the opposition was forced to criticise the *methods* of reform – usually choosing to attack the priorities of Leeman, Rowntree and the dominant members of the Liberal party, while always adopting a shocked attitude at the level of that most emotive of taxes, the rates, which reached 2s. in the pound in 1854. The *Gazette's* comments on proposals to build public washhouses and a library, while drainage work still remained to be done, have been quoted. There were other allegations, some of them of an unpleasant nature which, even if untrue, were not without effect. In 1852 it said that a 'notorious Whig-Radical', the largest shareholder in a local newspaper, had done a deal with the Board of Health, agreeing to set back his house on payment of £50 (which he wanted increased).[64] In June of the following year a letter writer wrote an 'exposure of corporate jobbing', in which he said that land had been bought from the manager of the *Yorkshireman* for an agreed sum of £50, and that more had then been handed over.[65] In 1857 there were complaints that the Board of Health were favouring Micklegate and Walmgate Wards,[66] and Joseph Rowntree came under severe attack. Husband exposed what he called a 'job' when he said that the council had refused to construct a main sewer in Layerthorpe (a poor area), unless the house owners there paid one-third of the cost of it, while Micklegate and the Mount had been drained at no expense to the inhabitants.[67] Later in the same year draining went ahead in the Pavement district, and thousands of pounds were spent on cleansing the Foss by intercepting the drains and routing the effluent into the Ouse, so fouling up that river. '. . . his will *must* be law', the *Gazette* said about Rowntree, and went on, nastily,

> Mr. Alderman Rowntree has no premises in Spurriergate, extending towards the River Ouse, and it is personally immaterial to him whether or not that river shall become an elongated cess-pool, spreading malaria and fever among the inhabitants of the district, and those periodically located in barges at the staithes near to Ouse Bridge.[68]

Leeman was undisputed leader of the Liberals from 1862, when James Meek died, and his methods of government also came under attack. He and his party monopolised the important committee places, as has been said; they frequently nominated opponents for the office of Lord Mayor and Sheriff, and forced them to pay the fines for refusing office;[69] and they used their patronage to secure posts for party supporters. In 1852, it was said that they deferred appointing a bellman because he was not a teetotaller (perhaps a wise decision);[70] and at the same time replaced the Registrar, Hewley Graham, a long serving Tory, by Francis William Calvert, a member of one of the most prominent local Liberal families.[71] In 1855 the council got some very bad publicity when it tried to fill six vacancies on the bench of justices with political nominees. Through death and resignations the York bench had dwindled to eight (as against a full-strength total of seventeen), while their work had doubled. The corporation sent in its nominations, and amongst them was Leeman himself! This was an incredibly indiscreet act, and it gave Robert Henry Anderson a glorious opportunity to attack his *bête noir*. Leeman, he pointed out, was a practising attorney, and it was the law, at least as far as counties were concerned, that no one should sit in judgement while practising law. On this occasion Anderson's will prevailed, but this was one of the last occasions on which he was able to torment his ex-employee.[72]

Leeman held complete sway over the corporation, and this led to him being referred to as a dictator, and a successor to Hudson. This seems to be unfair. His control over his party was not as complete as Hudson's had been, and there was no way it could be. Hudson was a Tory tyrant, whose power was based on graft and greed – if you did not bow the knee to the Railway King you got no inside information on the railways with which to make your fortune, no municipal or railway contracts, and you were victimised. Leeman had a very different following, a conglomeration of 'Old Whigs', Liberals, temperance and teetotal advocates, Quakers, Independents, Catholics and so on, as well as an increasingly vocal working-class element in the city. He had to balance the demands of all these, and he seems to have done so fairly well – at any rate he never seems to have irretrievably angered any important Liberal group. Certainly he used to fill vacant offices with Liberals (or teetotal bellmen), but every party leader did this – and there are perfectly logical explanations for doing so. Certainly Leeman loved power, but checked himself from abusing it as a rule. The business of allowing himself to be nominated as a J.P. illustrates his love of authority, but it was an untypical act. In 1851 he was said to have attempted a 'job' when he tried to replace a Mr. Buckle, a coal inspector, with a man named Britton, who was said to have been responsible for his 'dirty work' in Micklegate. Leeman ordered his followers to vote for Britton but was disobeyed and defeated.[73] It may well have been a salutary experience.

A controversy which illustrated the differences that existed in the ruling party in York occurred in 1852, when the corporation proposed to sell the Theatre Royal.[74] Leeman and others wanted to apply to the Lords of the Treasury for permission for the sale. During the debates he, Rowntree and Meek revealed that they were not theatregoers, and Leeman referred to the drama as a curse. Meek called the theatre 'Satan's synagogue' and said he had never seen a play in his life. 'It was high time the Theatre was pulled down', he said, 'and if ever it was pulled down, he hoped there would never be another raised in York'. This gave the *Gazette* a glorious opportunity to twit the sabbatarian Meek in the same way Hudson had done years before.[75] It called him a 'sanctimonious Alderman', and pointed to the fact that furnaces at his glassworks were kept in, and attended, on Sundays; and that Meek's gambling in shares was not beyond criticism. Meek and his like, however, did not get their way over the theatre; their followers refusing to go along with their proposals. There is a lovely report of a speech from E. R. Anderson, a Liberal, in which he quoted Shakespeare to Meek, and compared theatres and chapels in a most dramatic way (much to the latter's detriment). The theatre issue, incidentally, also illustrates how the power of Leeman and Meek differed from that of Hudson. If the latter had wanted to turn the Cathedral into a railway station, it was said, his lackeys would have agreed.

Parliamentary Elections

Leeman had parliamentary ambitions, and his interest in an election of the 1840s has already been mentioned. York was a two member constituency for the whole of the period covered in this study; and usually the contests followed a set pattern, with the Tories settling for one seat, and the Liberals split between those willing to share representation and those wanting both seats. Invariably the radical section of the Liberal party ran a more 'advanced' candidate, in opposition to the wishes of people like Meek, and usually he lost. Leeman got a chance to run when an election occurred in 1852, and it followed the traditional pattern.

The sitting Liberal member in 1852 was still W. M. E. Milner, who had become unpopular because he missed divisions,[76] and because of his attitude to reform. A new reform bill was in the air and the working-class, and what remained of the local Anti-Corn Law League, were pressing for the radical Henry Vincent to stand. Leeman announced that he stood for household, as against manhood, suffrage, and at one stage was a candidate himself.[77] There was a particularly long campaign in 1852 and Leeman was embarrassed by the attacks of R. H. Anderson, and found himself in the difficult position of being outbid on the left. The working-class preferred Henry Vincent, and Leeman was stung to attack the 'extreme party in this city'.[78] He eventually withdrew and left the field to Milner and Vincent. The *Gazette* said that Leeman had been made to retire because his decision to oppose Milner 'had given grave offence to a certain distinguished friend and patron of his own, resident not many miles from us'.[79] That was the kind of hint once used to refer to the Fitzwilliams. (The Poll book, strange to say, does not record Leeman voting in 1852.)

It is not possible to deal with Leeman's parliamentary election contests in detail, but he got another chance of obtaining a seat in 1857. Between 1852 and 1857 he spent much more time than before discussing national issues and taking part in national affairs. In February 1856, for example, he made speeches about the Shipping Dues Bill, and led a delegation from 150 local authorities to protest against Palmerston's Police Bill.[80] Those years also saw a great deal of activity by the National Sunday League, an organisation set up to end 'the rigid, sanctimonious, and tyrannical observance of the Sabbath', by opening parks and museums on that day and allowing Sunday band concerts. In York they were opposed by Rowntree, particularly, and Leeman lent his support to the opposition Lord's Day Defence Association.[81]

Leeman was apparently approached to stand (as was Meek) in 1857, but for reasons that are unknown he declined, and moved in a candidate of his own. Milner was not available, and Leeman obtained what the *Gazette* called 'a bag fox' from Manchester – a linen draper (like Hudson) and a Methodist class leader.[82] This was Joshua Proctor Brown-Westhead, who said he stood for civil and religious freedom, the ballot, national education, the Maynooth grant (still a hot political issue) and, like Leeman, for the sanctity of Sunday. Once again the radicals introduced a candidate: Malcolm Lewin, the brother of Sir Gregory Lewin of the Northern circuit. Lewin wanted a coalition with Brown-Westhead, but the latter refused. Lewin taunted Brown-Westhead with being the tool of others, a charge he denied, whereupon the crowd (at the hustings) shouted ' "You are, you are," "You said so yourself," "You're the tool of Leeman and party." ' Lewin was defeated. His chief supporters had been a Mr. Coning, a Quaker grocer of Goodramgate, and T. Monkhouse, an ardent supporter of the Sunday reform movement. Leeman plumped for Brown-Westhead.

The question of parliamentary reform had not been a great issue in 1857, when Leeman, for all his protests, adopted a very Whiggish stance. In 1859, however, the issue had come alive again. John Bright had produced a Bill, and the government had produced another with fancy franchises, which Meek's son called 'a cloven foot without trousers'.[83] What was going to happen was that a larger section of the working-class were going to get the vote, and Leeman (who now seemed to have doubts about the ballot) had to listen to the demands of people who would shortly be enfranchised. Brown-Westhead was a candidate again when an election was called; and it seems, from an editorial in the *Gazette*, that Leeman had been trying his luck, unsuccessfully, at Pontefract and Bever-ley (where he was said to have had great influence).[84] On this occasion the second Liberal candidate for York was the famous archaeologist Austin Henry Layard, who denounced the government reform bill as 'a mere sham, . . . unworthy of consideration'.[85] Layard, who was proposed by Leeman, was defeated. This time he had supported the more radical of the two Liberals.

From the time of Hudson's downfall to 1859 little had been heard about the methods of influencing voters at general elections in York, but in the aftermath of his defeat Layard spoke of the Tory candidate, J. G. Smyth, obtaining victory by 'calumny and intimidation'. Smyth himself spoke of workmen using the old Chartist method of threatening to withhold their custom from Tory shopkeepers, and a letter from William Hirstewood said there had been incidents of intimidation and person-ating, and that quantities of strong drink had been freely dispensed to thirsty electors.[86] The old traditional methods of conducting a campaign had not disappeared, and would not while voting remained open; and there are plenty of reports of similar techniques being used at the munici-pal contests (by both parties). Much later, Layard made a speech at Rotherhithe in which he referred to his York campaign.[87] 'At three o'clock on the polling day', he said, 'a gentleman sent to them and said that there were 30 voters who might be bought for £2 a head, and so secure his election. Of course he would not consent to so base an overture, and after waiting till within five minutes of the closing of the poll these 30 patriotic constituents voted against him.'[88]

The Liberals had been subjected to pressures from organised working-class reform movements at the election of 1857, and Brown-Westhead innovated annual 'reports back' to his constituents, where he gave accounts of his actions to people like Coning.[89] A York Reform Association came into existence, intending to keep the issue alive, but interest, as Leeman said, lapsed during midterm.[90] In 1865, however, it revived again. The York Reform Association, led by John Smith, a barrister and a 'Chartist Quaker', reported that the parliamentary revision was 'good' for the Liberals,[91] and declared its support for a £6 franchise. Leeman took this demand over when, in 1865, he was drafted to run in harness with Brown-Westhead. A letter said that the YRA was behind his nomination, and certainly that is suggested by the fact that Coning seconded him at the hustings. When the results were declared Leeman had come second in the Poll, and went to Westminster with James Lowther the Tory candidate. Brown-Westhead had been ousted by the man who had introduced him to the city,[92] and once again York had returned a member from each party. (Leeman was the first York resident to be returned since Robert Chaloner in the 1820s.) An analysis of the voting showed the following state of affairs:[93]

Number who voted	3,828
Number who plumped: for Lowther	1,919
for Leeman	22
for Brown-Westhead	13
Splits: between Brown-Westhead and Leeman	1,716
between Lowther and Leeman	106
between Lowther and Brown-Westhead	52

In the aftermath of the election some evidence appeared, again, to suggest that shady practices had been used. Brown-Westhead, it was said, had spent large sums buying freedoms (thus creating voters) since 1859, but at the Liberals' victory dinner John Smith said that the sitting Member had been ousted by bought votes. 'It was quite understood how the Tories won the election', he said, 'The fact was they had simply purchased the seat for Mr. Lowther, and they had paid a rather large price for it'.[94] The Liberals had certainly gone into the election with the belief, culled from their canvass book, that they would have a majority of over 300. Something happened to those pledges.

When Leeman became an MP he was an extremely influential man; leader of the Liberal party in York; a director of a major railway company;[95] a prosperous lawyer; and someone with wide business interests. During the famine caused by the American Civil War Leeman revealed that he had interests in a cotton spinning firm which employed 1,000 hands,[96] while his connections with the Rosedale iron workings are well known.[97] He also became a deputy lieutenant for the North Riding of Yorkshire.

The 1865 election was the last of its kind, the last fought under the system introduced in 1832. In 1867 an Act was passed which added 938,000 voters to an electorate of 1,056,000 in England and Wales. Leeman stood out against manhood suffrage during the debates on it, for which he came under severe attack from the reformers of Leeds.[98] In the aftermath of the Act (which did not have such far reaching effects in York as elsewhere, because so many were already voters as freemen), both parties set about organising in a way they had not done before, and the city's political organisations took on a more modern appearance. A York Working Men's Conservative Association came into being, and Liberal Registration Committees were set up on a ward basis.[99] When the next election came along in 1868, however, Leeman did not stand; and Brown-Westhead was called in once more to stand with John Hall Gladstone in the Liberal interest. One Tory and one Liberal were returned, as usual, the result being:[100]

Lowther	3,735
Brown-Westhead	3,279
Gladstone	3,038

Once again the 1868 election was the scene of corruption, even though a new Bribery Act was now in existence. Once more the Liberal canvass had led to a conclusion that the party would win both seats by a margin of 1,000 votes. 'How are we to account for the fact that the men who were working on the Liberal committees in May went over by hundreds to the other side on Tuesday?' asked the *Herald* on 21 November. 'From all that we have heard and seen, we are forced to conclude that influences have been in operation which we do not hesitate to say are at once immoral and illegal.' There had been more intemperance and bribery than ever before (they always said this). 'The "Conservative working man", of whom Mr. LOWTHER spoke . . . has been found, but he has been found through gold and silver, through intimidation, and through Bacchanalian revelry'.

The Liberals decided to petition against Lowther's return and a York Vigilance Committee was set up to obtain information. It received enthusiastic support from the Quakers, in particular Coning. Eventually the petition was abandoned and Lowther was safe, but during the weeks before it was given up, abundant information emerged to convince the unbiased reader that bribery was present.[101]

The 1868 election must have been a disappointment to many reformers who thought that a new influx of voters would purify the system, but it was the last under open voting. In 1872 the secret ballot was implemented and from then politics really were different in York. When the Ballot Act was passed Leeman was once more a York MP. Brown-Westhead became ill in December 1870 and resigned in February of the following year.[102] The writ was moved with tremendous haste; the Tories (they said) were unable to find a candidate; and Leeman, then Lord Mayor, went in unopposed.[103]

When Leeman eventually retired as an MP in 1880 his son succeeded him. Leeman was the second most important York citizen of the nineteenth century; Hudson was the first. Both were self-made men, and both were skilled party leaders, but there the similarity between them ends. When Hudson fell, men were discussing the possibility of erecting a statue to him. They did not do so, but when Leeman passed away, a statue to him was put up, and it now stands near the railway station. It looks very different from the *Vanity Fair* cartoon of Leeman (Plate 10), and is the subject of an oft-repeated piece of bad history, according to which it is really Hudson! Leeman presided over the city when great strides were made, and when it was changed from a fever pit into something much more like it is today. But building drains does not capture the imagination in the way that building railways does, and it is Hudson who is remembered, not Leeman. That is a pity.

Notes

1 Those who were had been 'elected' as a punishment. Most people selected in this way paid a fine not to sit, but a few, like Robert Cattle, who were rich enough to stand the expense of office, took up their seats. They were a tiny group.
2 Two who illustrate these better than any are Sir John Simpson and Robert Henry Anderson.
3 One of whom was a Tory.
4 There has been very little written on Leeman. The two following sources are very slight. R. Balgarnie, *In Memoriam. George Leeman, Esq. Late M. P. for York*, York, 1882. *Death, Biography and Funeral of Mr. George Leeman, late M.P. for the city of York*, York, 1882. There are long obituaries, however, in *Yorkshire Gazette* 4 March 1882 and *York Herald* 27 February 1882.

5 Leeman was known as 'The Deacon of Salem' to his Tory enemies. For the Salem chapel see also Chapter VIII above.
6 Anderson made a dreadful speech announcing his allegiance, saying he was proud to wear Hudson's 'livery'. At one stage Anderson was secretary of the York Whig Club. He was also the attorney for the defence of Jonathan Martin.
7 *Gazette* 5 August 1820. Anderson claimed that the Law Society was activated by 'political feelings' against him.
8 The case is reported in *York Courant* 18 February 1834.
9 Ibid.
10 None of these is in collections in York apparently. In the early 1830s Anderson (who signed himself 'John Justice') produced the *Freeman's Journal,* and in the fifties brought out another series of publications called, variously, *The Farmer's Friend and Freeman's Journal,* the *Free Press* and the *York Times.* Details of the last can be found from the report of *Anderson v. Fairburn and Ano.* in *Yorkshire Gazette* 22 March 1856. Details of the earlier journal can be gleaned from *Courant* 7 May 1833.
11 Anderson would make a marvellous subject for a biography.
12 *Herald* 8 December 1827.
13 *York Chronicle* 15 February 1837.
14 See e.g. his speech at an election in 1841. *Herald* 12 June 1841.
15 See e.g. his speech at a debate of the York Society for the Diffusion of Political Knowledge. *Yorkshireman* 28 March 1835.
16 See the editorial from John Duncan, urging Leeman and others to take up the reform cause. *Yorkshireman* 13 May 1848.
17 Letter from Henry Lyons, *Herald* 5 August 1848.
18 *Herald* 26 January 1850.
19 See e.g. *Herald* 18 January, 22 February, 15 March 1851.
20 The events of the 1848 election can be followed in all the local papers from 20 May 1848.
21 Charles Wilkins. Wilkins was apparently a Tory who stood for the complete Hume platform! Anderson's motives in introducing him can only be guessed at. Perhaps he was conned. Perhaps he was in the pay of Hudson. Perhaps it was simply an anti-Leeman move. That he was in cahoots with Hudson seems the most likely explanation.
22 For the history of Chartism in York see A. J. Peacock 'Chartism in York' *York History No. 3* (no date).
23 For example the Wakefield, Pontefract and Goole. He had shares in the London and York, *the* great anti-Hudson company.
24 The story of York politics in these years is told in A. J. Peacock *York in the Age of Reform* (unpublished York D.Phil thesis). Part of it is told in A. J. Peacock and David Joy, *George Hudson of York,* Clapham, 1971.
25 *Herald* 12 December 1846.
26 See e.g. *Herald* 29 September, 6 October 1849. See also the attacks on Pulleyn at elections for pasture masters reported in *Yorkshireman* 5 January 1850. See also *Gazette* 16 February 1850.
27 B. T. Wilkinson was Hudson's nominee as manager of the York Union Bank. He was caught using the bank's funds to speculate on his own behalf – and he

did this with Hudson's knowledge. See Peacock and Joy op. cit. (no. 24), and the pamphlet account of the trial of *Richardson* v. *Hudson* published by the *Yorkshireman*.
[28] William Hargrove was proprietor and editor of the *Herald*. He was succeeded by his sons, notably A. E. Hargrove.
[29] Leeman's actual connections with the *Yorkshireman* are not clear. Certainly he was a proprietor; he seems, also, to have written some of its leaders.
[30] *Yorkshireman* 10 November 1849. B. T. Wilkinson was also thrown off the council.
[31] *Yorkshireman* 24 November 1849.
[32] Ibid. 4 November 1848.
[33] This seems to be the correct figure (it is not always clear who was a Tory and who was not) and does not include the aldermen – who were mainly Tory. Husband got back on the council eventually, to become Tory leader, as has been mentioned.
[34] *Gazette* 3 November 1849.
[35] *Gazette* 27 October 1849.
[36] G. H. Seymour replaced William Stephenson Clark, a great Hudson supporter.
[37] *Yorkshireman* 2 November 1850.
[38] *Gazette* 16 and 23 November 1850.
[39] *Gazette* 8 November 1851. Walmgate Ward was 'the most important in the city from its large extent' and the number of registered electors (915). Ibid. 3 November 1859. John Walker, a famous ironfounder (see p. 123, above) was one of the Tories defeated in Walmgate in 1851.
[40] *Gazette* 6 November 1852 and 20 August 1853 (editorial).
[41] *Gazette* 4 November 1854. The *Gazette* ignoring 1852, said that this was the first time such a thing had happened since 1835.
[42] *Gazette* 8 November 1856.
[43] *Gazette* 14 November 1857.
[44] *Gazette* 3 November 1860.
[45] *Gazette* 2 November 1861.
[46] *Herald* 2 November 1861.
[47] *Gazette* 10 November 1860.
[48] *Gazette* 5 May 1849. *Yorkshireman* 5 May 1849. *Herald* 5 May 1849 (editorial). It had been in existence for some time before that however. See Lord Morpeth's letter to Leeman in *Gazette* 2 September 1848.
[49] See the analysis of it from the *Justice of the Peace* in *Yorkshireman* 26 May 1849.
[50] There is no adequate history of the management of the strays.
[51] J. Redlich and F. W. Hirst, *The History of Local Government in England*, 2nd Edition 1920, pp. 144-46.
[52] *Gazette* 19 October 1850.
[53] T. Laycock *Report on the State of York*, 2 vols., 1884. On the first epidemic see M. Durey, *The First Spasmodic Cholera Epidemic in York, 1832*, York, 1974. In 1832 185 people died, or 1 in 138; in 1849 163 died or 1 in 214 (taking the population at an estimated 35,000), *Gazette* 9 March 1850.

54 Laycock was involved with the H.O.T.A. and Richard Anderson, a journey-man currier, seems to have been its leading figure. See e.g. the report of its most important annual meeting (when it considered the 1848 Act) in *Gazette* 9 March 1850. A list of improvements that *were* made in the Liberal years can be found in the *Herald's* obituary of Leeman quoted earlier (n. 4).

55 It took three years, of course, to purge the council of Hudsonians. The reaction starting in 1849 therefore ended in 1851.

56 For details of the growth of population see Chapter V, pp. 110-17, above. For a description of the Irish areas see F. Finnegan, *Poverty and Prostitution. A Study of Prostitutes in York,* 1979.

57 Letter in *Gazette* 4 December 1852. For an analysis of the situation in 1857 see Ibid. 14 November 1857.

58 Reports of council meetings in *Gazette* 17 August and 7 September 1850.

59 *Gazette* 15 February 1851, editorial. The council decided it would *not* build a public library. *Gazette* 19 April 1851.

60 *Gazette* 16 August, 13 September, 15 November 1851.

61 *Gazette* 18 August 1860.

62 *Gazette* 4 July 1868.

63 *Gazette* 19 February 1870.

64 *Gazette* 14 August 1852. The paper was probably the *Yorkshireman* and the person was probably Shilleto, a butcher of Micklegate.

65 *Gazette* 4 June 1853. This looks as if it could be the same incident as that referred to in n. 64.

66 *Gazette* 18 April 1857. Long report of council debates.

67 *Gazette* 16 May 1857. See Rowntree's remarks, however.

68 *Gazette* 1 August 1857.

69 During the years under discussion there was only one Tory Lord Mayor – Husband – and he was bitterly attacked for taking an active part in an election during his term of office (something Meek had done). There are very good obituaries of Meek in the local papers. E.g. *Gazette* 20 December 1862.

70 In these years there were strong teetotal and total abstinence movements in the city, supported enthusiastically by people like the elder Joseph Rowntree. They were, therefore, important organisations in Liberal politics. Leeman never appears to have supported them. (Hudson certainly did not!)

71 The Calverts were particularly powerful in Micklegate, and were frequently involved in the rows over the strays in that ward (with R. H. Anderson opposing them as often as not). See the article in *Gazette* 9 October 1852 on corporate 'jobbing'.

72 For the debates and controversy see, e.g. *Gazette* 19 and 26 May, 16 and 23 June, 4 August 1855. R. H. Anderson's career ended when he became bankrupt. The proceedings, of course, dragged on over a long period. For details see, e.g. his final examination in Ibid. 24 April and 29 May 1858.

73 *Gazette* 26 April 1851.

74 *Gazette* 13 November, 18 December 1852, 1 January 1853. On this occasion R. H. Anderson was accused of trying to get the theatre site for the Roman Catholic church.

[75] Letter signed 'Anti-Humbug', *Gazette* 20 November 1852. Meek had once been a director of the York and North Midland Railway Company, when Hudson was chairman. He had wanted the company to close down on Sundays, and when he did not get his way he resigned. Hudson had then poked fun at him, drawing attention to the furnacemen working at his glassworks on Sundays, and saying Meek's domestic servants worked on the Sabbath.

[76] See the attack on him in *Yorkshireman* 21 June 1851.

[77] For details of the election see *Yorkshireman* 13 March 1852 et. seq. and other papers of similar dates.

[78] 'I hope there is nothing whiggish in me; but I will say that I would rather live in despotic Turkey than submit to the tyranny practised by some of . . . the "extreme" party in this city' *Yorkshireman* 5 June 1852.

[79] *Gazette* 1 May 1852. Milner withdrew, then reconsidered, stood, and got in.

[80] *Gazette* 16 and 23 February 1856.

[81] *Gazette* 18 October, 1 November 1856.

[82] *Gazette* 21 March 1857 and subsequent issues of it and the *Herald* for details.

[83] *Gazette* 19 March 1859. Meek's son was Lord Mayor three times.

[84] *Gazette* 16 April 1859.

[85] For details of the election see the press from 26 March onwards. On Layard see G. Waterfield, *Layard of Nineveh,* 1963.

[86] *Gazette* 7 May 1859. For Smyth's remarks see *Gazette* 30 April 1859.

[87] *Gazette* 1 December 1860.

[88] *Gazette* 1 December 1860. He made the same kind of remarks later. Ibid. 5 August 1865. Those who hung on to the last minute, hoping to put up the price of their votes, were always known as 'waiters on providence'.

[89] See e.g. *Gazette* 1 February 1862, 17 January 1863.

[90] *Gazette* 6 February 1864.

[91] *Herald* 11 March 1865, letter from Smith.

[92] For details of the election see the newspapers from 8 April 1865.

[93] *The Poll Book,* York 1865.

[94] *Herald* 15 July 1865.

[95] The North Eastern. He eventually became chairman.

[96] *Gazette* 18 October 1862. Meeting on the distress in Lancashire.

[97] Later on there were rumours that Leeman had held up the building of a line to Whitby in favour of one that opened up the Rosedale area. It is only fair, however, to say he had a complete answer to the charge.

[98] *Gazette* 13 October 1866. In 1867 Leeman was able to get passed what came to be known as his Sale and Purchase of Shares Act. See Ibid. 22 June 1867.

[99] See e.g. *Gazette* 9 March 1867, 25 July 1868.

[100] For the election see e.g. *Gazette* 12 September 1868 et seq.

[101] On the committee and petition see e.g. *Gazette* 12 and 24 December 1868, 30 January and 13 and 20 March 1869. See W. W. Bean, *The Parliamentary Representation of the Six Northern Counties of England,* Hull, 1890, pp. 1119-20 on the election and petitions.

[102] *Gazette* 31 December 1870, 11 February 1871.

[103] *Gazette* 18 February 1871. It was said the Tories tried to get Sir Henry Edward, Major Worsley and Viscount Down.

CHAPTER X

The City Council
and Electoral Politics,
1901-1971

by

Rodney Hills

THIS CHAPTER DESCRIBES AND EXPLAINS the social and economic characteristics of members of the city council, and the electoral politics of York,
between 1901 and 1971.[1] The period is divided into three: Edwardian,
interwar and postwar, with the main focus on the census years, within
each subperiod.

1901-1914

The modern municipal history of York dates from the Municipal
Corporations Act of 1835 under which the reformed city council was
given limited powers. Meetings of the council started to be reported in the
local press, and its powers were gradually extended until, in 1888, after a
substantial boundary extension (see Map 2, p. 112), York became one of
the first County Boroughs, an event celebrated by the building of a new
council chamber.[2] In 1889 a school board was established.

The parliamentary election of 1835 established a pattern when the
Conservatives, under the dynamic George Hudson, succeeded in capturing one of York's two seats from the Liberals; and until 1918, when it
became a single member constituency, the two parties generally shared

the seats. The first elections for the reformed council reflected this party conflict, and the practice of fighting municipal elections on party lines continued, especially after 1884, when the size of the six double-member wards made it difficult for independents to cover them without an organisation.[3]

Party conflict was, however, muted by 1900 with the council members only loosely grouped under their respective party labels. The 'Tory Party was committed by then to a policy of doing as little as possible and keeping down the rates: the Liberals stood for nothing at all'; though for the first time two Labour candidates had been returned.[4] Chairmanships and vice-chairmanships were shared, and aldermanic seats went to incumbents in perpetuity, with vacancies being filled from the former alderman's party. The parties were led by prosperous businessmen whose consensual views were buttressed by personal links developed over 20 years of council membership, by business and marriage ties, and through sharing the same chapel.[5]

The population of York in 1901 was 77,914 and, like Chester, it was a middle-class, cathedral and garrison city, though the Minster did not play an active part in local affairs. However, the high level of white collar employment was balanced by manual employment on the railway, where 5,500 men worked, and in confectionery, which employed 2,500.[6] The importance of the railway was such that the county town ethos (which lingered for a further 50 years in Chester) quickly altered, as the political system adjusted to the impact of working-class organisation and representation, led by railwaymen.[7]

As early as the 1880s local railwaymen had started to detach themselves from Liberalism, and their growing consciousness found expression in the formation of the Trades Council in 1890. By 1899, 18 out of 24 unions were affiliated, and it had close links with the ILP and the Cooperative Society. As early as 1895 the ILP ran a municipal candidate who was elected with a Co-operative Society candidate in 1900; and in the following year the three organisations established the United Labour Committee to secure 'Labour Representation on Public Bodies' and to share election expenses.[8] The growth of the desire for such representation is seen in the election of a Labour candidate to the school board in 1901, having come bottom in 1898.

The council during 1901-02 consisted of thirty Conservatives (eight aldermen and twenty-two councillors), fifteen Liberals (four and eleven) and three Labour (none and three). Those who were members during 1901 had served on average 17.3 years, with 43.6 per cent having entered aged under 41 years, and 7.7 per cent aged over 55 years.[9]

In terms of class and occupations the council members in 1901 were not typical of the city as a whole, with manual workers represented by only the three Labour councillors (see Table 1). The majority were the owners of small businesses (who tended to be Liberal) and self-made Conservative shopkeepers, though the size of the enterprises and the worth of members varied. This reflected the crucial importance of self-help through trade as a vehicle for social mobility during the nineteenth century. In the city there were few cultural barriers to social acceptance. Membership of the council and, to a lesser extent, the two ancient guilds – the Merchant Taylors and the Merchant Adventurers – socially legitimised the upwardly mobile. A further incentive to tradesmen to enter the council was provided by the rates, and one candidate stated that his qualification for membership was his 'responsibility for the payment of no small part of the city rates'.[10]

The number of professional men, especially lawyers, may have reflected the council's patronage and because membership served as a useful way of making a reputation, but it also reflected the occupational bias of the Conservatives nationally.[11] Seven of the eight lawyers were solidly middle-class, and provided an important link between the professions and trade.[12]

If the churches were the centre of community life, instrumental in bridging the gap between classes and thereby contributing to social cohesion, they also divided, and in York the Conservatives were Anglican and the Liberals Nonconformist (see Table 2).[13] However, religious conflict, seen in the battle to establish a school board and in its elections, was reduced as the activists met one another through membership of the council. Interestingly, in 1901 seven of the Nonconformists were Wesleyan and the one Primitive Methodist was Labour. Members were also divided over Freemasonry, with eleven Conservative brothers but only one Liberal. There were, however, social links between the parties, including guild membership and governerships of local hospitals, and also some business connections, usually between senior members.

Between 1901 and 1911 the final flowering of radicalism and the formation of the Labour Party changed local politics. The 1902 Education Bill brought the sectarian conflict over education to the fore with its proposal to give rate support to voluntary schools. The younger Nonconformist Liberals, especially the municipal candidates, led the opposition. Local Nonconformity felt so strongly that five of its leading Ministers, including two active in Liberal politics, refused to pay the education rate.[14] The position of the party's established leadership was undermined by the emergence of a group of radicals – most recruited by the younger Joseph Rowntree, the personification of a Quaker businessman, and his

Table 1   1901
       Social Class and Occupation of Council Members

	Conservative	Labour	Liberal	Total Council[2]
Social Class[1]				
No. of Members	29	3	16	48
% in Class[3]				
I	42	0	0	25
II	48	0	81	56
III	10	100	19	19
	100	100	100	100
Occupational Groups[1]				
No. of Members	30	3	16	49
% in Class				
Professional	37	0	0	22
Business	23	0	50	31
Shopkeeper	40	0	25	33
Non-manual	0	0	25	8
Manual	0	100	0	6
	100	100	100	100

Notes:
[1] For the purposes of this and subsequent tables the occupation of members when first elected was determined from newspapers, directories, election leaflets, etc., and then classified by social class and occupational group. The social class classification is that used in the 1971 census, which excludes women and retired men. The groupings represent:

    I Professional occupations.

    II Intermediate occupations (e.g. civil service executive officers, nurses, publicans and teachers).

    III Skilled occupations: manual and non-manual (e.g. clerks, shop assistants, travellers and typists).

    IV Semi-skilled occupations (e.g. caretakers, hawkers and telephone operators).

    V Unskilled occupations.

Continued on p. 259

son Seebohm – whose stand on the Bill and concern with social problems gave them widespread support in the party. The first practical result was the formation of the Health and Housing Reform Association in 1902 which obtained support from some Nonconformist clergy and ILP members. This was followed by the establishment of the Progressive Party in 1905 by those Liberals who 'wanted large reforms in health, housing and education'; this gave municipal Liberalism both organisation and a policy.[15] The Rowntree element was strong, with Oscar Rowntree and J. B. Morrell both directors; Crichton, a Quaker passive resister who was in charge of welfare; Davies, the firm's Quaker chemist; and Hogge, Joseph Rowntree's research worker who became a Liberal MP. They were joined by William Birch, a Wesleyan self-made builder, and Wilkinson, a Quaker solicitor. All the activists were under 35.

The Progressive Party's policy of the municipalisation of public utilities so that revenue could be generated to pay for educational, health, housing, sanitation and street improvements was published in the *Yorkshire Gazette* (the local weekly which Rowntree had purchased in 1903), and then in pamphlet form in 1905.[16] A common programme, an increased number of meetings and candidates – which annoyed the other parties – and Hogge's rumbustious campaign resulted in the capture of one seat. In the following two years the policy was expanded and expounded; three more seats were won in 1906, and a further four, rather against the national swing, the next year, bringing the total to 15.[17]

The Liberal advance imposed strain on the political system, not least because of their adoption of Labour's group system though without the whips. This, and their common programme, resulted in a greater degree of uniformity of action, and the Liberals, supported by Labour, were able to exercise more power than their numbers warranted. (Not all sitting Liberals approved, and at least one retired early, while Alderman McKay quietly disassociated himself.) It was, however, the aldermanic vacancies and committee placings which caused most stress. In 1904, on the death of a Liberal alderman, the Conservatives elected the senior Liberal, much against his party's wishes as they suspected his loyalty. They were correct, as the new alderman immediately left the party. (A similar thing had

---

Notes to Table 1 continued.

In the occupational groups 'professional' is restricted to professional occupations and directors of large companies. All other white-collar workers, if not the owners of a business or shop, are included in the 'non-manual' group.

[2] Three Conservative members are omitted from the social class classification and two from the occupational groupings because unknown or retired.

[3] There were no members in class IV and V.

Table 2   1901, 1911 and 1921
          Religious Affiliation of Council Members

	Conservative	Labour	Liberal	Total Council
1901				
No. of Members[1]	26	2	11	39
% of Members				
Anglican	92	0	27	69
Nonconformist	8	50	46	20
Quaker	0	50	18	8
. Roman Catholic	0	0	9	3
Presbyterian	0	0	0	0
	100	100	100	100
1911				
No. of Members[2]	25	1	18	45[4]
% of Members				
Anglican	72	100	17	49
Nonconformist	20	0	44	29
Quaker	0	0	33	14
Roman Catholic	4	0	0	4
Presbyterian	4	0	6	4
	100	100	100	100
1921				
No. of Members[3]	22	9	14	46[5]
% of Members				
Anglican	55	44	7	39
Nonconformist	27	56	58	41
Quaker	0	0	28	9
Roman Catholic	14	0	7	9
Presbyterian	4	0	0	2
	100	100	100	100

happened with the previous Liberal promotion in 1898.) The Conservatives then filled five of the six vacancies which occurred in the next three years, giving themselves a total of eight to the Liberal's four, despite a ratio of councillors of 18 to 15. At the turn of the century the committee placings had been in proportion to the respective party strengths, but by 1909 the Liberals were rightly complaining that though they had 42 per cent of the council's membership they had only 26 per cent of the major committee places.[18]

The municipal radicalism of the Liberals and their electoral success contrast with the performance of the party elsewhere, which generally failed to produce a constructive policy going beyond economy.[19] By taking over and refining Labour's programme the Liberals were able to beat back the socialist challenge, and labour lost four of its five seats between 1905 and 1908; but it also had wider appeal and took seats from the Conservatives until 1912. The Liberals succeeded in expanding municipal activity, especially in education, where the able Wilkinson and the energetic Medical Officer of Health, backed by new legislation, were able to make considerable progress.

The United Labour Committee became the Labour Representation Committee in 1903, after which associations were formed in all six wards (though only really effective in the railway Micklegate ward), and individuals accepted into membership. The committee was seen as the independent wing of the labour movement, and hence in 1904 the Trades Council wanted the national party's rules altered to allow individual parties to affiliate. It also strongly supported the view that delegations to selection conferences, and therefore power, should be based on the strength of the organisations affiliating to the local party; and successfully moved this at the 1912 conference.[20] The transfer of affiliation to the national party, from the Trades Council to the York Labour Party, was (rather unusually) achieved without difficulty, because the leadership of the Labour movement was small, tightly knit and committed to independent representation in defence of working-class living standards.[21] This independence was demonstrated in 1906 when Stuart, the Labour

---

Notes to Table 2:

[1] Six Conservative, five Liberal and one Labour member are omitted because their religious affiliation is unknown.

[2] Six Conservative, two Liberal and two Labour members are omitted.

[3] Seven Conservative, two Labour and one Independent member are omitted.

[4] The total includes one Independent Roman Catholic member.

[5] The total includes one Independent Anglican member.

parliamentary candidate, did badly because many Liberals refused to give him their second vote as a result of his independent stance.[22]

After 1905 and the Liberal offensive, when even two of the three Micklegate seats were lost, the Labour Party became moribund. The decline was exacerbated by the retirement of its two most active councillors, and this left effective expression of radicalism to the Liberals. Furthermore, over unemployment, which reached 2,500 in York in 1905, the Liberal alleviative policies were more in accord with the electorate's mood than Labour's fulmination against an unjust economic system.[23] It was not until 1911, when the squeeze on living standards found expression in industrial unrest with strikes at Leetham's flour mills, the glassworks, and the railways (where troops with fixed bayonets were used), that Labour began to recover. It found a new municipal leader in Dobbie, who already headed the Trades Council and the 2,700 shopmen members of the General Railway Workers Union, and who was later to enter Parliament.

Those who were members of the council in 1911 had served on average for 20.4 years, even though, especially for Liberals, defeat as a reason for leaving increased from 17.7 per cent in 1901 to 27.3 per cent. The impact of the Liberal advance and the Conservative reaction – younger and better quality candidates – was to reduce the average age of election, with 52.2 per cent having entered aged under 41 years, and only 4.3 per cent over 55 years, and between 1910 and 1914 26.7 per cent of Conservatives and 40.0 per cent of Labour entrants were under 36 years.

The most significant change in the 1911 profile was in the occupations of members (see Table 3). In the Conservative ranks the proportion of businessmen had increased at the expense of professionals. This reflected the growing importance in the party of small traders who were worried by the prevailing economic climate, not least the rising rates, which they blamed on the Liberals. (A parallel response was the formation of the Chamber of Trade in 1911.) Between 1900 and 1909 only three Conservative entrants were professionals, compared with 19 businessmen and four shopkeepers.[24] The substantial occupational differences between Labour and the other parties remained: from 1900 to 1914 all but one of the party's 11 councillors were manual workers, and eight were railwaymen, including a clerk.[25]

The occupational change was also reflected in a religious one, with a decline in Conservative Anglicanism (see Table 2). The link between the traditionally high status Wesleyan Centenary Chapel and Liberalism weakened, and of its nine pre-1914 members of the Council, five were Conservative, three Liberal and one Labour. Though this may have

Table 3   1911
Social Class and Occupation of Council Members

	Conservative	Labour	Liberal	Total Council[2]
Social Class				
No. of Members	30	3	19	52
% in Class[1]				
I	17	0	21	17
II	67	0	63	62
III	16	100	16	21
	100	100	100	100
Occupational Groups				
No. of Members	31	3	20	55
% in Group				
Professional	16	0	16	15
Business	45	0	47	44
Shopkeeper	39	0	16	28
Non-manual	0	0	21	7
Manual	0	100	0	6
	100	100	100	100

Notes:

[1] There were no members in classes IV and V.

[2] One Conservative, one Liberal and one Independent are omitted from the social class classification. They are included in the occupational grouping, the Independent under 'business'.

For definitions and source see Table 1.

reduced political conflict, it was also a portent of Liberalism's loss of the prosperous self-made Nonconformist.[26]

The respectability of the Labour leaders – Nonconformist and teetotal – and their links with working-class self-help institutions, should have caused the Liberals to mount a determined drive to recruit them into the party to counterbalance the loss of 'shopocratic' support. However, the Liberals were unable or unwilling even to run working-class municipal candidates, and only one was fielded between 1898 and 1914; this, allied to the Rowntree connection, resulted in the party becoming identified with the employing class.[27]

Freemasonry in 1911 remained a Conservative preserve, with no Liberal but 11 Conservative adherents; and, in general, the Liberal's social and business links with the Conservatives were limited to Agar. Except for bowls, sporting links were also rare: for the Conservatives it was angling, cricket and rugby, for the Liberals and Labour it was soccer.[28] However, one factor making for consensus was the existence of kinship ties: where a member was related to a current, past or future member. Seven members had such links in 1901 and 17 in 1911.

After the 1911 elections the Conservatives lost their overall majority, but this was reversed in 1913 when the Liberals, unfairly blamed for the prosecution of Sunday traders, and severely criticised for supporting a Labour nomination for Lord Mayor, lost five seats. Labour gained one. The clearest pointer to the future was in Micklegate, where the sitting Liberal came bottom with the winning Conservative and Labour candidates receiving largely plumped votes.

1918-1939

The war hastened change. In York, as nationally, Labour's aspirations were legitimised and it grew in power and influence. The local Liberal Party was permanently damaged by the war. The strong Quaker element, led by Arnold Rowntree, the city's Liberal M.P., was pacifist and this further alienated much of the middle-class Nonconformist element. The York party followed Asquith into the wilderness, and this repudiation of collectivism was to be permanent.

The electoral changes which gave most women over 30, and all men, the vote, also reduced York to a single member constituency.[29] In 1918 the sitting Coalition Conservative, basking in the glow of victory, ran an emotionally patriotic campaign, and outflanked the opposition with his promises of reform. Rowntree was decisively defeated, and Labour polled little more than it had in 1906. By 1921 the new alignment was somewhat clearer, though the rate of change was slow. The impact of the sharp inflationary and deflationary movements in money wages was severe, and industrial relations deteriorated; unemployment and housing became major political issues. Labour's appeal, couched in terms of defending working-class living standards, widened – as the promises of 1918, especially over housing, remained unfulfilled. The sharp rate increases caused by inflation, and the initial postwar organisational weakness of municipal Conservatism, resulted in the emergence of economy candidates. The Conservative Party responded, and by 1921 its chameleon-like conversion to radical reform was over. As the electorate slowly polarised along class lines the core support for Labour and Conservative – those willing to plump – increased, which further weakened the Liberals, whose own core vote was declining.[30] Furthermore, the Liberals lost most of their able leaders, and this made them even more vulnerable.[31]

In the municipal year of 1921 the Conservatives held twenty-eight seats, the Liberals ten, Labour nine, and the Independents one. Despite the increase in the number of contested elections, 44.6 per cent of those who were members of the council in 1921 ended their first term by retirement, and 27.5 per cent by promotion to alderman. The average length of service was 20.9 years, which is partly explained by the importance in local politics of the personal votes of incumbents. The average age on entry had risen, because of the increased number of Labour members: 37.5 per cent of whom were over 50 on entry; 47.9 per cent of all members had been first elected when under 41, and 20.8 per cent when over 50.

The class and occupational groupings were relatively unchanged, though the Conservatives, because they had absorbed the independent economy councillors, now included some non-manual workers (Table 4).[32] The religious affiliation of councillors and aldermen was also little different, though the number of Catholic Conservatives had increased (see Table 2). There were two inter-party links; the Centenary Chapel, where the Conservatives now predominated, and temperance.[33] Labour members tended to be less active in church affairs, especially the younger element. Kinship ties covered 19 members, but freemasonry, though on the decline, the guilds and the Chamber of Trade were solely Conservative. Overlapping social links were few, which partly reflected growing social and cultural diversity, though members did have contact with a wide variety of associations.

In the general elections of 1922 and 1923 Labour increased its vote, on swings of 14.2 per cent and 2.7 per cent. They campaigned on domestic issues against a backcloth of falling incomes, rising unemployment and a severe housing shortage. The Liberals were pushed into third place. In municipal terms, Labour held its own; while the Liberals found it increasingly difficult even to field candidates and in 1922 Wilkinson was defeated.

Though the 1924 Labour Government was not very successful it did give short-term help to the unemployed and passed an important housing

Table 4   1921
Social Class and Occupation of Council Members

	Con-servative	Labour	Liberal	Indepen-dent	Total Council[2]
Social Class					
No. of Members	28	9	14	1	52
% in Class[1]					
I	18	0	14	0	14
II	57	11	57	0	48
III	25	89	29	100	38
	100	100	100	100	100
Occupational Groups					
No. of Members	28	10	14	1	53
% in Group					
Professional	18	0	14	0	13
Business	46	0	50	0	38
Shopkeeper	18	0	14	0	13
Non-manual	14	30	22	0	19
Manual	4	70	0	100	17
	100	100	100	100	100

Notes:
[1] There were no members in classes IV and V.
[2] One Conservative and one Labour member are omitted from the social class classification, and the Conservative is excluded from the occupational grouping. Two women – one Labour and one Independent – are omitted from both sections.

For definitions and sources see Table 1.

act. The Prime Minister, Ramsey MacDonald, visited York in April 1924, and was received by York's first Labour Lord Mayor, Alderman Dobbie (Plate 11). In York, where Labour throughout the 1920s pressed the Council for work schemes and more houses, these issues were constantly used against the Conservatives. The 1924 election came at a most inopportune moment for both Labour and the Liberals, but the former were able to run a candidate who managed to hold his position.[34]

After 1924 the government's domestic performance became the touchstone of municipal politics and, with the General Strike, was to be instrumental in the rapid advance of Labour in York after 1926. The city was re-warded in 1925, with each ward annually returning one council-lor; and the pattern emerged of sitting Liberals and Conservatives being given a clear run against Labour. This maximised the electoral chances of Liberal incumbents, but crucially weakened their independence and made it difficult for the party to expand.[35] Labour continued to campaign on the issues of municipal enterprise, the unemployed and housing. The reduction in housing subsidies, the insensitive treatment of the un-employed, which pushed more of them onto the rates via the Poor Law, and the stagnation in money wages, were largely responsible for a steady swing to Labour.

The 1929 general election occurred as York's unemployment rose; in the first five months of the year it averaged 11.9 per cent. Lloyd George's radical manifesto made unemployment the key election issue, and this forced the Conservatives to defend their record. (The local Liberals were uneasy with their programme and were happier when expounding their traditional panacea of Free Trade.)[36] The electorate, especially the working-class, wanted protection from the vagaries of the economic system and this, coupled with a rising demand for social expenditure, was what Labour offered, though presented in rhetorical rather than practical guise. The Liberals were no longer a credible force, and Labour won York on a 9.8 per cent swing, with the Liberal vote, despite the increase in the electorate, only marginally up on its 1923 level, and the Labour majority coming from disillusioned Conservatives. In the municipal elections Labour won three seats on a 4.8 per cent swing and now had two aldermen and twelve councillors. After their defeat there was a Conser-vative coup, with a new and younger leadership emerging who unsuccess-fully tried to persuade wards to oppose sitting Liberals.[37]

During the 1920s class polarisation increased, depending on the movement in unemployment and money wages, and this accelerated after the General Strike. By 1929 there was a significant correlation between voting and class.[38]

As the Labour Government proved incapable of reversing the upward trend in unemployment – which averaged 16.9 per cent in York in 1931 – so its support ebbed. Its collapse and replacement by a National Government in 1931 was followed by a crisis election in which Labour was routed. The Conservatives recaptured the city on an 18.5 per cent swing, with the Liberal vote going to the victor.[39] In the local elections six days later there was a further municipal swing against Labour, making a total of 13.79 per cent since 1929.[40] By the end of 1931 Labour was reduced to 10 members to the Conservative's 27, the Liberal's 10 and Independent's one.

Those who were members of the council in 1931 had served on average for 22.3 years, and the importance of incumbents is clear, with only 20.7 per cent leaving because of electoral defeat.[41] Only five Liberals were newly elected between the wars, but three, once they had become entrenched, served for over 18 years.[42] Of the 1931 members 30.4 per cent were first elected when under 41 years, and 32.6 per cent when over 50; but for those entering between 1919-1929 the figures were 16.4 per cent and 45.2 per cent, which reflected the dominance of successful shopkeepers and businessmen. This was further reflected in the shift in Conservative members from social class III to II after 1921, with 65.5 per cent of their entrants coming from class II and only 20.7 per cent from III. Though the number and occupational range of Conservative non-manual members had increased, only one was from social class III, which meant that the mass of white-collar workers were even less well represented than they had been by the party 10 years earlier (see Table 5). Labour, though it had recruited one doctor, continued to be dominated by manual workers, including seven railwaymen. (The two Conservative manual workers had crossed the floor from Labour.) The sole member from social class IV was hardly typical: he had been commissioned during the war and later retired as a Rowntree's depot manager.[43]

Religious affiliations remained as before, though there was a decline in the number actively religious, again more marked on the Labour side. There were 14 members with kinship ties; and freemasonry, the guilds and the Chamber of Trade remained the preserve of Conservatives.[44]

The strains which had accompanied the Liberal revival were repeated as Labour increased in numbers on the council. It pressed for proportional representation on the aldermanic bench, but the Conservatives were unwilling to replace incumbents, and this helped the Liberals but hurt Labour.[45] There was tension over the allocation of major committee places, with the Liberals tending to be under-represented. However, Dobbie was given the Lord Mayoralty in 1923/24 (Plate 12), one measure of the party's acceptance since 1913, and Labour took chairmanships and vice-chairmanships; both symbolising the party's acceptance of the basic political norms. The Conservative response to Labour's organisation, and the growth of a mass electorate, was slow; but after 1928 their group meetings became more formalised, and the new leadership encouraged hesitant steps to develop common election programmes and to share expenses.[46]

Table 5   1931
Social Class and Occupation of Council Members

	Conservative	Labour	Liberal	Total Council[2]
Social Class				
No. of Members	26	12	10	48
% in Class[1]				
I	12	8	0	8
II	77	0	60	54
III	11	84	40	36
IV	0	8	0	2
	100	100	100	100
Occupational Groups				
No. of Members	26	13	10	49
% in Group				
Professional	12	8	0	8
Business	23	0	40	20
Shopkeeper	34	0	20	22
Non-manual	23	23	30	25
Manual	8	69	10	25
	100	100	100	100

Notes:

[1] There were no members in class V.

[2] Three Conservatives and one woman – an Independent – are omitted from both sections. One Labour member is excluded from the social class classification. For definitions and sources see Table 1.

After 1931 Labour made a rapid local recovery, as high unemployment – for men over 20 per cent in 1932 and 1933 – falling money incomes and the treatment of the unemployed became the dominant political issues, more than offsetting the 10 per cent growth in real incomes since 1929. The exchanges between the Conservatives and the Liberals over protection appeared sterile to an electorate worried about wages and job security. This benefited Labour, which continued to emphasise slum clearance and public works, and which was seen as the

working-class living standards.[47] The Liberal weakness, which had prevented them from fielding any candidates in 1932, was worsened by the
national split; and by 1933 both Oscar Rowntree and Morris, the influential Chairman of the Streets and Buildings Committee, seem to have
become Simonite Liberals.

Between 1934 and 1936, though the upward movement in real
incomes was halted, unemployment fell and money wages rose. In the city
employment, especially on the railways and in confectionery grew, the
latter by 30 per cent (see also Chapter V, pp. 142-3, above); and in the
three years to 1937 unemployment fell by 1,900 and the labour force
expanded by 4,500. The political repercussions were seen in the 1935
general election, fought during the Abyssinian crisis, when despite a 7.9
per cent swing to Labour, its share of the two-party poll was no higher
than that achieved in 1924.[48] Labour's recovery from the debacle of 1931
was swift but limited, with the party failing to match its 1929 general and
municipal performances; and by 1934 the tide was once again on the turn
as economic recovery weakened its appeal.[49] If Labour started to lose
municipal seats as its supporters abstained, so reducing turnout, then the
Liberals were in a worse situation, being reduced to eight members. This
would have been even fewer but for the failure of the Conservative
leadership to persuade its ward associations to oppose sitting Liberals.[50]

The change in the economic and political climate by the late 1930s
was symbolised in the Trades Council's preoccupation in 1937 with
holidays. The sustained rise in individual and family incomes during these
years overshadowed the persistence of unemployment, which at 8.5 per
cent in 1937 and 8.2 per cent in 1938 – over 2,700 – was still high
compared with the pre-1914 era. Labour's programme, which continued
to stress unemployment and housing, was of decreasing relevance to
much of the electorate; and this, together with the party's failure to lead
public opinion on the new social issues, caused many of its supporters to
vote with their feet.[51] Furthermore, Labour's internal divisions over
constitutional reform, rearmament and Spain increasingly gave the public
the impression of a party likely to drag Britain into war. The Parliamentary by-election in York in 1937, fought on the issues of peace and the
government's domestic record, resulted in only a small 2.0 per cent swing
to Labour from 1935.[52] In 1937, Labour lost one municipal seat in York;
but the election was more important for what it revealed about the
Liberals. One of their sitting members retired, and the Conservative
leadership was able to persuade a divided ward association to break its
unofficial pact with the Liberals. The Conservative candidate duly won,
with the Liberal last with 11.4 per cent of the poll; the retiring councillor

having endorsed Labour. During the elections three incumbent Liberals endorsed Conservative candidates, and this formally marked the end of traditional municipal Liberalism. The *Anschluss* and the Czechoslovakian crisis of 1938 threatened war, and Chamberlain's return from Munich waving his piece of paper was vindicated within six weeks in the local elections. In York, Labour defended five seats, losing three where there were new candidates, and its poll share was even lower than in its previous nadir with a −1.0 per cent swing from 1931. The sole Liberal candidate ran a poor third.

There were some alterations to the norms of the Council during the 1930s which benefited Labour, especially the belated non-partisan appointment of its representatives to major chairmanships. The Lord Mayoralty was brought within the grasp of most Labour members by the payment of a realistic allowance, though allocation still depended upon the Conservatives' informal willingness to accept rotation. However, the aldermanic bench remained an irritant, with the Conservatives refusing to unseat incumbents or to accept proportional representation.

Municipal Conservatism also altered with the acceptance of formal organisation, common election programmes and shared expenses, though all were delayed by traditional opposition. Furthermore, because central control was weak, with candidates being selected and financed by wards, the leadership was unable to oppose sitting Liberals though they ceased receiving Conservative endorsement.[53]

The composition of the council changed between 1914 and 1939, with the Conservatives increasing from 26 to 32 members, Labour from six to nine, and the Independents from one to four while the Liberals decreased from fifteen to seven.[54] This was echoed in the characteristics of those first elected between 1900-1914 and 1930-1939, where (beside obvious changes, such as electoral defeat replacing retirement as the main reason for leaving) there were significant modifications in the age of entry and in occupational structure. The average age of new members increased (especially on the Conservative side) with none being elected under 41 in the 1930s, compared with 37 per cent pre-1914. This was partly due to the impact of the young Edwardian Liberals, but also to changes in the occupations of members, with non-manual and manual workers expanding at the expense of businessmen, though manual workers remained few in number.[55]

1945-1974

The war completed the political realignment, with the slight but significant paradigm shift in attitudes benefiting Labour, which was identified as the party of social reform. The serious and sustained interest

of the 1945 electorate in reconstruction (especially housing), employment, pensions and social insurance, resulted locally in Labour winning
the parliamentary seat; and gaining control of the council for the first
time after capturing 19 of the 21 contested seats.[56] Though political
fortunes after 1945 varied, with York being marginal both in municipal
and national terms – Labour lost the parliamentary seat in 1950 and did
not regain it until 1966 – the realignment was complete, with Labour
firmly established as the alternative party.[57] Furthermore, the political
battles were fought within a new consensus, which at local level was
reflected in changed municipal norms and voting behaviour.

In 1945 Labour took the chairmanships of the Finance, Education
and Public Assistance Committees, and in the following year took them
all, thus ending the non-partisan tradition.[58] The vexed question of
aldermanic elections took longer to resolve. Labour settled old scores by
taking all seven available seats in 1945, and the Conservatives retaliated
on regaining control in 1949. It was not until 1953 that a new consensus
emerged, based on proportional representation.[59] The city's marginality
meant that until 1964 the Lord Mayor came from the majority party, and
in 1947/48, 1958/59 and 1963/64 control rested on his casting vote. It is
surprising that the office was finally de-politicised when routine alterna-
tion was accepted.[60]

After the war the dominance of national political considerations in
municipal politics became overwhelming. There were two early manifestations of this in York: the reduction in the size of personal votes, with the
consequential narrowing of inter-ward swings, which was clear by 1951,
and the disappearance of the Liberals after 1948.[61]

After the elections of 1945 just 50 per cent of the Council remained
from pre-war and by 1951 only 20 per cent. However, the new generation
in York and elsewhere was to be a long serving one.[62] The average for the
1951 council was 15.1 years, with 60.0 per cent of Labour members and
29.3 per cent of Conservatives serving over 20 years, though 40.4 per
cent eventually left because of electoral defeat.

The change in the mechanism of social mobility, from trade and
commerce to education, and geographical mobility was apparent by
1951. This weakened the interest of the middle class in local politics and
was accompanied by a decline in the importance of council membership
as a means of conferring social prestige.[63] However, the council in 1951,
especially on the Conservative side, did contain a substantial number of
members from social classes I and II, though the city's economic leaders
were not represented (see Table 6).[64] The Conservatives remained predominantly small local traders and businessmen, having lost even those

Table 6   1951
Social Class and Occupation of York City
and of Council Members

	York City[1]	Conservative	Labour	Total Council[2]
Social Class				
No. of Members		37	10	47
% in Class				
I	2	19	0	15
II	11	59	20	51
III	58	22	80	34
IV	13	0	0	0
V	16	0	0	0
	100	100	100	100
Occupation Groups				
No. of Members		37	10	47
% in Group				
Professional		16	0	13
Business		51	0	40
Shopkeeper		19	10	17
Non-manual		11	40	17
Manual		3	50	13
		100	100	100

Notes:
[1] The figures for the city are taken from the 1951 census, and recalculated using the 1971 definitions.
[2] Five women – four Conservative and one Independent – are omitted from both sections.
For definitions and sources see Table 1.

clerical workers they had obtained prewar.[65] Labour politics, especially council membership, provided a crucial field in which manual workers could exercise their talents, gain public recognition and social status. In York, because of the long tradition, this was especially true for railwaymen, and eight out of the ten Labour councillors were so employed, with five being skilled men.

There was a decline in the role of councillors as leaders of associations, though they did tend to belong to a wide range of social institutions,
even if Freemasonry was less popular. After the war it became increasingly difficult to infer the religious commitments of members from their
secular activities – by 1951 York candidates had ceased to signal their
religious connections – and, in line with the continued decline in church
attendance, fewer members were religiously active.

From 1951-61 the two-party municipal battle resulted in three
changes of control, with the Conservatives losing after five years in 1954,
and again in 1961 after winning in 1959; though only twice were local
issues strong enough to prevent York's swing from following the national
pattern.[66] In 1954 the Conservative proposal to introduce economic rents
and a rebate scheme aroused spontaneous hostility, and this was fanned
by Labour, resulting in the loss of eight seats on a 4.8 per cent swing.
Despite a national swing to the Conservatives in 1960, there was a 2.8 per
cent swing to Labour in York, where the Conservatives were blamed for
delaying the introduction of measures designed to relieve the city's
chronic traffic congestion.

The total length of service of the 1961 council members remained
high at 16.6 years.[67] The age of entry to the council was, however, lower
than in 1951, with 25.9 per cent entering under 41 years and 14.8 per cent
over 55, compared with 20 per cent and 26.7 per cent.[68] As with previous
councils a majority – 56 per cent – of members, especially on the Conservative side, were elected at the first attempt, and the number of women
continued to be derisory.

The overall social class and occupational characteristics of the 1961
council was close to the national average except for Labour members[69]
(see Table 7). Though the Labour group did have one lecturer and two
self-employed men within its ranks, it remained predominantly drawn
from social class III, with 13 manual workers among its 22 members (59.1
per cent). This was a reflection of the working-class characteristics of the
constituency party and neither were typical of the party in larger urban
areas.[70]

The reforms of Maxwell Fyfe and Woolton designed to widen the
appeal and membership of the Conservative Party did have some success
nationally, but in York the new middle class, especially office workers,
were not recruited. The 1961 council reflected this, with the Conservative
members continuing to be largely shopkeepers and businessmen (70 per
cent), with a declining proportion of professionals and few employed
white-collar workers.[71]

Table 7   1961
Social Class and Occupation of York City
and of Council Members

	York City[1]	Conservative	Labour	Total Council[2]
Social Class				
No. of Members		30	20	50
% in Class				
I	3	10	0	6
II	11	53	15	38
III	54	37	75	52
IV	21	0	10	4
V	11	0	0	0
	100	100	100	100
Occupational Groups				
No. of Members		30	20	50
% of Groups				
Professional		10	0	6
Business		47	5	30
Shopkeeper		23	5	16
Non-manual		13	25	18
Manual		7	65	30
		100	100	100

Notes:
[1] The figures for the city are taken from the 1966 sample census and recalculated using the 1971 definitions.
[2] Two Conservative and two Labour women are omitted from both sections.
For definitions and sources see Table 1.

From 1961 until the abolition of the County Borough Council in 1974, municipal elections continued to echo national trends, with differential voting being of importance though turnout generally fell. The contests were close, with four changes of control until the large anti-government swings gave the Conservatives substantial majorities after 1967.[72] One consequence of this marginality was the development of

Table 8   1971
Social Class in England and Wales, York City,
Birmingham Council, and York Labour Party's,
General Management Committee

	England and Wales[1]	York City[1]	Birmingham Council[2]	York Labour Party General Management Committee
% in Social Class				
I	5	4	22	6
II	18	15	44	10
III	51	51	28	84
IV	18	19	6	—
V	8	11	—	—
	100	100	100	100

Notes:
[1] Figures from the 1971 Census of Population.
[2] Newton (1966, p. 246).
[3] The classification covers 49 members who attended at least one meeting during the year; 20 men and 20 women were omitted.
For definitions see Table 1.

bipartisan approaches, most notably towards comprehensive education, traffic management and housing administration; this did, however, delay both policy-making and execution. Labour's 1960 commitment to the abolition of the eleven-plus was eventually shared by the Conservatives, but the time taken to formulate a political and professional consensus meant that when York's County Borough status ended in 1974 it still awaited implementation, as it does today. This development was challenged, and by the late 1960s there was growing conflict between the Labour Party and their council representatives which reached a symbolic height in arguments over the 1972 Housing Finance Act.[73]

The Liberals reorganised in 1961 and ran candidates in the two following years, winning one seat in 1962, but the revival soon petered out. It is important to note that these candidates were recruited from those white-collar groups where the other parties were weak, and that

Table 9   1971
                    Social Class and Occupation
                       of Council Members

	Conservative	Labour	Total Council
Social Class			
No. of Members[1]	34	14	48
% in Class[2]			
I	9	—	6
II	59	21	48
III	32	72	44
IV	—	7	2
	100	100	100
Occupational Groups			
No. of Members[1]	34	14	48
% in Group			
Professional	9	—	6
Business	44	—	31
Shopkeeper	12	7	11
Non-Manual	23	36	27
Manual	12	57	25
	100	100	100

Notes:
[1] 5 women (3 Labour and 2 Conservative) are omitted.
[2] There were no members in Class V.
For definitions and sources see Table 1.

five of the nine subsequently became active in either Conservative or Labour politics.[74] There was another revival in 1971, which, unlike the first, was firmly based on a distinctive style – community politics – though both relied upon a single dynamic individual.[75]

The members of the 1971 council completed on average 14.3 years of service, though in that year, because of electoral volatility, twelve Conservative and four Labour councillors had sat for less than three years.

More Conservative (59.5 per cent) than Labour members (47.1 per cent) were elected at their first attempt. This party difference was also apparent in entry ages, with 52.9 per cent of Labour members joining the council when under 41 and 7.7 per cent when over 50, compared with 25.0 per cent and 16.7 per cent of Conservatives, but the overall average age was lower than elsewhere.[76]

There continued to be a wide difference between the class and occupational structures of the city and the council, with only 25 per cent of the latter being manual workers, compared with 68 per cent of the population; as well as between the parties (see Tables 8 and 9). During the 1960s the Conservatives absorbed the threat posed by potential municipal rivals, as they had after 1918; and by 1971 their proportion of non-manual workers had increased at the expense of shopkeepers.[77] This development culminated during 1971 in the deposing of the leader and two senior aldermen by younger men, more in tune with the changes.[78]

Manual workers continued to predominate among Labour members, with only three employed in intermediate occupations; and the railway tradition continued with ten representatives, the same as in 1961, including four skilled men.[79] The Group's composition reflected the character of the local party, which, despite the establishment of a university in 1963, remained an organisation of the skilled working class, both manual (51.0 per cent) and non-manual (33.0 per cent).[80]

Conclusions

The municipal history of York after 1900 is not unique, because it was part of the general class transformation of British electoral politics which resulted in a new two party alignment. However, the process in the city did have distinctive features, most notably the Edwardian Liberal revival and the continued characteristics of the local Labour Party. What is perhaps important about York's history is that it shows how the fundamental recasting of the political system was achieved at local level with the minimum of conflict. The party battle was, in reality, a reflection of the underlying societal consensus on norms and values which the political activists shared. Though there was friction as the adjustments occurred, conflict was muted, and the consensus was buttressed on the Council by the longevity of service which made for conservatism.

The Edwardian Liberal revival merely postponed the inevitable. The party was middle class and, as the 1906 and 1913 elections showed, its supporters were suspicious of the organised working class. The consequential failure to widen the party's class base was to be fatal. The war, the extension of the franchise and the economic travails of the interwar years accelerated the class polarisation of the electorate, and during the

1920s this was aided by the strident anti-socialism of the Conservatives. The Liberals, deprived of a class base, crumbled. After 1945 York became a marginal city as the realignment was completed, but a growing uniformity of electoral behaviour accompanied the loss of the council's independent power.

The class and occupations of members of the County Borough Council changed relatively little between 1901 and 1974, and they were always unrepresentative of the city as a whole. There was an alteration in the balance of membership away from the professional and intermediate social classes (I and II) towards those in skilled occupations (class III). This was caused by the change in the general occupational structure, as well as by the alteration in the mechanism of social mobility and in the utility of council membership to the socially mobile. It was also the result of political developments, in particular the rise of Labour, which gave the skilled artisan access to political power, and the widening of Conservative membership during the 1960s.

Footnotes

[1] The author wishes to thank Mr. R. Beedham and Mrs. E. Sutcliffe of the Institute of Social and Economic Research, University of York for their most generous statistical help.

[2] J. B. Morrell and A. G. Watson, *How York Governs Itself*, 1928, p. 8.

[3] K. E. T. Wilkinson, *Seventy Years of York*, Unpublished memoirs, pp. 5-8. In 1891 the wards ranged in size from 1,443 electors to 2,669, covering populations ranging from 7,014 to 16,566.

[4] Ibid., p. 61; *Yorkshire Herald* 30 November 1896, 2 November 1898.

[5] The leader of the Conservatives in the city and on the council was Sir Joseph Sykes Rymer, a coal merchant, colliery owner and farmer, who was a devout Wesleyan. One of his sons married a daughter of Alderman Agar, the Liberal leader, who owned a family leather business and also farmed. Both were directors of the York Waterworks Company. Rymer had been on the council from 1867 and Agar from 1880.

[6] M. Kinnear, *The British Voter: An Atlas and Survey Since 1885*, 1968, pp. 122-123; H. Pelling, *Social Geography of British Elections 1885-1910*, 1967, p. 308; B. S. Rowntree, *Poverty: A Study of Town Life*, 1901 (1922 edn.), p. 32.

[7] M. Lee, 'Chester' in L. J. Sharpe, *Voting in Cities*, 1967, p. 76.

[8] Both Councillors were active trade unionists and Co-operative Society directors, and argued for municipalisation and the building of working-class housing under the 1890 Act. See *York Equitable Society Report and Balance Sheet for the Quarter Ending 5th June 1900, 4 March 1902; Yorkshire Herald* 23, 28, 31 October 1900.

[9] All the comments on the census years relate to members who sat during part or all of the relevant calendar year.

[10] Rhodes Brown's Election Address, 1910.

[11] One legal member became Town Clerk. For a discussion of professional members see: G. W. Jones, *Borough Politics,* 1969, pp. 106, 292-296.

[12] They were the sons of professional workers, three with education at major public schools, two held important directorships outside York and one became Under Sheriff of Yorkshire. The other was a self-made draper who, after he purged the taint of trade, read for the bar.

[13] A. H. Birch, *Small Town Politics,* 1959, p. 181. There were important overlaps between members. The Centenary Chapel was used by two Conservative and two Liberal members, and the Anglican Alderman McKay, the last Liberal Lord Mayor and vice-chairman of the Finance Committee, worshipped with a Conservative councillor, alderman and senior party officer. There was some mobility, with two members moving from Methodism to Anglicanism, one as he left trade for the bar, and the other as he crossed to the Conservatives.

[14] In 1900, 65 per cent of York children attended voluntary schools, compared with the average of 45 per cent in England and Wales. Passive resistance to paying the rate continued until 1908.

[15] Wilkinson, op. cit. (n. 3), p. 62, Arnold Rowntree, Seebohm's cousin, became the Liberal Association's Secretary in 1901, President in 1904, and MP in 1910.

[16] D. S. Crichton, et al. *Towards a Municipal Policy for York,* York, 1905; *York Labour News* November 1905; *Yorkshire Evening Press,* 31 October 1905.

[17] T. Anderson, et al. *Towards a Municipal Policy for York,* 1907. Four seats were won from the Conservatives and three from Labour.

[18] *Yorkshire Gazette* 20 November 1909.

[19] Jones op. cit. (n. 11), pp. 42-44; C. Cook, 'Labour and the downfall of the Liberal Party' in A. Sked and C. Cook, *Crisis and Controversy: Essays in Honour of A. J. P. Taylor,* 1976, p. 62.

[20] Conference Reports, 1904 and 1912.

[21] For a general discussion see R. McKibbin, *The Evolution of the Labour Party,* 1974, pp. 33-47.

[22] York was one of the constituencies in the LRC- Liberal pact and the only one where the Liberals plumped. The Liberal polled 6,413, of which 2,082 were plumpers, and Labour 4,573 and 421. There were 4,042 Liberal-Labour splits. Labour was outraged when Crooks urged Labour to vote for the Liberal as well 'thus making Stuart's independent stand seem like mere intransigence'. P. P. Poirier, *The Advent of the Labour Party,* 1958, pp. 263, 267.

[23] See report on the ILP-Liberal debate: *Labour News,* June 1904.

[24] Though from 1910-14 the figures were five, six and four.

[25] The occupations of the eleven defeated candidates were six manual, two clerical and insurance agents, and one doctor. Four were railwaymen.

[26] The first secretary of the LRC also worshipped at the Wesleyan Chapel. One prosperous Catholic milliner, a Guardian for 20 years, who was a Liberal candidate in 1900, was a Conservative one in 1910.

[27] In 1913 the firm had three directors on the Council and a departmental manager. Morrell's brother, brother-in-law and solicitor were also members.

[28] The first chairman of York City AFC was a Labour Councillor, and three Liberals also became directors.

29 Pre-war 66 per cent of York's men had the vote and it was the less affluent who were disenfranchised.

30 In Monk Ward, for example, the percentage of Labour's vote obtained by plumping rose from 44 per cent in 1903 to 74 per cent in 1922, and over 80 per cent in 1923 and 1924.

31 Davies retired from the Council in 1915, Hogge in 1913 and Wales in 1919. The one working-class former councillor joined Labour. Arnold Rowntree retired from politics after his defeat. Crichton died in 1921 and significantly his wife left the party in 1918, and won a Council seat as an Independent.

32 Three were clerks and one an insurance agent.

33 Three Conservatives and one each from the other parties. Three Labour members, two Liberal and one Conservative were active in the temperance movement.

34 Despite the fervent anti-socialist campaign, Labour took 54.3 per cent of the 1923 Liberal vote, with 24.3 per cent going to the Conservatives and 21.4 per cent abstaining; and its share of the two-party poll fell by 0.2 per cent to 43.8 per cent.

35 It also made it difficult for the Liberals to win seats, though an engine driver, after nursing Holgate for two years, won it from Labour in 1927, and held it until 1945.

36 This was partly because of their dislike of Lloyd George, even though the Liberal report *Britain's Industrial Future* (1928), which was the basis of the manifesto, had been written by Wallace (later a Rowntree director), and Seebohm Rowntree was active in the Inquiry. The party shared with the Conservatives a belief in thrift, independence, and self-help, and shied away from unconventional remedies.

37 The coup against the President since 1906 – an Anglican solicitor of 71, was engineered by Wragge (aged 75), the Group Leader, and Alderman Todd (69), but power passed to Dodsworth, an Anglican solicitor aged 38, and Terry (51), Chairman of the family confectionery firm. Wragge and Todd were consoled with the Lord Mayoralty in 1931/32 and 1930/31.

38 For 1929 Spearman's rank correlation coefficient $r_s=0.742$, and is significant at the 0.01 level; and for the years 1926-29 $r_s=0.703$, significant at the 0.05 level.

39 Labour took 36.8 per cent to the Conservative's 63.2 per cent.

40 The anti-Labour swing averaged 4.2 per cent from 1930, which ranged from −14 per cent in Monk, where a popular Labour member defended, to 11 per cent in Castlegate, where a popular Conservative defended.

41 Two Conservatives, two Labour and one Liberal served for less than ten years (9.6 per cent) but three Conservatives, five Labour and three Liberals served over 30 years (21.2 per cent).

42 Watson 1919-1946; Hutchinson 1920-1921, 1924-1927, 1930-1945; Kay 1920-1926; Harwood 1927-1945; and Roberts 1931-1934.

43 He left an interesting unpublished memoir: A. Simpson, *All In A Worker's Lifetime.*

44 Three Conservatives, and one Liberal and Labour members worshipped at the

Centenary Chapel. Morrell was a guild member and Oscar Rowntree became a freemason during the 1920s, as he was moving towards the Conservatives.

[45] In 1929 the ratio of aldermen to councillors was Conservative, 7 to 16; Labour, 2 to 12; and Liberal, 3 to 5.

[46] In the 1920s there was growing criticism of the lack of interest shown in the Association by Conservative councillors.

[47] The 1931/32 swing was 6.5 per cent to Labour (−3.5 per cent from 1929), but despite a 14.9 per cent increase in the party's vote, no gains were made because turnout, though it fell by 5.9 per cent, was still above the 1929 level. The 1932/33 swing was 0.5 per cent.

[48] The patriotic appeal of a National Government in the midst of a crisis was also important. The two-party poll shares were for Labour 44.0 per cent in 1923, 43.8 per cent in 1924, 54.3 per cent in 1929, 35.1 per cent in 1931, 43.0 per cent in 1935, and 44.9 per cent in 1937.

[49] In terms of seats, Labour, with 14 in 1934, did equal its 1929 performance, but its poll share was below that peak. The swing from 1933/34 was −0.9 per cent, from 1934/35 +2.5 per cent (the General Election increasing turnout), and from 1935/36 −0.8 per cent.

[50] Labour lost one seat in 1930 and three in 1931; regained four in 1934, but again lost one in 1935 and two in 1936.

[51] In 1936 Labour responded to the demand for a new hospital, but it was not the initiator of the idea or leader of the campaign.

[52] The swings from 1929 were −10.6 per cent to 1935 and −8.7 per cent to 1937.

[53] Individuals with local support and/or money could gain nomination in most wards even against an association's wish.

[54] In 1937 the city had expanded and Acomb was incorporated as a new ward. This increased the number of aldermen by one, to 13 and councillors by three, to 39. The three Acomb councillors were elected as Independents, though one was an active Liberal, and are so included because they were only really concerned with ward affairs.

[55] Only 15 manual workers were elected between the wars, 11 Labour (eight railwaymen), two Conservatives (both ex-Labour members), one railway Liberal and one railway Independent (also ex-Labour).

[56] R. B. McCallum and A. Readman, *The British General Election of 1945*, 1947, p. 50. The general election swing was 9.7 per cent from 1937 and 0.8 per cent from 1929. The municipal swing was 8.1 per cent from 1938 and 1.3 per cent from 1929.

[57] In the Acomb and Clifton wards Labour's breakthrough in 1945 was permanent.

[58] Significantly, the Labour Group leader established a pattern by taking the chairmanship of the co-ordinating Finance Committee.

[59] The proportions were based on the representation of councillors in the preceding three years. The candidates were chosen by the respective groups, usually by seniority. *Council Minutes* 1952-53, pp. 883, 887.

[60] In 1962/63 and 1973/74 Labour took control with 26 of the 52 seats, though the Lord Mayor was Conservative, because the balance was held first by a Liberal and then by two Independent Conservative aldermen.

⁶¹ The 1936/1937 swing was 2.9 per cent from Labour, ranging from −15.1 per cent to +5.3 per cent, with four out of seven wards following the swing. The 1950/1951 swing was −1.9 per cent (−4.5 to +3.9 per cent), with 11 of the 12 wards swinging from Labour. Having finished a poor third in 1945 and 1950, the Liberals did not run a Parliamentary candidate until 1964.

⁶² G. W. Jones and A. Norton, *Political Leadership in Local Authorities*, University of Birmingham, 1978, p. 25.

⁶³ Birch, op. cit. (n. 13), pp. 11, 115-116.

⁶⁴ There continued to be no representatives from the railway's senior management, and the Rowntree connection was broken with Morrell's defeat in 1945.

⁶⁵ The four Conservative non-manual workers held managerial positions and Labour's four were clerical workers.

⁶⁶ After 1946 the Liberals did not run candidates. There were a few Independent councillors, who, if they remained members, joined the Conservatives. For issues and swings see: F. Bealey, J. Blondel and W. P. McCann, *Constituency Politics*, 1965, pp. 381-382; W. Hampton, *Democracy and Community*, 1970, pp. 246-271, 312-314; D. M. Hill, 'Leeds' in Sharpe, *Voting*, op. cit. (n. 7), pp. 185, 315; K. Newton, *Second City Politics*, 1976, pp. 15, 195, 259-262.

⁶⁷ The averages for 1961 and 1971 include the continuing service, of respectively the 17 and 24 members on the new authorities 1974-1980.

⁶⁸ In 1961, 38.5 per cent of Labour members were aged under 41 years when first elected (16.7 per cent in 1951) and 7.7 per cent were over 55 (50.0 per cent), compared with the Conservatives' 14.3 per cent (21.7 per cent) and 21.4 per cent (21.7 per cent).

⁶⁹ For details of the 1964 members of English and Welsh County Borough Councils see: Committee on the Management of Local Government, vol. 11, *The Local Government Councillor*, H.M.S.O., 1967, pp. 15-43. (The five social class percentages were 9, 48, 30, 10 and 3.)

⁷⁰ The percentage of Labour members who were manual workers was 70.5 in Newcastle-under-Lyme, though it was lower for party 'stalwarts' (1960), 28 in Sheffield (1966), and 20 in Wolverhampton (1963/64) and London (those elected in 1961). Bealey et al., op. cit., (n. 66), pp. 271-272, 305; Hampton op. cit. (n. 66), p. 190; Jones op. cit. (n. 11), pp. 107, 368; J. Sharpe, *A Metropolis Votes*, 1962, pp. 29-42.

⁷¹ Of the three professionals, one was first elected pre-1939, one was a surveyor developing his own construction company and the third was an accountant who became an M.P. in 1974. The non-manual workers were two salesmen, an insurance broker, and an organiser for the deaf.

⁷² Labour were in control in 1961/2-1964/5, 1966/7 and 1973/4.

⁷³ The tension is highlighted by the fact that in 1967, for example, none of the six Labour aldermen and only nine of the 17 councillors attended any of the party General Management Committee meetings.

⁷⁴ Three joined Labour – one becoming a councillor – and two were elected as Conservative councillors.

⁷⁵ At his third attempt the leader of the later revival wrestled one safe seat from Labour in the 1973 elections for the new District Council. By 1980 the party held 10 of the District seats and had run parliamentary candidates in 1974 and

1979. The tactics have been to concentrate on ward issues, accompanied by a steady stream of similarly directed leaflets.

[76] In Birmingham 53 per cent were aged under 45, compared with 56.0 per cent in the Maud sample, and 69 per cent in York; Newton, op. cit. (n. 66), p. 117.

[77] Six of the non-manual workers were from social class II and two from class III. One manual worker later joined Labour, and another went into business with the son of his ward colleague.

[78] Two were first elected in 1949 and one in 1946.

[79] Two of the women members, however, were from social class II. In 1980 nine of the Dictrict Group were from class III (six of whom were manual workers) and six were railwaymen.

[80] The figure is based on the 89 activists who attended at least one General Management Committee meeting during 1971. They appear to have been representative of the membership of 1,900. Though there were three lecturers and three students active in 1971, the most influential period of university involvement was in the mid-sixties when the International Socialists worked inside the party.

CHAPTER XI

'Newman, Palladio and Mrs. Beeton': the Foundation of the University of York

by

Christopher Storm-Clark

'A Rude and Barbarous People'

For its 121st meeting, the British Association returned in 1959 to York, its place of birth, only a few weeks after the first public announcement of an application from the city for a new university. Apportioned among 2,903 visitors during an exceptionally fine spell of September weather, the prodigality of 16 presidential addresses, 345 lectures and papers, and 138 excursions did not diminish the generosity with which the President, Sir James Gray, endorsed York's candidature:

> York has all the virtues and attributes of a great university city. Tell your citizens, every one of them, to work and talk unceasingly for your university, which you will assuredly get – for you have the most lovely city in the kingdom in which to set it.[1]

York had other, more prosaic claims. These had been 'humbly' represented in a petition to Parliament in 1652 as 'its healthful situation, cheapness of victual and food' and 'the convenient distance of it from

other universities and the borders of the kingdom'; but there were
various motives for the three, possibly four, petitions for a university
which (beginning with James I's passage through York on a Royal Progress to Scotland in 1617) were politely received and ignored during the
seventeenth century. The petitioners of 1652 lamented 'the deplorable
want of a learned and faithful ministry in very many congregations', but a
university would not only help to maintain an intellectual cutting edge in
the reformed church: it would also provide an outlet for the professional
aspirations of the younger sons of the nobility and gentry. Deprived of a
place in the bureaucratic apparatus of the King's Council in the North
since Parliament had declared it to be 'illegal, unprofitable, and inconve-
nient' in 1641, and thwarted by 'the distance and dearness of the southern
universities, whose charge we are, by continual impoverishments,
rendered daily more unable to bear', the petitioners sought, not for the
first time, a remedy for their growing sense of economic and cultural
inferiority:

> As we the inhabitants of the northern part of this kingdom find our
> share in this common want and calamity to be very great, insomuch
> that we have been looked upon as a rude and barbarous people . . .
> so we cannot but be importunate in this request; in which, if we may
> prevail, we hope it will be a special means of washing from us the
> stain of rudeness and incivility, and rendering of us, to the honour of
> God and this kingdom, not so much inferior to others in religion and
> conversation.[2]

If York's academic aspirations had a materialist edge, it was not
surprising that they should fall into abeyance during periods of prosperity. Although the city's population grew from around 12,000 at the
beginning of the eighteenth century to 16,846 by the time of the census in
1801, it was the result less of indigenous industrial growth than of the
impact of agricultural improvement on the spending-power of the landed
gentry in the three contiguous Ridings. 'Here is no trade indeed', Defoe
observed during his Tour through England and Wales between 1722 and
1724, 'except such as depends upon the confluence of the gentry'.[3]
Symbolised by the opening of Lord Burlington's Assembly Rooms, modelled on Palladio's Egyptian Hall, in 1732, the city became a resort of
fashion and social discourse: in the words of Dr. Patrick Nuttgens, 'a
landscape of gentility and wealth'.[4]

But York's prosperity was precarious. Eclipsed by the growth of the
textile towns on the exposed coalfield of the West Riding, the city was
particularly vulnerable to the prolonged and severe economic depres-
sions that tormented both industry and agriculture after the Napoleonic
Wars. 'Our present state is described in a few words', wrote Sir William

Strickland, a Malton landowner, to the Board of Agriculture in 1816; 'the cultivation of the land is daily declining, the labourer, the mechanic, and the shopkeeper are unemployed; the occupier of the soil cannot pay his rent and the owner of it cannot pay his bills'.[5] Once again, as corn prices fell, the expense of sending young gentlemen to Oxford or Cambridge became unconscionable, threatening not only the career prospects of those who had to substitute a profession for an inheritance, but also the supply of educated clergy required to promote (or to resist, depending on one's point of view) the contemporary evangelical revival in the Church of England. 'Why will you not hasten to be the first since the Reformation', asked the signatory, Philoprepos, of a series of letters to the *New Times* and the *Yorkshire Gazette* between 1825 and 1827, 'in founding a university in England?' Republished in 1831 as *An Appeal to True Patriots for an University at York,* the letters set out York's claims in familiar terms:

> . . . Those ancient walls would seem to combine, in a manner and degree not perhaps to be found elsewhere in the three kingdoms, all the advantages of a city, with academical quiet and ecclesiastical dignity of the first order.[6]

It may not have been entirely by coincidence that the *Appeal* was published in August 1831, only a few weeks before the first meeting of the British Association in York; but on that occasion no endorsement was forthcoming. The geological museum built by the Yorkshire Philosophical Society between 1827 and 1830 became the focus of attention; and any further aspirations towards the foundation of a university were overtaken by Durham in 1832 and London in 1836. If the Yorkshire Philosphical Society satisfied the desire for an active nucleus of intellectual discourse and scientific inquiry in the city during the nineteenth century,[7] George Hudson's railway projects in the city and the profits of land drainage schemes in the agricultural hinterland reduced the economic anxieties that had once reinforced York's academic importunity.

J. B. Morrell and the Civic Trust

The city's commercial renaissance from the 1840s onwards did, however, furnish the movement for a university, when it was revived immediately after the Second World War, with indispensible sources of financial support and personal initiative. This is illustrated by the career of John Bowes Morrell, a director of Rowntree's from 1897 to 1943, Chairman of the Westminster Press from 1933 to 1953, Lord Mayor of York in 1914/15 and 1949/50, and one of the moving spirits of the campaign for a university in York after 1945 (see Plate 16). Morrell's connection with

Rowntree and Company began in 1884 when Joseph Rowntree, in search of finance for a new factory to produce fruit gums, turned to the York City and County Bank for a loan of £10,000. The loan was arranged by the Bank's general manager in York, William Wilberforce Morrell; and in 1890 his son, John Bowes Morrell was taken into Rowntree and Company as a trainee manager. Later a delicate private arrangement between Joseph Rowntree and W. W. Morrell, involving a second loan of £10,000 for the construction of a still larger factory in Haxby Road, helped to overcome the firm's reluctance to admit an outsider and potential competitor to the family caucus, the existence of which, as in other branches of the industry, had safeguarded the secrecy of Rowntree's recipes and processes.[8]

When the firm was reconstructed as a limited company under Joseph Rowntree's chairmanship in 1897, Morrell became a director at the age of 25. From his father, who had played an influential part in the foundation of a new School Board in 1889 and of York Public Library in 1891, Morrell derived a modest interest in civic improvement which neatly complemented Joseph Rowntree's wider concerns of temperance, pacifism, education and the relief of poverty. In 1906 he was appointed to the directorate of the Joseph Rowntree Social Service Trust, one of three trusts for which Rowntree, in the belief that philanthropy should be well-planned, had set aside about half his property between 1901 and 1903. One of the Trust's first ventures was the provision of finance to the North of England Newspaper Company, formed in 1903 as a rescue vehicle for ailing provincial newspapers, for the purchase of the *Northern Echo,* a Darlington paper, which Morrell had offered to print in York after the apostasy of the *York Herald* at the time of Gladstone's Home Rule Bills had left the Liberals without a local newspaper of their own. In 1906 Morrell took a controlling interest in *The Speaker,* a Liberal weekly paper which, under the new title of *The Nation,* was merged with *The New Statesman* in 1931.[9] In this way the Trust, with the benefit of a constitution devised to permit activity in political as well as social matters, gave Morrell access to resources which, after his election to the City Council in 1905, reinforced his rapidly-growing influence on York's civic affairs.

In the *City of Our Dreams,* written in 1935 at the invitation of York Round Table to mark the centenary of the Municipal Corporations Act, Morrell had suggested that the preservation of the city's historic buildings might be enhanced by their adaptation for educational purposes.[10] But the pressures of local government and newpaper management prevented the crystallisation of Morrell's idea for a university until after the Second World War. The credit for an actual moment of inspiration was later claimed by the Dean of York, Eric Milner-White, who arrived from

Cambridge, where he had been Fellow and Dean of King's College since 1918, to take up his office in 1941. As he himself later recorded, York's eminence as a city of learning since the time of Alcuin had always made it an appropriate site for a university:

> But its renewed claim in the twentieth century started from a remark of a Dean straight from Cambridge, ignorant of this long history. In the early days of his appointment, delighted with the city, and when his words were still 'news', he publicly expressed his admiration thus: 'What a place for a University!' That fired the imagination, amongst others, of Oliver Sheldon, a Director of Rowntree & Co. Ltd., whose enthusiasm had already founded a Society to protect our Georgian glories. It was not forgotten, and directly the War ended, the Dean and he joined with Noel Terry to found a Civic Trust for York; which should assist the preservation of its ancient treasures; but more, should look ahead to its hopes, developments and standards for the future.[11]

Although the Civic Trust, under J. B. Morrell's chairmanship, had an enthusiastic nucleus of university promoters and a constitution flexible enough for Sheldon and Milner-White to pursue their aims, its immediate concern was with the reconstruction and preservation of old buildings. In spite of the destruction of St. Martin-le-Grand and the Guildhall during the Baedeker raids, the city had not suffered as had Hull or Coventry. It was felt that the city's landscape had been scarred as much by commercial vulgarity and abortive traffic schemes in the interwar period as by bombs. Moving the formal resolution to establish the Trust at an inaugural ceremony in the Mansion House in July 1946, the Archbishop of York spoke not only of 'the weather' and 'the malice of man' as the 'great enemies' of the city but also of 'the greed of man as expressed in commercialism, which destroyed beautiful buildings and put up hideous advertisements which ruined the landscape'.[12] It was left to Morrell, seconding the Archbishop's resolution, to hint at future academic developments in which 'a city of York's artistic wealth might well become the cultural centre for the north and some of its historical buildings be preserved for the educational requirements of the new generation'.[13]

The prospects for the foundation of at least one new university in the United Kingdom were good. The proportion of 17-year-olds in full-time education in 1938, although still a modest 4 per cent, had doubled since the establishment of a national system of schooling in 1902. The expansion of the managerial and professional classes in response to opportunities in government, industry and education between the wars had created an enlarged constituency from which students might be expected to be drawn. The war had created a climate of opinion favourable to educational reform as well as an awareness of the military and industrial utility of university research. In 1946 the Barlow Committee on Scientific Manpower recommended that the number of qualified scientists should be doubled within 10 years, and, reflecting the insistence of the university reformers of the late nineteenth century that there should be no segregation of scientific from liberal studies, declared that, 'we are attracted by the conception of bringing into existence at least one University which would give to the present generation the opportunity of leaving to posterity a monument of its culture'.[14] In fact, Dr. Hugh Dalton, Chancellor of the Exchequer, had indicated in Autumn 1945 that he was prepared to support some degree of university expansion, if only to cater for those whose academic careers had been interrupted by the war. This hint that there might be an opportunity for a new foundation was seized immediately by the secretary of the Workers' Educational Association in North Staffordshire, Miss Gladys Malbon, who, with the support of the two local Members of Parliament and the Vicar of Etruria, organised a deputation to the University Grants Committee as early as May 1946.

The foundation of the University College of North Staffordshire at Keele owed its success to the promoters' reinforcement of their local claim by an appeal to current educational concerns. York, by contrast, had no firm plans which could be presented to the University Grants Committee and, unlike the Potteries, no special claim on the social conscience of the Committee's most influential member, R. H. Tawney. Undeterred, Oliver Sheldon had written to *The Times* in August 1946 to suggest that 'the University Grants Committee should, in its review of available facilities, as requested by the Chancellor of the Exchequer, bear in mind the possibilities in cities and towns which have so far not been afforded the opportunity of sharing in university work'.[15] Sheldon's appeal aroused the enthusiastic support of the Lord Mayor, Alderman Frederick Gaines, a former branch secretary of the National Union of Railwaymen who had begun his working life as a porter in 1904. Gaines persuaded Morrell, Sheldon and Milner-White, none of whom was entirely convinced that it was an appropriate time to act, to form a joint deputation to the UGC from the City Corporation and the Civic Trust. At their meeting in London in April 1947, as Milner-White later recalled, 'the deputation had nothing to offer the UGC except their desire; nevertheless, their reception by that body was exceedingly kind, and in particular its Scottish members gave notable encouragement'.[16] Neither side had envisaged an immediate commitment, but the Committee's subsequent letter had an unexpectedly animating influence. While the demand for university places could be met by the extension of existing institutions, 'it is open to the local community to work out details of a scheme which might form the basis of a long-term policy if conditions should materially change after, say, five or ten years'.[17]

York Makes Its Own Beginnings

At variance with some of the other applicants, who had relied upon the initiative of local authorities (they included Brighton, Norwich, Canterbury, Coventry and Lancaster by the end of 1947), York interpreted the UGC's reply as a challenge rather than as a polite rejection. As Milner-White wrote in 1948, 'In all discussion we have always come back to the necessity of York *making its own beginnings* . . . to prove in fact what all admit in theory, the peculiar suitability of York as an academic centre'.[18] Having made a series of contacts with influential sympathisers in Oxford and Cambridge, the Civic Trust established an Academic Development Committee, which under the chairmanship of Milner-White began to prepare a list of activities, including a series of summer schools in architecture and history, which might exemplify the vigour of York's desire to be a university city. Fortified by a gift, arranged by Morrell, of £1,000 from the Joseph Rowntree Social Service Trust (to be followed by a convenanted grant of £5,000 from the North of England Newspaper Company in 1948), Sheldon approached C. W. C. Needham, a York architect who had been working on York's postwar Civic Plan, and W. A. Eden, of the Leeds University School of Architecture, to discuss the foundation of a 'John Carr Institute of Architecture' which would offer vacation courses on architectural history and measured drawing to students in existing schools. At the same time, the Committee commissioned Dr. J. S. Purvis, a trained archivist who had started on the exhausting task of cataloguing the Minster's archiepiscopal records, to engage a panel of lecturers for a 'Summer School of Archives and Historical Research'.

At the opening in August 1949 of the first two summer schools in the Merchant Adventurers' Hall, to the restoration of which the Pilgrim Trust had contributed £2,000, J. B. Morrell, then in his second term of office as Lord Mayor, made the objective of the enterprise quite explicit. The summer schools, he said, 'are an educational venture upon which a university may eventually be built'.[19] During the first two years, the schools incurred a small financial loss, but this was made up by grants from the Pilgrim Trust and the York Education Authority. By 1952 the Academic Development Committee felt strong enough to embark upon a programme of activities throughout the year. In September Dr. W. A. Singleton, of the Manchester University School of Architecture, who had replaced Eden as director of the architectural summer school in 1951, organised the first of a series of courses on the protection and repair of ancient buildings at a small hotel in Bootham. As the Civic Trust observed in its Annual Report in 1952, the course was 'designed to assist in remedying the very serious deficiency of expert architectural advice and specialised craftsmanship in relation to ancient buildings which exists throughout the country'.[20] It reflected a special interest of the Trust, which in 1946 at the instigation of C. J. Minter, the City Engineer, had tried to set up a Guild of York Craftsmen to attract impecunious skilled workmen who could associate themselves with the work of the Trust without the payment of an annual subscription.[21]

In 1951 John West-Taylor, a graduate of Trinity Hall and the London University School of Librarianship and Archives, was appointed as secretary to the Academic Development Committee. In 1953 he directed a new course, 'Civic Patterns in York', under the joint sponsorship of the Committee and the British Council. At their meeting with the Lord Mayor's deputation in 1947, the UGC had mentioned 'the special requirements of overseas students'; and West-Taylor's course, the title of which was altered to 'Life in a Historic City' in 1954, was designed to introduce overseas students to the pattern of life in a representative English city. Milner-White evolved a more ambitious scheme for a 'School of Britain', a residential college at which students from Africa, America and Australia could study 'the rock from which they were hewn'.[22] Although the Dean's idea was not taken up, it was clear that these early achievements could sustain their momentum only in a more permanent form. This was provided by the foundation of the Borthwick Institute of Historical Research and the Institute of Advanced Architectural Studies. In 1939, Archbishop Temple had invited Dr. J. S. Purvis to examine the contents of the Diocesan Registry. Purvis found a collection of records covering the history of the Diocese and Province of York from 1220 onwards which amounted to over a million documents. There was no general index, and a large part of their content was simply unknown. In 1949 Professor E. F. Jacob, Sub-Warden of All Souls and one of the York summer schools' most distinguished lecturers, inspected the Registry muniments and confirmed that they were of inestimable historical value. Purvis quoted Jacob's words to the Civic Trust's Annual Meeting in 1950:

A fuller examination of these records will call for a revision, or even a correction of many views long published and accepted as of authority of the Reformation period in particular, since without such a study of hitherto unworked material no history, especially of Tudor times, can be considered complete.[23]

Shortly before the war, Dean Bate, Milner-White's predecessor, had proposed to enlarge the Minster Library to house the documents in safer and more convenient surroundings, but the site proved to be too small for the miles of shelving required by a properly-ordered archive. In 1947 Archbishop Garbett and Col. Innes Ware, the Diocesan Registrar, turned to the Civic Trust for help. The Trust was aware that St. Anthony's Hall, a medieval building with a history as protean as that of the city itself, had recently been vacated by the Blue Coat School for boys as a result of the 1945 Education Act; and a small group from the Academic Development Committee led by Oliver Sheldon appealed to the Hall's owners, the City Corporation, for its restoration as a 'Repository of Historical Muniments'. By 1950, it was agreed that the Corporation should lease the Hall to the Civic Trust for 21 years at a peppercorn rent, and that the whole body of records should be deposited there as an indivisible loan in the care of an archivist to be appointed by the Trust. With a grant of £12,000 from the Pilgrim Trust, work began (after a short delay due to a national shortage of building materials) in the first half of 1952. Meanwhile, shortly before his death in August 1951, Sheldon had approached the Trustees of William Borthwick, a resident of Bridlington, who had bequeathed £60,000 for an unspecified enducational foundation in Yorkshire. The trustees agreed to assign the income from the legacy to the Academic Development Committee for the running-expenses of what had originally been conceived as the York Institute of Historical Research. With further financial support arranged by J. B. Morrell, the Borthwick Institute, under Purvis's directorship, established the St. Anthony's Press, which between 1951 and 1959 produced no less than five books and seventeen monographs.

The Institute was opened on 15 May 1953 by the Princess Royal. Preceded by a lunch at the Merchant Adventurers' Hall, the inaugural address was delivered by the Vice-Chancellor of Oxford, Sir Maurice Bowra, to an audience which included the chancellors and vice-chancellors of six universities. The symbolic importance of the occasion did not go unnoticed by Milner-White, the compiler of the Civic Trust's Annual Report for 1953:

> On the platform stretching the entire width of the Hall was seated such a body of eminent academics as was never before seen in York, the huge yellow curtains behind them providing a perfect foil to the scarlets and blues of their robes.[24]

The foundation of the Institute of Advanced Architectural Studies also reflected the fortunate consonance of the Civic Trust's academic aims with its conservationist policies. Since the introduction in September 1952 of the first course on the protection and repair of ancient buildings, the Academic Development Committee had begun to look for a permanent base from which its architectural courses and summer schools could be expanded for the benefit of laymen as well as specialists. Once again, there was a building to hand: St. John's, Ousebridge, at the corner of Micklegate and North Street. In fact, the Trust had turned its attention to Micklegate, a street containing a number of distinctive Georgian frontages on a rising curve from Ouse Bridge to the Bar, as early as 1946, when it noted a complaint from the Vicar of Holy Trinity to the York Georgian Society about the physical decay engendered by the area's loss of social esteem. 'Fish and chip shops, doss-houses and tenements are rapidly paving the way for the ultimate demolition of some of York's most interesting houses'.[25] The threat of demolition in 1950 made St. John's the focus of the Trust's anxieties even though the building itself had always lived dangerously. In 1551 its steeple collapsed; in 1818 it lost part of its churchyard to a road-widening scheme; and in 1850 it was attacked by the Victorian cult of church restoration which resulted in the reconstruction of its south and east walls to widen the entrance to North Street. Eventually deconsecrated in 1938, it was unlikely to survive unless some other use could be found for it.

The conversion of a redundant church was an appropriately imaginative venture for the 'York Institute of Architectural Study', launched by the Academic Development Committee in November 1953. An appeal for £12,000 attracted four immediate contributions of £1,000 each from the Pilgrim Trust, Rowntree's and two local building firms. By 1955, the Institute was running four technical courses and three summer schools, including one on 'The Country House' intended 'chiefly for Americans'.[26] Its new quarters in St. John's were opened by the Minister of Works in March 1956; and in the following year the Carnegie United Kingdom Trust gave £2,800 for the incorporation of a 'national reference centre' for the protection and repair of historic buildings. By 1958, the Institute had evolved into a nationally-recognised postgraduate training body, and it was reconstituted, with a further grant of £35,000 from the Social Service Trust to meet its running costs up to 1962, as the Institute of Advanced Architectural Studies.

Both Institutes were now under the sponsorship of the York Academic Trust, established as an independent charitable institution two years earlier, when the Academic Development Committee had recognised that the scale of its activities had outgrown the Civic Trust's capacity to contain them with its other responsibilities of preservation and urban improvement. Under Milner-White's chairmanship, the Academic Trust inherited a committed nucleus of university promoters who made up its Governing Council, around which there was a wider membership of sympathisers drawn from the overlapping constituencies of industry, politics, law, newspapers, education and the arts.

The New Universities

York's own efforts were reinforced by developments elsewhere. In February 1956 Brighton Borough Council, which had made two further approaches to the UGC for a university since 1947, submitted a Memorandum drafted by its Director of Education, W. G. Stone. The Memorandum contained more than a local claim: in his examination of the way in which the demand for higher education would be affected by the postwar peak in the birth-rate and by the trend, which had then only just become apparent, towards a higher school-leaving age, Stone made out a case for a complete departure from what Lord Annan later described as 'the orderly, decorous expansion of the system in the 1950's'.[27] Even so, the advantage of Brighton's application for a University College of Sussex, as the UGC perceived it, was not that it would be the first of a new wave of university foundations for the requirements of the next decade but that it would provide some relief for London from the pressure of applicants from the South East.

Inhibited by doubts about the future employment of graduates, the availability of accommodation and equipment, and the maintenance of academic standards, the UGC had hitherto relied upon expansion within existing institutions, especially the civic foundations, the last of which, Leicester, received its independence with a charter in 1957. In so far as 82,000 places in 1954 (compared with 50,000 in 1938), distributed among 21 universities, made provision for 73 per cent of qualified applicants (but only 4.3 per cent of the age group as a whole), this policy had had some moderate success.[28] But the UGC's announcement in their quinquennial Report in September 1958 of a plan for 124,000 places by 1965 failed to satisfy the expansionists. A few months earlier, the Association of University Teachers had suggested a target of 145,000 (a figure which the York Academic Trust, during its final preparations for a submission to the UGC in 1959, thought 'may have been idealistic'): but even if each of the existing universities were to accommodate 4,500 students by 1965, there would still be a deficit of 23,000 places. Their solution was the foundation of at least five new universities in places such as Norwich, York and Leamington, 'because the existing town or city provides a nucleus of cultured life'.[29]

When in 1963 the Robbins Committee proposed that there should be 346,000 university places for home and overseas students by 1980, it warned that, 'These figures involve what to many will seem a startling increase in numbers . . .'.[30] But there had already been a substantial change of outlook. As the proportion of 17-year-olds remaining at school rose from 6.6 per cent in 1952 to 11.1 per cent in 1960, higher education attracted a growing volume of political support in the face of invidious comparisons with other countries, evidence of industrial decline, and the belief that there would be substantial economic returns from skill and training. As A. H. Halsey and M. A. Trow wrote in 1971, 'Statistics of inequality of educational opportunity have become popular knowledge and have turned access to the universities into an almost commonplace criterion of distributive justice'.[31] The proportion of 18-year-olds possessing qualifications for university (two or more passes at GCE Advanced Level in England and Wales) grew from 4.3 per cent in 1954 to 6.1 per cent between 1954 and 1959; while the proportion actually admitted to university fell from 73 per cent to 66 per cent. The changed climate in which Lord Robbins began his work was later described by Lord Annan:

> Like several commissions set up to effect change and mass the guns which would blast the positions of the unthinking, the Robbins Committee spent a great part of its energy winning a battle against an enemy that had retreated from the field. The commissioners believed that they would have to convince a sullenly conservative academic profession and a sceptical Conservative government that their academic standards could still be preserved if universities expanded, because the growing sixth forms in schools would fill to overflowing the pool of ability in whose existence the opponents of growth declined to believe. But in fact the progress of the inquiry itself convinced the government, who accepted the expenditure envisaged in the Robbins Report overnight, and the diehards decamped.[32]

Some pre-emptive decisions were taken long before Robbins; and due credit must be given to the UGC for its innovatory attempt at long-term planning during the course of 1959, when it revised its estimates of the demand for university places for 1965 from 124,000 to 168,000; with a further increase to almost 230,000 by 1976. Even though the government promised a first instalment of only 175,000 places by 1970, it was thought that existing universities would be able to account for only 155,000 of them. Accordingly, in April 1959, the UGC set up a Sub-Committee on New Universities, a year after its approval of the University College of Sussex.[33]

Although the York Academic Trust was unaware of these figures at the time, it felt sufficiently confident to ask the Archbishop to invite Sir Keith Murray, chairman of the UGC, to 'an informal meeting' at Bishopthorpe Palace, in preparation for which John West-Taylor drafted a fourteen-page brief setting out the Trust's case. Aware that the UGC's acceptance of Sussex had been offset by their rejection of applications from St. David's College, Lampeter, and Bradford Institute of

Technology, West-Taylor made a careful summary of the UGC's views on university expansion, the size and scope of possible new foundations, sponsorship by other universities, catchment areas, residence, and overseas students which had been set out in the *Report on University Development, 1952-1957* published in September 1958. He concluded that York would have to show that it had the physical and cultural amenities to support an institution of not less than a thousand students from a catchment area that 'would be the English speaking world'. The Trust was already negotiating for a site of 50 to 100 acres at Heslington; it had the use of St. John's and St. Anthony's Hall (and was hoping to take over another centrally-situated group of buildings at the King's Manor); it had raised over £125,000 on capital and revenue account since 1950; its record of training and advanced study in historical research and architecture had been supplemented by courses and conferences for overseas students, social scientists and industrial consultants; and it had the support of the most influential members of the local community. This last achievement, which the UGC had emphasised to the Lord Mayor's deputation in 1947, was of crucial importance, since York was the only candidate not to have the direct sponsorship of a local authority. The Trust had to conform to the procedure which the UGC had adopted for new foundations in the light of its experience with Sussex, which had been given an endowment of £12,000 a year together with a site of over 200 acres by Brighton Borough Council and additional endowments amounting to £38,000 from Sussex, Surrey and Kent County Councils. Its immediate task, therefore, was to form a Promotion Committee which would include representatives of York Corporation, the three Ridings and the Rowntree Trusts. This came into being, under the chairmanship of the Archbishop, at a gathering in the Mansion House convened by the Lord Mayor; and after one further meeting in November 1959, a final memorandum was sent to the UGC early in December. With the exception of some purely tactical arguments, this document incorporated a substantial part of West-Taylor's earlier brief for the discussions with Sir Keith Murray at Bishopthorpe Palace; but there was an additional paragraph which said that the Trust would like York to be a 'collegiate university'.

The belief that York, apart from the magnetism exerted by the visible evidence of its history, might have a special and mutually beneficial claim on students from overseas formed a cardinal point in the appeal for a university as it was expressed in the promoters' final memorandum to the UGC in December 1959:

York is a microcosm of the British way of life and, as existing courses have shown, has much to offer them; and particularly to students from the Commonwealth who will later become leaders of their countries when they attain self-government, and replace more primitive ways of life by new systems modelled on Western democracy and technology.[34]

The 1959 memorandum also highlighted York's interest in social science. As a city of 125,000 close to the industrial conurbations of the West Riding, Teesside and the Humber, surrounded by an agricultural region as heterogeneous as its own industrial structure, it was 'an admirable centre for sociological and scientific research'. During a visit to the city at the invitation of the University Promotion Committee in June 1959, the chairman of the UGC, Sir Keith Murray, had remarked that he 'welcomed special stress on social studies in a city where Seebohm Rowntree (Plate 14) had done so much to illuminate them . . .'.[35] But York's case had a degree of strength perhaps more apparent to the UGC than to the promoters: the imminence of a national crisis of student numbers. The UGC's response was not long delayed. In April 1960 Sir Keith Murray announced that the government had given its approval in principle to two new universities: East Anglia and York.

Unlike their civic counterparts of the previous generation, which as 'university colleges' had remained under the tutelage of London for many years, the new universities understood that, in the words of Sir John Fulton, the first Vice-Chancellor of Sussex, 'they were not only free to innovate but also that they would fall below the level of their opportunity if they failed to experiment through new approaches to university government, curricula and teaching methods'.[36] The instrument of their emancipation (and another element of the procedure devised for the foundation of Sussex in 1958) was the Academic Planning Board, a small body composed of three or four persons of exceptional academic distinction, a vice-chancellor from another university, a lay representative of industry or the professions, and an eminent member of the local community from which the foundation had sprung. In York's case, these last three elements were represented by Professor (later Sir) William Mansfield Cooper, Vice-Chancellor of Manchester; Sir Francis Hill, a former Mayor of Lincoln, Chairman of the Association of Municipal Corporations and President of Nottingham University Council; and Harold Oldman, Chief Education Officer in York since 1944 and an active member of York Academic Trust.[37] The chair was taken by Lord Robbins, who was Professor of Economics in the University of London (at the London School of Economics) from 1929 until 1961, when he became Chairman of the Committee on Higher Education. Appointed by the Promotion Committee from a list of nominees prepared by the UGC, the Board began work in September 1960 to prepare a petition for a Royal Charter and to appoint a vice-chancellor.

The Academic Brief

The preparation of a design for the general academic character of the university was a delicate task: as Lord James later pointed out, an inadequate plan would leave too much to the discretion of the first vice-chancellor, while an attempt to project a mass of pre-emptive details on the curriculum and government of the university would circumscribe both its governing body and its newly-appointed staff. Thus the Board's Interim Report, produced in April 1961 after six meetings, adopted a restrained and tentative approach to academic planning:

> The question of the composition of degree courses is a matter on which we think it undesirable to make very precise recommendations at this stage. In our judgement, any description in detail is better left until the nucleus of an establishment of teachers has been appointed.[38]

The suggested pattern of courses involving a fairly conventional range of 'major subjects', each of which might be studied (but not under compulsion) with one of six 'subsidiary subjects', such as architecture, music or modern European languages, represented a compromise between the demand for innovation and an awareness that, as the Robbins Committee was to observe in 1963, the 'urge to knowledge for its own sake, pursued in depth, is one that inspires students of many levels of ability'.[39] It was a pattern which had been introduced by a number of universities during the preceding 15 years in the form of combined honours courses in humanities; but it stood at some distance from the extreme breadth of Keele's foundation year or the Schools of Studies at Sussex and East Anglia. In practice, York did come quite close to the idea of a 'school', considered as a cognate group of subjects within a general field of study, in one area: the social sciences. From 1963 until 1968 the social science degree consisted of a common course of seven subjects taken by all students for five terms, followed by only four terms of specialisation in one or two of three main subject-areas of economics (including statistics and economic and social history), politics and sociology, under the direction of a single Board of Studies.[40] Such an arrangement might not have commended itself to those who believed that it was insufficient to provide the specialist knowledge and technical virtuosity required, for example, by a future professional economist or statistician; but the Academic Planning Board anticipated these anxieties with a suggestion that students who obtained first or upper second class honours should be allowed to proceed to a master's degree by papers after one year's further training. Reinforced by the existence of two embryonic graduate schools in architecture and historical research, the simultaneous introduction from the outset of graduate and undergraduate teaching 'would be a solution, at any rate in part, of the vexed question of excessive specialisation at an early stage'. If the academic staff were to have 'an outlet at graduate school level for their desire to participate in highly specialised research and teaching, it should be much easier to demand of them, at the under-graduate stage, that they should restrict their activities to forms of teaching which are appropriate to the needs of their pupils'.[41]

The university's system of government was designed to reflect, at least at its lower levels, the academic pattern of major and subsidiary subjects. 'Courses of this sort would almost inevitably cut across the traditional divisions into large faculties.' Each subject or closely related group of subjects would be administered by a Board of Studies responsible to a General Board, which, as a 'General Academic Board', emerged as an elected body of 40 members of the academic staff under the chairmanship of the Vice-Chancellor. Although the system of election reserved one-fifth of its places for professors, the General Academic Board was one element in a bicameral arrangement by which discussion of appoint-ments, salaries and promotions was hived off to a separate Professorial Board. It was an ingenious compromise, possibly derived from Lord Robbins's experience at the London School of Economics, which tried to avoid the tensions of a traditional Senate, which in the older universities had to accommodate not only the entire professoriate – victors of the struggle for emancipation from control by charitable donors and sponsor-ing local authorities in the latter half of the nineteenth century – but also an increasing proportion of other staff demanding the right to participate in academic government. An unspoken advantage of a separate Profes-sorial Board was that it would act as a counterweight to the lay majority which the Academic Planning Board had assigned to the Council, a body of 21 members (excluding the officers), of whom six would be elected from within the university. The Council, in turn, required a substantial lay element not only to provide the university with influence in the surround-ing community but also to protect it from a system of inspection and control by its new paymaster, the state. As the Robbins Report later observed: 'Academic autonomy is more likely to be safeguarded where the public has a guarantee that there is independent lay advice and criticism within the universities'.[42] In practice, there has been little evi-dence of any conflict between academic and lay elements either on the Council or on the Court, which, as at Kent, has been retained as a supreme governing body.

The third principal area of concern to the Academic Planning Board was residence. Sussex had owed its early success partly to the assurance given to the UGC, who were not prepared to provide capital grants for residential buildings, that there was an ample supply of lodgings in out-of-season Brighton; East Anglia could fall back on Great Yarmouth; while Blackpool, in a three-cornered contest with Chester and Lancaster, considered itself as a serious candidate for a new university for the same reason. Although the York Academic Trust had envisaged a university 'catering ultimately for about 2,000 students' it was clear by 1961 that the new universities would be required to make a contribution of not less than 3,000 places each within the next decade – a figure mentioned by the Academic Planning Board but qualified (wisely, as it turned out) by the expectation that circumstances might change. York could provide, it was thought, lodgings for only 500 students, so that although there was no suggestion that it could be a completely residential university like Keele (which had reached its original target of 800 students by 1961), it seemed essential that at least half of the student population should be housed on the site.

The choice was either halls of residence or colleges. Other universities, such as Sussex and East Anglia, went to great lengths not to tarnish their innovatory principles with any suggestion of a college system (although the Vice-Chancellor of East Anglia believed that they had rediscovered the 'secret strength' of the college: the staircase). No new university, with the possible exception of Kent, which from the time of its opening in 1965 tried to revive the tradition of high table, ever envisaged reproducing the lifestyle of Oxford or Cambridge, still less the nightmarish administrative complexity of London. It is true that the York Academic Trust's desire for a collegiate system, first expressed in its memorandum to the UGC in December 1959, may have been open to misinterpretation when it referred to 'a widely held opinion (difficult to substantiate by quotation, as it rarely figures in speeches and similar pronouncements) that Oxford and Cambridge owe much of their pre-eminence to this system'. But the Trust's request that 'this possibility be examined', reinforced by the suggestion that it might attract greater endowments for a university 'founded in a city whose environment for this purpose we believe to be second only to Oxford and Cambridge', was not meant, as the Academic Planning Board's Report emphasised, to resurrect the idea of the college as 'a unit of academic decentralisation' with its own system of admissions, teaching and staff appointments. It was envisaged as a much simpler unit of residence and catering which, Lord James later wrote, 'seeks to provide the valuable intimacies and loyalties of the life of a smaller community to a degree which is scarcely possible if the unit is a whole large university'.[43] Thus when the first two colleges, Derwent and Langwith, were opened in 1965, great care was taken not to impose an instant body of tradition to which staff and students would be expected to conform. Although one might have detected a difference of social tone between two senior common rooms severally frequented by members of the arts and social science departments, the college buildings, separated by only a few yards of canopied pavement, were so contiguous as to be scarcely distinguishable from one another.

Apart from its delineation of a collegiate system, the Academic Planning Board made no suggestions about the physical form of the university. Nor did it specify methods of teaching. Its list of major subjects was 'provisional', with the 'possibility', to be investigated, of a degree in Education. The only definite exclusions were Latin and Greek, although Sociology and International Relations were considered as 'subjects the study of which might appropriately begin at graduate level'. In the construction of its academic brief the Board may have been influenced by the view, as it was later expressed by the Robbins Committee, that while it was permissible to try 'new combinations of subjects which have recognisably organic connections', it was also advisable to remember that 'undergraduates should not be made the guinea-pigs of experiments with totally new subjects without textbooks or a commonly accepted core of methods of thought'.[44]

The Development Plan

With the presentation of its Interim Report, contained in 15 pages of foolscap, in April, 1961, the Board had completed the major part of its work. Transformed into an Academic Advisory Committee (another step in the procedure derived from the foundation of Sussex) after the University received its Charter in October 1963, it continued to monitor academic standards through its influence on senior appointments until its dissolution at the end of 1968. The responsibility for interpreting the academic brief to the architects and, in conjunction with newly-appointed staff, for translating its recommendations into a workable curriculum of studies fell upon the first vice-chancellor. For this task, the Board chose Lord James of Rusholme (Plate 17). A graduate of Queen's College, he obtained a doctorate in Chemistry in 1933 and taught at Winchester College until 1945, when he was appointed High Master of Manchester Grammar School, the most famous and academically the most distinguished of the town grammar schools of Tudor foundation. Under his leadership the school had achieved an exceptional reputation for the number and calibre of its successful candidates for university entrance; and he brought to York an insistence on high standards of teaching and a belief that while genuine scholarship deserved respect, there were some subjects where, as he himself expressed it, 'what we should really be concerned with is not so much research as normally understood, as the process of reflection on material that is already known'.[45] One result of these views was that a number of staff were recruited, until the mid-1960s, directly from the ranks of the teaching profession; another was that York became widely known for its emphasis on a system of tutorial teaching, involving small groups of four or five students, which Lord James believed to be a natural corollary of collegiate life.

Lord James foresaw that some of his ideas might be questioned by a later generation of staff and students. The collegiate system, for example, was not immune to a preference for different styles of communal life. In his final report to Court in 1972 he commented:

> A reaction against paternalism, a desire for independence, the reduction of the age of majority, all of these have led students at some stage to prefer to the amenities of college and the security of lodgings, the often extreme squalor of a shared flat.[46]

Over the same period, the small tutorial group had given way in some departments to a seminar of six or more students:

> . . . Its use dictated not so much by a bad staff-student ratio as by a genuine conviction that the devotion of some of us to the very small tutorial arises rather from tribal loyalties than from hard evidence of educational efficiency.[47]

Thus the University's Development Plan, published in May 1962, after a period of exceptionally close collaboration between the consultant architects and the vice-chancellor – a process later described by Lord James as one of 'architectural dialectic'[48] – tried to incorporate the same degree of flexibility as the Academic Planning Board's brief:

> The future of an organisation so complex and liable to change as a university can never be predicted except within broad limits. It is indeed extremely important that the future of a university should not be restricted by enforced compliance with a rigid plan. . . . We have tried not to make any more firm proposals than are essential to provide a workable basis for the first phase of construction.[49]

The Development Plan had two principal aims:

> . . . It is necessary to try to discover the characteristic forms and relationships of the buildings in their setting which correspond to the academic and social ideals of the University on one hand, and to the social and geographic context of the York district on the other. If such a harmony is achieved, the University may become in a relatively short time as memorable as some of the older and more influential university establishments of the world have become over the years of slower growth.[50]

The site consisted of 180 acres of green belt on the south-east side of the city. It was an extension of Walmgate Stray, one of a number of areas of common land left untouched by the city's concentrated radial development during the previous century. Its nucleus, from which the architects proposed to allow building operations to proceed in a series of four broad arcs represented as self-contained 'Phases' of development over the following 10 years, was situated at the south-east extremity of the site in the form of a large house and 17 acres of garden. Built shortly before 1570 for Sir Thomas Eynns, Secretary to the Council of the North, Heslington Hall passed in 1708 into the hands of the Yarbrugh family. In 1852, Nicholas Yarbrugh bequeathed the Hall to a nephew, Yarbrugh Graeme, who transformed his modest Elizabethan country house into a Victorian mansion of 109 rooms.[51] At the outbreak of the Second World War, the family left the house, which became the headquarters of 64 Group, Bomber Command and then remained empty until 1955, when after a chance meeting at a bus-stop in York, it was purchased from its last private owner, Lord Deramore, by J. B. Morrell on behalf of the Joseph Rowntree Social Service Trust.

Morrell's original intention was to turn the house and grounds into a 'folk-park' containing a village green with a cross and maypole, around which would be grouped a water mill, cottages, a maze and a lake supporting a Celtic coracle and a Viking ship. But York Corporation refused to assume financial responsibility for the project, and in 1959 the Social Service Trust announced its intention of handing over Heslington Hall (together with a gift of £150,000 to be spread over 10 years) to the university immediately after its formal establishment. After York Academic Trust's public announcement of its plans for a submission to the UGC in August 1959, a small group led by Eric Milner-White began negotiations with Lord Deramore for the purchase of an additonal 137 acres of land adjacent to the Hall. But this was not sufficient. Another building was needed in the city in time to absorb the first intake of students in 1963, two years before the projected completion of the first two colleges at Heslington. In 1947 an article in *Country Life* drew attention to a conference organised by York Civic Trust and the Council for the Preservation of Rural England to discuss the future of York's old buildings:

> During the discussions it will be strange if something is not said of the project for establishing a university in York. . . . In the King's Manor – the old administrative seat of the Council of the North – there exist admirably suited premises for a foundation that would be nourished by, and nourish, York's perennial youth.[52]

By 1950, the Academic Development Committee was negotiating for an option on King's Manor from which the Wilberforce School for the Blind, occupants since 1835, proposed to move to new premises in Dringhouses in 1956. King's Manor was almost a ready-made collegiate building. Originating as a residence for the Abbot of St. Mary's in the 1280s, it had been enlarged into a U-shaped house of brick and stone by Abbot Sever in 1490. After the dissolution of St. Mary's it became the headquarters of the Council of the North. At the height of its activity, the Council employed a staff of 300 and dealt with over 450 lawsuits and 2,000 suitors and petitioners a year; and, conveniently situated just outside the conflicting jurisdiction of the City, the building was continually adapted and enlarged until the impeachment of Strafford in 1640. Like St. Anthony's Hall, it suffered from a variety of iconoclastic indignities during and after the Civil War, but after a short period of use by a 'Weekly Assembly' for dancing and card-games in the early years of the eighteenth century, it was leased to a succession of boarding schools until its acquisition by the Diocesan National Society who opened a boys' school in 1813.

Unfortunately, J. B. Morrell's purchase of Heslington Hall in 1955 had left the Social Service Trust disinclined to take over the King's Manor after it had been vacated by the School for the Blind in 1956. In November 1958, the buildings were brought by York Corporation: from then until 1961 negotiations with the York Academic Trust and its successors dragged on, complicated by the continued presence of the York Workshops for the Blind, in spite of the suggestion, incorporated into the UGC Memorandum of 1959, that the King's Manor could be converted by the University into a college for senior officers in local government. Finally, in November 1961 the City Council's Finance and General Purposes Committee recommended that a 99-year full repairing lease should be granted to the university at an annual rent of £3,250. This was hardly a generous arrangement (J. B. Morrell had proposed to buy the buildings outright for about £30,000 in 1956) either for the establishment of a new university in the city or for the preservation of an historic building of national importance, but if the university was to open on time in October 1963, there was no alternative but to accept these terms.

The conversion of both the King's Manor and Heslington Hall was entrusted to a Norwich architect, Bernard Feilden, who subsequently became Architect to Norwich Cathedral and Surveyor to the Fabric of York Minster. Meanwhile, in June 1960, Sir Linton Andrews visited the site at Heslington, shortly after the Promotion Committee had decided to take up an option to purchase. Under the heading of 'A Scene to Kindle Enthusiasm' he later wrote in the *Yorkshire Post*:

> ... The glowing sunshine, the shade of the great trees, the chestnut candles, the exceptional display this year of lilac and laburnum, sought and soothed the eye in every part of the estate and Heslington itself. We could not have inspected the site under happier conditions. A festal sun lightened up the blossom. Not a tuft of cloud, not a wisp of swan's down whiteness, varied the Mediterranean blue of the sky.[53]

In fact, parts of the site were almost intractably waterlogged. A solution was found in the creation of a 'balancing reservoir', which, intended to catch the run-off of rainwater from the higher parts of the site, roofs, and paved areas, eventually became the most distinctive feature of the university's landscape. Here, as in the Development Plan as a whole, Robert Matthew, Johnson-Marshall and Partners, the consultant architects appointed by the Promotion Committee in April 1961, showed a remarkable degree of imaginative versatility in matching the necessities of the site to its buildings. Their decision to adopt a method of prefabricated construction known as CLASP (Consortium of Local Authorities' Special Programme) avoided not only the expense of deep piling in wet ground but also the need to import wet-trade building labour from outside the city. The initial development of CLASP, a dry technique made up of external panels of light aggregate cladded on to a steel frame over slab foundations, is credited to the County Architect of Nottinghamshire, Sir Donald Gibson; but it was foreshadowed by a system of prefabricated school-building developed after 1946 by Hertfordshire County Council, where Stirrat Johnson-Marshall had been Assistant County Architect. His experience was complemented by Sir Robert Matthew's achievements as Chief Architect to the London County Council from 1946 until 1953, symbolised not only by the Royal Festival Hall but also by the Roehampton Estate, begun in 1952, an impressive blend of housebuilding and landscape architecture. Thus the partnership brought to York two major developments in British postwar architecture – prefabrication and the use of landscape – which, interpreted by the senior project architect, Andrew Derbyshire, were indispensable additions to the general principles of compactness, visual coherence, linear planning, and the segregation of traffic which had spilled over from urban redevelopment into university design.

The Development Plan envisaged, by July 1970, a university of eight colleges (with an average membership, including staff, of just under 400), three groups of laboratories and workshops, a library, a boiler house, a concert hall and a sports centre; all connected by a network of covered footpaths within a 'ten-minute walking circle'. It projected a total working population of 4,000 for 1972. Even though the Development Plan's numerical targets were almost fulfilled by 1972, the loss of two colleges – partially compensated by additional residential wings and the development of loan-financed housing around Heslington Village – had blighted the prospects of further growth in conformity with the Academic Planning Board's academic and social philosophy. But the university could take comfort from the fact that, allowing for the alteration of its financial schedules, the use of the CLASP system had resulted in the completion of every single building within the limits of time and cost projected by the Development Plan.

The Promotion Committee's decision to accept the architects' recommendation to use CLASP may be considered as Eric Milner-White's last great contribution to the foundation of the university. At a meeting shortly before his death in June 1963, he made a vigorous defence of the architects' designs for the first two colleges, reminding those who wanted a more traditional setting of stonework, gothic arches and ivy, of Sir Henry Wotton's dictum that what architecture required was 'commodity, firmness and delight'.[54] Although CLASP has been criticised for its apparent lack of aesthetic versatility, Derbyshire and Johnson-Marshall tried to mitigate the impression of uniformity with a variety of devices. College buildings were grouped asymmetrically around a central nucleus, while roofs and side-elevations were embellished by romantic details in the form of pyramid-shaped rooflights and box bay windows. More striking in their effect on the surrounding landscape were the boiler house flue stack, contained by three linked concrete legs splayed at the bottom, and the water tower, mushrooming out from its centre support in the middle of a group of laboratories. But these – together with the Central Hall, cantilevered out over the lake, its roof suspended by two stays anchored to a concrete support, and the Library, named after J. B. Morrell – have been isolated monuments and exceptions to the fundamental principle of compact domesticity demanded by the college system. As Lord James remarked during his final year as Vice-Chancellor, 'The ideal university would no doubt rest on a triumvirate consisting of Newman, Palladio and Mrs. Beeton'.[55]

With the completion of Feilden's work on Heslington Hall and the King's Manor by the autumn of 1963, the University was ready to accept its first intake of 215 undergraduates and 13 graduates, at that time the highest number of students with which any university had ever started. By September 1965, when the first two colleges and a group of laboratories were opened at Heslington, over 8,000 applications had been received for only 420 undergraduate places. York had already acquired a reputation for its adherence to traditional academic standards and a common social life. From 1965 onwards, the University's architectural distinction became a major attractive force – signalised by Sir Nikolaus Pevsner's verdict on its physical fabric: 'conceptually, constructionally, and, to add this with all emphasis, visually the most successful of all the buildings of the New Universities in Britain'.[56] With the establishment of such a distinctive physical presence in the city, the successors of Morrell, Sheldon and Milner-White could be satisfied that York had finally 'made its own beginnings'.

Footnotes

[1] York Civic Trust, *Annual Report 1958-59,* p. 4.
[2] C. B. Knight, *A History of The City of York,* York 1944, pp. 467-9.
[3] Daniel Defoe, *A Tour through England and Wales,* vol. 2, 1724, reprinted by Everyman's Library 1927, p. 234.
[4] P. Nuttgens, *York the Continuing City,* 1976, p. 70.
[5] Board of Agriculture, *The Agricultural State of the Kingdom, 1816,* reprinted, with an introduction by G. E. Mingay, 1970, p. 366.
[6] A. J. Peacock, 'A Nineteenth Century York University', *York History,* I, York Educational Settlement, 1974.
[7] For further discussion of the Yorkshire Philosophical Society and of the first meeting of the British Association, see Chapter I, above.
[8] A. Vernon, *Three Generations; the Fortunes of a Yorkshire Family,* 1966, pp. 127-132. Morrell's salary of £50 was to be paid by a deduction from the interest on the second loan.
[9] Ibid., pp. 144-5, 151.
[10] J. B. Morrell, *City of our Dreams,* 1940.
[11] E. Milner-White, 'The University of York: Sketch of the Preparatory Work towards its Establishment 1941-1962', appended to York Civic Trust, *Annual Report 1962-3,* p. 20.
[12] York Civic Trust, *Annual Report 1946-7,* pp. 1-2.
[13] Ibid., p. 2.
[14] *Report of the Committee on Scientific Manpower,* Cmd. 6824, 1946, p. 17.
[15] *The Times,* 14 August 1946.
[16] E. Milner-White, op. cit., n. 11, p. 21.
[17] Ibid., p. 21.
[18] York Civic Trust, *Annual Report 1947-8.*
[19] E. Milner-White, op. cit., n. 11, p. 21.
[20] Academic Development Committee, *Secretary's Report,* appended to York Civic Trust, *Annual Report 1951-2.* The pages of this report are not numbered.
[21] 'Proposed Guild of Craftsmen'. York Civic Trust, *Annual Report 1946-7.*
[22] York Civic Trust, *Annual Report 1953-4,* p. 4.
[23] 'The St. Anthony's Scheme'. York Civic Trust, *Annual Report, 1950-1.*

24 York Civic Trust, *Annual Report, 1952-3*, p. 3. The opening of the Borthwick Institute was also described in *The Times*, 16 May 1953.

25 York Civic Trust, *Annual Report, 1947-8*. The pages of the Report are not numbered.

26 Academic Development Committee, *Secretary's Report*, appended to York Civic Trust, *Annual Report, 1954-5*, p. 16.

27 Lord Annan, 'The University in Britain', in M. D. Stephens and G. W. Roderick, eds., *Universities for a Changing World*, 1975.

28 Report of the Committee on Higher Education, Cmnd. 2154, 1953, pp. 12, 15-16.

29 Association of University Teachers, *Report on a Policy for University Expansion* (1958).

30 *Committee on Higher Education*, p. 65.

31 A. H. Halsey and M. A. Trow, *The British Academics*, 1971, p. 57.

32 Lord Annan, op. cit., n. 27, p. 27.

33 H. J. Perkin, *Innovation in the New Universities of the United Kingdom: a Report for the Organisation for Economic Cooperation and Development*, Paris, 1968, pp. 98-9.

34 York University Promotion Committee, *Memorandum to the University Grants Committee*, December 1959, p. 7. I am indebted to the Registrar of the University, Mr. John West-Taylor, OBE, for having drawn my attention to this and other documents and for his help and consideration during the preparation of this chapter. Needless to say, errors of fact and judgement are entirely my responsibility.

35 York Civic Trust, *Annual Report 1958-9*, p. 3.

36 Sir John Fulton, 'The University of Sussex', in M. G. Ross, ed., *New Universities in the Modern World*, 1966, pp. 18-19.

37 The other members of the Academic Planning Board were: Professor Sir William Hodge, FRS, Master of Pembroke College, Cambridge; Lady Ogilvie, Principal of St. Anne's College, Oxford; and Professor J. G. Wilson, Professor of Physics, University of Leeds.

38 University of York Academic Planning Board, *Interim Report, April 1961*, pp. 5-6.

39 *Committee on Higher Education*, p. 91.

40 The social Science Part I course comprised Economics, Economic and Social History, Statistics, Politics, Sociology, Logic and Scientific Method, plus a 'Supplementary Subject' chosen from another department.

41 Academic Planning Board, *Interim Report*, p. 4.

42 *Committee on Higher Education*, p. 218.

43 Lord James of Rusholme, 'The University of York', in M. G. Ross, op. cit., n. 36, p. 39.

44 *Committee on Higher Education*, p. 94.

45 Lord James of Rusholme, op. cit., n. 43, p. 49.

46 *University of York, Vice-Chancellor's Report for the Year 1971-72*, p. 11.

47 Ibid., p. 5.

48 Lord James of Rusholme, op. cit., n. 43, p. 38.

49 *University of York Development Plan 1962-1972*, 1962, p. 7.

[50] Ibid., p. 13.
[51] *Heslington Hall: Introductory Notes on the Building and its Owners,* University of York, 1977.
[52] *Country Life,* 6 June 1947. It is possible that the article was inspired by Oliver Sheldon.
[53] *Yorkshire Post,* 7 June 1960.
[54] Sir Henry Wotton (1568-1639), better known perhaps as a secret diplomatist, published *The Elements of Architecture* in 1624.
[55] Vice-Chancellor's Report 1971-72, p. 2. John Henry Newman published *On the Scope and Nature of University Education* in 1852.
[56] Sir Nikolaus Pevsner, *The Buildings of England, Yorkshire: York and the East Riding,* 1972, pp. 70-71.

CHAPTER XII

The University
and the Community

by

Jeremy Whiting

THE MAIN BUILDINGS of the University of York are concentrated on a 200-acre site in the village of Heslington, about three miles from the city centre. Thus it would be easy for the University to have relatively little interaction with the neighbouring community other than as a modest employer of labour and as a limited source of demand for local facilities. However, though much of the University's work is inevitably self-contained (or has national and international rather than local connections) it would have been to the University's detriment if it had allowed itself to become isolated from its immediate surroundings and opportunities.

It is the purpose of this chapter to outline a number of University projects which are based on links with the local community and promote contact with firms and organisations in and around York.[1] It is confined to scientific and sociological projects, and thus excludes the University's extensive and lively participation in the social, artistic and pedagogical activities and endeavours of the community. Furthermore the selection of topics represents only a small part of the total research effort and excludes many projects which have gained international interest and recognition, such as the work on membranes, organelles and real population management in the Department of Biology; on insulin, laser-induced reactions and hydrogen storage (the hydrogen economy) in the Department of Chemistry; on the development of high-level programming languages in the Department of Computer Science; and on x-ray crystallography and surface studies in the Department of Physics.

The survey begins with two of the longest-established projects, both of which have been concerned with the environment. The first is a study of how environmental blight associated with colliery tips may be ameliorated; whilst the second has to do with the preservation of places of natural beauty. The theme of conservation is pursued in the third topic but in a very different context, namely how to prevent the weathering of medieval glass. The fourth topic breaks away from this theme; it is concerned with improving communications between computers so that the capacity of a local computer can be effectively enlarged. The final three topics illustrate a different aspect of the interaction between the University and the local community in that they are associated with industrial or commercial interests. The first in this group is very specific in scope, being concerned with the development of novel, high-technology instrumentation for the food industry in conjunction with a single local firm; whereas the second, the Electronics Centre, is an example of a consultancy service which is likely to be of use to a wide range of local firms and businesses. Such direct involvement and co-operation can have a marked influence on the local community as witnessed, for example, by the extensive development of advanced technology industrial sites adjacent to a few universities. The consequential effect on an area of rapid changes in industrialisation is the subject of the final topic, in which a sociological study is being made of the development of a large new coalfield in the predominantly rural environment of Selby.

Of the selected topics, some have been completed whilst others, such as the Electronics Centre, have only just been launched. One or two are modest in effort and depend on a single member of the academic staff; in contrast, the Selby Coalfield Development project has involved the establishment of a special research team.

Reclamation of Colliery Spoil*

Spoil from coal mining operations disfigures many parts of the United Kingdom, including major areas in Yorkshire. Some natural revegetation of colliery spoil as a medium for plant growth is desirable if areas are to be reclaimed to high biological productivity. Such a study has been undertaken in the Department of Biology at the University of York since 1966. Initially the old county of the West Riding of Yorkshire was the focus of attention, but in 1968 four other local authorities joined in sponsoring the work: Derbyshire and Nottinghamshire County Councils, and Rotherham and Barnsley County Boroughs. A Colliery Spoil Reclamation Research and Advisory Unit was established under the direction

* Head of Derelict Land Reclamation Research Unit: Dr. M. J. Chadwick.

of Dr. M. J. Chadwick in the Department of Biology to deal mainly with the provision of advice on specific reclamation projects within the five authorities.

As a result of this collaboration a vigorous Local Authorities' Standing Panel was in being by 1974, and the Vegetation and After-Management Sub-Group identified a number of problem areas that required research activity. Research into some of these problems was undertaken by a group in the Department of Soil Science in the University of Newcastle-upon-Tyne and other aspects assigned to the (renamed) Derelict Land Reclamation Research Unit at York.

The research at York concentrated on four main areas of enquiry: the nitrogen economy of colliery spoil; phosphorus relationships of colliery spoil; grass species cultivar differences in growth and nutrient recovery; and a survey of colliery spoil reclamation schemes and natural revegetation throughout England and Wales.

Spoil fertilisation studies had indicated that phosphorous was more important for sward establishment than nitrogen. Colliery spoil is always deficient in phosphorus and fertilisation produces good growth responses (at least with applications of up to 300 kg ha^{-1} P$_2$O$_5$). The addition of lime increases the availability of phosphorus, although very high applications (30 tonnes ha^{-1}) can depress phosphorus availability and hence herbage yield. High levels of limestone also depress the nitrogen content of herbage. Field trials showed that recovery of applied phosphorus from the shoots of herbage did not exceed 10 per cent.

Higher recovery levels (15-20 per cent, 35 per cent at best) were realisable for applied nitrogen fertiliser with about 10 per cent remaining in the spoil. These figures indicate a need for annual nitrogen fertilisation whether slow-release fertilisers or other nitrate- or ammonium-based fertilisers are used. Legumes prove difficult to establish initially on colliery spoil and there is little evidence that they contribute significant amounts of nitrogen to the sward over the first few years. Recovery of applied nitrogen in the herbage is usually highest where perennial ryegrass (S23) has been grown on spoil with adequate phosphate levels.

Yield studies, between varieties within a single grass or legume species, showed little variation. The differences that did occur (within red fescue or the bent grasses) were highly correlated with morphological characteristics. It appears that the choice of a cultivar within a species is not likely to give rise to greatly different site yields, and cultivars of a single species always give similar yields on spoils which have had similar fertiliser treatments. However field trials using perennial ryegrass always demonstrated the need for a balanced fertiliser application.

314 YORK 1831-1981

The differences between 'amenity' grasses and those bred for agricultural purposes (mainly high-yield) was shown in the lack of yield-response to high rates of fertiliser application, rather than in the ability of the 'amenity' grass to yield better under low levels of fertilisation than the agricultural varieties. Perennial ryegrass varieties grew poorly at low levels of fertilisation, in contrast to varieties of the fescue species.

A different but complementary study of spoils was a survey of over 200 sites throughout England and Wales, although progress since reclamation tipping had ceased was difficult to gauge for many sites because of the lack of records. From the large number of sites 36 were chosen to include a range of vegetated and non-vegetated sites. The vegetated sites included those with and without trees, many of the latter being agriculturally managed.

Sites that become naturally revegetated show little evidence of a gradual succession to a closed vegetational cover with age. There seems to be more evidence for control of the successional process through the nature of the substrate. Some naturally revegetated sites support a level of production that is rather superior to productivity encountered on the better agricultural sites that had been reclaimed. Sites reclaimed for agriculture often show evidence of regression due to acidity, but studies were able to determine which of the sown species were successful on a site and which made a reduced contribution. Most often *Agrostis tenuis* and *Festuca rubra* showed excellent qualities of persistence. Where seed mixtures containing a wide variety of grass and legume species were sown, only a few of the original species remained. Where sites are not carefully managed after reclamation a high percentage of non-sown species enters the sward.

It was found that at certain sites the change in chemical characteristics of spoil with depth proved more useful in assessing the progress of spoil changes than absolute values. These 'profile characteristics' need careful interpretation in the light of local conditions and past spoil-management practice.

Much of the research conducted by the Derelict Land Reclamation Research Unit is included in the encyclopaedic work on land restoration by Bradshaw and Chadwick (1980).

People, Wildlife and Conservation*

A review of the whole subject of Biological Conservation (Usher, 1973) indicated several areas where research could profitably be undertaken: two of these areas have been developed into research projects with

* Project Director: Dr. M. B. Usher.

teams of graduate students. One concerns the effect of wildlife on visitors to the countryside and to nature reserves in particular. The other concerns the quantification of ideas involved in the selection of reserves, and hence is central to conservation strategies. The field work for both these projects has been undertaken in Yorkshire (see Diagram 1 for locations).

Early work on the influence of the countryside on visitors (Usher, Taylor and Darlington, 1970; Usher, Pitt and de Boer, 1974; Usher and Miller, 1975) was based on questionnaire surveys, and concentrated on general attitudes. These studies, based on a lowland heath (Strensall Common), moorland and forest (Bridestones) and the coast (Spurn), indicated that 12-16 per cent of visitors were interested in natural history, the remainder having a day out in the countryside. In later studies (Everett, 1978; Haffey, 1978) visitors were questioned more closely both on what they hoped to see and what they had in fact seen. The expectations and observations of visitors to Dalby Forest, an extensive forest area

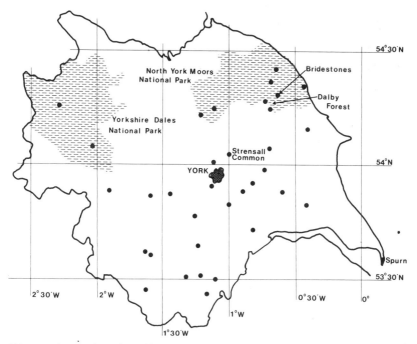

Diagram 1 A plan of the historic County of York showing the National Parks and nature reserves referred to in the text. The locations of the series of nature reserves whose data are included in Diagram 2 (p. 319) are shown by black circles.

within the North York Moors, are shown in Table 1. It is clear that animal life makes a much greater impact on visitors than plant life. Many people (up to one visitor in four) hope to see large mammals, but few visitors actually see them. Likewise many people hope to see the more spectacular bird species such as hawks, owls, woodpeckers and the kingfisher, but relatively few visitors actually do so. Far more visitors see the more prominent pheasant, the chaffinch that frequently approaches parked cars, or the loud and noisy jay. The only 'popular' flowers are the orchids, and it is surprising how few visitors mentioned the heathers which are dominant in parts of Dalby Forest.

Haffey (1978), also working on the North York Moors, studied areas of open moorland. Although the animals again completely dominated the wildlife aspirations of visitors, there are some interesting differences from the Dalby Forest Study. In the open moorland the large mammals are less likely to be found, hence replies to the questionnaire tended to be more general (i.e. 'animals', 'wildlife'), or to name domesticated animals such as sheep. Birds were more popular, with the grouse heading the list of species which visitors hoped to see (65 out of 791 visitors interviewed) or which they had seen (253 visitors). Heather, which frequently grows as a monoculture, had only been seen by 118 visitors (30 came to see it), and was the only higher plant other than bracken to be mentioned specifically.

These studies clearly indicate what visitors wish to see. The use of Information Centres and displays helps visitors to realise these aspirations, although there is no real substitute for the species seen alive in its real, wild setting. Gauging public opinion in this way is important in understanding how to 'sell' conservation, as well as in gaining financial resources when conservation has to compete with many other forms of land-use. Although an aim of conservation is to safeguard wildlife as a whole, it is politically important that conservation attracts popular support so as to obtain a reasonable share of land and financial resources. These studies in Yorkshire are possibly the only ones that quantify the public interest in wildlife.

However, public interest is only one criterion that can be used in assessing conservation value. A survey of the literature on criteria (Margules and Usher, in press) indicates that, during the last decade, a series of 18 different classes of criteria has been proposed and used, most studies only using about one half of the total suggested. To quantify the importance of these criteria, a study of a variety of habitats on the North York Moors has attempted to analyse the mental processes of conservation experts. Eight sites were then shown to members of staff of the Nature Conservancy Council, Institute of Terrestrial Ecology, North York Moors National Park Authority, colleges and universities, and the

Table 1   Sightings by Visitors to Dalby Forest

Species/ groups	Animals Hope to see	Have seen	Species/ groups	Plants Hope to see	Have seen
Mammals			*Trees*		
Deer	671	37	Pine	0	3
Fox	208	15	Beech	0	2
Badger	267	4	Birch	2	0
Squirrel	180	76	Hazel	0	2
Rabbit	120	169	Holly	2	0
Others	48	51	Oak	2	0
			Others	4 .	4
Birds			*Flowers*		
Pheasant	20	92	Heather	0	9
Kingfisher	15	3	Primrose	4	8
Jay	13	43	Strawberry	0	6
Chaffinch	1	57	Bilberry	2	3
Woodpecker	34	19	Bluebell	0	4
Birds of prey	32	26	Honeysuckle	0	4
Others	66	242	Orchids	12	14
			Others	15	39
Adder	22	12			
			All fungi	10	12
Other reptiles	15	8			
			All mosses	2	1
All amphibians	3	7			
			All lichens	2	2
All fish	3	6			
All insects/ spiders	20	78			

From a questionnaire survey of 2,816 visitors to Dalby Forest in 1975/6, the table shows the numbers of visitors who hoped to see various species (or groups) of wildlife and the number of people who had seen these species/groups. The data are summarised from Everett (1978).

Table 2   Use made of Criteria for Assessing
                 Potential Conservation Value

Index Score	Criteria
0.9	Diversity, Rarity
0.8	Area, Representativeness, Scientific value, Uniqueness, Ecological fragility.
0.7	Naturalness.
0.6	Threat of human interference, Position in Ecological/Geographical unit.
0.5	Potential value, Wildlife reservoir potential, Management considerations.
0.4	Replaceability.
0.3	Amenity value.
0.2	Education value, Recorded history.
0.1	Availability.

An index score, indicating the extent of general use (a score of 1 indicates complete use) made of 18 separate criteria for assessing potential conservation value. The data are derived from a study of the reaction of experts to eight sites on the North York Moors.

Yorkshire Natualists' Trust. These experts assessed the sites as they would do professionally, completing one questionnaire in the field and another, more detailed, afterwards. The results, shown in Table 2, indicate that seven criteria are particularly important (these are the ones with an index of 0.8 or more: the index is essentially the proportion of times that the criterion was used in the conservation potential assessment by all experts at all sites). Two of these criteria, diversity and area, can be measured quantitatively, and hence have been subjected to further research.

A study of the higher plants occurring on 35 nature reserves in Yorkshire (shown in Diagrams 1 and 2) indicated that the number of species, which is related to diversity, increased with area according to the equation

$$S = 60.18 \, A^{0.291}$$

where S is the number of species and A is the area in hectares (Usher,

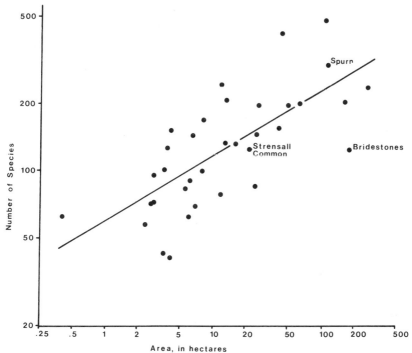

Diagram 2   The species-area relationship for the higher plants occurring on 35 nature reserves in Yorkshire (note that the axes are on a logarithmic scale). Reserves referred to in the text are named on this diagram.

1979). Recognition that such species-area relationships, well known in studies of island fauna and flora, might apply to nature reserves has opened up further fields of research. 'What conservation strategy maximises the number of species on reserves?' is a question that was analysed by Higgs and Usher (1980): there are situations in which a number of small reserves is preferable to one large reserve, the key being the proportional overlap in species between the two areas. 'How does one choose highly diverse areas when diversity is related to size? What are representative areas?' are questions analysed by Usher (1980): the position of points on a species-area diagram, as demonstrated by data for limestone pavements in the Yorkshire Dales National Park, answers such questions.

Wildlife, increasingly, interests many people. The studies on wildlife conservation being undertaken in the University of York show that many aspects of conservation, both selection of sites and management of reserves, can be based on scientific principles. It is, however, important that the duality of the theoretical foundation of the subject, and the understanding of its role within society, are preserved since conservation is essentially a practical, long-term discipline.

Weathering and Conservation of Stained Glass[*2]

A visitor to York Minster could be forgiven for believing that glass is a highly durable material since comparatively large areas of medieval stained glass survive in the windows of these buildings. It may seem surprising, therefore, that concern is currently being shown about the urgent need to conserve stained glass if it is to continue to enrich our heritage.

The late twelfth-century panel shown in Plate 9 illustrates the gravity of the problem. Constant attack of the glass by centuries of rain, frost and other agents, including pollutants, has brought about the complete breakdown of certain areas, whilst others have suffered less badly.

At the University a group of physicists is interested in the properties of ancient glass (Cox, et al., 1979). The long term aim of the group is conservation, but its initial objectives were to establish why certain specimens of medieval glass have proved to be much more durable than other contemporary pieces, and to correlate the weathering characteristics of glass to its chemical composition. Glass does not deteriorate in a unique manner. On some specimens pits develop which, in time, deepen and expand laterally, while on other pieces a layer of decomposition products builds up, reducing the transparency of the window. Other modes of decay are known.

Scientific examination of historically important glass clearly has to be non-destructive and for this reason the composition of selected specimens is determined by x-ray fluorescent analysis. A small area of each sample is polished to expose unweathered material which is then irradiated with 'white' x-rays. The intensities of the secondary x-rays thus produced, characteristic of the atoms forming the glass, are measured by means of an energy-dispersive spectrometer fitted with a Si(Li) detector. To obtain accurate quantitative analyses, the recorded intensities are corrected for selective absorption effects which occur within a specimen.

To date some 250 pieces of glass have been studied, principally from York Minster, ranging from the twelfth to the sixteenth centuries. Although it is probably still premature to draw firm conclusions, a number of significant facts has emerged. It is commonly believed for example that good durability is associated with soda-rich glass and our

* Project directors: Dr. G. A. Cox and Professor O. S. Heavens.

research has substantiated this view. This, however, is by no means the whole story. Medieval soda glass has proved to be extremely uncommon and most of the early durable material in York Minster is potash rich.

Table 3   Analyses of Twelfth-Century Glass
From York Minster
(weight per cent)

Constituent as oxide	Glass A. Blue, durable	Glass B. Pink, durable	Glass C. White, poorly durable
Na_2O	12.6	1.2	3.0
MgO	2.1	4.8	6.7
Al_2O_3	2.3	1.6	1.4
SiO_2	62.8	59.3	51.6
K_2O	8.0	17.5	17.6
CaO	8.9	10.4	12.9

Note: Only major constituents are shown.

The highly durable specimens A and B (Table 3) are of interest since clearly their Na_2O and K_2O contents are markedly different. By contrast, glass C is a badly pitted example of the same date, but the amount of K_2O is almost identical to that of glass B. The roles played by these two oxides and their bearing on durability are still uncertain and form the subject of debate. Further work remains to be done, particularly on the statistical analysis of data.

Possibly a more certain measure of durability is provided by the ratio $SiO_2 : CaO$, or more generally $SiO_2 : RO$, where RO is the total concentration of oxides or of divalent metals. A high silica content (about 60 wt per cent) together with a moderate amount of lime (about 10 wt per cent) confers good weathering characteristics. Large quantities of CaO generally give rise to poor durability. Medieval glass is a complex material, frequently inhomogeneous, and containing ten or more major constituents. One fact, however, which is clearly established is that the colour of the glass has little or no influence on its ability to withstand the British climate.

Over the past three years, the group's interest has turned increasingly towards the practical conservation of ancient window glass. As previously indicated, rain and other forms of moisture, such as water vapour in the atmosphere, actively promote the corrosion of glass. It is therefore of importance to protect the surface of poorly durable specimens from this form of attack. Several forms of protection are currently either in use or being investigated, ranging from the 'double glazing' of entire windows on the outside – thus preventing rain water, for example, from coming into direct contact with the stained glass – to applying thin transparent coatings of organic materials directly onto the surface of the individual pieces of glass which make up a window. The degree of protection offered by such methods varies widely, for example loosely applied organic coatings may serve merely to trap moisture in contact with the glass and to accelerate the decay processes!

In the Physics Department we are seeking to develop forms of protection which will withstand several centuries of York's weather before further attention is required. The principal technique under investigation at the moment involves the deposition of a thin film of *highly durable* modern glass (about $1/1000''$ in thickness) onto the ancient material by means of a method known as radio frequency sputtering.

Briefly, this entails exerting a high-voltage electrical discharge in an atmosphere of low-pressure argon gas in which are situated the specimens to be coated and a 'target' of durable glass. By controlling appropriately the conditions under which the discharge occurs, energetic argon ions may be accelterated violently towards the 'target' and on impact displace tiny molten globules of glass. Careful positioning of the specimen to be coated results in such globules adhering firmly to its surface, and the gradual build-up of a thin film of the target material on the specimen. If the rates of thermal expansion of the film and ancient glass can be matched, such protective layers of modern glass can be made to stick very firmly and so exclude totally water in all its forms – and corrosive gases in the atmosphere such as sulphur trioxide.

To date the problem of how to deposit thin films of glass onto *simulated* medieval speciments has been solved. There still remains, however, the tasks of assessing the quality of these very thin coatings, and of determining precisely how durable they are and how well they will stand up to several centuries of York's weather. To this end the modern techniques of x-ray and electron spectroscopy are being employed.

Inter-Computer Networking Developments*

The power and versatility of a computer run by a university or firm can be greatly extended if a system of inter-linking computers is readily

* Project director: J. D. Service, Department of Computer Science.

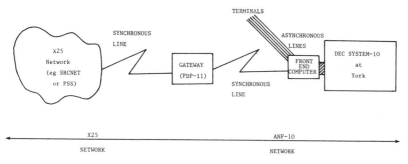

Diagram 3   The Gateway Inter-Computer Networking System.

available. Such a system would allow different computer centres to specialise and yet be available to any user as would a range of data stores. The Post Office is in the process of commissioning a 'packet switched' network to achieve such links which will use the series rules or 'protocols' known as X25 as its logic controls. The complete network is called PSS. British universities are strongly committed to using PSS and PSS-like networks (such as SRCNET) and several projects have been undertaken to ensure that most types of computers in use in universities are capable of connetion to PSS; all new computers must have a PSS capability.

The University of York has a DEC system-10 computer which does not have standard software for connecting the X25 networks, though it does have its own sophisticated network known as ANF-10 (Advanced Network Functions). The project outlined here was undertaken to enable DEC system-10 computers to be connected to PSS and SRCNET. Initially the project was directed towards producing an interface between ANF-10 and an X25 network for SRCNET and then subsequently for PSS. This interface is known as a 'Gateway' (see Diagram 3). The function of the gateway is to allow users of the DEC system-10 to obtain access to systems connected to the other network as though they were local systems and, similarly, for users of the other network systems to obtain access to the DEC system-10. This requires the ability to (a) switch a terminal to any system on either network, (b) move data between computers and (c) create a control file on one computer, run it on another and have the output printed or plotted on a third. (Service 1980.)

A production version of the Gateway has been in use between York and SRCNET for some time, and a copy of it has been installed at Edinburgh to link the Edinburgh and UMIST (University of Manchester Institute of Science and Technology) DEC system-10's to SRCNET. At

York the gateway is used to obtain access to the IBM machines at the Rutherford and Danesbury laboratories and also, via another gateway, to use computers on the ARPANET in the USA. Development is continuing, and work is now progressing on the conversion of the gateway to make it compatible with PSS.

Analytical Instruments for the Food Processing Industry*

The principal aim of this project is the development of new types of analytical instrumentation for use in the food-processing industry. In particular, it is concerned with developing novel ways of using infra-red radiation for both qualitative and quantitative analysis of those components of food products which are important in determining their nutritional value.

The project is being run in conjunction with a small local company, headed by a York graduate, which is mainly concerned with the manufacture of instruments for the analysis of milk. The project has attracted a substantial grant from the Wolfson Foundation under its scheme to promote university research linked with industry.

The technique, which is based on the absorption or reflection of infra-red radiation by different constituents in food products, is being adapted to the rapid and automatic determination of fats, proteins, carbohydrates and water. The initial phase of the work is concentrated on improving the accuracy, and increasing the speed, of analysis of milk and other dairy products. Rapid analysis of milk is essential to the operation of any large dairy or marketing organisation, for quality control in the blending of milks from many different farms and for payment purposes.

The passage of infra-red radiation through most materials is characterised by a highly individual wavelength-selective partial absorption. The spectrum of specific absorption acts as a 'fingerprint' by means of which each component of a complex mixture may be identified and quantitatively analysed. For such analysis a number of wavelength regions is selected by means of custom-built interference filters. These are based on substrates of germanium with multilayered thin films of various dielectric materials deposited on one side. They have the properties of high specificity and high energy throughput which are important to this application, and are incorporated in an optical system of novel design which is well adapted to rapid recording of absorption intensities. Electronic systems are also being developed, and micro-processor techniques

---

* Project directors: Dr. R. E. Hester, Department of Chemistry, and Mr. J. Shields, Shields Instruments Ltd.

are used to control the basic instrument functions and for data-processing.

The wavelength range of interest is from approximately 1-10 μm. Within this region all fats, proteins and carbohydrates have a number of characteristic absorption-bands and there is sufficient differentiation for each to be analysed in the presence of the others with good sensitivity. However, cross-interferences due to band overlaps do occur and these need to be determined by calibration procedures using standard samples. Procedures for the analysis of samples of milk and other foodstuffs by wet chemical methods are well known, although slow and tedious to perform, and these are used in standardisation and calibration of the infra-red instruments.

With automated sampling devices attached to the infra-red milk analysers which have already been built, it is possible to make complete fat, protein, lactose and solids-not-fat or total solids analyses at the rate of 240 samples per hour. Although the techniques and instrumentation are of sophisticated design it is intended that relatively unskilled operators will be able to use them. Co-operation with organisations such as the milk marketing boards ensures their acceptability to users. The high cost of the advanced technology employed is offset by the high productivity, and the cost per sample of an analysis is kept low.

While the transmission method is well suited to most fluid samples which may be pumped through the measuring beams of infra-red radiation, solid foodstuffs such as grain, meat products, etc. are better analysed by reflectance techniques. This Wolfson research project is concerned with evaluating all possible infra-red methods and with achieving maximum flexibility and adaptability of the instruments produced. Thus it is expected that a basic electro-optical design will ultimately be coupled with a variety of sampling devices and a micro-processor will provide calibration factors for a large number of different food products.

Electronics Centre*

Electronics is perhaps the branch of applied science in which new developments of potential value to industry arise most often, since the cost of sophisticated electronic devices, such as silicon chips, has been falling for many years. The obvious example is the micro-processor, which is remarkably cheap, versatile and powerful but cannot be used without considerable knowledge of electronics and computer programming. The use by a firm of modern electronic techniques of this kind can

---

* Director of the Centre: Professor G. G. Bloodworth; Manager: Mr. P. G. Long.

give new life to an established process or product and markedly improve
its competitive position. Many firms which could exploit such techniques
have few or no electronic engineers, and could benefit considerably by
using the expertise of the staff of a nearby university.

For some time the University of York has been actively engaged in
making its expertise in electronics available to local firms. Although the
Department of Electronics is small and started only in 1979, the older
Departments of Physics and Computer Science have considerable
resources of staff and equipment in the fields of electronics, optics,
computers, etc. They have been working with local industrial firms for
many years. However, when the Department of Electronics was
launched, the University decided to set up an industrial unit with full-time
staff to extend and co-ordinate this work. Thus the York Electronics
Centre was launched in September 1980 to undertake research,
development and design work for firms having insufficient engineering
resources of their own. Although the Centre is based in the Department
of Electronics, it works closely with the Departments of Physics, Computer Science and Chemistry and can call on their expertise and facilities to
assist in an industrial project.

The Centre was established with the aid of a grant of £60,000 from the
Wolfson Foundation and is intended to become financially self-
supporting after about three years, by undertaking work on a contract
basis at normal consultancy rates. During this initial period the Centre is
building up its links with local firms, particularly those which are not
already using up-to-date electronic techniques and may not appreciate
their potential value. In this missionary phase, the Centre is holding
informal meetings and presentations on industrial premises as well as
inviting engineers from industry to attend lectures at the University on
subjects such as microprocessor applications, accompanied by facilities
for gaining practical and programming experience.

A centre of this kind is not only a means by which the University
forges links with the local community and helps the local economy. It also
has significant value for the academic staff, since many of the projects
have considerable intellectual challenge and provide opportunities for
new uses of their scientific knowledge and practical expertise. It is not
normally possible for undergraduates to work directly on an industrial
project since they have insufficient experience and cannot work full-time
on it to meet the necessary deadlines. However, such projects frequently
generate incidental problems that are entirely suitable for students. By
bringing industrial work into the academic science departments the
Centre will undoubtedly broaden the scope of teaching and research; and
it will also help staff to give students a more realistic and accurate

impression of applied science and engineering in industry before they face a choice of career.

Industrialisation in the Selby Area*

The area around Selby, ten miles south of York, is experiencing rapid change. The predominantly rural environment, characterised by a medium-sized town, a number of small village communities and a substantial amount of good quality farmland, will be transformed by accelerated industrial expansion during the 1980s. The chief factors promoting social change and population growth in the area are as follows:

(a) The development of the Selby coalfield, the largest of its kind in Europe, which will produce ten million tons of coal a year when in full production. The coalfield extends over 110 square miles of the Selby area and will require a total labour-force of up to 4,000 by the late 1980s.

(b) The development of Drax 'B' power station to the south of Selby town. The power station, which will be fired by coal extracted from the Selby coalfield and delivered by rail, will eventually provide employment for an additional 600, plus operational staff, by the mid-1980s.

(c) To complement these two major initiatives, the development of services and industries which are required to support the increased population expected to move into the area.

(d) The influx of commuters and retired people into the area which has already led to a rise in population and to changes in the structure of existing communities.

The social effects of the anticipated growth in population and the planned process of industrialisation cannot be foreseen entirely, but what is beyond doubt is that the character of life in the villages in the area will experience fundamental changes, and there will be increased demands for services of all kinds.

Similar developments are likely to occur in other parts of the United Kingdom; indeed, the Vale of Belvoir is the subject of a development plan proposal from the National Coal Board, which has stated that further large coal deposits will have to be opened up during the remainder of this century.

Thus the University's research project aims firstly to study a number of questions that planners and members of the public have been asking

* Principals: Professor K. Jones and Dr. M. Hirst, Department of Social Administration and Social Work.

about developments in the Selby area; and secondly to provide a detailed case study and to devise models of social change which may be applied to similar industrial developments in comparable areas of Britain. The research project offers an exciting opportunity to study social structures and activities during the early stages of rapid change, and a wide range of social issues will be examined. In general, the research project will monitor current events in the Selby area, evaluate and report on the social implications of rapid industrialisation, and offer short-term information. To this end a number of interrelated studies has been initiated.

Community Studies

A comparative study of social change in village communities in the Selby area will be based upon social surveys conducted in several villages which vary in size, and which will be affected to a greater or lesser extent, both directly and indirectly, by the development of the Selby coalfield and associated industrial initiatives. A substantial influx of workers and their families into an essentially rural environment may become one of the most important effects to be considered. Apart from the scale of the impact in terms of the number of people moving in, its importance will be evaluated by an analysis of:

(a) the character and tradition of the existing communities, to determine how the developments are changing people's attitudes and affecting their lives;

(b) the differences, if any, in the way of life practised by the newcomers, and the difficulties they experience in adjusting to a new and unfamiliar environment, often without family support;

(c) the nature of demand, arising from social and demographic changes, which will be placed upon the housing, schools, shops, transport and leisure facilities, as well as health and social services.

Employment

A study of the local labour market will examine the consequences for employment opportunities of the industrial developments already planned for the Selby area. Labour-force characteristics and turnover, recruitment and training problems, the recent pattern of employment, and any anticipated future developments will be explored with reference to three main aspects:

(a) the responses of local firms in the service, transport and construction sectors to the possibilities for an expansion of their activities, and the reaction of local employers to a possible aggravation of a local labour shortage for certain skills;

(b) the strong pressure that is likely to arise for job opportunities for women, given that most of the coalfield and power-station jobs will be taken by men;

(c) the consequential changes for local farming interests arising from the industrial developments and induced employment, and perhaps from inability to compete with changes in wage levels.

Planning

An examination of the response of social planners to the development of the coalfield should have implications for any attempt to promote more effective and efficient planning through greater co-ordination. A study of the planning process will examine two important aspects:

(a) the structure of the planning machinery in terms of territorial boundaries and functional responsibilities;

(b) the decision-making in the planning process and the perceptions of elected representatives and officials.

The development of the coalfield is essentially a long-term project, and stable new social patterns are unlikely to be established until some time after the coalfield comes into full production in the late 1980s. Meanwhile the research team, which is funded until 1982, is issuing a series of 'Factsheets'[3] as the study progresses.

Footnotes

[1] The author is indebted to his colleagues Professor G. C. Bloodworth, Drs. M. J. Chadwick, G. A. Cox, R. E. Hester, M. A. Hirst, M. B. Usher and Mr. J. D. Service for the material contained in this chapter.

[2] Part of this section is reproduced by permission of the Institute of Physics, the copyright holders. Acknowledgment is made to the Dean and Chapter of York Minster for making available specimens of glass for examination and to Mr. T. Gibson of the York Glaziers' Trust for his kind co-operation in this project.

[3] Selby Factsheets published by the Selby Research Team, Department of Social Administration and Social Work, University of York, York, YO1 5DD.

References

BRADSHAW, A. D. and M. J. CHADWICK (1980). *The Restoration of Land*. Blackwell, Oxford.

COX, G. A., O. S. HEAVENS, R. G. NEWTON and A. M. POLLARD (1979). A study of the weathering behaviour of medieval glass from York Minster. *J. Glass Studies*, 21, 54-75.

EVERETT, R. D. (1978). *Conservational Evaluation and Recreational Importance of Wildlife within a Forestry Area*. D.Phil. Thesis, University of York.

HAFFEY, D. (1978). *A Recreational and Ecological Assessment on the Moorlands of the North York Moors National Park*. M.Phil. Thesis, University of York.

HIGGS, A. G. and M. B. USHER (1980). Should nature reserves be large or small? *Nature*, 285, 568-569.

MARGULES, C. R. and M. B. USHER (in press). Criteria used in assessing wildlife conservation potential: a review. Biological Conservation.

SERVICE, J. D. (August 1980). *Pocket switching and the DEC system-10*. University of York, Department of Computer Science.

USHER, M. B. (1973). *Biological Management and Conservation*. Chapman and Hall, London.

USHER, M. B. (1979). Changes in the species-area relations of higher plants on nature reserves. *Journal of Applied Ecology*, 16, 213-215.

USHER, M. B. (1980). An assessment of conservation values within a large site of special scientific interest in North Yorkshire. *Field Studies, 5*.

USHER, M. B. and A. K. MILLER (1975). The development of a nature reserve as an area of conservational and recreational interest. *Environmental Conservation*, 2, 202-204.

USHER, M. B., M. PITT and G. DE BOER (1974). Recreational pressures in summer months on a nature reserve on the Yorkshire coast, England. *Environmental Conservation*, 1, 43-49.

USHER, M. B., A. E. TAYLOR and D. DARLINGTON (1970). A survey of visitors' reactions on two Naturalists' Trust nature reserves in Yorkshire, England. *Biological Conservation*, 2, 285-291.

Index

338 YORK 1831-1981

St. Mary's Abbey, 12, 15, 54, 64, 72, 73, 74, 78, 305, Plate 5
St. Mary's, Bishophill Junior, 66, 68, 207, 209, 210
St. Mary's, Bishophill Senior, 66, 207, 209, 210, 211, 231 n.
St. Mary's, Castlegate, 68, 173
St. Maurice's, 205, 207, 211
St. Michael-le-Belfrey, 207, 227, 229, 231 n.
St. Michael, Spurriergate, 173
St. Olave's, 205, 207, 211, 227, 231 n.
St. Paul's, 211
St. Paulinus, 229
St. Peter's Cathedral Church, 205
St. Sampson's, 207, 219
St. Saviourgate, 173, 178, 212, 215, 216, Map 5
St. Saviourgate Chapel, 212, 213
St. Saviour's, 207, 208, 211, 219
St. Saviour's Place, 212
St. Stephen's, Acomb, 227
St. Thomas', 211, 217, 222
St. Thomas', Osbaldwick, 228
St. Wilfrid, Mission of, 214
St. Wilfrid's, 214, 229
St. William's College, 75
Salem Chapel, 212, 213, 222, 228, 235
Salem Mission, 178, Map 5
Salmond, William, 6, 7, 8, 13
Salvation Army, 223-4
Schools, see Education
Science, 1-2, 5, 7, 10-12 passim, 14, 16-25 passim, 30, 50-1, 54, 55, 57-8, 78, 91, 100-2, 104, 107, 311-27
Aeroplane (Cayley), 31-8, Plate 4
Lens (Taylor), 40-7
Micro-telephone (Hunnings), 47-50
Telescope (Cooke), 38-40
Science Research Council, 80
Scott, Sir Walter, 3, 26 n., 55
Sedgwick, Adam, 24, 25
Selby, 312, 327-9
Service, J. P., 322, 329 n.
Sessions, William, II, 132
Sessions, William, Ltd., 132, 147
Seymour, G. H., 252 n.
Sheldon, Oliver, 289, 290, 291, 293, 308
Shepherd Building Group Ltd., 152
Shepherd, Colin, 151
Shepherd Construction Ltd., 105
Shepherd, Donald, 151
Shepherd Engineering Services Ltd., 151
Shepherd, Frederick, 150
Shepherd, Frederick, and Son Ltd., 150-1
Shepherd, Frederick Welton, 150, 152
Shepherd, Michael, 151
Shepherd, Sir Peter, 151, 152
Shepherd, William, 150

Shetelig, H., 70
Shields, J., 324
Shilleto, A., 253 n.
Sigsworth, E. M., 153 n.
Simpson, A., 268, 281 n.
Simpson, Sir John, 250 n.
Singleton, W. A., 291
Skaife, Robert, 61, 74
Skeldergate, 66, 78, 148, 150, 163, 215, 223, 224
Skeldergate Bridge, Map 1
Smith, John, 248
Smith, Reginald, 70
Smith, R. H. A., 235, 236
Smith, Robert, 62
Smith, Sydney, 2, 26 n.
Smith, William, 2, 11, 12, 26 n.
Smyth, J. G., 247
Snowdon, Edward Thomas, 243
Society for the Encouragement of Female Servants, 168
Society of Antiquaries, 54, 64, 70, 73
Soup Kitchen, 177, 181
Southlands, 217
Speaker, The, 288
Spen Lane, 147
Spence, Joseph, 123
Spillers Ltd., 148
Sproule, Lt. Cmdr. J., 36-7
Spurn, 315
Spurriergate, 70, 244
Stead, I. M., 60, 65, 67
Stephens, Ken, 105
Stewart, F. D., 194
Stonebow, the, Map 1
Stonegate, 30
Stourton, Lord, 11
Strafford, Earl of, 305
Street, George Edmund, 94
Streets and Buildings Committee, 270
Strensall Common, 315
Strickland, Sir William, 286-7
Stuart, George Harold, 261-2
Subscription Library, 6
Summer School of Archives and Historical Research, 291
Sunday School Society, 210
Surgeons, College of, 7
Sycamore Terrace, 62

TADCASTER ROAD, 228
Tang Hall, 205, 222, 228, 229
Tanner's Moat, 63, 124, 125
Tate, E. Risdale, 73
Tawney, R. H., 290
Taylor and Taylor, 68, 75
Taylor, Edward Wilfrid, 46
Taylor, H. Dennis, 40-6, 50, 51, 130
Taylor, Robert, 33, 34

Wotton, Sir Henry, 307, 310 n.
Wragge, Robert H. Vernon, 181, 281 n.
Wright, Wilbur, 37-8

Yarbrugh, Nicholas, 304
Yates, R., 150
York:
  Anglo-Saxon, 58, 61, 66-9, 70, 72, 75, 77, 92, 95, 97
  Anglo-Scandinavian, 67, 69-72, 76
  Medieval, 58, 61, 72-8
  Norman, 58, 73, 75, 92, 95, 96, 97, 98
  Roman, 6, 14, 57-8, 61-6, 67, 70, 71, 74, 76, 78, 92, 95, 97
  Viking, 61, 67-72
York Academic Trust, 294-8 passim, 301, 304, 305
York and North Midlands Railway, 57, 129, 238, 254 n.
York Archaeological Trust, 65-6, 71, 76, 78, 79-80, 81, Plate 6
York Auxiliary Bible Society, 222
York Benevolent Society, 177
York Board of Guardians, 165, 166, 170, 171, 173, 174, 175, 176, 177
York Central Mission, 223
York Charitable Society, 223
York City and County Bank, 288
York City Corporation, 237, 290, 293, 297, 304, 305
York City Mission, 178, 222, 223
York Civic Trust, 288, 290-4 passim, 304
York Co-operative Society, 176
York County Hospital, Map 5
York Courant, The, 6
York Daily Herald, see Yorkshire Herald
York Dispensary, 6, 162, Map 5
York Education Authority, 291
York Equitable Industrial Society, 63
York Excavation Committee, 63, 65
York Excavation Group, 66, 81
York Festival, 139
York Flint Glass Company, 123
York Footpath Association, 55
York Georgian Society, 294
York Glass Works, 131, 147
York Glaziers Trust, 329 n.
York Herald Newspaper Company, 131
York Institute of Architectural Study, see
  Institute of Advanced Architectural
  Studies
York Institute of Historical Research, see
  Borthwick Institute

York Institute of Popular Science and
  Literature, 6
York Literary and Philosophical Society, 6
York Medical Society, 6
York Minster Archaeology Group, 78, 80
York Minster Excavation Group, 75
York Mystery Plays, 139
York Poor Law Union, 164, 165, 166, 170, 171, 174
York Public Library, 288
York Reform Association, 248
York Religious Tract Society, 223
York Round Table, 228
York Savings Bank, 6, 176, Map 5
York Tavern, the, 20
York Union Workhouse, 170-6, 174, 182, 222, Map 5
York Vigilance Committee, 250
York Waterworks Company, 161, 279 n.
York Wesleyan Visiting Agency, 223
York Working Men's Conservative
  Association, 249
York Workshops for the Blind, 305
Yorke, Henry Redhead, 237
Yorkshire Agricultural Association, 15
Yorkshire Antiquarian Club, 59
Yorkshire Architectural Society, 6, 15, 22, 59, 73, 81
Yorkshire Dales National Park, 319
Yorkshire Evening Press, 131, 147
Yorkshire Gazette, 6, 21
Yorkshire Herald, 131, 238, 288
Yorkshire Law Society, 235
Yorkshireman, the, 236, 238
Yorkshire Museum, the, 6, 7-9, 11, 12-14, 15, 16, 18, 19, 22, 38, 54, 57, 59, 60, 61, 62, 63, 64, 67, 69, 70, 72, 74, 77-8, 80, 81, 287, Map 5, Cover
  Handbook, 57, 59
Yorkshire Observer, the, 6, 26 n.
Yorkshire Penny Bank, 176
Yorkshire Philosophical Society, 2, 6, 8, 9-16, 17, 18, 19, 21, 22, 23, 30, 31, 38, 53, 54, 55, 57, 58, 59, 60, 61, 62, 64, 68, 70, 72, 73, 77, 79, 80, 81, 82, 287, Map 5, Cover
Yorkshire Roman Antiquities
  Committee, 64
Yorkshire Scientific and Antiquarian
  Society, 8-9
Yorkshire Sugar Company, 149
Young, J. E. M., 219

ZERNIKE, Frits, 46